How the Bible Became Holy

Yale UNIVERSITY PRESS

New Haven and London

How *the* Bible Became Holy

MICHAEL L. SATLOW

Published with assistance from the foundation established in memory of Calvin
Chapin of the Class of 1788, Yale College.

Yale University Press books may be purchased in quantity for educational, business, or
promotional use. For information, please e-mail sales.press@yale.edu (U.S. office) or
sales@yaleup.co.uk (U.K. office).

Designed by Nancy Ovedovitz and set in Monotype Bembo type by Newgen North
America. Printed in the United States of America.

The Library of Congress has cataloged the hardcover edition as follows:
Satlow, Michael L.
How the Bible became holy / Michael L. Satlow.
    p.   cm.
Includes bibliographical references and index.
ISBN 978-0-300-17191-4 (hardcover : alk. paper)   1. Bible—Canon.   2. Bible—
History.   I. Title.
BS465.S285 2014
220.1—dc23

                                                                            2013042751

ISBN 978-0-300-17192-1 (pbk.)

A catalogue record for this book is available from the British Library.

10 9 8 7 6 5 4 3 2 1

For my children,
Daniel, Penina, and Jeremy

Contents

Part III

Note on Documentation and Sources

This book is neither comprehensive nor exhaustive. Inevitably, the arguments wind their way through contentious and complex scholarly debates, full discussions of which would make the narrative too unwieldy. In the notes I have attempted to provide both basic bibliography for readers interested in learning more as well as brief indications of areas of particular scholarly controversy and my own evaluation of them.

Translation editions are generally indicated in the notes, with the exception of biblical quotes (including the Apocrypha), which follow the New Revised Standard Bible, although I sometimes make minor modifications, primarily for the sake of clarity or style. I have kept the names of ancient religious compositions that are not part of the modern canon in roman type to signal that these works often had the same or more religious authority at the time as texts that would later become canonical. In direct citations of fragmentary ancient texts, parentheses are conventionally used to indicate explanations supplied by the translator, whereas brackets indicate text that the editor has reconstructed, often due to physical damage or illegibility of the fragment. Translations of classical literature usually follow the *Loeb Classical Library,* and those of rabbinic literature, except where indicated, are my own. Transliterations of foreign terms follow colloquial usage.

CASPIAN
SEA

N

M E S O P O T A M I A

R. Tigris

R. Euphrates

PARTHIA

Babylon •

• Susa

• Persepolis

PERSIAN GULF

A R A B I A

How the Bible Became Holy

Introduction

The first time I tried to read the Bible I was thirteen. I had received a two-volume set of the Hebrew Bible, or Old Testament, for my bar mitzvah, and it was the first Bible that my family possessed. The print was small and the English translation stiff, but I was excited to finally have the opportunity to read it. The first three and a half chapters, with their dramatic accounts of creation, sin, sex, and murder, were great. That's as far as I got. The mind-numbing list of names, of who begat whom, was jarring; it was simply too boring and weird. I put the book down and turned to other, more interesting pursuits.

Over the next several decades, I made many more attempts to read the Old and the New Testaments. Sometimes I would start at the beginning and try to read through; at other times I would begin in a particular book. Each time would end in failure, and I confess that to this day I have not read the Bible, or even a single testament, cover to cover. Engaging stories come to a screeching halt at extended genealogies or detailed descriptions of buildings. Lists of peculiar laws, sometimes strung together incoherently, suddenly appear. Stories repeat, but in versions that contradict each other. Admonitions to be kind and compassionate are belied by approving accounts of almost unspeakable cruelty. Beautiful statements are buried in incomprehensible and cryptic oracles. The historical narrative lurches back and forth. The Good Book is very hard to read.

The reason for this is that the Bible is an anthology of diverse writings that have been patched, stitched, and strung together over the course of about a millennium, from 800 BCE to 150 CE. This is the primary insight of two centuries of biblical scholarship that began with the Enlightenment and its fundamental recognition that the Bible was not simply given by a perfect God but written and edited by imperfect humans. Its contradictions, repetitions, strange jumps of logic, and even spelling mistakes can all be understood as the inevitable results of a long process of different people at different times with different interests revising, rewriting, and adding to a received collection of texts.

The question that has stayed with me since my initial attempt to read the Bible, then, is not, How did the Bible achieve its present, peculiar state? Biblical scholarship, with its extraordinarily sophisticated tools, has supplied a generally convincing explanation for this. Rather, it is, How and why did individuals and communities in antiquity regard the texts that would become part of the Bible as authoritative? The Bible, as we are all well aware, has become arguably the most important book in the history of human civilization. Who would give such a strange book such outsized authority, and why?

The standard answer to this question is that the texts that are now part of the Bible became authoritative at, more or less, their moment of composition. The laws of the Pentateuch, in this telling, are seen as reflections of the (perhaps ideal) laws of the kingdom of Judah, administered by a state legal system. Its stories were well known and thought of as sacred. Its psalms and other hymns were regularly recited in public and given a special status. By the Hellenistic period (fourth to first centuries BCE), almost all Jews knew of most of the books of the Old Testament (some through its Greek translations, the Septuagint) and thought them sacred. Christian literature emerged from this matrix. Both Jesus and his followers saw Jesus as a fulfillment of scripture, and the early Christians quickly accepted the divine authority of the books that they created, which would become the New Testament. By the time the rabbis actually canonized the Jewish Bible, or Tanak, in the third century CE, they were merely formalizing what most people already thought.[1]

I have always found this narrative intellectually unsatisfying. To be fair, I don't think it actually exists as such and I have simplified it here. But the general idea, that the Bible quickly gained an ironclad authority among Jews and then Christians in antiquity, shoots through much contemporary public discourse, religious education, and even scholarship. As far as I can tell, it is based primarily on the Bible's own strong claims to authority. How could a text that so self-consciously asserts its own origin as the divine word not have been taken seriously?

Yet one problem with this narrative is that it is improbably flat. In its account, the Hebrew Bible's authority was secure already in the sixth century BCE and then changed little, despite the vicissitudes of history that followed. There is no development and no contestation over a millennium. What doesn't change in a millennium?

Another, more serious problem with this standard answer to the question of when and how the Bible became authoritative is the evidence. Over the past few decades, new texts and archaeological discoveries have come to light and scholars have changed the way that we think about much of early Jewish and Christian history. When I began this book, I thought that I could simply refresh the standard answer and bring it up to date according to these new discoveries and insights. I thought of it as a refurbishing, making the narrative a bit spiffier and maybe changing some things around the edges, but leaving it essentially intact. As I plunged into the research and writing, though, increasingly I began to doubt this narrative; it was not holding up against the evidence. It was as if, to continue the metaphor, I set out to resurface the cabinets and found that the studs were rotted. The standard answer needed a gut rehab.

This book proposes a very different answer to the question of when and how the Bible gained authority. I will argue here that *Jews and Christians gave to the texts that constitute our Bible only very limited and specific kinds of authority until well into the third century CE and beyond.* The "peoples of the book" did not know their book very well.

This is a book primarily about the people who considered, or not, certain ancient texts as authoritative. It is a story that takes with more than a substantial grain of salt the claims of the texts and puts people at the center. I am interested in the Israelites, Jews, and Christians who over the course of a thousand years developed a variety of attitudes toward textual authority. Unsurprisingly, these attitudes did not simply emerge and freeze in time, to be passed on to each succeeding generation that faced its own very different set of challenges and opportunities. Tracing the authority of the Bible is much less about the Bible itself and much more about the historical communities that created, read, and copied—or not—these ancient texts.

To understand the approach I take in this book we must first dwell briefly on the word *authority* and what it implies. The word is inherently vague, and I believe that it is more useful to consider three different types of authority that I will call normative, literary, and oracular.

For most readers and in the standard answer that I sketched above, the phrase "authority of scripture" most readily brings to mind *normative* authority. This means its authority to dictate our behaviors. When today people invoke the Bible in political discourse (for example, what does the Bible say about homosexuality?), they are almost always assuming that the Bible has such normative authority; it tells us what we should or must do. Yet, as I will argue here, for most Jews and Christians in antiquity the Bible had very little normative authority. Until the first century CE, most Jews, particularly in the land of Israel, had only a very fuzzy knowledge of scripture and certainly would not have turned to it for practical guidance.

By *literary* authority I refer to the common phenomenon of authors using earlier texts as models for new ones. Much of biblical literature, I will argue, was produced by and for scribes, who constituted a tiny fraction of the population. Scribes trained by copying and revising earlier texts, and it is thus not surprising that they would use these texts as models for their own original compositions, despite the fact that nobody was making them do so. These earlier texts need not necessarily be "canonical" to serve as a model; ancient scribes, just like modern authors (or, in different media, painters or composers), might follow or allude to an earlier text without declaring it authoritative. Just as today a writer might draw from and elliptically reference Homer's *Odyssey* in a story about homecoming, so too writers in antiquity used earlier texts as models but freely modified them. Another, more pointed, modern example might be Bible stories written for children. These stories clearly depend on an earlier text, but also rework it so as to render it unnecessary for understanding the new composition.

The third and probably most common type of authority given in antiquity to biblical (and other) texts was *oracular*. Oracular authority is assigned to a text that is thought to deliver a message, usually about the future, from the divine realm. This is the authority that in antiquity was most commonly linked to the term "holy." Technically one can make a distinction between oracles and prophecies, as the latter, as found in several of the surviving prophetic books in the Bible, also contain moral exhortation. Nevertheless, it was the oracular content of those compositions that most concerned their ancient readers.

When applied to the Israelite, Jewish, and Christian communities that wrote and read the texts that would become part of the Bible, this approach to "authority" yields a far more dynamic and accurate understanding of how the Bible emerged as a holy text. As we will see, this did not happen in any particularly straightforward or predetermined way.

This book tells a chronological story that begins in the ninth century BCE in the northern kingdom of Israel and ends in Galilee in the early third century CE. Part 1, which covers the Israelite, Judahite, and Persian periods (ninth to fourth centuries BCE) shows how most biblical texts were produced by and for scribes, mainly as academic exercises. To the extent that these texts had any authority at that time, it was mainly literary. These scribes also produced a group of texts that recorded the oracles of the prophets. Both kinds of texts were kept in the temple and the court, where they were accessible only to the elite. There were two or three attempts during this period to give normative authority to some of these texts, but they largely failed. Religious life was centered on the temple, its sacrifice, and local customs, not a text.

Part 2 moves to the Greek period, from Alexander the Great's conquests to (approximately) the Roman ascent in the Near East (330–63 BCE). During this time textual authority developed along two very different trajectories. Beginning with the translation of the Pentateuch into Greek around 250 BCE (the Septuagint), the Jewish intelligentsia in Egypt and other Greek-speaking areas increasingly began to turn to it as a foundational literary or cultural text. They engaged it much as their non-Jewish neighbors did with Homer, and toward very much the same goal: the attainment of social and cultural prestige. The desire to share in this prestige trickled down to lower classes, and by the first century BCE produced the regular public reading of the Pentateuch in the synagogue. Even with this widespread knowledge of biblical texts, though, it still had little normative authority in these communities.

In Jerusalem, on the other hand, almost the reverse situation developed. In the mid-second century BCE a revolt in Jerusalem led to the establishment of a new ruling Jewish dynasty, known as the Hasmoneans. Within this new ruling court two competing political parties rose, which would become known as the Pharisees and the Sadducees. The Sadducees claimed that texts had normative authority, which they then used to argue against the traditional temple practices of those allied with the Pharisees. This debate about the normative authority of texts was hardly known outside of these rarefied political circles, and would hardly be known to us as well had not a dissatisfied group of Sadducees broken off in the first century BCE to establish its own community in Qumran, leaving behind for us the Dead Sea Scrolls.

Part 3 deals with the Roman period. In the first century CE, the synagogue would migrate from the Greek-speaking world to Jerusalem, with the support of the Sadducees. It would be one of the major channels through which knowledge of scripture would spread to the wider Jewish community in Judea (as it was known at that time). For most Judean Jews, the real value of scripture was its oracular authority. Jesus himself, growing up in Galilee, had very limited knowledge of scripture. After his death, his Jewish followers (such as Paul) would understand his life and death as the fulfillment of scriptural oracles. To his early Gentile followers, however, this seemed rather bizarre. They understood Jesus's importance in terms of his actions and message, which were unconnected to strange-looking Jewish texts. This would set up a fierce battle in the early church over the authority, oracular or normative, of Jewish scriptures, one that would reach a critical turning point in second-century Rome.

Our story concludes with the rabbis, the heirs and successors to both the Sadducees and Pharisees. They forged a compromise position that paradoxically elevated scripture to a cherished, normatively authoritative position while at the same time marginalizing that authority. If the second-century Christians were emerging with a position that elevated the message of scripture above its actual text, the rabbis went in the reverse direction, almost fetishizing the text and its actual physical form.

While I of course have relied heavily on the research of many of my academic colleagues, I have built my arguments primarily from my own rereading of the primary sources. These primary sources generally fall into two types, literary and archaeological, and the nature of these sources as well as how I use them warrant a brief word.

I deal in this book with three main kinds of literary evidence, but the most important one is the Bible itself. The truth is that the Bible is a very poor historical source, but for many of the questions that interest us about Israelite and early Christian history and religion it is also one of our only sources. The problem with using the Bible as a historical source is that it isn't one; its writers and editors never set out to write an objective historical account of anything. My intent is not to disparage, but only to note, as scholars have for a very long time, that while the Bible might sometimes look like it is telling history, its shapers, like those of most ancient literature, had no interest in maintaining a critical distance from the stories they told. It thus presents a challenge to the modern reader who seeks to penetrate its words in order to recover the historical contexts in which it was shaped.

The second kind of literary evidence is quite similar to the Bible, texts that present themselves as authoritative (or "scripture") but that were not included in either the Jewish or the Christian canon. These provide a window into different, often vibrant and important, Jewish and Christian communities and their approaches to the Bible. Some of these texts are found in the semicanonical Apocrypha (although all were originally Jewish works, this is part of the Catholic Bible); some in modern scholarly collections known as the Pseudepigrapha (for both the Old and New Testaments); some among the Dead Sea Scrolls; and others that popped up in peculiar manuscripts or inscribed on stone. By the end of our story, these texts were largely marginalized and made secondary to those that would enter the Bible. Part of our story is seeing how that process happened, given that in an earlier time many Jews and Christians granted a great deal of authority to some of them, like 1 Enoch, Jubilees, and the Gospel of Thomas. Like the Bible, these works do not easily reveal their authors and contexts and must be read suspiciously. These texts, particularly the Dead Sea Scrolls, have received a surge of scholarly interest in recent times, and these texts and new insights into them will play a critical role in my reshaping of the standard narrative presented above.

The third, looser category of literary evidence is composed of various documentary, philosophical, and historical tracts that (at least when found complete) bear a clearer indication of their author and context.

These include writings such as a fifth- to fourth-century BCE cache of papyri belonging to the community of Persian Jewish mercenaries stationed in Egypt; Greek ethnographic writings about Jews in the fourth-third centuries BCE; fragments of Jewish writings in Greek that were based on the Septuagint (Greek translation of the Bible), from the second and first centuries BCE; the philosophical tracts of the Philo (who lived in Alexandria, first century BCE–first century CE); the histories of Josephus (who lived in Jerusalem and Rome in the first century CE); and writings of early church fathers such as Justin. Rabbinic sources are primarily used in the last chapter; they sometimes contain reports of earlier periods, but these cannot generally be trusted. These are just a few of the many kinds of texts that we will encounter and that will greatly aid us by providing both some relatively firm dates and also perspectives that are quite different from the pseudonymous "scriptural" texts.

Recent archaeological finds, and new reevaluations of old finds, also provide a different perspective for understanding the history of this period. New demographic studies, for example, give us a much clearer picture of the relative standings of the kingdoms of Israel and Judah, from which we can better see how Israelite scribal culture might have been imported to Jerusalem in the eighth century BCE. Similarly, we will better understand the scribe Ezra's failed attempt to argue for the normative authority of the Torah when we see him within the context of a city that contained only a few hundred people organized in tightly knit clans. Remains of synagogues and the inscriptions that they contained allow us to better trace the development and movement of the institution from the Greek-speaking world to Jerusalem and elsewhere in Judea, and a very recent redating of the settlement of Qumran, when seen against the Dead Sea Scrolls, provides new insight into the development of the community that produced those texts.

This is primarily a story about the development of textual authority in antiquity. More broadly, though, it also points toward the story of how it is that we, in the modern West, have come to live in a textual world. We read texts for information and entertainment. Our lives are ordered by the legal documents that we are expected to be able to read, understand, and consent to. Our pantries, cupboards, beds, and clothing contain words that claim our attention. We read the labeling on our food to discover what we are buying and refer to written recipes to prepare our dinners. Our streets are marked with texts. Words, not pictures, inform us whether we are passing a fabric shop or a butcher. And for many of us, a workplace without texts would be unimaginable.

This was not the case in antiquity, when texts and their authority played a marginal role in the lives of the vast majority of people. It did, however, grow directly out of the mentality that had developed around the emerging Bible of the second century BCE. This notion that texts and their interpreters have power is, I believe, the real enduring and important legacy of the Bible.

Part I

I The Northern Kingdom: Israel, 922–722 BCE

Reflecting on the fall of the kingdom of Israel in 722 BCE, a historian from the kingdom of Judah could not resist a bit of gloating. The Assyrian conquest of Israel, the historian wrote, "occurred because the people of Israel had sinned against the Lord their God, who had brought them up out of the land of Egypt." They sinned, and despite God's warning to them, "they would not listen but were stubborn, as their ancestors had been, who did not believe in the Lord their God" (2 Kings 17:7, 14). The historian goes on to provide a rich and detailed list of the many ways that Israel sinned against the Lord and thus brought disaster upon itself. "None was left but the tribe of Judah alone," the historian from Judah concluded (v. 18).

This historian, of course, can hardly be trusted to provide an objective or critical account. For the past several centuries, the kingdom of Judah had looked to the far larger, stronger, and richer kingdom of Israel to the north with a combination of fear and envy. Yet not only had Israel fallen, but two decades later Jerusalem had withstood the fierce assault of its conqueror, the Assyrian army. The Lord had vindicated Judah despite the fact, as the historian nervously notes, that "Judah also did not keep the commandments of the Lord their God but walked in the customs that Israel had introduced" (v. 19). Even in the future, should the Lord abandon Judah, too, it would still be Israel's fault.

The Bible as it exists today sees Israel through the triumphalist eyes of Judah. Israel is a place of sin, a caricature important primarily as a moral warning of what happens when you displease the Lord. The story of the Lord's promise to care for the people of Israel takes place in Judah.

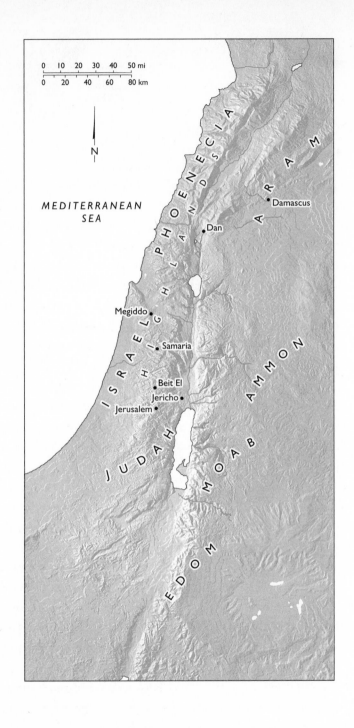

0 10 20 30 40 50 mi
0 20 40 60 80 km

N

MEDITERRANEAN
SEA

• Damascus

A R A M

P H O E N E C I A

• Dan

I S R A E L

H I G H L A N D S

Megiddo •

• Samaria

Beit El •
Jericho •

Jerusalem •

J U D A H

A M M O N

M O A B

E D O M

Because the vast bulk of evidence about ancient Israel derives from the Bible—whose texts have been filtered and worked over from a Judahite perspective—historians who wish to achieve a less biased understanding of the ancient kingdom of Israel face a significant challenge. Over the last few decades, however, these historians have made significant progress by carefully teasing apart the biblical stories; analyzing linguistic clues in our extant texts; conducting linguistic analysis; studying the few ancient inscriptions that mention Israel; and comparing what we know about Israel with other local cultures and communities. They have also, most important, been aided in their task by new archaeological finds. Combined, these approaches allow us to see the basic contours of the history of Israel at this time, even if we must still use a fair bit of speculation to fill in the gaps.

And the picture of Israel that continues to emerge is very different than the one found in the Bible. Israel, not Judah, was the cultural powerhouse and political player. Judah was merely a small speck on the cultural and geopolitical map of the region, a tiny, struggling, and relatively resource-poor kingdom in the Judean hills. It is to Israel, not Judah, to which we need to look in order to understand the origins of the Bible.

Israel was the place that first gave birth to some of the earliest stories and texts found in the Bible, but these texts had little authority. The large and heterogeneous population of Israel developed stories and legends that helped its people to see themselves as part of a single people. Most of these texts and legends, traces of which can be found throughout the Bible, were far from what we would call authoritative or "holy." Nor was written law as important as it would come to be. In Israel, as in Judah and all the surrounding kingdoms, authority and the will of the Lord were not to be found in a text but in the oral pronouncements of elders, priests, and prophets. When lawsuits arose, they were solved not by a judge consulting and applying to a case a set of written legal rules but by a process of negotiation; even the much older famous code of Hammurabi should be thought of less as a modern, authoritative legal code and more as a combination of scribal exercise and set of legal guidelines that elders could use, or not, in resolving disputes. The oracles of prophets were sometimes preserved in written form, but they were used academically, as reference works. A few poems and psalms, some that could have had liturgical purposes, may also have survived the Assyrian destruction, but these would have been "authoritative" only by virtue of their antiquity, and even then mainly as part of a curriculum of study for the highly educated.

Israel was also far more culturally developed than Judah. More important than the actual texts that its refugees would bring to Judah were their skills, technologies, and ideas. These skills would transform Judah, and the scribes and administrators who found a new home in Judah's royal court created the conditions that would allow for the birth of authoritative texts in the seventh century BCE. To understand how this happened we must first go back a step to the beginnings of the kingdom of Israel in, if the Bible is to be trusted, the tenth century.

According to the Bible, the first Israelite monarch was Saul, who reigned in the late eleventh century BCE. Unable to establish a lasting a dynasty, he was usurped by David (ca. 1000–961 BCE). King David united the tribes and established his capital in Jerusalem, where he also purchased the land that would become the site of the central temple. He bequeathed his kingdom to Solomon, one of his many sons, who continued to rule the "United Monarchy" (as many scholars call it) from 961 to 922. Solomon built the temple in Jerusalem and greatly expanded Judah's territory.[1]

The kingdom of Israel emerged after Solomon's death. Solomon was succeeded by his son, Rehoboam, who attempted to hold Solomon's kingdom together by force. Israel, though, revolted and chose another king, a certain Jeroboam, son of Nebat, from the tribe of Ephraim, who had served under Solomon (1 Kings 12). Thus began the two-centuries-long rift between the northern and southern kingdoms.

Such is the biblical account—but is it true? There is precious little evidence outside of the Bible to support it. An inscription found in the Israelite city of Dan dating from around 800 BCE celebrates a victory of a king named Hadad over the kings of "Israel" and "the house of David." The inscription indicates that there was a dynastic line, separate from Israel at that time, that traced its lineage back to a figure named David. Beyond that, however, the inscription does not indicate anything about David or the extent of his power. The evidence for the existence of

Solomon is even more tenuous, with the biblical account sometimes in tension with archaeology. Later biblical accounts, for example, describe Solomon's palace as enormous and luxurious (1 Kings 7). The excavations in the "City of David" in Jerusalem, however, have failed to unearth any such structure. Some scholars have thus concluded that neither a United Monarchy nor a king named Solomon ever existed.[2]

Whatever the precise origins of Israel and its connection to Judah, Israel began to emerge as a powerhouse in the mid-ninth century. The Israelites, who had been centered in the hill country of Ephraim, established a capital in Samaria (in lower Galilee). The city was magnificent, and although the fortunes of the kingdom of Israel varied over the next century, the city of Samaria itself remained the prosperous seat of the royal court of Israel. The Israelite palace in Samaria has been located by archaeologists; it is a large and elaborate structure and the many expensive ivory carvings found within it testify to the wealth of Israel's kings (figs. 1 and 2). Samaria was also the residence of many of the local elite, whose estates were located outside of the city and from which they received regular shipments of agricultural goods for their support.[3]

However, it would be misleading to think of Samaria as the seat of a modern-day empire, such as London in the eighteenth and nineteenth centuries with its wealth and monuments pillaged from its colonies. The "kingdoms" of the ancient Near East, with the exception of the great world powers of the day, Egypt and Assyria, were often little more than cities with a few dependencies. In many cases we might better compare the role and power of these kings to modern-day American mayors, except that they administered far smaller budgets. While such kings were not, of course, democratically elected, they ruled largely by the consent of the city's clans. Their power was dependent on keeping the clans either satisfied with their rule or disorganized enough that they could not agree on an alternative ruler.

The kings of Israel in the ninth and eighth centuries managed to forge a confederation that went somewhat beyond this model. In expanding toward both the north and the Mediterranean coast, the Israelite kings did not conquer existing Canaanite settlements as much as they incorporated them into a single, diverse polity. The nominal seat of power resided

Figures 1 and 2: Ivory carvings from excavations in Samaria. (Courtesy of Palestine Exploration Fund)

with the Israelites in the Samarian highlands, but the functioning and integrity of the kingdom as a whole depended on the support of other peoples in the lowlands. It was a fragile union.[4]

The Israelites established strongholds at important locations throughout the kingdom. Dan and Beit El, on the northern and southern borders, were particularly important royal cities and cultic centers. Hasor (in the north) and Megiddo (in a central location in the Jezreel Valley) too were royal strongholds. They served as strategically important defenses against external threats but also projected in a concrete and visible way the power of the Israelites to this heterogeneous population.

As in most successful political entities, though, soft power played a far more effective role in establishing group identity and cohesion than did the threat of force. Over the course of a little more than a century, the diverse peoples of Israel developed a common historical narrative that knit them into a single polity while at the same time providing an opportunity for them to acknowledge their diversity. Out of the several dialects that they spoke, they forged a common language with which they could communicate with each other. And they came to largely accept the primacy of a single god, whom they called Elohim or YHWH, as the protector of their federation.

More than any other biblical narrative, the story of Jacob and his sons might provide a model of the Israelite strategy of forming a single identity out of a heterogeneous population. While in its present form it has been extensively reworked and edited, its core narrative appears to have been formed in Israel and is, in fact, well suited for the political situation of the ninth to eighth centuries.

According to this story, Jacob—Isaac's son and Abraham's grandson—fathers twelve sons (and one daughter) whose names become equated with the tribes. It is no coincidence that Jacob also acquires the name "Israel." The Bible reports that this renaming occurred after Jacob spent the night wresting a mysterious being. As daybreak came, the man begged to be let go: "But Jacob said, 'I will not let you go, unless you bless me.' So he said to him, 'What is your name?' And he said, 'Jacob.' Then the man said, 'You shall no longer be called Jacob, but Israel, for you have striven with God and with humans and prevailed'" (Genesis 32:26–28).

From then on in the Bible's narrative, *Israel* and *Jacob* are used interchangeably and apparently randomly. The northern (antiestablishment) prophet Hosea also knew of a version of this legend (Hosea 12:4). Rather than being read as a genuine historical account, this legend is best understood as a post facto attempt by Israel to understand its own name, which can be parsed in several different ways. Here it is seen as referring to "one who wrestles" with the god "El." It thus suggests that a united northern kingdom of Israel emerged out of struggle, which again, whether historically accurate or not, was (and remains) a common national narrative.

The story of Jacob's twelve sons, their internal disputes, and their alliances is an etiological one: it is meant to explain the origins of the tribal system operative at the time it was told. Judah and Benjamin were identified with the southern polity of Judah, and the biblical scenes that depict them as groveling before Joseph were most likely meant as a dig at their neighbors (Genesis 44).[5] Joseph receives two tribal shares; there is no tribe of Joseph but instead his sons Ephraim and Manasseh become the tribal ancestors. The legend that elevates Ephraim above his older brother Manasseh (28:13–20) establishes the supremacy of Ephraim, the original Israelites from the hill country. The tribe of Manasseh, whose large territory bordered Ephraim's, was put in the position of near equal. Such a legend could help to placate the tribe of Manasseh if it felt resentment at Ephraim's political supremacy.

The myth of the "children of Israel" served a necessary strategic function. It created a collective imagined community under the direction of Ephraim, the favored descendent of Joseph, Jacob's favorite son. At the same time, it acknowledged differences between the tribes, each of which could, under the myth, have its own distinctive customs. Such a legend, current in some form, helped the members of this confederation to connect to each other. They thought themselves (whether accurately or not) to share blood, which would transcend whatever social and cultural differences they might have.[6]

History in antiquity was about stories, and stories were meant to be told. As with the bards in ancient Greece who recited the poems of Homer, the stories of Israel were performed by professionals, undoubtedly with local variations. Although it is sometimes tempting to see these histories as royal propaganda created and propagated by authorities to justify their own power, these stories—which were constantly being recited and modified in light of the interaction between the bard and his community—are better seen as the fluid creation of a historical memory. It is a memory that could play a very useful role in establishing the community known as Israel.[7]

In addition to a myth of a common past, language too helped to hold together this loose Israelite confederation. The peoples of Israel, like those of most other kingdoms in the region, spoke a Semitic language. The most common vernacular language was Aramaic (which had different forms), but over time kingdoms developed their own distinct dialects or languages. Hence, speakers of one Semitic dialect were often able to recognize some vocabulary and grammatical structures of another. The kingdoms around Israel spoke different forms of what scholars call Northwest Semitic. For instance, Ugarit, a city-state that existed in modern-day Syria beginning around the middle of the second millennium BCE, developed Ugaritic, and Moab (located in modern-day Jordan) spoke Moabite. Ammon (in modern-day Jordan) and Edom (also in Jordan) developed distinctive Northwest Semitic dialects. These languages were all close enough to each other that it would not have been too difficult for their speakers to understand each other.

Hebrew—if we can use the term a little loosely for the moment—was the vernacular language of both Israel and Judah. The very first written evidence of Hebrew is an inscribed limestone tablet known as the Gezer calendar, which dates from the tenth century. This fragment is a partial list of months and the agricultural activities associated with each one. Several scholars believe that it served no practical purpose; according to one, the calendar "has the appearance of a non-scribal learning tool, teaching writing as an entertainment, not an instrument." The Gezer calendar (found in Judah) is written in a script that most think can be called paleo-Hebrew, although it shares close affinities to, and was probably derived from, Phoenician. The Gezer calendar is similar enough to the few other Hebrew inscriptions that date from this time to suggest that the writers of these texts formed a loose craft network, like potters and metal workers.[8]

There are very few extant written artifacts from the kingdom of Israel. Our most extensive evidence for language and writing in Israel, in fact, is a large cache of eighth-century ostraca (ink writing on shards of pottery) from Samaria that record the delivery of jars of goods to the city. The linguistic features of these ostraca differ somewhat from those found in the other evidence, leading some scholars to argue that Israel developed its own dialect of Hebrew. Rather than talk of "Hebrew" as a unified language, the argument runs, we should instead refer to the language of Israel as Israelian and that of Judah as Judahite. Whether they should be termed different languages or dialects of the same language, then, is open to debate.[9]

The Israelian hypothesis is an intriguing one, although many scholars remain skeptical; there is still not enough evidence to know for certain. Without getting too far into this debate, though, it is certainly plausible to think that the incorporation of several formerly Canaanite cities into a single polity would, over the course of time, have led to a smoothing out of local dialects into one that could be understood more easily in neighboring cities within the same kingdom. Like writing and the oral telling and refining of historical legends, this would have been an organic process, not one that was imposed top-down from Samaria.

The peoples of Israel thus grew to see themselves as a single people sharing a single language. They also grew to worship the same deity.

This deity bore the name Elohim or YHWH. The Canaanite cities that entered into the kingdom of Israel had, like their language, different but roughly shared pantheons. They all believed (as did the Greeks) in the existence of several gods who interacted with each other. Many believed as well in a variety of lesser deities, often associated with specific places or natural phenomena. Individual city-states sometimes gave different names to their gods, although they were quick to identify an unfamiliar god in one city with a more familiar one in their own. The name might be different, the reasoning went, but the god was the same.[10]

The gods were involved in the lives of both the individual and the community. The distinction was important. The god or gods of the city protected the population from communal disaster, such as famine or a military defeat. Accordingly, each citizen was expected to show the proper respect to these gods in order to stay on their good side and thus ensure continuing divine protection. Individuals, though, were also free to worship, or not, whichever additional deities they thought would give them, as individuals and families, health and prosperity. The community as a whole had no direct stake in these personal religious practices.

The first Israelites had a single national god they called YHWH. We are not entirely sure how this name was pronounced, and later traditions would in fact declare it unpronounceable, a name too powerful and holy to utter. Conventionally today the name is written as Yahweh or Jehovah, and often is translated into English as "Lord."

As the Canaanite cities joined Israel, they confronted a very practical problem: what deity or deities protected this new polity? The Israelite kings, for the most part, looked to YHWH as the sole protector of their kingdom, but they were also wise enough to know that simply stamping out traditional local cults was not a way to win the hearts and minds of a population. At the same time and from the other direction, local peoples would have sought a way to find common ground with each other and Israelites. One result of this was an identification of YHWH with the traditional Canaanite deity El, a god who (like Zeus) was sometimes portrayed as the first among the gods. Call the deity YHWH or El, by the eighth century this was thought to be the same god and the protector of Israel.[11]

Worship of the national deity was a highly ritualized and serious business. The public cult of YHWH involved regular and highly regulated sacrifice offered by priests. The Israelite priesthood appears to have been hereditary, with the line being thought to go back to Moses (not Aaron, as the Judahites would come to believe). One practical effect of such a belief was to limit this important role to the descendents of the original Israelites. They made their sacrifices in official temples and shrines. Israel had two primary shrines located at opposite ends of its territory, one at Dan and the other at Beit El, although there were other official places of worship as well.

YHWH was the "official" god of Israel but not always the only one. One Israelite inscription that dates to around 800 BCE mentions YHWH,

El, and Baal (a Canaanite god) together. Some thought that YHWH had a female consort named Asherah.[12] Kings and their subjects wanted to make sure that their bases were covered.

Contact between the Israelites and their god(s) occurred mainly through the act of sacrifice as mediated by the priest. On occasion, though, it could also happen more directly via the prophet. The prophet, like the priest, was usually a functionary of the temple and served to directly convey the divine will. The temple's prophet functioned much like an ancient oracle: the office was institutionalized; questions could be submitted to it; and the answers were often poetic, if not completely obscure. Temple prophets were part of the establishment and their continued employment and enjoyment of the perks that went along with the position exerted a pressure on them to tell the monarch what he wanted to hear.

Unlike priests, though, prophets existed outside of the established cult. In Israel, legends of the prophets Elisha and Elijah, both described as having extraordinary powers and being willing to take on the official priests, were apparently popular. Narratives in the Bible describe them as both resurrecting the dead and confronting the priests of Baal in the name of YHWH.[13] Amos and Hosea too were Israelite prophets who were critical of the establishment.

There were official cultic holidays that would have been particularly auspicious times for Israelites to visit their local temples and shrines. They also came to the temples and shrines to ask for health, prosperity, love, and fertility, and to give thanks when their requests and vows were fulfilled. In a story set in Israel prior to King David but most likely reflecting much later religious practice, a man is said "to go up from his town every year to worship and to offer sacrifice to the Lord of Hosts at Shiloh" (1 Samuel 1:3). As in this case, people would ordinarily worship and beseech YHWH by means of sacrifice. The priests would slaughter and cook the animal. YHWH would get the "sweet savor" of the cooking flesh, the priests would take a portion, and the rest would be consumed in or by the shrine by those who had brought the animal.

Israelites, and Judahites too during this period, did not see any contradiction (as the later writers of the Bible would) between the public worship of YHWH and the private worship of other deities. The most visible sign of this were figurines of the household gods. The Bible alludes to the use of such figurines (Genesis 31:19, 33–35). Archaeological finds amply confirm the domestic use of figurines: scores of these clay figures that date through the sixth century have been found in Israelite settlements.[14] Few if any would have seen such private worship as a betrayal of YHWH.

Throughout antiquity the categories of ethnicity and religion were inextricably bound. Part of what made an ethnicity distinctive was precisely the devotion that it gave to its protecting deity. For Israelites, this devotion manifested itself in a variety of practices that we would call religious. Israelites most likely restrained from work on the Sabbath, however they might have defined "work," and observed some other common holidays. The Israelite prophet Amos, reflecting the wealth of Samaria, rails: "Listen to this, you . . . saying, 'If only the new moon were over, so that we could sell grain; the sabbath, so that we could offer wheat for sale, using an *ephah* that is too small and a shekel that is too big, tilting a dishonest scale, and selling grain refuse as grain! We will buy the poor for silver, the needy for a pair of sandals'" (Amos 8:4–6). Reflecting what would become a common theme among biblical prophets, Amos condemns punctilious ritualism in which proper ethical behavior is absent.

Israelites shared a few other visible and distinctive practices. They restrained from eating pork. Maybe they wore fringes on their garments. They almost certainly circumcised their sons. These were all seen as things that would please their god while at the same time creating shared practices through which they could establish ties with each other.

Narrative, language, and the cult were all strategies that helped to unite the diverse Israelite population into a single entity. These strategies may have had royal support, but they also developed organically from the bottom up, as small city-states themselves wanted to be a more integral part of Israel.

As a confederation with a centralized seat of power, the kingdom of Israel needed a government which, in turn, required functionaries. Among the most important class of such governmental functionaries were the scribes. These scribes were a necessary part of the administration of the kingdom and played a particularly important role in international relations. An educated and elite class, Israelite scribes would later bring their knowledge and, more important, their skills to Judah, where they would continue to play a significant part in society.

The role of scribes must be understood primarily within the context of imperial politics. The small kingdoms of West Asia at this time did not operate in a vacuum. To survive, they had to ally themselves with one of the two great powers, Assyria or Egypt. Both Israel and Judah were at the very edge of the Egyptian sphere, and their rulers made the safer and smarter decision of allying themselves with the Assyrians.

Israel and Judah became Assyrian vassal states. Vassal states were largely autonomous, with their own rulers and military, but were bound by treaty to the ruling empire. The terms of these treaties, or covenants, were largely formulaic, so while the exact treaties between Israel and Judah and their Assyrian overlord are not extant, other similar treaties that do survive show the rather one-sided terms under which they operated: in return for Assyria's military protection, the vassal state vowed to stay loyal. Breaking the vow resulted in both a curse and, of course, Assyrian military retribution.[15] In order to maintain good relations with their overlords, the Israelite monarchs would have regularly sent "gifts" back to Assyria.

One of the primary jobs of the scribes was to manage the communication between the vassal state and the Assyrian authorities. In addition to mastering proper diplomatic language and protocols, scribes had first to deal with the basic linguistic barrier. In Israel, Hebrew served as the local vernacular language. Correspondence with the Assyrians, however, had to use the Akkadian language, written in complex cuneiform script. We assume that there was a class of Israelite scribes based primarily in Samaria that handled not only matters of internal administration but also relations with Assyria.

In truth, we know almost nothing specifically about Israelite scribes and scribal activity. The only indirect testimony to their existence is the repeated reference in the biblical (and Judahite) book of Kings to the "Annals of the Kings of Israel," apparently a chronicle (now lost) that was kept by the court in Israel (2 Kings 15:11). This composition, a telltale sign of the presence of skilled scribes, was brought to Judah, presumably by scribes, after Israel's fall.

About scribes generally throughout the ancient Near East we know a good deal more. Being a scribe at this time was more akin to being part of a class than a profession. In Assyria and Egypt, most scribes came from families of scribes. They underwent an extensive and rigorous training, primarily in Sumerian, a language that had long been dead by the eighth century. Sumerian was seen as a "classical language," and much as an upper-class education in England used always to include Greek and Latin, scribal training involved the copying and revising of ancient Sumerian literature. This (along with education in mathematics, astronomy, astrology, and history) was seen as preparing them for a life of civil service, the practical skills of which they would learn on the job. They were draftsmen, diplomats, lawyers, and professors rolled into one.

Scribes throughout the Near East formed a loose network. Scribes from one royal court would write not to the king of another but to his scribe. The receiving scribe would then translate the message to the king. This "translation" could be far more involved and complex than the word implies. Scribes might send a set of notes to another scribe, who would then reconstruct and orally communicate the message in his own language. They would be present in most locations that had a governing or military presence.

We do not know if the scribes of Israel received the same "classical" education as the scribes that were closer to the seat of power in Assyria and who are better known to us. Yet there are traces of evidence that whatever the precise content of their training, Israelite scribes functioned in ways similar to these other scribes. One indication of this can be seen in their treatment of law and prophecies.[16]

One of the traditional exercises of a scribal education was the copying of the Code of Hammurabi (ca. 1775 BCE). The purpose of such copying was not to spread practical knowledge of the code; it was a training exercise. It allowed scribes to practice their handwriting while learning how to engage creatively with this kind of written text. Instead of being expected to slavishly copy the texts in front of them, scribes instead engaged with and revised them. They did this with legal as well as with literary texts. Even the legal texts had more literary than normative authority at this time.

There is fragmentary evidence that such activity occurred in Israel as well. A fragment from Hazor created prior to this city-state's incorporation into Israel contains a set of laws that were similar to Hammurabi's in form, although they differed in content; they could well have been the result of some kind of scribal exercise. So too, a short fragment of an ostracon from Khirbet Qeiyafa—a location that could have been in either Israel or Judah—is part of a larger list of short laws of the same kind.[17]

But the most interesting, and tangled, bit of evidence for this kind of scribal reworking of laws is from the Bible itself. Exodus 21–23 appears to be an independent collection of short laws, mostly dealing with civil matters and containing a festival calendar that was embedded within a narrative. This collection is known by scholars as the Covenant Code. It appears to have been created in the kingdom of Israel and then brought south to Judah, where it was revised and ultimately found its way into the Bible.[18]

The language of the Covenant Code suggests that it originated in Israel. What, though, was its purpose? Did it serve as a source of normative authority, much as we look to written legal codes for authority? While this possibility cannot be categorically excluded, the social context of adjudicating legal disputes would seem to make this unlikely. Disputes were brought to local leaders and elders who would negotiate settlements in line with the possible and practical rather than according to some abstract ideal of justice. Some of these elders, perhaps themselves trained as scribes, might have turned to written texts to help guide them, but these were not binding laws. It is this context that helps us to better understand the purpose of the Covenant Code.

The Covenant Code was a scribal exercise, much like the Laws of Hammurabi and the fragmentary set of laws from Hazor. This also helps us to make sense of its occasionally less than practical and unenforceable idealism. Scribes or other administrators may have occasionally turned to the Covenant Code (whether in written form or, more likely, as a memory from their days of training) when called upon to judge, but they would not have cited it as an authority for their decisions. Like the Annals, the Covenant Code was taken to Judah by scribes (or even a single one) fleeing from the Assyrians, where (as we will see in the next chapter) it continued to be reworked.

The scribes also had a hand in recording prophetic activity. Prophets, both those who worked within and outside the established temples, shrines, and government organs, delivered their oracles orally. At least sometimes a scribe would then write them down. A fascinating parallel to this activity can be seen in an inscription found in Deir Alla, a site now in Jordan that was not far from Samaria. This Aramaic inscription was written in the ninth-eighth centuries BCE on plaster and records a series of pronouncements of a prophet named Balaam, who received a nocturnal communication from the gods. One biblical writer would later transform this revered prophet Balaam into a buffoon in order to denigrate him (Numbers 22–24). Here I simply want to note that the inscription attests to the writing down of prophetic oracles, probably for reference. Over time, those oracles that demonstrably never came to pass fell away, whereas those like Amos and Hosea—whose views, not very coincidentally, confirmed the Judahites' suspicions about their northern neighbors—were preserved. Only from their positions within the official establishment or from the fact that their radical and unlikely predictions came true would the written records of the prophets have gained oracular authority.

The kingdom of Israel reached the height of its power in the mid-eighth century, but from there things went quickly downhill. For unknown reasons, in 731 BCE the Israelite king Hoshea, son of Elah, revolted against Assyria and allied with Egypt, an unforgivable and not very smart act. When the Assyrians sent their troops, as they had to, the Egyptians were nowhere to be found.

The Assyrian campaign against Israel was devastating. Its first stage, the Assyrian king Tiglath-pilesar III decimated lower Galilee. In his annals, Tiglath-pilesar reports that he carried away 13,520 captives. This was almost certainly an exaggeration; modern archaeologists estimate the population of this area prior to his conquest at around 17,600. In 722 BCE another Assyrian king, Shalmanseer V, conquered Samaria and, according to the Bible, deported another group of Israelites. Only two years later, Shalmanseer's successor, Sargon, launched a final crushing attack on Israel. In a cuneiform inscription he boasts, "I besieged and conquered Samarina [the Assyrian spelling of Samaria]. I took as booty 27,290 people who lived there. I gathered 50 chariots from them. I taught the rest (of the deportees) their skills. I set my eunuch over them, and I imposed upon them the (same) tribute as the previous king (i.e., Shalma-neser V)."[19] Archaeological excavations confirm both the devastation of the Israelite settlements and the Assyrian repopulation of the land with other conquered peoples.

The fate of the deported Israelites almost certainly depended on their skills. According to Assyrian records, some Israelites—identified as such by their theophoric names, which contain elements of YHWH's name— attained positions of authority in the Assyrian royal court and army. Many more, we assume, became agricultural slaves.[20] We have almost no record of the fate of the Israelite elite, the royal family, priests, proph-ets, and scribes. Many were deported. According to the Bible, one de-ported Israelite priest was sent back to Samaria to teach (unsuccessfully) the newly settled residents how to worship properly the God of Israel (2 Kings 17:27–41). The implication of the passage is that Israelite priests remained distinctive; there was some continued recognition of social roles and classes among Israelites in Assyria.

Other refugees, though, fled south to Judah. The evidence can be found in the archaeological record. At the end of the eighth century the number and size of settlements in Judah grew dramatically. Jerusalem more than doubled its area at this time, expanding its population some tenfold, to around 20,000. Prior to the Assyrian conquests, the popula-tion of Israel was around 350,000 and the population of Judah 110,000.[21] Even if the war was bloody and the numbers of captives recorded in the Assyrian records are accurate (they almost always exaggerate), that would still leave a large number of Israelites for which to account. It is clear that many of them went to Judah.

Today it is easy to imagine that the Israelite refugees saw some of the texts discussed above, such as the Covenant Code and the prophecies, as an important part of their cultural inheritance. That, however, would be anachronistic. There was nothing particularly "sacred" about these texts. As the potter gathered whatever tools were on hand that he could carry to his new home, so too would scribes have grabbed easily accessible scrolls for the journey—this was the stuff of their trade and learning. Like all refugees, they were simply hopeful that they would have the opportu-nity for a new start in their new home. That opportunity came to them sooner than they might have thought.

2 The Writings of Judah:
Judah, 722–586 BCE

The Israelite refugees to Judah would not have been met with a particularly warm welcome. Judah was not Israel. Lacking large areas of flat land, it depended on the hardscrabble terrace farming of its hilly terrain for subsistence. Judah also lacked easy access to the sea or major trade routes. Jerusalem, its capital, was a small city that in the mid-eighth century still lay largely within the confines of what is today called the City of David. The palace of the king of Judah was unlikely to have contained the kinds of rich ivories found in that of the Israelite king. At minimum, the Judahites would have been apprehensive at the prospect of housing and feeding the refugees. In many villages and towns in which they arrived, particularly if they did so in large numbers, they would have been met with hostility.

But the Israelite influx also presented an opportunity. Among them were engineers, builders, scribes, and experienced bureaucrats, all possessing potentially useful skills and knowledge. These were all skills that Judah could use, and it did. By the end of the eighth century BCE, twenty years after the destruction of Samaria, the Israelite elite had established a presence in Jerusalem. The very fact that the kingdom of Judah ultimately came to identify itself as "Israel," while hardly definitive, certainly suggests that these new immigrants had a powerful impact on their adopted home.

In the century and a half or so between the 730s, when Israelites began to flee from the encroaching Assyrian forces, and 587/586 BCE, when the Babylonian army destroyed Jerusalem, Judah developed a remarkable literary culture. More important than the actual quantity of texts produced during this period (still relatively few) or the number of people who could actually read them (almost certainly tiny) was the development of a particular attitude toward written texts among Judah's elite. The ability to read, write, and interpret complex texts conferred status. As the status of the scribes grew, so too did the status that they conferred on the texts upon which that status depended.

By 586 BCE, the scribes of Judah had produced a variety of texts that advanced their own authority. But a claim to authority is not the same as actual authority and, as we will see in this chapter, some texts were better received than others. As Jerusalem smoldered and many of its elites began their long march into exile in Babylonia, there was neither a Bible nor a strong sense of the reliance on the authority of texts. The seeds, however, had been planted.

Put yourself, for a moment, in the place of King Hezekiah of Judah at the end of the eighth century. Assyria, your own overlord, is in the process of destroying Israel. Refugees—how many we do not know—begin to trickle, maybe even flood, into Jerusalem. Among them are members of the Israelite elite, now penniless, who come to you offering their skills in exchange for a place to live and a livelihood for their families. On the one hand, you might think they present a risk. They are part of a regime that revolted against your protector and their commitment to you and your own line of succession might be less than absolute. Their incorporation into positions of power would certainly cause jealousy among the more established bureaucrats and their clans, unsettling delicate power relationships. On the other hand, though, they have knowledge and skills you could use. With perhaps some jealousy you consider what you have heard about the great cities of Israel, with their architecture, water instillations, and trade. You of course maintain your own scribes, but they now may look to you a bit provincial when compared to the more skilled and worldly Israelite scribes now at your doorstep.[1]

Hezekiah decided to accept the risk, and at least at first it appeared to pay off. A tantalizing hint of just how close he brought the Israelites, or wanted to, was the name that he gave to his son and heir—Manasseh (2 Kings 21:1). In Israelite lore, Manasseh and Ephraim were brothers (the sons of Joseph), and it would be hard to imagine that any Judahite king would have used that name lightly.

One of the most striking and concrete payoffs of Israelite know-how may have been the waterworks often known as Hezekiah's Tunnel. Jerusalem depended on two sources for its water: rainwater (stored in cisterns) and the spring of Gihon, which was located outside the walls of the city. Around this time a long tunnel was constructed that brought the water from this spring inside the city walls, the existence of which may have saved Jerusalem from its Assyrian assailants just a few years later. The construction of this tunnel, dug simultaneously from the two ends, was quite an engineering achievement. The engineers commemorated their feat with a well-formed inscription (known as the Siloam inscription) in the middle of the tunnel—far from where anyone could read it—that celebrates their own technical triumph without even bothering to mention who actually funded the project (figs. 3 and 4).[2]

We cannot know for sure that Israelites were directly involved in this project, but Israelite cities contain extensive waterworks, whereas such instillations did not previously exist in Judah. The inscription, which is paradoxically both monumental and placed where nobody could see it, also points to a level of professional or craft literacy not typically found in Judah. By snubbing the monarch under whom the tunnel was built, the engineers might also have been attempting to assert their own independence and superiority. Just to be safe, though, such assertions were better left where the king could not see it.

Hezekiah built his waterworks because he expected war. He built a massive fortified wall around Jerusalem at the same time. The enemy was the Assyrians. It is difficult to know exactly why Hezekiah prepared for

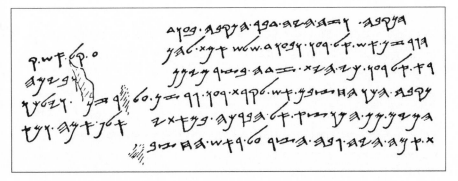

Figure 3: Copy of the Siloam inscription. (© Copyright Carta, Jerusalem)

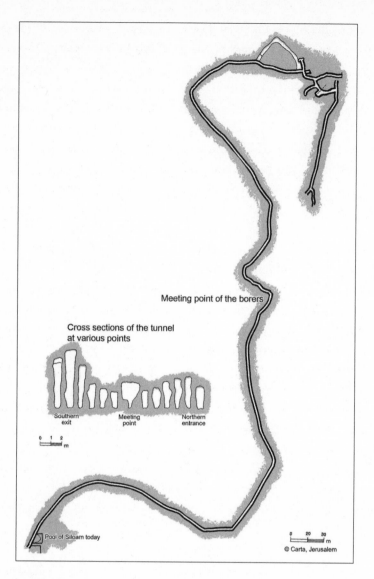

Meeting point of the borers

Cross sections of the tunnel
at various points

Southern
exit

Meeting
point

Northern
entrance

0 1 2
m

Pool of Siloam today

0   20   30
m

© Carta, Jerusalem

Figure 4: Map of Hezekiah's Tunnel, with location of the inscription. (© Copyright
Carta, Jerusalem)

this assault. Was he planning, perhaps under Israelite influence, to forgo
his own alliance with Assyria and throw his lot in with Egypt? Or did he
see that Sennacherib, the Assyrian king, was intent on conquering all the
kingdoms in his path during this campaign? Whatever motivated Hezekiah, he made the right choice. The walls and the waterworks saved Jeru-

salem. The Assyrians would level the rest of Judah in 701 BCE and exact a heavy tribute from Hezekiah, but Jerusalem withstood his assault.

Just as Israelite engineers may have helped to save Jerusalem, so too their scribes may well have achieved positions of influence and power within Hezekiah's court. According to a story recorded in the Bible, shortly before the Assyrian assault on Judah, Sennacherib sent an emissary to Jerusalem to publicly threaten King Hezekiah. He addressed the crowd in Hebrew. Three of Hezekiah's court officials were present. One was in charge of the palace (chief of staff); one was "the recorder" (presumably a note taker); and the other was a scribe named Shebna. They replied to the emissary, "Please, speak to your servants in the Aramaic language, for we understand it; do not speak to us in the language of Judah (*yehudit*) within the hearing of the people on the wall." Hezekiah's officials did not want the residents of Jerusalem to understand the threats, but the Assyrian emissary knew precisely what he was doing: "Has my master sent me to speak these words to your master and to you, and not to the people sitting on the wall, who are doomed with you to eat their own dung and drink their own urine?" He then loudly denounced Hezekiah in "the language of Judah" (2 Kings 18:26–27). The scribe would ordinarily have expected to conduct official business in Aramaic, whereas most bystanders would have understood only Hebrew.

Hezekiah's officials were multilingual. As in Israel, Hezekiah's scribes worked as diplomats and administrators, and it is possible that some of them learned their craft there, or from their Israelite fathers. A small, seemingly incidental detail might also be significant: the presence of the scribe named Shebna. Shebna is an otherwise unattested name and it is possible that his name indicates an origin outside of Judah.

The emissary was probably meant more to provide diplomatic cover for the Assyrian assault than to find a compromise that would keep the peace. The Assyrian attack was swift and furious, quickly leveling the second most important city in Judah, Lachish, which was on Judah's southern border. Sennacherib himself was probably there for that conquest, and in his new palace in Nineveh he commemorated it with a massive wall relief. This relief, placed in a suite of rooms probably used for administrative purposes, was the most prominent of the several reliefs in this suite that commemorated Sennacherib's victories during this campaign.[3]

In this relief and his other written inscriptions, Sennacherib crowed about his victory over Lachish and Hezekiah's forty-six walled cities. He claims he deported over two hundred thousand Judahites, took a huge amount of gold and silver, and captured Hezekiah's "daughters, his palace women, his male and female singers." But he could not capture Jerusalem.[4]

Jerusalem's success against the mighty Assyrian army had a traumatic and galvanizing effect. The survival of all of Israel was at stake, and the Israelite refugees especially would have known it. Had Sennacherib succeeded in taking Jerusalem, it is likely that Israel would have ceased to be a living community; like the kingdoms of Ashdod, Ekron, and Gaza, it would have entered the dustbin of history. Surviving Sennacherib's siege, even if it involved the payment of an enormous amount of tribute, was seen as a miracle, a sign that the God of Israel really did protect his people.

Isaiah, the son of Amoz, successfully predicted this outcome. Isaiah was an official prophet in the court of Hezekiah. As the Assyrians approached the city, Hezekiah naturally consulted him about the outcome. Isaiah's response ended with an unambiguous prediction: "He shall not come into this city, shoot an arrow there, come before it with a shield, or cast up a siege ramp against it. By the way that he came, by the same he shall return; he shall not come into this city, says the Lord" (2 Kings 19:32–33). Isaiah did not get this entirely right—the Assyrians did appear to make it to the city. He was right enough, though, to be seen as an authentic prophet bearing good news. This served to add weight to his other, more cryptic oracles, which were written down and collected.

Prior to the Assyrian invasion Hezekiah had tried to centralize the public cult. Hezekiah wanted worship of only the single God of Israel, and then only in the temple in Jerusalem. "He removed the high places, broke down the pillars, and cut down the sacred pole. . . . He trusted in the Lord of the God of Israel; so that there was no one like him among all the kings of Judah after him, or among those who were before him," his much-admiring biblical historian wrote (2 Kings 18:4–5). This was imperial propaganda, meant to counter those who may have argued that the Assyrian assault itself was the result of divine displeasure with Hezekiah's reforms. The fact that Hezekiah's own son, Manasseh, immediately restored the shrines, pillars, and posts upon his ascension to the throne indicates that even he was not convinced by his father's interpretation.

Whether or not one accepts the idea that Israelite scribes deeply influenced and transformed the nature of scribal culture in Hezekiah's time, it is clear that there was an explosion of literary activity in Judah then. Whereas there were just a few shards of written material from Judah prior to this time, suddenly inscriptions on jars and weights—both of which are connected to royal administration—started to appear in relatively large numbers. Like the ostraca from Israel, these inscriptions are never very exciting; they almost all merely indicate ownership or contents. But they, along with fragments of what appears to be a monumental inscription, show the expanding role of writing connected to the administration of Judah.[5]

Throughout the Near East, many scribes employed by the royal and cultic organs of state would have spent most of their time on bureaucratic functions. At least some, though, were (also?) expected to engage in more "academic" activities. Supported by the monarch, they engaged in traditional scribal activities such as the reworking of older texts and the production of new wisdom. The royal court, and perhaps very rich noble families, would become patrons of these scribes. Patrons of scribes might well have enhanced their own prestige in a society that increasingly valued writing and literacy.

The biblical book of Proverbs was produced in such a context. As it exists today, Proverbs is a collection of traditional "wisdom." That is, most of the book is composed of relatively short and pithy sayings that urge proper and good behavior, similar to the suggestions found today in popular self-help articles. The target audience was the upper class. The saying "Honor the Lord with your substance and with the first fruits of all your produce," with the further promise that doing so will bring even more material gain, is clearly not addressed to the destitute (Proverbs 3:9). Other chapters personify wisdom: "Take my instruction instead of silver, and knowledge rather than choice gold; for wisdom is better than jewels," wisdom exclaims (8:10–11). Such advice is best understood as functioning within a community that already has a choice between gold and wisdom, that is, the upper strata of the educated elite.

Proverbs repeatedly develops this theme of the tension between the pursuit of wealth and wisdom. Scribes faced this tension: they could become more involved with the administration of the state and by so doing gain greater material reward, or they could spend more of their time pursuing wisdom. Within the court they seemed to have at least some degree of freedom in how to divide their time. "When you sit down to eat with a ruler, observe carefully what is before you, and put a knife to your throat if you have a big appetite," one aphorism reads (23:1–2). The passage goes on to explain in series of aphorisms that the royal table is a trap that will remove you from the true pursuit of wisdom. The more you partake, the more you desire fleeting pleasures.

Deep into the book of Proverbs, close to the end, a remarkable passage appears: "These are other proverbs of Solomon that the officials of King Hezekiah of Judah copied" (25:1). The very first line of Proverbs ascribes everything to that point to Solomon—why does the text not simply continue that claim? The verse introduces a distinct collection of proverbs for which the "officials" (literally "men" but really to be read as "scribes") who copied and reworked earlier material wanted credit. Since this activity was funded by the king, why not give him a little credit? The attribution of Proverbs to King Solomon must in any case be taken with a grain of salt, but it could well be that the scribes who were reworking earlier scribal material believed that they went back to what at least in their imagination was the great and wise king.

Proverbs casts an oblique light on one aspect of scribal culture, although it leaves some critical details in the dark. For example, how did these scribes store and access their writings? Did they rely on their own libraries and those of their friends, or was there a more centralized library?

We are here mainly reliant on comparative material. Assyrian temples appear to have frequently contained libraries, several of which have been unearthed in archaeological excavations. A cache of tens of thousands of clay tablets that were found in a single archaeological site in Nineveh constituted the library of Ashurbanipal, who ruled Assyria circa 685–627 BCE. Temples in the ancient Near East also sometimes had more modest libraries. Collections of scholarly texts found in both Egypt and Assyria have been identified as the libraries of local temples.[6]

Did the temple of Jerusalem have a library? According to much later and unreliable testimony, it did. There is one tantalizing clue in the Bible itself. According to a biblical account, the prophet Samuel, after acclaiming Saul as king, recited the "rites and duties of the kingship; and he wrote them in a book and laid it up before the Lord" (1 Samuel 10:25). Saul was said to be the first king of the nascent Israelite monarchy (ca. 1050 BCE) prior to the construction of the temple, and this passage is unlikely to be true. Rather, it is far more likely that the later writer of this incident, who was familiar with a library at the Jerusalem temple, created this anachronistic scene. Similarly, the "book of the law" is said to have been stored "beside the ark of the covenant of the Lord," which presumably was located at the Jerusalem temple (Deuteronomy 31:26). The plausibility of the existence of a library in or by the temple is buttressed by the archaeological finds in Jerusalem that identify concentrations of bullae (clay stamps used to seal documents). These finds attest to the practice of storing of collections of (probably administrative) documents.[7] Despite the tenuousness of this evidence, though, I think that it is likely that a library did exist in the temple. Administered by priests and scribes (undoubtedly some were both), this would have served as the central resource and repository for the city's small community of scribes.

Scribes were scholarly and creative, not human photocopy machines. When they did sit down to copy older texts—whether because the text was in poor physical condition or because they wanted a copy for their own enjoyment—they "corrected" and revised them according to their tastes. This is the process that, I believe, led to the creation of the core of the book of Deuteronomy.

The Israelite scribes had brought with them the Covenant Code, a collection of laws that are now found in the biblical book of Exodus. Whether or not these laws were ever enforced in Israel, they served a role in the education of Israelite scribes—the code was another text to know, copy, and learn to rework. Different scribes undoubtedly reworked the Covenant Code in different ways. It was a kind of training exercise, and the resulting copy could be discarded, circulated or, if the scribe was well connected enough, deposited in the temple library. One of these copies resembles the central chapters (12–26) of Deuteronomy.

Scholars have long recognized that the core of Deuteronomy reworks the Covenant Code. There is a coherent logic to the revisions. The Covenant Code seems to assume a weak central authority, whereas one of Deuteronomy's most characteristic features is its insistence on very strong central institutions, with political authority situated with the king and religious authority in the one temple in Jerusalem. At the same time, the revisions tend to humanize the cultic practices found in the Covenant Code. Three short examples will illustrate these tendencies.

First is the treatment of the Passover celebration. The Covenant Code notes two related holidays. One is the Passover itself, in which individual families were to "slaughter" (not "sacrifice," which is a technical term), roast, and eat a lamb, smearing its blood on the doorposts to keep away evil forces. The other is the Feast of Unleavened Bread, a seven-day festival during which the Israelites were not to eat any form of leaven (Exodus 12:1–20). Deuteronomy, though, collapses these two holidays into one seven-day holiday to be celebrated at the Jerusalem temple (Deuteronomy 16:1–8). Two local, decentralized holidays have been brought together under tight control of the priests.[8]

Second, Deuteronomy—and in the Torah, only Deuteronomy—assumes a strongly centralized political authority headed by a king (Deuteronomy 17:8–20). It is Deuteronomy that creates the class of the "Levitical priests," which on the one hand gives priestly power to the entire tribe of Levi (not just the descendents of Moses and/or Aaron) while on the other disenfranchises all of them from owning ancestral plots of land. The priests, who in a centralized temple would always threaten the authority of the king and his court, are chopped down to size.

A third example, one that demonstrates the humanizing tendency of Deuteronomy, can be seen in its treatment of sacrifice. Most other biblical texts seem untroubled by the idea that YHWH consumes or enjoys the sacrifices. Deuteronomy shrinks at the idea of YHWH acting so corporeally. "God has no need of the sacrifice itself," one scholar summarizes; "it is only an expression of gratitude to the Deity, and this constitutes its entire significance."[9]

What could account for these revisions? As a whole, Deuteronomy powerfully supports the centralizing agendas of Hezekiah and, a bit later, his descendent Josiah. It also reflects the miraculous sense of YHWH's unconditional election of Israel, a natural outcome of surviving the Assyrian assault. Its self-designation as "book of the Torah" and its images of the importance of writing suggest scribal circles. Many scholars have thus supported the idea that Deuteronomy was produced by scribes close to either Hezekiah or Josiah, with most preferring Josiah. For reasons that will become clear, I believe it was more likely to be produced in Hezekiah's time.[10]

Some have seen Deuteronomy as a form of royal propaganda meant to support the centralization of the cult, but one problem with this interpretation is that the book, at best, is ambivalent about the institution of kingship: "When you have come into the land that the Lord your God is giving you, and have taken possession of it and settled in it, and you say, 'I will set a king over me, like all the nations that are around me,' you may indeed set over you a king whom the Lord your God will choose" (Deuteronomy 17:14–15). The passage goes on to limit who can be king (a kinsman chosen by YHWH) and what he is allowed to do and, more important, not to do (have too many possessions or wives). Then it adds a remarkable rule: "When he has taken the throne of his kingdom, he shall have a copy of this law written for him in the presence of the Levitical priests. It shall remain with him and he shall read in it all the days of his life, so that he may learn to fear the Lord his God, diligently observing all the words of this law and these statutes" (17:18–19). The king is subservient to the law, an idea unprecedented in the ancient Near East. It is difficult to think that Hezekiah, however good and pious he was, would have commissioned such a passage.

So if the book was not authorized by Hezekiah, how do we understand it? I want to suggest that it was an academic exercise composed by scribes who worked either for Hezekiah or (just feet away) in the Jerusalem temple. These scribes either were from the north, were descended from scribes from the north, or worked with scribes from the north who had access to older Israelite documents. They rejected the Aaronide priesthood and they approved of much of Hezekiah's program. Hezekiah, though, did not commission the scroll that they produced, nor did he likely see it. It was a scribal fantasy, a learned vision of how the world should be if they were in charge. In their world, the king would be subject to their law; everybody would annually give away 10 percent of his crop; and every seven years all debts would be forgiven (Deuteronomy 14:22; 15:1). They—or maybe just one single scribe—wrote this on a scroll and deposited it in the temple, where it lay buried for the next century. They could hardly have suspected that it would come to serve as a powerful, if ultimately ineffectual, basis for the religious reforms of Hezekiah's great-grandson, Josiah.

Hezekiah survived his brush with Assyria and apparently died peacefully in 698 BCE. Manasseh was twelve at the time, and he would rule for fifty-five years, apparently in peace. This alone must have caused no small annoyance to the later biblical historian, who portrayed him as the worst king in Judah's history: he "has done things more wicked than all that the Amorites did," the Bible reports (2 Kings 21:11). His real sin, in the writer's eyes, was to restore the shrines and practices that his father had worked to discontinue. Manasseh and his advisors, of course, would have seen their actions as a restoration of the traditional pious practices that Hezekiah disrupted. His long and peaceful reign, in contrast to the tumultuous events under Hezekiah, might have validated his actions. The biblical historian, writing later and from a perspective directly opposed to Manasseh, tried to sidestep this problem (2 Kings 21:1–18).

Although he continued the religious policies of his father, Manasseh's son Amon fared far worse. He was twenty-two when he began to rule, in 641 BCE, and was killed by his advisors two years later. The Bible does not tell us why they killed him, but it does report that "the people of the land" were outraged at the regicide and "killed all who had conspired against King Amon" (2 Kings 21:24). They immediately installed his eight-year-old son, Josiah, as king.

Running the kingdom of Judah in 640 BCE was no job for an eight-year-old. Josiah's geopolitical world was in transition. When Josiah ascended the throne, the great empire of Assyria was beginning to totter. The Egyptians had freed themselves of direct Assyrian control by 653 BCE. Around the same time, the Babylonians led a loose coalition into revolt against Ashurbanipal, the Assyrian king, which he put down savagely. The suppression succeeded only in deferring rather than crushing Babylonian aspirations. Sometime after Ashurbanipal's death circa 630 BCE, a new king of Babylon, Nabopolassar, led the Babylonians again in revolt against Assyria. The Assyrians, who were in internal disarray, could not suppress this revolt. By 612 BCE the Babylonians had succeeded in routing the Assyrians back to Nineveh, which they and their allies conquered and sacked. Three years later the Babylonians destroyed the remaining Assyrian army and took control of what was left of the Assyrian Empire.[11]

In the midst of this tectonic transition, according to the Bible, in 622 BCE, when Josiah was twenty-six years old, the "scroll of the Torah" was discovered during renovations in the temple. The political waters were treacherous, and he undoubtedly would have wondered what the Babylonian revolt against Assyria would mean for Judah.

The discovery of the scroll was seen as an oracle, and not only because it came at a time of political uncertainty. Throughout the Near East it had become customary to inscribe oracles and omens, which for all practical intents are the same. The last great king of Assyria, Ashurbanipal, had collected an enormous library of cuneiform tablets, among which were many such oracles. Isaiah's oracles were written down in the days of Hezekiah; one passage in the book of Isaiah even describes an oracle that was intimately connected to the very act of writing (Isaiah 8:1–4). Oracular writing was a recognizable genre.

When the high priest Hilkiah found the scroll, according to the biblical account, he immediately gave it to the scribe to read. The scribe then brought the scroll to the king and read it to him too (2 Kings 22:8–10). While the high priest and king may have been too busy to read it themselves, it is also possible that they couldn't, or at least did not trust themselves to read an extensive document. Josiah's ministers next "authenticated" the scroll with a local prophetess, Huldah, one of the very few women to appear in our story. She reinforced the oracular message: Judah was doomed, but through adherence to the God of Israel the doom could be delayed. The troubled political situation added additional gravity to the oracle.

Josiah then had all the people of Jerusalem assembled, along with the "priests and prophets," and read them the scroll: "The king stood by the pillar and made a covenant before the Lord, to follow the Lord, keeping his commandments, his decrees, and his statutes, with all his heart and all his soul, to perform the words of the covenant that were written in this book. All the people joined in the covenant" (2 Kings 23:2–3). Soon after, Josiah commanded them to observe Passover. The biblical writer comments, "No such Passover had been kept since the days of the judges who judged Israel, even during all the days of the kings of Israel and of the kings of Judah" (2 Kings 23:22). Josiah appears to innovate here, acting as "the royal patron of the cult," assiduously supervising its correct observance.[12]

I think that Josiah had here found the core of Deuteronomy, the reworked Covenant Code produced by Hezekiah's scribes. It had lain buried in the temple library for a century; this was why its discovery and its contents caught Josiah and his court completely by surprise. Josiah thus took this scroll, a text that Hezekiah's scribes originally wrote as a utopian scribal fantasy, and read it as a living and relevant oracle. The key to national well-being was divine favor, and gaining divine favor, according to this oracle, required convincing the priests and prophets to change the status quo and persuading the people to accept a new set of religious norms. He was attempting to implement a somewhat amped-up version of Hezekiah's reforms, but hopefully more successfully.

This is the context in which we must consider Josiah's covenant ceremony. It was an unprecedented and bold act that sprang from a combination of Josiah's relatively youthful optimism and his panic. Josiah convened the people and asked (compelled?) them to promise their compliance. One wonders just how truly willingly the people did so.

Such a covenant ceremony was itself radical. This is the earliest such ceremony known to us in which the members belong to the same political entity. More significant, it was centered on a *written scroll*. In one brief act, a written document was given official religious authority.

The attempt to move religious authority to a written scroll had wider ramifications. Scrolls themselves never intrinsically possess authority; that power belongs to the people who possess, interpret, and make them public. In this case, rather than the scribes claiming the text's authority, it was Josiah himself. Josiah used the new scroll to add authority to his ensuing violent campaign against the traditional priests, their shrines, and their livelihoods. Even the holiday of Passover was brought under the control of the state, its celebration centralized in Jerusalem. This was something Hezekiah's scribes could only have dreamed about.

Josiah could not have launched a wide-ranging war on what most of his subjects would have seen as their traditional religion without their consent. This is why he called for a large-scale public reading of the new scroll and asked his listeners to give their consent to his program. Without their support, he could never have begun. The priests and prophets stood awkwardly through the ceremony; not all would be sure what this would mean to them.

According to the biblical account, Josiah's attack on traditional religion was swift, violent, and successful. He destroyed cult sites, burned images of gods, desecrated the gravesites of his enemies, and killed rebel priests. His reforms culminated with the communal celebration of Passover in Jerusalem. "Before him there was no king like him," the biblical historian summarizes, "who turned to the Lord with all his heart, with all his soul, and with all his might, according to the law of Moses; nor did any like him arise after him" (2 Kings 23:25).

Despite the biblical claims, it seems that the war of words waged by Josiah and his court was more successful than his actual cultic reforms. There is no archaeological evidence, or any other evidence outside the Bible, for Josiah's reforms. Some scholars have argued that this indicates that the entire story of Josiah's discovery and reading of the scroll was a later fable.[13] Most scholars, though, think that there really is a historical core to this account. Josiah had full control over only a very small number of people and institutions. The fact that the seals of his officials no longer contained images, as was the custom under the previous kings of Judah (the lion is especially well represented in these seals), may indicate that Josiah implemented reforms in his court. On the other hand, the quick reversal of his acts by his successor, the continued use (attested in archaeological finds) of figurines of household gods, and the apparent lack of knowledge of Deuteronomy among Jews more than a century later all suggest that his success was quite limited.

Josiah's failure should not surprise us. A written oracle cannot go far against centuries of entrenched traditional religious practices. More surprising is the intense use of writing used by Josiah and his followers. The oracle that forms the core of Deuteronomy was not just read and preserved; it was also embedded in a newly created historical narrative. Scribes from Josiah's time created a narrative prologue to the scroll, a historical account of the wanderings of the Israelites through the desert and to Sinai. The effect of this prologue was to place the legal oracle in hoary antiquity.

The Deuteronomistic historian, as this writer or school of writers is often called, also added the last chapters of Deuteronomy, which continue the historical narrative, and the next six books of the Bible: Joshua, Judges, First and Second Samuel, and First and Second Kings. This entire history has a pronounced and distinctive theological agenda that drives primarily at two points. First, the entire history of Israel, from the Israelite conquest of Canaan (again, whether this was actually true or survived only as a created memory) to the present days of King Josiah, can be reduced to the simple evaluation of whether the people followed YHWH's rules (as the historian understood them) or not. The leaders who did prospered, as did their people. YHWH punished those who didn't. If good leaders were punished, it was because their ancestors had sinned. Throughout this history, it is naturally the kings of Israel who are portrayed as particularly bad, although the author also does not pull punches with the kings of Judah whom he dislikes. Even Josiah's father, Amon, and grandfather, Manasseh, are harshly critiqued.[14]

The second thrust of this history is that it culminates with Josiah. The author of this history either worked for or was strongly sympathetic to Josiah. Josiah's scribes, loosely construed, created a history that authorized their patron and his actions. They used historical sources—they frequently mention that they had access to royal annals—but they spun the narrative strongly and relatively consistently.

Why would Josiah's scribes rewrite the history of Israel? For whom were they writing? Unlike the slightly later Greek historians, the Deuteronomistic Historian gives no general statement about the audience, method, or goals of the work. We have no evidence about the reception of this work other than *perhaps* a glancing reference by the later prophet Jeremiah: "How can you say, 'We are wise, and the law of the Lord is with us,' when, in fact, the false pen of the scribes has made it into a lie?" (Jeremiah 8:8). Jeremiah here might be condemning not the core of Deuteronomy itself—whose basic message and language he echoes—but the Deuteronomistic history that appropriates it.

This was a history intended not for the masses but for the court itself. It contained stories and ideas that were widely known (for example, the legends of Samson in Judges 13–16), but as a written work of history it would have circulated only among a small group of officials. Its primary purpose, then, would have been to instruct the future rulers of Israel on good governance, which depended largely upon their sole adherence to YHWH.

Among the extant works of history from antiquity, the Deuteronomistic history is unique. It combines different genres known in antiquity to create an original kind of historical narrative that makes an original claim: YHWH elected all of Israel as his chosen people, not just its rulers.[15] It is hard to imagine, though, that the author of the Deuteronomistic history intended his work to be recited publicly to the masses in order to encourage them to obey YHWH and reinforce their sense of a single national identity. Even with the inclusion of well-known folk tales, the history is too long and tedious; much of it sounds very much like the royal annals from which the author drew. It lacks the punch delivered by the prophets, who did seem to exhort the people toward better behavior. Rather, the Deuteronomistic history seems intended for the rulers, demonstrating to them that they share the same fate as their people, and that that fate lies in their hands.

The original Deuteronomistic history was quickly overtaken by events. Josiah confronted the Egyptian army on its march north at Megiddo in 609 BCE and was killed in battle. From the perspective of the author of the Deuteronomistic history, his death—and the slide that over the next two decades would lead to the destruction of the Jerusalem temple—was quite the anticlimax.[16]

A few decades later the Deuteronomistic history was revised to reflect this unanticipated turn of events. Some of the revisions were subtle premonitions of disaster, others less so: "Still the Lord did not turn from the fierceness of his great wrath, by which his anger was kindled against Judah, because of all the provocations with which Manasseh had provoked him," the author says, trying to explain how Josiah and Judah could have met such an ignominious end (2 Kings 23:26). Writing after the destruction of the Jerusalem temple in 586 BCE, the revisers of the Deuteronomistic history tried to explain YHWH's wrath as the result of the sins of Judah's previous leaders, certainly not those of Josiah and his spiritual predecessor, Hezekiah.

Josiah believed that the discovery of the scroll of Deuteronomy was a divine message, signaling to him that the scroll itself was to be read as a divine oracle. The fact that Josiah's people discovered this scroll at an auspicious moment was not coincidental, and its authentication by scribes and a living prophetess was vital to the claim that it was authoritative. Whereas many scholars for this reason have argued that the story of the discovery was a pious fraud meant to boost the scroll's authority, I see no reason to reject this account out of hand. Maybe Josiah's people really did find the scroll, regard it as a message from YHWH, and then take it seriously. Whether this is correct or not, though, Josiah's (failed) argument that this oracle gave him authority to disrupt traditional religious practices was but one, if extreme, manifestation of a broader phenomenon that was taking place in Judahite society: the increasing use of writing and the prestige associated with it.

The scribes of the kingdom of Israel had previously recorded some of the prophecies delivered there. This practice now spread to Judah. Scribes wrote down, collected, and edited prophetic oracles. The prophet Isaiah in the early seventh century is commanded to write, although it is not precisely clear what he is supposed to be writing (Isaiah 30:8–11). In the late seventh century, the prophet Jeremiah was said to have dictated to a scribe, Baruch, son of Neriah, his prophecies and commanded him to read them aloud in the Jerusalem temple (Jeremiah 36:1–8). (Remarkably, a clay bulla was found in archaeological excavations bearing this very scribe's stamp.) A contemporaneous prophet, Habbakuk, was instructed to write his prophecy on tablets that could be easily carried (Habbakuk 2:2). Beyond this, much of this process remains obscure. We can assume that not all prophets had their oracles recorded, and for those that did, not all of their oracles would have made it into writing. Many oracles would not have been fulfilled, and we can assume that these ceased to be preserved.

Most striking, though, is the way images of writing begin to appear in the prophecies, even in the very beginning of the seventh century. Isaiah is instructed to write a few words on a tablet, not in order to preserve them but to illustrate his prophecy (Isaiah 8:2). Later in his prophecies the image of writing is used metaphorically: "The vision of all this has become for you like the words of a sealed document. If it is given to those who can read, with the command, 'Read this,' they say, 'We cannot, for it is sealed.' And if it is given to those who cannot read, saying, 'Read this,' they say, 'We cannot read'" (Isaiah 29:11–12). Ezekiel is shown an image of a scroll written on both sides and told to eat it (Ezekiel 2:9–3:3).

Prophecy has become a scribal activity or, perhaps better, the scribes who provide our only access to these oracles are themselves flirting with prophecy.

Scribes also intersected with priests. Traditionally, young Judahite priests would have learned the proper rituals from their fathers. Sometime in the eighth or seventh centuries, though, some of these rituals were written down—which kinds of sacrifices are to be made for what reasons (for example, Leviticus 1–7). These writings, called by scholars the "P source," were largely technical in nature. They were, however, later copied and revised by others with a different outlook; the revisers fused the technical details of the cult with their own moral vision of society. These texts are known today in scholarly circles as the "H" (or "Holiness," after the focus of these texts on holiness) source. Whether the actual authors and revisers of these texts were scribes or priests, they reflect the penetration of writing into cultic practice. At the same time, though, we have no evidence of the role that they may have played or the authority, if any, that was given to them.[17]

Scribes also wrote down hymns or psalms. Some of the songs that are now embedded in the narratives of today's Hebrew Bible were composed, independently of the narrative, around this time.[18] About liturgical hymns, we are far less well informed. Almost half of the psalms in the biblical book of Psalms are ascribed to "David," but these attributions are now considered late additions and there is great scholarly reluctance to date any of the psalms to the period of the first temple.

Writing grew to carry a numinous quality. The earliest attestation of a biblical text outside of the Bible is an amulet that was found in Jerusalem. Dating from around 600 BCE, the amulet is composed of two small silver scrolls with writing etched on them. Part of the text is nearly identical to the "Priestly Blessing" that is found in the Bible (Numbers 6:24–26). Like the inscription in the water tunnel, this too was not meant to be read. The amulet was found in a burial cave; perhaps it originally was carried by its owner to protect him in life, but certainly now it was supposed to protect him in death.[19] We should not see this as a text excerpted from the Bible; it is almost certain that this, and other texts like it, circulated first and independently of the narrative context into which they were eventually placed.

The growth of the presence and power of writing would have inevitably enhanced the social status of the scribe. At the same time, though, other professional classes (such as the engineers who built Hezekiah's Tunnel) increasingly saw writing as an important, or even necessary, marker of status. Evidence for this is in a letter found in Lachish that dates to shortly before its destruction by (this time) the Babylonians, in the early sixth century. Apparently, a military commander, Hosayahu, had received a letter from his superior in Jerusalem accusing him of not being able to read—the superior's previous orders were not followed to his liking. This hurt Hosayahu's feelings: "The heart of your servant is ill," he writes back. "In it my lord said: 'You don't know how (to read)—call a scribe!' As the Lord lives, no one has ever tried to read *me* a letter! Moreover, whenever any letter comes to me and I have read it, I can repeat it down to the smallest detail."[20] He saw illiteracy as a stigma for a man in his position.

The independent kingdom of Judah did not survive for long after Josiah's death. Judah stood between the emergent power of Babylonia, which had defeated Assyria, and the crown jewel of the region, Egypt. In 597 BCE, the Babylonians, under Nebuchadnezzar, deposed the Judahite king Jehoiachin. Nebuchadnezzar's forces plundered the temple and sent Jehoiachin, his court, and several other elite families into exile in Babylonia (2 Kings 24:8–16), among them Jehozadak, the high priest and a descendent of Aaron (1 Chronicles 5:41). The size of this deportation was modest, with literary sources providing figures that range between three thousand and ten thousand (Jeremiah 52:28; 2 Kings 24:14).

Jehoiachin, who was only eight when he went into captivity, outlasted his enemy. Nebuchadnezzar died, leaving his empire to his son, Evalmerodach, who released Jehoiachin from his imprisonment. He was provided with regular food rations for the rest of his life (a detail confirmed by a clay cuneiform tablet) and, presumably, was allowed to collect a small court in exile around him (2 Kings 25:27–30).[21] To the reviser of 2 Kings, all was not lost—the seed of David yet lived.

The Jerusalem temple continued to stand for another decade after Nebuchadnezzar's capture of Jehoiachin in 597 BCE. The Babylonians finally burned it to the ground on the seventh day of Av (commemorated in Jewish tradition, for not entirely clear reasons, on the ninth day of Av, or Tisha B'Av), 586 BCE, following an ill-considered revolt. The revolt and its aftermath were followed by further displacements, with the Babylonians expatriating hundreds of elite Judahite families to Babylonia, while others escaped the Babylonian wrath by fleeing to Egypt.

In 722 BCE, when the kingdom of Israel fell, writing and written texts played little role in Judah. Over the next 136 years this changed; the Judahite elite not only began to produce written documents, but there developed also a culture of literacy that gave status to the literate and their ability to work with texts. Several factors lay behind this transformation: the introduction of new knowledge and skills brought south by the Israelite refugees; the sense after 701 BCE that YHWH had truly saved and chosen Judah, which in turn led to taking oracles more seriously; and simple human envy, as those lower in status sought to emulate those above them on the social ladder.

Despite this transformation, however, the only texts that were seen as authoritative were those that were considered oracles, accurate records of the words of YHWH. And even then, these oracles were not widely accepted as normative commands; they were authoritative in the sense that a well-respected encyclopedia might be. Josiah attempted to push the normative reach of one of these texts, but this was both anomalous and by and large a failure. The texts remained important primarily to scribes, not prophets, kings, and all the more so the larger community.

We have to assume that in the chaos between 597 and 586 BCE, and especially with the burning of the temple with its (assumed) library, most of these scrolls were lost forever. Some, though, were scooped up by the scribes who went with Jehoiachin or later joined him and his court in exile. Here they would have to start again, but this time without the power they had wielded in Jerusalem and under a very different set of social and political conditions.

3 The Second Commonwealth: Babylonia, Persia, and Yehud, 586–520 BCE

"Israel are scattered sheep, harried by lions," Jeremiah lamented in the beginning of the sixth century (Jeremiah 50:17). A significant number of Judahites, particularly those outside of the major areas of fighting, remained in the old province of Judah, now under Babylonian control. Others fled to Egypt ahead of the Babylonian assault. And, of course, many found themselves deported to Babylonia itself.

It is easy to imagine that the destruction of the temple and the physical dislocations of the Judahite population caused religious trauma. Now outside of their native land and without a place in which they could sacrifice to their god, they would have been forced to develop other ways to worship YHWH. They might, for example, have elevated the writings that they brought with them as a focal point for their religious activity, studying them and developing the institution of the synagogue to publicly read them. They might have begun to restructure their religious understandings and behaviors according not to the words of priests and prophets but to written texts. This is exactly how many modern scholars and interpreters have imagined it. In this narrative, the second temple, first built in 520 BCE, pales against the first as lesser and inferior, a kind of atavistic and primitive throwback in the face of a more rational and advanced Judaism.

This is a narrative that is largely based on a speculative fantasy. There is no doubt that the temple's destruction and the Judahite deportations did lead to social and theological trauma. Exile is hard. People lost everything; many had to build new livelihoods in foreign lands. The experience was profoundly disorienting. "By the rivers of Babylon, there we sat, sat and wept, as we thought of Zion," one psalmist wrote (Psalms 137:1). The sadness was accompanied by fantasies of violent vengeance: "Fair Babylon, you predator," the psalmist continues, "a blessing on him who repays you in kind what you have inflicted on us; a blessing on him who seizes your babies and dashes them against the rocks!" (vv. 8–9).

Those who had the energy, time, and sophistication to contemplate the theological ramifications of what had happened would also have been discomfited. The Jerusalem temple was YHWH's house—how could it be destroyed? Either the Babylonian gods were more powerful than YHWH and had defeated him, or YHWH had intentionally abandoned his house as a punishment for Judah's disobedience. Neither option was very palatable.

Yet the kind of wholesale transformation imagined in the narrative above did not, in fact, occur. The exiles—or at least those who did not abandon their god and community and fade in among their neighbors, as we should probably imagine many of them doing—continued their ancestral practices. To our knowledge, the communities in Babylonia would have been missing a public cult at which sacrifices were made to YHWH. (Jewish communities in Egypt, as we will see in a later chapter, did establish new temples.) Perhaps over a longer period of time, the lack of a public cult would have sufficiently weighed upon the community to the point where its members would have thought about finding substitutes for it. It never came to that point, though. Forty years after the destruction of the temple, Babylonia fell to Persia, and the Persians, working through the old Judahite elite, allowed the temple to be rebuilt. Priests and prophets resumed their former roles. There was little room in this "second commonwealth"—now a small, struggling, and semiautonomous Persian province of Yehud—for a strong scribal culture and the development of textual authority. That time would come, but it would not be in Yehud in the sixth century.

In 539 BCE, only forty-seven years after Nebuchadnezzar destroyed the Jerusalem temple, Cyrus, the king of Persia, easily captured Babylonia. To the Judahite elite, among whom were some who remembered the Jerusalem temple, Cyrus's easy conquest of Babylonia would have been more than sweet revenge. It was also a sign of divine punishment.

Nebuchadnezzar was no longer alive to receive his just desserts (he died in 562 BCE), but God still favored his people by avenging their conquerors. This belief was, incidentally, a bit more complicated theologically than it might at first appear. The same people who explained the destruction of the temple as YHWH's punishment now had to show that the agent of that punishment—Nebuchadnezzar—had done something wrong (Jeremiah 25:9). His sin, these writers asserted, was pride: he believed that he was himself the one who destroyed the house of YHWH rather than humbly acknowledging that he was merely YHWH's agent. This little twist allowed later biblical (and Jewish and Christian writers) to roundly condemn Nebuchadnezzar and to hold him up as a paragon of evil.

We know nothing about the state of the Judahite community in Babylonia in Cyrus's time. Many apparently found peace and prosperity in their new home. The prophet Jeremiah himself, after Nebuchadnezzar's first deportations but before he fled to Egypt, advised the exiles to prepare for the long haul: "Build houses and live in them, plant gardens and eat their fruit. Take wives and beget sons and daughters; and take wives for your sons, and give your daughters husbands, that they may bear sons and daughters. Multiply there, do not decrease. And seek the welfare of the city to which I have exiled you and pray to the Lord in its behalf; for in its prosperity you shall prosper" (Jeremiah 29:5–7). Perhaps they really did. When Cyrus issued an edict allowing the Judahites to return to Jerusalem, he would have addressed it to a community that had both an administrative structure (the Judahite court in exile) and at least some means to act on it. The fact, as we will soon see, that many (probably most) members of that community did not in fact leave for Jerusalem at this or any subsequent opportunity suggests that they were quite comfortable where they were.

There is more direct evidence, albeit from a slightly later period, that also shows the success of the descendents of the Judahite exiles in creating a comfortable life for themselves. Among the many cuneiform tablets unearthed to date was a cache in Nippur of about 730 tablets, records of a fifth-century banking family known as the Murashu. Within these documents there are about seventy names that contain some reference to the God of Israel, almost certainly of Judahite origin. The documents are themselves unremarkable, and the transactions entered into by these individuals do not differ at all from those of their neighbors. At least in the very limited perspective reflected in these tablets—that of banking and commerce—these Israelites were doing well and had fully integrated into their larger community.[1]

For these well-off and well-integrated families, Cyrus's Persian conquest of Babylonia in 539 BCE would not have made much of an impact; they would simply have given their taxes to somebody else. For the crust of the Judahite elite, though, the ramifications of Cyrus's defeat of Babylonia were far more pronounced. If he were still alive, the exiled Judahite king Jehoiachin would have been only sixty-seven, and even if he were dead, his sons would have claimed royal descent and legitimacy stretching back to David.

The Bible portrays King Cyrus of Persia as close to the polar opposite of Nebuchadnezzar. He is YHWH's anointed, according to one prophet (Isaiah 45:1). Whereas Nebuchadnezzar destroyed YHWH's house and then asserted that he had conquered YHWH, Cyrus accepted and acknowledged YHWH's desire to use him to rebuild the temple. In 539 BCE, according to the Bible, Cyrus issued a proclamation: "The Lord God of Heaven has given me all the kingdoms of the earth, and has charged me with building Him a House in Jerusalem, which is in Judah. Any one of you of all His people, the Lord his God be with him and let him go up" (2 Chronicles 36:23).

On its face, the biblical report is suspect. Would Cyrus really acknowledge the God of Israel? Would it have been written in the Hebrew in which the Bible reports it? Did the biblical authors report a historical source, or did they create a fiction in order to legitimize their own desires and wishes?

We cannot be certain, but a chance archaeological discovery adds a good deal of credibility to this biblical report. This famous discovery, made in 1879, is known as the "Cyrus Cylinder" and is now owned by the British Museum. The clay cylinder is tightly inscribed in Akkadian in cuneiform script and served as a "foundation deposit" for a temple of the Babylonian god Marduk in Babylon. According to this text, Marduk, who had previously (under the Babylonians!) been worshipped improperly, "took the hand of Cyrus, king of the city of Anshan, and called him by his name, proclaiming him aloud for the kingship over all of everything." The cylinder soon shifts to the first person, and Cyrus states that he returned the Babylonian gods to their sanctuaries.[2]

The cylinder is a masterful work of Persian propaganda. Cyrus is positioned as a pious ruler who respects all gods. Indeed, his conquests were made at the very behest of the gods. The proclamation was also politically shrewd. By reversing the exilic policies of the Babylonians, he reckoned, he could earn a great deal of good will throughout his now rapidly expanding empire. Jerusalem was relatively uninhabited at this time, and allowing the exiles to return to and rebuild it would have both earned their loyalty and advanced settlement in his empire.[3]

The response to Cyrus's decree to the Israelites was not overwhelming. Some of the exiles set out from Babylonia under the guidance of a man named Sheshbazzar, "the prince of Judah" (Ezra 1:8). Apparently Sheshbazzar was a descendent of the exiled King Jehoiachin, and his Babylonian name indicates that he (and whatever court to which he may have been attached) was or until recently had been located in Babylonia. Sheshbazzar was appointed "governor" (of which land precisely we don't know) and entrusted with the vessels that Nebuchadnezzar had looted from the Jerusalem temple and brought back to Babylon (5:14). With the support of a prophet and some money collected from the exiled Judahites, he led a group of exiles back to Jerusalem and laid the foundations (but no more) for the temple (Isaiah 55:12–13). Then he disappeared from the historical record.

As later events will show, there is every indication that Sheshbazzar's mission was a failure. This is hardly surprising. Jerusalem had been thoroughly destroyed half a century earlier and had lain more or less desolate since then. Although part of the collapsed Babylonian Empire, Jerusalem was also located just a little too close to the Egyptian Empire for full comfort. The Persian administration in the area was also loosely structured, reflecting its distance from the center of Cyrus's empire. Who would want to leave the rich and fertile rivers of Babylon for this land?

Presumably, not many. We have no idea how many people accompanied Sheshbazzar on his long journey, but one biblical author hints that many within the exilic community preferred to give the returnees monetary resources rather than actually join them (Ezra 1:5). Even with hundreds of returnees and a decent treasury collected from voluntary donations (the temple vessels, of course, could not be sold or bartered, and Cyrus does not appear to have provided any other government support), this community could hardly have been expected to thrive in the challenging situation in which it found itself.

Indeed, the next signs of life that we hear from this community come seventeen years later. Much had happened in the Persian Empire during those years. Cyrus had died in 530 BCE, succeeded by his son Cambyses II, who in 525 conquered Egypt. Cambyses died in 523 and after a brief internal struggle Darius (who was not descended from Cyrus) emerged as the new Persian "king of kings" in 522.

At the Louvre today in Paris are the incredible monumental remnants of Darius's palace in Persepolis (located in modern-day Iran), transported there by the French archaeologists who excavated the site in the beginning of the twentieth century. Darius had his palace adorned with rich reliefs, in which lions were especially prevalent, and gold and silver plates on which his exploits were inscribed. To enter into these rooms in the Louvre is to catch a glimpse of the Persian Empire at its height and to get a sense of Darius's enormous task of running the administrative structure necessary to keep this empire functioning.

If Cyrus and Cambyses can primarily be seen as conquerors, Darius excelled at consolidation and administration. It is not as if Darius did not engage in warfare; he expanded the empire into the Balkans and other parts of modern-day Iran and put down numerous rebellions. His real efforts, though, were focused on figuring out ways to run his far-flung empire. Darius minted the first Persian coins, although most of the trade during his reign was conducted through barter or precious metals. He further solidified his fiscal policy by instituting a census. He confirmed the older practice of keeping Aramaic as the lingua franca, or the language of official business. Darius also established an administrative structure. He divided the empire into satrapies, each of which was ruled by a governor. By 502 BCE, the satrapies and their governance were relatively well established; it is less clear what the term as applied to Sheshbazzar (if he really did hold this title) meant. The entire area between the Euphrates and Egypt became its own satrapy, called Beyond the River, which contained smaller satrapies run by governors.

One of the more important roles that these governors played in the empire was to act as judges and to administer the "law of the king." Here again we find Darius attempting to consolidate his far-flung empire. Persian authorities attempted to take control of the legal systems of the places that they conquered *not* through the imposition of a single legal code but rather through the appointment of their own judges. This is an important and crucial difference between the functioning of law in antiquity and today. In our legal system, the role of the judge (or jury in some cases) is to apply the established law to a particular case or set of facts. By contrast, in antiquity the role of the judge (there was no jury) was to use common sense and follow precedent as he understood it to reach a just decision in each case. When "law codes" were written, their function was either to collect records of past cases—which would be useful to but were no way binding upon future judges—or to serve to set an ideal and thus also advance the claims of their royal authors to be just. So when Hammurabi created his law code, its purpose was to show that Hammurabi was a just ruler, not to bind judges to a set of laws. When, much later, Darius collected the "laws" of Egypt, he was really cataloguing traditional customs and values of the Egyptians and translating them into Aramaic, the new imperial language.[4] They helped to establish Darius's legitimacy as a just ruler. The Persian governors and the judges they appointed walked a fine line between being responsive to the needs and traditional practices of the local people they ruled and responding to the "law of the king," decrees issued by Darius in this case.

In 522 BCE the Persians sent a new governor to their new satrapy Yehud (Judah), part of Beyond the River. His name was Zerubbabel, and he was the grandson of King Jehoiachin. His name, like Sheshbazzar's, is obviously Babylonian and might be a hint that the Judahite elites were still mainly concentrated in Babylonia. In any case, he left for Yehud with high expectations. The prophets refer to Zerubbabel as the "branch," alluding to both his Davidic ancestry and the messianic hopes they had for him (Haggai 2:2). He took with him Joshua, the son of Jehozadak, the high priest who was exiled with King Jehoiachin.

If Sheshbazzar had made any progress at all, you wouldn't know it. Zerubbabel and Joshua arrived in the seventh month. About their return, the Bible states: "Then Jeshua son of Jozadak, with his fellow priests, and Zerubbabel son of Shealtiel with his kin set out to build the altar of the God of Israel, to offer burnt-offerings on it, as prescribed in the law of Moses the man of God. They set up the altar on its foundation, because they were in dread of the neighbouring peoples, and they offered burnt-offerings upon it to the Lord, morning and evening. And they kept the festival of booths, as prescribed, and offered the daily burnt-offerings by number according to the ordinance, as required for each day" (Ezra 3:2–4).

This short passage contains three striking details. First, there was no temple when they arrived; indeed, there wasn't even an altar on which to offer sacrifices! The fact that the first thing they did was to set up the altar demonstrates that their understanding of the temple as the central feature of the worship of the God of Israel had not waned in the course of the exile.

Second, they—or, perhaps more likely, the later author of this passage—thought that the altar and the sacrificial rite had to conform to the written record of the "law of Moses." They are depicted as looking to a written scroll for guidance and authority. More specifically, this is a scroll that contains technical details of the sacrificial rite. I will return to this detail in the next chapter, as I believe it better reflects the perspective of the author of this narrative, writing in the mid- to late fifth century, than it relates to what actually happened in 522 BCE.

Third, who were these "neighbouring peoples" whom they feared? Most were undoubtedly the descendents of the Judahites who were not exiled by the Babylonians, who may have been trickling back into the city in the seventeen years since Sheshbazzar had arrived. Some, of course, may have been non-Judahites who had resettled, either voluntarily or forcibly by the Babylonians, in Jerusalem. Those who had come back with Sheshbazzar, who may have felt that this new wave was usurping them, would have joined both of these other populations comprising the "people of the land."

So the people began to build, but not for long. As soon as the rebuilding began, a group of local residents appealed to Zerubbabel to allow him to let them join them; they too, after all, worshipped YHWH (Ezra 4:2). Zerubbabel and Joshua, though, wanted nothing to do with the locals. The desire on the part of the locals to join in building and worshipping at the temple is perfectly understandable. They saw themselves as part of the same religious community as the new returnees. But Zerubbabel, Joshua, and the other elders did not see it that way.

Why? Something had clearly changed in the mentality of the Judahite exiles in Babylonia. In order to understand what, we must briefly return to the Judahite court in Babylonia before resuming with the story of Zerubbabel and Joshua.

Through the sixth century BCE, most Israelites and Judahites were, to various degrees, ambivalent about the existence and efficacy of deities other than YHWH. By attempting to consolidate the public cult around YHWH alone, the reforms of Hezekiah and Josiah tended toward one end of the spectrum. For most of the population (and maybe for Hezekiah and Josiah as well), though, the existence of other deities and the propriety of their private worship were never very much in question. They may have seen the images of these gods as ridiculous, but what they ridiculed was the idea that a deity could take material form, not the existence of the deity itself.[5]

Beginning in the mid-sixth century, the exiled Judahite elite in Babylonia began to develop a more robust idea of divine exclusiveness. The most prominent extant source for this line of thought was a prophet whom scholars label Deutero-Isaiah. We know nothing about the prophet himself. What we do know is that the biblical book of Isaiah contains three sets of oracles, delivered at different times. The first set, comprising chapters 1–39, are the eighth- to seventh-century oracles attributed to the prophet Isaiah who lived in the time of Hezekiah. The second set, chapters 40–55, was delivered in the mid-sixth century as Cyrus was expanding his empire. The third set, chapters 56–66, was given in the late sixth century. It is possible that the later two sets of oracles were delivered by the same prophet, but that is not certain. (Some scholars argue that we should speak also of a Trito-Isaiah.) At some relatively early point, for unclear reasons, these sets of oracles became part of the same scroll, all attributed to Isaiah.

One of Deutero-Isaiah's primary themes is that YHWH is in fact the only god; it is the pure monotheism that we often mistakenly attribute to the Pentateuch itself. "Thus said the Lord, the King of Israel, their redeemer, the Lord of Hosts," the prophet declares: "I am the first and I am the last, besides me there is no god" (Isaiah 44:6). The same prophet clearly knew that his view was a minority one; that not all recognized YHWH as the sole god. But they would. Isaiah imagines a time, to begin imminently, in which all peoples, Israelite and not, will acknowledge the sovereignty of the one true God whom they will come to worship in Jerusalem (Isaiah 65–66). This is an exclusionary vision that leaves no room for other gods or their worshippers.[6] In this vision, YHWH still has a name, but that name—previously used to differentiate this god from others of different names—is less relevant, because no other gods are acknowledged. To mark this shift in thought, I will begin from here to use the English word "God" to denote YHWH, as seen from this perspective. (Needless to say, Cyrus or any later Greek or Roman would take affront at such usage.)

Another distinctive feature of the extant version of Deutero-Isaiah is its use of texts. The prophet, we presume, delivered the oracles orally. It was left to a scribe to put them into written form. However the prophet himself phrased the oracles, the scribe who recorded them did so according to literary convention, even drawing upon the earlier prophet Jeremiah. Deutero-Isaiah never actually cites Jeremiah by name but through several allusions engages and reworks the prophecies. For this author, Jeremiah is thus quasi-authoritative, an important resource to respect and use rather than one that is evoked for normative authority. This is precisely the kind of creative and academic use of earlier sources that we saw in previous scribal activity and its intersection with prophecy.[7]

The prophet(s) who delivered the oracles in Deutero-Isaiah, the scribe(s) who molded them into the form in which they now exist, and Zerubbabel and Joshua all came from the same circle that was linked to the Judahite court in exile. They shared a certain emerging vision of the one God and the authority of the Davidic line and the priests of one particular clan to implement that God's will. They also had an inchoate notion of the authority of older texts, although the impact of this notion would not be felt for another seventy years.

The "neighbouring peoples" whom Zerubbabel and his companions encountered did not share these commitments. To Zerubbabel and his followers, these natives may have claimed to be worshipping the same God, but they had no real understanding of how God desired to be worshipped. They were precisely the sinners that their prophet railed against. They, on the other hand, must have been struck by the gall of these newcomers, especially when they would have seen themselves as having a certain right to participate simply by virtue of their continual presence in the area.

"Bad" behavior alone is rectifiable. Zerubbabel, though, seemed to make no effort to win them to his side, most likely because the differences between those who had remained and those who returned went beyond practice and belief. The biblical accounts of how many actually returned with Zerubbabel and Joshua are confused, and there is little agreement among modern scholars. While open to debate, the archaeological evidence suggests that around this time Jerusalem had a population of about 2,750, with perhaps the entire province of Yehud containing an additional population of 25,000.[8] This is far below the figure of tens of thousands indicated in the biblical account. However, more significantly and plausibly, the Bible categorizes the returnees by genealogy. At least the later writers had a concern for genealogical purity, and it is possible that Zerubbabel himself led a relatively aristocratic group that had no interest in working with those of lesser and untraceable descent. They would do this on their own, with God's help.

God's contribution to this building effort apparently fell a little short. Zerubbabel and his cohort first, expectedly, hit resistance from the local population. These locals, thoroughly annoyed now, set about undermining the work of rebuilding the temple. According to the authors of our histories, who were of course on the side of Zerubabbel and Joshua, the "adversaries of Judah and Benjamin," as they called them, bribed the Persian authorities to stop the work. They appear to have been largely successful.

Two years apparently passed with almost no progress on the temple. On the twenty-fourth day of the sixth month of the second year of the reign of King Darius (520 BCE), the returnees began again to build. About a month later, "the word of the Lord" came to the prophet Haggai, who must have accompanied Zerubbabel and Joshua when they returned to Jerusalem. The message was not a pretty one. God rebuked the people for building their own houses before his house. As the prophecy continues, the reason for this neglect becomes clearer. There has been little rain, and things have not been going well for the returnees. "You have sown much, and harvested little; you eat, but you never have enough; you drink, but you never have your fill; you clothe yourselves, but no one is warm; and you that earn wages earn wages to put them into a bag with holes," God says through Haggai (Haggai 1:6). But the people, he goes on, have it all backwards. The drought, God declares, is the result, not the cause, of neglecting the rebuilding of the temple. Once the temple is rebuilt God's favor will return, and the land will prosper.

About a month later, Zechariah began to prophesy, presumably also in Jerusalem. His prophecy included words of encouragement to Joshua and Zerubbabel. God compares the high priest Joshua to a brand plucked from the fire; Zerubbabel is "my servant, the Branch," referring to a messianic figure from the Davidic line. Zerubbabel was to complete the work he began: "Moreover, the word of the Lord came to me, saying, 'The hands of Zerubbabel have laid the foundation of this house; his hands shall also complete it. Then you will know that the Lord of hosts has sent me to you. For whoever has despised the day of small things shall rejoice, and shall see the plummet in the hand of Zerubbabel'" (Zechariah 4:8–10).

Another month passed, and then Haggai prophesied again. The foundation of the temple was established and God promised that now he would begin to send blessings on the crops (Haggai 2:18–19). That same day Haggai confirmed Zerubbabel as God's signet on the quickly approaching day of God's judgment.

What caused this flurry of prophecies? It is likely that the building was not going well. Even with Haggai's help, it was hard for Zerubbabel and Joshua to motivate the people and marshal resources, especially after or during a drought and in the continuing face of local opposition. Zechariah added a bit more weight, attempting to give even further authority to Zerubbabel and Joshua; Haggai then affirmed them again. Unlike Jeremiah, Haggai and Zechariah were "company men," prophets working on the same side as the institutional leadership.

Yet the opposition to the building project did not cease. The Persian governor of Beyond the River, the biblical account relates, was alarmed by the construction of the temple. Maybe the locals convinced him to interfere; perhaps he suspected that their rebuilding project would somehow sow seeds of rebellion against Persia. He, though, did his job responsibly. Upon being informed by the "leaders" that they were acting in accord with King Cyrus's decree, the governor allowed them to continue as he wrote to Darius for confirmation.

According to the biblical book of Ezra, upon receiving the letter the Persian authorities searched the records in Babylonia and found King Cyrus's decree (Ezra 6). This Aramaic decree goes well beyond the short Hebrew report at the beginning of the book of Ezra. The document, if authentic at all, is almost certainly embellished, as is the document that follows in which Darius confirms Cyrus's decree and guarantees Persian monetary support for the rebuilding of the temple and the sacrificial service. Thus reassured, the governor allowed the building to continue.

Assuming that the governor's intervention occurred close to the time that the foundation was completed, the temple took another four years to complete. The temple was completed on the third of Adar in the sixth year of Darius's rule—516 BCE. The celebration was raucous and bloody, with hundreds of animals sacrificed (Ezra 6:16–17). The people also appointed priestly courses and Levitical divisions to take turns serving at the temple. A little over five weeks later the returnees, joined by those who had separated themselves from the "pollutions" of the people of the land, celebrated Passover at the new temple (Ezra 6:21). The chapter of Sheshbazzar, Zerubbabel, and Joshua ends on this upbeat note.

The narrator of this story ended with the story of the joyous Passover celebration in order to highlight the continuity of this second Jerusalem temple with the first. For Haggai, Zechariah, Zerubbabel, and Joshua, the second temple—complete with the implements from the first temple that Nebuchadnezzar had fortunately preserved and that Cyrus had returned to the exiles—was not only authentic but would become more glorious than the first (Haggai 2:9). By noting the Passover celebration, the account linked this story with the reforms of both Hezekiah and Josiah, the last two "good" preexilic Judahite kings, whose stories (preserved in the Deuteronomistic history, which they as leaders knew) also contained such a celebration. The prophets were only partially correct. Zerubbabel would not become the anointed one whose coming would herald a new phase in world history. Rather, he would fade away into history, his task incomplete, much like Josiah. Yet the temple that he built, as modest and out of the way as it was, would some five hundred years later truly become more glorious than the first.

The basic structure of religious authority had not changed. A monarchic leader from the line of David handled state relations. The priests—understood as all Levites rather than just the descendents of Aaron, qua Deuteronomy and led by a high priest of proper family—were the primary religious authorities. Their first and primary goal was to get the Jerusalem temple up and running in order to restore the sacrifices and to allow God to return to his home and dwell among his people. When Haggai wanted to make a point, he told the people to "seek a ruling from the priests"—ask them about the law concerning a certain case of purity (Haggai 2:11). Excepting the later writer's appeal to the written "law of Moses," there is no consultation with written texts or even a hint of their existence as a source of authority. God still spoke to the people through prophets, who were official members of the administrative apparatus.

The biblical book of Esther, at least in its very general vision of life at the center of the Persian Empire, paints a similar picture. In the author's world, it is at least plausible that Persian Jews could live a full and satisfying life close to the royal court with no knowledge whatsoever of any authoritative writing and perhaps even without any distinctive religious customs.

The book of Esther is a bit of an enigma. A story purportedly about an event that occurred sometime in the fifth century in Persia, the book offers few clues about its author or actual date of composition, although scholarly consensus might lean now toward the late Persian period. Without using it to make any strong historical arguments, though, it still provides a picture at least of what some author around this time thought was plausible.[9]

The book tells how two Jews, Esther and Mordechai, rescued their compatriots in the Persian Empire from destruction. To summarize briefly: the king of Persia, Ahasuerus, has deposed his wife and seeks another. This comes to the attention of a hanger-on of the court, a "Judean" named Mordechai, who urges his relative Esther to compete for the job.

She wins the competition and is installed in the king's harem. In the meantime, the king's evil viceroy, Haman, becomes incensed at Mordechai because he will not bow down to him. In order to get rid of Mordechai, Haman plots to kill all of the Jews in the Persian kingdom and convinces the king (who comes across as a bit dim) to allow him to proceed. Mordechai gets wind of the plot and tells Esther. Esther invites the king and Haman to her quarters and there reveals her identity as a Jew. The king stalks out in anger and Haman begs Esther for his life, at which point the king returns and thinks that Haman is making a pass at her. He has Haman and his family killed and allows the Jews to defend themselves against their enemies. Mordechai, meanwhile, is recognized for his services to the king, and the Jews live happily ever after.

As many commentators from antiquity on have noted, there is a striking absence in this narrative of both God and the Torah, or of any authoritative documents other than those of the Persian king. Perhaps the author simply thought that this was not relevant to the plot, but the absence of any appeal to sacred documents is at least worthy of note. The only reference that might be read this way—Haman's accusation to King Ahasuerus against the Jews that "their laws" are different than those of other groups and from those of the king (Esther 3:8)—is instead a reference to distinctive ethnic customs. There is no specific evidence through the book of any distinctive customs that we might call religious: there are no Sabbaths or holidays, no mention of the God of Israel, and even Mordechai's refusal to bow to Haman is not justified in the book, although later interpreters would see it as motivated by religious scruples.

This is consistent with another feature of the story, the lack of communal organization. Mordechai, at Esther's request, arranges for a three-day fast, but this is ad hoc. It is Mordechai's sending of the festal letter at the end of the book to the scattered Jewish communities that establishes the holiday of Purim as a day of "feasting and merrymaking" (Esther 9:20–23). He does this not as a leader of the Judahites in Babylonia—a role that he does not appear to have at the beginning of the book—but as an officer of the royal court. Mordechai's letter, in fact, was not quite enough. Queen Esther dispatched her own letter only to confirm Mordechai's, again meant to establish its royal backing (9:32). The point is not that these events really happened, but that the author of this book found it more plausible to have these letters sent by Persian authorities than by anybody else. To the extent that these exiles had power and influence, in this author's mind, they held and exercised it as individuals who were close to the Persian authorities. They were not independent religious or communal leaders of the "Judeans."

The book of Esther also signals a terminological shift. The Hebrew Bible (Old Testament) almost always uses the term "Israel" or "children of Israel" to refer to its community. I have been using the term the "Judahite" here to highlight their geographical and political origins and continuing identity. Esther and the other literature from this period, though, begin to use the term *yehudi* in this same sense, to denote a member of the collective whole. The term, for example, is used to identify Mordechai (2:5). The term clearly derives from the name of the new Persian province Yehud, the successor of Judah. It can hence be translated as "Judean" or "Jew." "Judean" emphasizes geographical origin; "Jew" has come to be in our times more associated with religious identity. In truth, in antiquity as today, the two ideas were intertwined; this is why never, to my knowledge, do we have clear evidence from antiquity of a *yehudi* (whether masculine or feminine, singular or plural) who is not part of the community that worships the God of Israel. From this point I will begin to use both terms rather than Judahite. This points to the growing ambiguity between "Judean" identity, which is rooted in a specific geographical-political territory, and "Jewish" identity, which comes to have a wider meaning that includes following certain common customs and is less connected to the territory of Yehud. Jews and Judeans, as we will come to see, developed different notions of scripture and its authority. Which of these translations I use in each particular instance depends on which aspect of this identity that I wish to emphasize.[10]

Just a little over seventy years after the mission of Zerubbabel and Joshua, another mission to Jerusalem would take place, this time by a man named Ezra. Ezra was no prince of the Davidic line, like Sheshbazzar. He was, rather, a Persian functionary, much like the fictional Mordechai, who derived his power from his relationships with the royal court. By the middle of the fifth century, the Judahite court in exile located in Babylonia had apparently collapsed; we never again hear of a living, historical descendent of David until the claim is made for Jesus. At least some of its scrolls, though, did survive, now in the hands of a new generation. We do not know the precise relationship between this new generation and the older Judahite elite; the very fact that they do not reveal this in their own writings might point to more discontinuity than continuity. But whatever the relationship, it would be up to them to write the next chapter of our story.

4 Ezra and the Pentateuch: Persia and Yehud, 520–458 BCE

By the beginning of the third century CE, Ezra the scribe had gained a status among Jews that was second only to Moses. Books of his visions circulated widely and he was so well known that a portrait of him can be found on a synagogue fresco located in a dusty town on the fringes of the Roman Empire. The rabbis bluntly declared, "Ezra would have been worthy to have received the Torah had not Moses preceded him." It is Ezra, they say, who instituted the regular liturgical reading of the Torah.[1]

Ezra's reputation sprang from the one thin book in the Bible that bears his name. In this biblical narrative, Ezra reads the "Teaching" aloud to a public assembly, an account that has been taken as the first evidence both for the existence of the Torah and for its promulgation as a normative body of laws. One scholar has gone as far as to suggest, perhaps a little tongue in cheek, that it was Ezra himself who redacted the Torah into the form in which it now, more or less, exists.[2]

Ezra would thus seem to be a watershed figure in the story of how the Hebrew Bible acquired authority. And in a sense, he was. His achievements, though, were far more limited than later writers thought, as a close reading of his account will show.

With the single coy phrase "after these things" (Ezra 7:1), the Bible leaves more than sixty years of Jewish history in darkness. The biblical report of Zerubbabel's mission ends around 520 BCE; it resumes the story with the appearance of Ezra in 458 BCE. By now not only Darius I but also his son, Xerxes I, had died and the Persian Empire was in the hands of Darius's grandson, Artaxerxes I (v. 11).

Perhaps not so coincidentally, this "dark age" in Jewish history coincided with the epic war between the Greeks and the Persians. For some fifty years, between 499 and 449 BCE, the Persians were locked in a struggle with the Greek city-states (the Delian League). The conflict would ebb and flow, but it clearly absorbed most of Persia's energy; Artaxerxes had more important matters to attend to than the tiny and insignificant province of Yehud. The conflict also created tensions between Athens and Sparta that erupted into the First Peloponnesian War in 460 BCE. It is possible that the internal conflict among the Greeks gave Artaxerxes enough breathing space to consider the petition of the obscure foreign priest named Ezra.[3]

The very first thing that the Bible tells us about Ezra is that he was a priest. He was not just any priest: his direct lineage included Zadok (King David's high priest); Pinhas (who was noted in the Bible for his devotion to God; Numbers 25:1–13); and Aaron, the progenitor of all priests (in the Judahite tradition) (Ezra 7:1–5). More than a century after the destruction of the temple, the exiled community preserved the idea that priests should remain identifiable (and, presumably, respected), despite the fact that they would seem to have few if any functions to perform. Other than this genealogy, we know nothing at all about his youth.

How, though, did this Judean priest come to the attention of the Persian court? Throughout the biblical book of Ezra, Ezra himself is repeatedly identified as a "scribe." Ezra's letter of commission from the Persian authorities explicitly identifies him as "priest, scribe in the law of the God of Heaven" (Ezra 7:12–21).[4] Ezra is to appoint judges in Beyond the River, according to the "law of your God" (7:14, 25). Being a scribe was not like being a priest, an inherited title, or a modern Ph.D., who earns the title "doctor" whether he or she ever actually does anything with it. After the intensive training it required actual employment; it was a job almost always associated with political authority. Who, though, would have hired a "scribe in the law of the God of Heaven"?

The Judahite court seems to have dissolved at some point between Sheshbazzar and Ezra, and Ezra never presents himself as working through an intermediary body. He reports directly to the Persians. Some years later, Nehemiah is portrayed as working within the Persian court, and it is possible that Ezra originally worked as a scribe within this bureaucratic apparatus (Nehemiah 1:11). If so, Ezra would have had two jobs. One was to continue the Persians' efforts to collect and categorize the laws and customs of the people they conquered, as Darius did in Egypt. The second would have been to serve "as a kind of high commissioner for Jewish affairs in the Trans-Euphrates satrapy."[5] Ezra worked not for the exiled community but for the Persians, although he apparently requested the appointment. Perhaps he convinced his higher-ups that he could better fulfill his job if he were on the ground in Jerusalem.

Ezra, that is, was first and foremost a Persian functionary. His mandate was to revitalize the Jewish cult in Jerusalem and to establish a judicial system based on the "law of the God of Heaven," with, of course, the king's law. He also must have had access to the coercive organs of the Persian state, since Artaxerxes authorizes Ezra to punish those who won't obey him: "All who will not obey the law of your God and the law of the king, let judgment be strictly executed on them, whether for death or for banishment or for confiscation of their goods or for imprisonment" (Ezra 7:26).

Ezra with his retinue set out for Yehud in the spring of 458 BCE with 1,513 men, according to the biblical account, enumerated by clan (Ezra 8:1–14). It is possible that this reflects the continued importance of organization by clans among the exiles in Persia, but it is also possible that it instead reflects the political situation of the later redactor of this work who was living in Yehud. In any case, clan politics would come to play an important role in subsequent events. If we assume that each of the returnees also brought a family, the biblical account suggests that the real size of this caravan was five thousand to ten thousand individuals. As we will see below, though, there are good reasons to doubt these figures.

A few days out on their way to Jerusalem, Ezra stopped at a river and declared a fast to beseech God for a safe trip. But, given the secular authority bestowed on Ezra by the king, why should Ezra be afraid? He soon tells us: "For I was ashamed to ask the king for a band of soldiers and cavalry to protect us against the enemy on our way, since we had told the king that the hand of our God is gracious to all who seek him" (Ezra 8:21–22). Ezra, it seems, had talked himself into a corner. He used the argument that God cared for the Judeans in order to get the proclamation from Artaxerxes, but once he did so he thought that asking the king for protective troops would undermine his argument. Now, though, Ezra was concerned—he realized the potential danger in which he put the exiles as they started their long trek. Although the Persian road system was good and relatively secure, any long trip in antiquity faced numerous hazards, especially the threat of bandits (although it is hard to imagine a real threat to a caravan as large as the Bible claims it was). In addition to fasting and praying, Ezra divided the treasure that they were carrying among different camps, presumably to assure that were they to be attacked they would not lose everything.

Fortunately for Ezra, the trip was uneventful. The party arrived in Jerusalem on the first day of the fifth month, the month of Av, five months after they left Babylonia. They stayed for three days before bringing their precious cargo to the temple (Ezra 7:8–9, 8:32).

Ezra would have seen a temple very different from the grand structure that Herod built some 450 years later. According to archaeological finds (or more properly often their lack) and in contrast to the impression that the Bible gives, at that time Jerusalem was little more than a village. It had no fortifications, although remains of the walls destroyed by the Babylonians were still visible. Its inhabitants appeared to have lived immediately around and south of the temple, in the area now known as the City of David. Although the Persian authorities built strong urban centers along the Mediterranean coast and the plains immediately to the west, they invested few resources in the hill country in which Jerusalem is located. In the fifth century, even more so than two hundred years earlier in the days of Josiah, Jerusalem was in the hinterland, difficult to access and far from major roads and trade routes, with a fairly dependable source of water but flinty land that was hard to cultivate. Its economic position was precarious.[6]

Jerusalem was thus also sparsely populated. In Ezra's time, the total population may have been anywhere between 500 and 3,000 in an occupied area that constituted only about 5.5 acres. By contrast, my small city, Providence, Rhode Island, contains 11,840 acres; Manhattan is 14,528 acres; and the current Old City of Jerusalem is 224 acres. These numbers contrast sharply with the impression given by the Bible. According to the Bible, a previous wave of migration from Babylonia to Judah in 516 BCE consisted of 49,897 Israelites (Ezra 2:64). If the archaeologists are correct, there is surely a problem with this number: where did they all go? Perhaps those who returned quickly scattered to areas where life was easier or experienced an extraordinary rate of mortality. Perhaps the archaeologists, whose case rests more on the absence of finds than their presence, are mistaken.

More likely, though, it is the biblical author who is mistaken. The author, who clearly promoted Ezra and those associated with him, had an interest in exaggerating these numbers. If the archaeologists are correct, then the size of Ezra's entourage would have dwarfed the existing population of Jerusalem, which contrasts with the impression given by the rest of the narrative of Ezra's mission. Ezra's entourage was likely significantly smaller than the numbers that the Bible gives. We must instead imagine a small retinue, led by Ezra, a Persian functionary, arriving at a very modest settlement.

There is no description of the temple, but we must imagine that it too was a modest structure, hardly sturdier than the tabernacle described in the Bible that the Israelites took with them in their wanderings through the desert. It would have had an altar for the sacrifices and a tent or small structure, perhaps made of stone, that would have served as the "holy of holies." There would also have been some structure in the compound to house the temple's treasures, including the holy vessels used for the sacrifices. The temple was fifty-eight years old by the time Ezra arrived, but given Jerusalem's small population and poverty it would not have progressed much beyond the original structure.

Jerusalem's religious life centered on the temple and its sacrifices, performed by its priests and Levites. The Persians tended to interfere little, if at all, in local village life. They probably established their own administrative center on a hill outside of and overlooking the city, on the modern site of Ramat Rachel.[7] The small Jerusalem population was organized in clans, each of which was led by a patriarch, and there is no indication that any of these patriarchs held exceptional power. There is no evidence of centralized authority, and we must presume that communal decisions were reached by consensus of the clan heads.

The arrival of Ezra and his entourage on that summer day in 458 BCE must have come as something of a shock, and it is easy to imagine that the local population would have met the newcomers with some ambivalence.

On the one hand, the priests and Levites would have welcomed the sacrifices and treasures that Ezra brought, and the villagers might have welcomed the attention that they were finally receiving from Persian authorities. On the other hand, after sacrificing, Ezra and the leaders of the returnees presented their royal commission (Ezra 8:36). Ezra, it was clear, had come to shake things up.

On the first day of the seventh month, the Hebrew month of Tishri, two months after Ezra arrived, he assembled the population to read to them the "book of the law of Moses, which the Lord had given to Israel" (Nehemiah 8:1). Ezra, identified here as both a scribe and a priest, climbed a wooden platform and, flanked by several leaders, read all morning, with the Levites translating and explaining the reading (Nehemiah 8:8).[8]

We have now arrived at the critical part of the story. What was this "book of the law of Moses"? Were the locals of Jerusalem familiar with it? Did they understand it to be authoritative? In order to better answer these questions, at this point we need introduce what scholars call the documentary hypothesis.

The documentary hypothesis, in what can be called its standard form, was proposed in 1878 by a German scholar named Julius Wellhausen. It is a simple and brilliant answer to a very puzzling question: Why is the narrative of the Pentateuch (in particular) so strange? Why does it seem to contain so many contradictions, repetitions, and unexpected jumps? The question had long been recognized and addressed in different ways by Christians and Jews, whose theological answers reflected their a priori religious commitments to the text. Removing those commitments (which, for example, assumed that the text was authored by God)—an approach that had been in the air since the seventeenth century but was expressed more robustly in the Enlightenment—reopened the question. Clearly it was not enough to say that the text was imperfect because it was authored by imperfect human beings.[9]

The documentary hypothesis proposes that the Judahites living in Babylonia in the sixth–fifth centuries created the Pentateuch from earlier sources. More specifically, they used three to five sources, depending on how one counts. The two oldest sources were termed E and J. E was a set of Israelite (northern kingdom) legends that predated Israel's fall in

722 BCE and frequently calls God Elohim (beginning with an E). J was an overlapping set of legends that originated in Judah and that uses YHWH for the name of God (Y transliterates as J in German). J and E were combined into a single textual source, JE, sometime prior to 586 BCE. The core of Deuteronomy, discussed earlier, is termed D. The priestly material is termed P, and there is significant scholarly debate about the existence of another source that has connections to the priests, called H for the "Holiness Code." In Babylonia, then, a scribe (or group of them) molded these documents, cutting, splicing, and recombining many of them (although leaving D largely intact) into the whole as it now more or less exists.

The documentary hypothesis is just that, a hypothesis; there is no direct evidence for it. We have yet to uncover a single piece of evidence, outside of Deuteronomy, for the actual preredaction existence of these hypothetical sources. Over the last two decades some scholars have thus proposed replacing the documentary hypothesis with other theories that, for example, understand the formation of the Pentateuch as the result of a continual process of growth, accretion, and modification.[10]

As such hypotheses go, however, it has also been tremendously enduring and productive. It accounts for many of the narrative problems of the Pentateuch. It explains particularly well why there are consistencies and patterns to certain narrative disruptions that occur throughout the Pentateuch.

Let me offer just one example of the hypothesis in action. The problem is the biblical festival calendar. We will look first at the Pentateuch's varied descriptions of the festival calendar and then at how modern biblical scholars have tried to explain its discrepancies using the documentary hypothesis. That, in turn, will help us to better understand the significance of the narrative in Ezra.

In the Pentateuch, the calendar appears in four places. Exodus 23:12–17 mentions the Sabbath and the three pilgrimage festivals, Feast of Unleavened Bread, harvest or first fruits (Shavuot or Pentecost), and ingathering (Sukkot or Tabernacles). For each of these holidays one is commanded to "appear before the Lord God."

The calendar given in Leviticus 23 is far more involved. In addition to the Sabbath and pilgrimage festivals (two of which, Passover—which has been combined with the Feast of Unleavened Bread—and Tabernacles, are to be observed for a week), it mentions two other holidays: a "holy convocation commemorated with trumpet blasts" (v. 24; today called Rosh Hashanah) and a "day of atonement" (v. 26; Yom Kippur). This discussion of the festivals ends with a description of Tabernacles, which it dates to the fifteenth day of the seventh month. Tabernacles is to last seven days, during which time the Israelites are commanded to live in booths and "to rejoice before the Lord your God" with vegetation. This is all to be done in commemoration of the Israelite sojourn in the desert after God redeemed them from bondage in Egypt (vv. 39–40, 42–43). Numbers 28–29, the third relevant passage, has the same holidays but specifies very precisely the sacrifices that are to be made on each of the days.

Deuteronomy 16:1–17 contains yet another festival calendar. Like the passage in Exodus, it lists only the pilgrimage festivals (but without the Sabbath); it has no mention of Rosh Hashanah and Yom Kippur. Like the Leviticus passage, it specifies that Passover and Tabernacles are to last for seven days. It insists, repeatedly and unlike the other three passages, that the pilgrimages are to be made "before the Lord your God at the place that he will choose" (v. 16). The specific observances of Sukkot found in Leviticus (gathering vegetation, dwelling in booths) are not mentioned here.

What is the relationship between these passages? Source critics tend to assign the first, Exodus 23, to E. It describes a ritual in which the Israelites would "appear before the Lord" at their local shrines. Whatever they did there is not specified, but it probably varied somewhat according to the established practices of each particular shrine. The last passage is obviously assigned to D, and reflects this author's concern about the centralization of the cult in "the place that he will choose," by which Jerusalem is meant. D might here be revising E.

Some assign the other two passages to P, although Leviticus 23 might be better assigned to H. They contain mention of two holidays not mentioned in E and D sources, Rosh Hashanah and Yom Kippur. How do we explain the appearance of these holidays here but not in the other two passages? Did the authors of those two other passages—E and D—know of Rosh Hashanah and Yom Kippur but not mention them simply because they felt that they were not relevant to their description of the three pilgrimage festivals? Or were they in fact unaware of the two holidays, which would go on in our day (and maybe also in antiquity) to become the most well known and best observed of all Jewish holidays? To answer this question, we need to return to Ezra.

So Ezra read all morning. The people wept as they heard, but Ezra and his assistants shushed them. It was the first of Tishri, and they were not to weep or mourn. Instead, they were now to go home, rejoice, eat well, and treat the day as holy. In our terms (it does not bear this name in the account in Ezra), it is Rosh Hashanah (Nehemiah 8:9–12).

The next day a similar discovery was made. This time just the leaders gathered to study the scroll, and they discovered the existence of the festival of Tabernacles. They commanded people to bring vegetation and to make booths with it, "as it is written" (vv. 8–15). The entire community, we are told, did so, and dwelt in the booths for seven days, which, as we are told further, "from the days of Jeshua son of Nun to that day the people of Israel had not done" (v. 17).

What was this scroll that Ezra read? Why could the people not understand it? Why were they unaware of these two holidays?

Ezra clearly was familiar with the festival calendar of P. There are, though, several anomalies. This account mentions the holidays of Rosh Hashanah and Tabernacles, but not Yom Kippur, the holiday that falls between them. Unlike Leviticus 23, which seems to prescribe two practices for Sukkot (gathering vegetation to rejoice with and dwelling in booths), Ezra orders that vegetation be gathered in order to construct the booths. For neither of these holidays does Ezra mention sacrifices, which are of primary importance to P in particular. The timing of the reading also resonates with the Deuteronomistic history, which associates Tabernacles with the time when (every seven years) the people are to listen to the "Teaching," and with the date on which Solomon dedicated the first temple (Deuteronomy 31:10–13; 1 Kings 8:2).

Elsewhere too Ezra cites texts that closely resemble passages from the Pentateuch that modern scholars consider to be from the P and D sources (Ezra 9:11–12). For this reason, it seems likely that Ezra's scroll contains passages from both P and D (and H) sources, although not necessarily in the order or way that they survive in the modern Pentateuch.[11]

Ezra was a priest and a scribe, and it is not impossible that he himself composed the scroll that he brought back to Jerusalem. He would have had access to the old Judahite library and have been interested in priestly writings. D, as embedded in the Deuteronomistic history, was by that time a scroll that would have held an important place among elite Judahite circles in Babylonia and Persia. Ezra shows no familiarity at all with J or E materials. This does not mean that he did not know them or that they did not exist, but that it is likely they were not part of his scroll.

There is another, more mundane reason to think that Ezra's scroll did not in fact contain the entire Pentateuch. Such a scroll would simply have been too large. Today, for Jewish ritual purposes the Pentateuch, or Torah, is written on a single scroll. In antiquity, though, scrolls of that size were unheard of; they were far too unwieldy to be useful. Ezra, of course, might have had other scrolls with him as well, but it seems that the "law of Moses" was composed of some subset of P and D materials in not quite the version that we now possess.

Ezra's Torah was written in Hebrew. This was natural enough; D for sure and arguably P as well (or at least the part that Ezra knew) dated from before the exile, when Hebrew was the language of Judah. By Ezra's time, though, Hebrew was primarily a scribal language, having been supplanted as a living spoken language by Aramaic. Although Hebrew and Aramaic are related Semitic dialects, the gap was clearly too wide for most listeners to handle. The Hebrew reading had to be translated into Aramaic before being explained.

And the Torah, whatever its precise form, would need explaining. The people would have had some acquaintance with Moses, "the prophets," and other characters in their foundational myths. They would have been familiar with many of the distinctive laws as well, which in some form were simply part of their lives. What they would not have known was the text as such—a single narrative that puts this altogether, and adds on top of it many more details and laws with which they would have been unfamiliar. It would have been a tremendous amount to take in during the reading, even if it did span over a week (Nehemiah 8:18).

According to the biblical account, upon hearing the recitation of the Torah the Judeans were stunned and submissive, grateful for now knowing God's law. Surely, though, this strains belief. Ezra had had only two months to establish his credibility. At that point he introduced to the Israelites a text that claims authority to modify what they knew about themselves, their holidays, and the proper way to follow God's will. Over two days, according to this account, the Israelites discovered that neither they nor their parents observed or had even heard of two major holidays.

Today we take for granted the religious authority of texts. Religion, as it is commonly understood, comes out of a book. This approach, however, testifies much more to the influence of the Bible itself than it does to the nature of religion. Rather than deriving from written texts, most religious practices at most times and places were learned mimetically—I do what my family and community do, because that is simply the traditional way that we do things. Prior to Ezra, nobody (except, perhaps, priests) would have thought to turn to a book or text in order to learn proper religious behaviors. Questions might be addressed to a parent, priest, or village elder, but they too would appeal to communal memory rather than an authoritative text. The Torah introduces not just a set of new rules but also a new source of religious authority that is rooted in texts. Josiah had experimented with this claim, but it did not lead very far.

The author of the account of Ezra's reading wants his readers to believe that the Israelites immediately accepted this new source of authority, even when it might have gone against their traditional practices. Yet the actions recorded in the account suggest quite the opposite. The assembly of Israelites did not hear the whole Torah in one day; Ezra got only to the description of Rosh Hashanah before they adjourned for the day. The next day only the leaders assembled to continue studying the law. The author of the chapter does not tell us why the people did not reassemble to continue their reading, but it is likely that the public reading—in contrast to what the author wants us to believe—was a failure. Ezra misjudged his audience.

Two months after this reading, Ezra launched an attack on Israelite intermarriage. This was not Jewish "intermarriage" in the way that we might usually think of the term, as marriages between Jews and non-Jews. Instead, Ezra attacked marriages between the descendents of those who had returned from Babylonia to Jerusalem in 516 BCE and earlier and the descendents of those Israelites who were never exiled in 586 BCE, when the Babylonians destroyed the first Jerusalem temple. These are "intermarriages" between different groups of Israelites, and Ezra's condemnation points to the emergence of a new genealogical understanding of Jewish identity that would come to play an important role among Jews at a later time.

Ezra ideologically opposed these intermarriages, but not for the reasons we might suspect. According to the biblical account, Ezra was upset with the offenders (especially those in leadership positions) because they had intermarried with the locals, whose "practices *are like those* of the Canaanites, the Hittites, the Perizzites, the Jebusites, the Ammonites, the Moabites, and Egyptians, and the Amorites" (Ezra 9:1–2; my emphasis). This passage clearly echoes one in Deuteronomy. In our version of Deuteronomy, the people of Israel are not to intermarry with the Hittites, Girgashites, Amorites, Canaanites, Perizzites, Hivites, and Jebusites (Deuteronomy 7:1–2). There is no general prohibition here (or anywhere in the Pentateuch) against intermarriage, only against intermarriage into these particular tribes. The problem with intermarriage, in Deuteronomy as well as all related biblical texts that date from before 586 BCE, was the potential for being led astray to worship one's spouse's gods (Deuteronomy 7:4). This is exactly what happened to King Solomon, whose seven hundred foreign wives and three hundred concubines "turned away his heart after other gods" (1 Kings 11:4). The problem in these preexilic texts is what intermarriage leads to, not intermarriage itself.[12]

Somewhere in the background of either Ezra's or his biographer's thinking, this passage from Deuteronomy lurked, as it does behind a similar initiative made by Nehemiah, a governor of Yehud thirteen years later. But that is far from the whole story.

Ezra's real concern stems from his conception of "holy seed" and its ability to become polluted through intermingling (Ezra 9:2). Ezra believes that Jews—more specifically, Jewish men—have "holy seed." Ezra thinks that the semen of the Israelite returnees from Babylonia is pure, and that sex between a pure man and an impure woman leads to an impure "intermingling."

We are so accustomed to other arguments against intermarriage that we might miss the gap between our thinking and Ezra's. Since the time of the emancipation of the Jews in Europe in the nineteenth century, the massive immigration of Eastern European Jews to America in the nineteenth and twentieth centuries, and especially since the Holocaust, Jews have framed the argument against intermarriage in terms of survival of the people. This is perfectly understandable. The Jewish community was and remains fearful that Jews would marry non-Jews, that their children would not be raised as Jews, and that ultimately the population of Jews in America and across the world would dwindle or disappear. The fight against intermarriage is often framed as the fight for the very survival of the Jewish people.

This, though, is a modern argument—it is not the Bible's, and it certainly is not Ezra's. Ezra's concern is far more peculiar to a modern reader. He is horrified at the idea that genealogically pure semen would end up in the wombs of the impure daughters of the land.

Ezra's notion of "pure" seed is a sign of a more comprehensive ideology. In Judah before 586 BCE, only priests and Levites were concerned with genealogical purity. The P source forbids a priest to marry a prostitute or a divorcée (Leviticus 21:7) and commands the high priest to marry a virgin (7:13–15)—both in order to be holy to God and "that he may not profane his offspring among his kin" (21:15). Later biblical books, including Ezra, are punctilious about listing the genealogies of priests.

Yet at the same time priestly sources (perhaps of H) declare all Israel, not just the priests, to be holy. As God says to Moses, "Speak to all the congregation of the people of Israel and say to them: 'You shall be holy, for I the Lord your God am holy'" (19:2). Elsewhere the Bible goes even further: "All the earth is Mine," God commands Moses to tell the people of Israel as they camped at the base of Mt. Sinai, ready to receive the Ten Commandments, "but you shall be to Me a kingdom of priests and a holy nation" (Exodus 19:5–6). Is this to be taken metaphorically or literally? Is every Israelite to be considered a priest, with all the legal ramifications that go with this status?

Ezra, himself a priest, took the idea that Israel was a kingdom of priests as something more than a metaphor, if falling short of full legal status.

Just as priests were to be genealogically pure, so too all of Israel was to remain pure by following the same or at least similar marital restrictions as priests.[13]

This understanding of Ezra's notion of "pure" seed helps also to explain the earlier actions of Zerubbabel and Joshua, the leaders of the returnees in 516 BCE. These were all elite men from the same circle. They developed and shared an elitist ideology in which they saw themselves as the vanguard or, in their own language, as a "remnant": the small, genealogically pure true worshippers of the God of Israel. To be a member of true Israel it was no longer sufficient to be simply a member of the polity; one needed to be the child of proper, pure members of that polity. This was a sectarian, or at least proto-sectarian, ideology.

The challenge for the adherents and leaders of proto-sectarian ideologies is applying them to real life. Ezra had the ability to use the coercive power of the state to dissolve these marriages. Yet he didn't, and it is easy enough to surmise why. He had just arrived in a small community with established norms and power structures. For him to have immediately begun using Persian power to break apart families would have been so disruptive and have created so many enemies that it would have destroyed his ability to be effective. He wanted to dissolve these marriages, but he had enough political savvy to know that he needed the clan leaders on his side.

Ideology was probably the primary reason behind Ezra's opposition to intermarriage, but there also were political considerations. Ezra needed the clans, but he also wanted to weaken them in order to increase the authority of the returnees and the temple establishment. Since an attack on these marriages was transparently an attack on the clans and their leaders, he needed to tread very carefully. The clan leaders, on the other hand, could not openly defy Ezra since he held royal privileges, enforced by Persian power. Much more than marriage was at stake here.

Ezra's strategy was brilliant, even if ultimately ineffective. Although Ezra surely knew about these intermarriages from the time of his arrival, he waited until the ninth month to strike, four months after he arrived. Perhaps having learned from his public reading of the Torah that the direct approach is not always the most effective, and knowing that the issue would be particularly delicate for the clans who still exercised power,

Ezra began his attack with an exaggerated public display of piety. "When I heard this," Ezra says, "I tore my garment and my mantle, and pulled hair from my head and beard, and sat appalled" (Ezra 9:3). In full public view, he made a confession on behalf of the people and prayed for forgiveness. Praying, making confession, weeping, and prostrating himself, he must have made quite a sight, and soon a crowd gathered around him. The situation was volatile.

A certain Shecaniah stepped forward out of this mob to confess and to urge others to make a covenant with him to expel the foreign women and their offspring (10:2). I suspect that if this is an accurate account, it was a setup, but in any case Ezra took full advantage of the opportunity. He summoned the leaders to take a public oath to act accordingly and then, having gathered public support, he fell back on his coercive authority. He commanded all of those who had returned from Babylonia, including presumably those who had returned earlier and their descendents, to assemble at the temple for a meeting, and threatened to confiscate the property of anyone who did not attend (vv. 7–8).

The meeting took place three days later, on the twentieth day of the ninth month (v. 9). Ezra called on the assembled returnees to repent and dissolve the improper marriages. The returnees were sympathetic, but they were also tired and cold; this was the month of Kislev, which falls in November or December in our calendar. "Many people are involved and it is the rainy season," they said. "It is not possible to remain out in the open, nor is it the work of a day or two" (v. 13). They and Ezra agreed that they would return home, and Ezra would form a committee with their officers to resolve the matter.

A little over a week later, the committee began to meet. Two months later the committee did what committees did and continue to do best: it issued a report. The book of Ezra ends with this report, a list of the men who married foreign women. One hundred and fourteen men are on the list. If seen against the numbers given by the Bible—some forty-two thousand people returning over the last seven decades—the number of intermarriages was miniscule. If seen against the actual population of Jerusalem (at most two thousand), it was more substantial.

We do not know what happened next, if anything. Did these men turn out their wives and children? One would think that the author, who was certainly sympathetic to Ezra, would have informed us if Ezra was successful; perhaps the absence of any notice that Ezra actually achieved his aim of breaking up these families is evidence that he wasn't. These men could be shamed and their descendents immortalized as impure, but Ezra, who was brushing up against the limits of his power, could not actually punish them.

Even more interesting, we don't know what happened to Ezra. He too disappears. Some scholars suggest that he, having gone too far, was recalled to Persia. Maybe he suddenly died. Maybe, properly chastened, he chose to continue in a less confrontational style (although that does not seem to suit his character). Maybe he ended up marrying an attractive daughter of the people of the land. This whole remarkable story took place within a single calendar year and then Ezra disappears from the historical record.

Ezra, the scribe, priest, and functionary in the Persian court, was familiar with some of the preexilic writings of his ancestors, particularly texts of priestly concern and the Deuteronomistic history. Clearly he and the members of his elite circle took these texts seriously. He gained through his standing in the Persian court the royal (or "secular") backing for his mission to Jerusalem. His attempt to establish the written text that he brought with him as law—his claim that the text had normative authority—was his own idea. It was largely a failure.[14]

With Ezra gone, things in Jerusalem largely returned to normal. Thirteen years later, another Persian functionary, named Nehemiah, arrived in Jerusalem. Nehemiah, who emerged from Ezra's circle, was more ambitious and politically savvy than Ezra. Whether he was more successful, though, we will see in the next chapter.

5 Nehemiah to Chronicles: Yehud and Elephantine, 445–350 BCE

Ezra had come and gone, his tumultuous year in Jerusalem having made little, if any, impact. Over the next thirteen years things in Yehud quickly slid back to the way they had been. Yehud remained a semiautonomous territory that was governed by the very Judean local elite that Ezra sought unsuccessfully to undermine. It would not be until 445 BCE that the same shadowy group that produced Ezra would get another chance to mount a serious challenge to the established elite. This time a more politically savvy leader named Nehemiah had a chance to establish a polity in line with his and Ezra's vision. He too would fail.

During the last century of Persian rule of Yehud, before the conquest of Alexander the Great, the Judean elite were able to establish a very different kind of polity than the kingdom of Judah. Although part of the Persian Empire, they were free to administer their local affairs more or less as they saw fit, assuming of course that they met with Persian approval. They did this, increasingly, from Jerusalem, and the priests in the temple assumed increasing authority. A Greek ethnographer, Hecataeus of Abdera, noted around 300 BCE that the priests, under the direction of the high priest, administered all the local affairs in Judea, the old province of Yehud.[1]

For these priests, though, the old written texts would play little role. While they had been successfully moved from Persia to Jerusalem, they remained almost unknown outside of the rarefied circles of Jerusalem priests and scribes. Even in these circles they functioned less as normative law or a collection of oracles to be consulted in order to assure the welfare of the nation than as almost academic texts, ancient histories to be worked over by scribes. These academic exercises, however, were consequential: they generated the Pentateuch. I doubt they could have imagined the authority and power that text would, much later, come to have.

In the winter of 446 BCE, twelve years after Ezra's failed mission, a group of Judeans limped back from Yehud to the Persian palace of Susa. They came to bring a downbeat report to one of the king's cupbearers, a fellow Judean named Nehemiah. Jerusalem was struggling and the "remnant" was demoralized (Nehemiah 1:1–3). The effort of Sheshbazzar, Zerubbabel, and Ezra to revitalize the temple cult and establish the law of the God of heaven was clearly failing. Upset, Nehemiah, he himself tells us, approached the king and succeeded in gaining appointment as "governor of the land of Yehud" (5:14).[2] He would serve in this position from 445 to 432 BCE.

Nehemiah was neither a priest nor a scribe. He was an ambitious politician who was sympathetic to the circles to which Ezra had belonged. Like Ezra, he encountered an entrenched establishment when he arrived in Jerusalem. Unlike Ezra, though, he was able to make some inroads, however short lived, against them.

As Nehemiah tells it, upon arriving in Jerusalem he was soon confronted by three local nobles, Sanballat, Tobiah, and Geshem. Nehemiah's narrative consistently treats these three characters as his evil archenemies, although we must be careful to remember that they would have seen things differently. About two of these characters we in fact possess information from outside of the Bible that allows us to see them in a very different light.

Sanballat was a Samaritan whose family, as we now know from papyri, retained an important official position under the Persian authorities until Alexander's conquest in Samaria. Sanballat and his family were also faithful worshippers of the same God as Nehemiah and his; Sanballat's family regularly took theophoric names that used the word *yah*, the name of the Israelite God.[3] Moreover, Nehemiah reports scornfully, Sanballat's daughter married the son of Eliashib, the Jerusalem high priest at the time that Nehemiah arrived (Nehemiah 13:28).

In fact, Sanballat was so devoted to the God of Israel that he built his own temple to him on Mt. Gerizim.[4] Mt. Gerizim is located by the modern city Nabulus just north of the border of the Persian province of Yehud and has a storied place in the tales of Israel's history. According to Deuteronomy, when Israel crossed over into Canaan, representatives from several of the tribes were to stand on Mt. Gerizim and deliver to the assembled Israelites below the blessing to come on Israel should it adhere to God's covenant (Deuteronomy 28:12). The fact that this hoary myth survives in Deuteronomy is somewhat ironic. Sanballat knew the traditions that ascribed sanctity to Mt. Gerizim, but almost certainly did not know Deuteronomy, which emphasizes that the God of Israel is to have but one place of worship.

The temple on Mt. Gerizim was larger and more impressive than the one in Jerusalem. Its sacred precinct was approximately 315 by 322 feet and had tall and thick walls. Sanballat spared little expense to honor his God. The temple was also no simple political stunt. Large quantities of animal remains and Aramaic inscriptions testify to its wide usage. Samaria had a large number of people who wanted to worship the God of Israel, and who had no reason to think that YHWH would not accept offerings on Mt. Gerizim. Despite Nehemiah's sputtering protests, Sanballat's desire to join in helping to enhance YHWH's worship in Jerusalem too might well have been sincere. Nehemiah's rebuff of a fellow devotee of YHWH, who happened also to be the governor of the neighboring Persian province, would have been confusing and offensive.

Tobiah too worshipped the God of Israel. As with Sanballat, independent archaeological evidence testifies to his existence. In his case we possess remains of a palace that dates from the fifth or fourth centuries BCE and papyri from the Hellenistic period. The palace is located over the Jordan River and contains an inscription in Aramaic script with the name Tobaya. The papyri testify to the continuing importance of the family for centuries. Like Sanballat, Nehemiah admits, Tobiah's relatives had married into priestly families (Nehemiah 6:18). The Tobiads were in fact so well connected that Tobiah himself had a permanent chamber in the Jerusalem temple (13:4–5). The Tobiads were another powerful family, devotees of the God of Israel.[5]

Nehemiah sought the support of the mob in his struggle with these fellow adherents of the God of Israel who also had close relations to the Persian authorities. One of his first official acts was to attempt to rebuild the walls of Jerusalem—the account of which takes up an inordinate amount of space in the book of Nehemiah—in order to enhance the prestige of the city and provide work to its populace. Nehemiah assigned the work on the basis of the clans, presumably with the goal of enhancing their loyalty (3). He then coerced the local nobles to annul their debts (5:1–13). Nehemiah's intentions were patent: by seeking the welfare of the debtors he was also seeking their political support.

There is yet another power base whose support Nehemiah thought crucial: the prophets. Sanballat, Tobiah, and Geshem are said to accuse Nehemiah of buying off the prophets: "You have also set up prophets in Jerusalem to proclaim about you, 'There is a king of Judah,'" they are reported to have written him (6:7). Nehemiah strenuously denied the charge, but then immediately reported that his enemies have schemed with the prophets to lure him into a trap. Nehemiah tells of a prophet who advised him to shut himself up in the sanctuary. Had he done so, Nehemiah quickly realizes, he would have committed a sacrilege and, as he puts it, "provide them a scandal with which to reproach me" (6:13). He then also names a prophetess—one of only four female prophets named in the Hebrew Bible—as in on the scheme. The outcome of this battle for the support of the prophets is unclear; Nehemiah does not explicitly tell us that he succeeded in removing the prophets who were opposed to him. It would certainly have been understandable if the institutionalized prophets saw Nehemiah as an upstart and remained loyal to the established elite.

At some point thereafter Nehemiah called an assembly. At this solemn assembly, we are told, "they read from the book of the law of the Lord their God" (9:3). What follows is an extensive and remarkable, but highly condensed and selective, version of the history of Israel. In twenty-five verses, the Levites recounted the history of Israel. The high points are: God created the world and made a covenant with Abraham; the Israelites sojourned in Egypt (in just a few words) and then left; God gave the laws to the people at Mt. Sinai and continued to care for their welfare, despite their creation of a golden calf; the Israelites conquered Canaan; Israelite stubbornness led to their conquest; and God has now returned to them (vv. 6–31). Nehemiah's reading reflects far more knowledge of the narrative arc of the Pentateuch as it now exists than did Ezra's about two decades earlier.

There are several ways to understand Nehemiah's scroll, and each of them is highly speculative. It is possible that both Ezra and Nehemiah really did possess the same text. The fact that Ezra cites from it selectively reflects only his aims, not his knowledge. It is also possible that the narrative arc of the Pentateuch developed in the time between Ezra and Nehemiah; such a narrative would have been previously known in a loose form (and transmitted in the legends of J and E and the Deuteronomistic history), but Nehemiah's group in exile tightened the narrative and combined scrolls that had previously existed only separately. It is also possible that the creation of the narrative is linked closely with Nehemiah. In telling this story Nehemiah wanted to emphasize that he and the Jerusalem community were an integral part of the sacred narrative of Israel's history. That is, Nehemiah's community stands in the direct and legitimate line of the divine promise.

Whatever the precise historical reconstruction, it is clear that by Nehemiah's time most, perhaps even all, of the content that would find its way into the Pentateuch as well as the general narrative arc existed. Its general authority, however, had yet to take root.

The continuation of Nehemiah's narrative of the assembly illustrates the limited authority of this text. Nehemiah calls on the assembly to enter into "a unilaterally binding promise" to adhere to eight specific laws.[6] The assembly, though, does not include everybody. Only the "priests, the Levites, the gatekeepers, the singers, the temple servants, and all who separated themselves from the peoples of the land" along with their families, "all who know enough to understand," are invited to enter into this agreement (10:29). A later editor added that the eighty-three leading families verified their agreement with their seals (vv. 2–28).[7] This was to be a pact for the "brothers," those who separated from the "peoples of the land" (that is, the descendents of the Israelites who were never exiled). It was meant to create a small, committed, and self-styled elite group among the residents of Yehud.

Predictably, then, the very first stipulation was to avoid intermarriage (v. 31). Nehemiah here shows the same concern as his predecessor, Ezra, who had made little headway. Like Ezra, Nehemiah had both practical and ideological goals. One very practical effect of this stricture would be to rupture alliances between the established elite and members of his own group. At the same time, though, there is no reason to doubt that Nehemiah genuinely thought that God abhorred admixtures, including those between the genealogically pure returnees and the peoples of the land. The other laws concern the Sabbath, the sabbatical year, the temple, priests, and Levites. They commit themselves, for example, in order to support the temple service, and obligate themselves to bring first fruits, the first-born, and other tithes to the Levites.

The two primary themes of these stipulations are separation from (genealogically) impure Jews and the establishment of a proper cult centered in the Jerusalem temple. The genealogical lists included in the book of Nehemiah reinforce this focus on separation by enumerating the pure families (11:1–12:25). The second theme of the stipulations, the temple, converges with Nehemiah's interest in reestablishing Jerusalem as a viable city-state within the Persian Empire. The temple stood for more than the central place for the worship of the God of Israel, although that was no small thing in itself. Nehemiah seems to want to position it as the economic engine of the city and the province as a whole. The temple was to trigger an influx of capital from the countryside in the form of annual monetary taxes and produce that undoubtedly would not only enrich the priests and Levites but would also generate economic activity throughout Jerusalem.

Despite his efforts, Nehemiah never achieved a clear victory over his rivals. Nehemiah's relationship with the family of Tobiah remained strained. Near the end of the book of Nehemiah, a broadside is launched against intermarriage with Ammonites (13:1–3). The reason for this sudden condemnation becomes clear when seen with the story that immediately follows it. A certain Eliashib, a priest related to Tobiah—whom he calls the Ammonite slave—had given Tobiah a room in the temple. The Tobiads were not going to give up their entrenched positions easily.

There was another, final sign that ultimately he lost his struggle with the establishment. Twelve years after Nehemiah arrived in Jerusalem, in 434 BCE, he returned to the court of King Artaxerxes (13:6). Nehemiah does not tell us why, and he does not tell us how long he stayed. It is certainly not inconceivable that he was in fact recalled, perhaps at the urging of political enemies. Whether away for a long time or short, he was dismayed upon his return to Jerusalem. The first thing he says he did was to strike against Tobiah, ejecting him from the sanctuary and purifying the rooms he inhabited.

During Nehemiah's absence those who entered into the new covenant began to neglect their commitments. "In those days," Nehemiah protests, "I saw Jews who had married women of Ashdod, Ammon, and Moab; and half of their children spoke the language of Ashdod, and they could not speak the language of Judah, but spoke the language of various peoples" (13:23–24). Nehemiah gave them a thorough tongue-lashing, and then drove away precisely one intermarried priest—who was also, not very coincidentally, the son-in-law of his enemy Sanballat (v. 28).

And so the book of Nehemiah ends: "Remember me, O my God, for good" (v. 31). But did Nehemiah succeed, and if so, at what precisely? Like Ezra's reforms, Nehemiah's did not endure. The trajectory of the narrative is not hopeful; it is very easy to imagine that as soon as Nehemiah leaves the scene the people revert right back to what they were doing. Tobiah and Sanballat retained their power.

Nehemiah's most lasting legacy might be the very fact of the covenant that he made. However ineffective it ended up being, the effect of this covenant was to create a subgroup within Israel. The group's identity was based upon purity and separation, thus constituting a kind of proto-sect. These themes would reappear with particular force in later Jewish sects.[8]

Sociologically, there is no evidence that this group continued after Nehemiah. Instead, Yehud largely fell back to old ways as a small, out-of-the-way province in the Persian Empire where day-to-day power was largely concentrated in the hands of the traditional noble families, clans, and powerful priests. Ezra and Nehemiah did not make their Torah the "law of the land." They may have brought the scrolls that would eventually become part of the Bible to Jerusalem, but they read only selections from them aloud publicly, and even that was done only a handful of times over the course of a couple of decades. The scrolls entered the temple library, accessible primarily to priests and scribes should they be moved to consult them.

The next century under Persian rule was relatively peaceful. Yehud continued to function as a semiautonomous Persian province, with its governmental center in and around Jerusalem. Its governor was a Judean who was appointed by the Persian authorities. The priests, and particularly the high priest, as the keepers of the public cult at the Jerusalem temple, played an important role in governance. The Persians maintained administrative centers throughout Yehud (including one at Ramat Rahel, south of Jerusalem, on the site of a palace that was used in the preexilic period) at which they collected their taxes, which we presume were largely given as agricultural produce.[9]

There must have been a scribal class to handle the diplomatic and administrative issues of governance. The official language of governance was Aramaic, used in all correspondence with major Persian authorities. At the same time, though, Judeans were using a paleo-Hebrew script in some administrative contexts. Hence, on the small silver coinage that they were allowed to issue they stamped the name of their province, "Yehud," in this script. Throughout the fourth century the script was also increasingly used on the handles of jars that carried official goods. This was not accidental or aesthetic; it was an official statement that sought to connect Yehud to the former glorious days of Judah, at least as they wished them to be remembered.[10]

It was in this context that the biblical books 1 and 2 Chronicles were written. These two books—which really should be considered as a single work—retell the story of the Deuteronomistic history. The book opens with nine mind-numbing chapters of genealogical lists; devotes one short chapter to Saul; and then dives into its real subject for the remaining fifty-five chapters, the story of David and his line, down to the decree of King Cyrus restoring the second temple. Despite the fact that the story itself ends in 539 BCE, the actual account of Chronicles was written 150–200 years later. It is written in a late dialect of biblical Hebrew and mentions several generations of David's descendent "Jeconiah the captive"—that is, Jehoiachin (1 Chronicles 3:17). Although the genealogical list is corrupt here, many scholars think that it ends sometime in the fourth century.

Chronicles portrays a Jewish society firmly entrenched in the land of Israel with a well-functioning cult. Chronicles does not even mention the story of Israel's sojourn in and exodus from Egypt. Israel, according to the Chronicler, did not "settle" the land of Canaan; it was always there.[11]

Israel's presence in and right to the land is presented as an unproblematic and established fact. So too is the cult. In a passage that has no parallel in the Deuteronomistic history, King David organized the descendents of Aaron, the priests, into twenty-four subgroups, and assigned by lot to each group a time during the year at which its members served in the temple. "Shemiah son of Nathanel, the scribe, who was of the Levites, registered them" in front of the other royal officials (24:6). The Levites too were organized into twenty-four subgroups (vv. 20–30). The priests and Levites were to serve side by side in the temple, each with their distinctive tasks.[12]

Unlike the authors of the Deuteronomistic history, Ezra, and Nehemiah, the Chronicler was also unfazed by intermarriage. The Chronicler's view is an inclusive one, acknowledging Judean links with groups that earlier authors had condemned.[13] The Chronicler thus appears to be rewriting history with the present in mind. The Chronicler's circle and vision, we can surmise, was not like the small and insular one of Ezra and Nehemiah but one that exercised true authority and thus had to deal with the messier business of forging and nurturing political relationships, both internal and external.

The book of Chronicles has such a consistent style that aside from a few small emendations that appear to have been made later, it is most likely the work of a single scribe. He rewrote history; he didn't invent it. The Chronicler hews closely to the narrative of the Deuteronomistic history. The Chronicler also explicitly mentions other sources, such as the "book (or law) of Moses," the "writing" of David, the "writing" of Solomon, and a wide variety of other previous chronicles (2 Chronicles 35). The Chronicler must also have used genealogical lists, and his language at times is very similar to that of the priestly sources found in today's Pentateuch.[14]

For the Chronicler, these written documents, along with the directives of the "good" kings of the past (such as David, Solomon, Hezekiah, and Josiah), constituted a source of religious authority. Yet, as in the cases of Ezra and Nehemiah, when the Chronicler refers to the book or law of Moses, it is not entirely clear to what book he is referring. That is, the Chronicler's citations of the book of Moses are not always found in the Pentateuch as it now exists, and sometimes even seem to contradict it. For example, Chronicles assumes that the Passover sacrifice is to be performed at the Jerusalem temple, following Deuteronomy. The priests were then to follow the law of Moses by sprinkling the blood of the sacrificial lamb (30:16). The Pentateuch, though, never commands the sprinkling of blood. Where the Chronicler explicitly cites "the book of Moses," he cites Deuteronomy in somewhat different language (2 Chronicles 25:4; Deuteronomy 24:16). At the very end of the work the scribe (or perhaps a later copyist) explicitly mentions that the building of the second temple fulfilled Jeremiah's prophecy that the temple would lay destroyed for seventy years (2 Chronicles 36:21; Jeremiah 25:11–12).

The Chronicler rewrote the Deuteronomistic history to better accord with his times. In his recasting the settlement in Yehud is taken for granted and the (relatively recent) organization of the priests and Levites is authorized by the legendary King David himself. It was a newer and better version of the history, meant to replace the older scroll.

The fact that there were other scrolls of the Deuteronomistic history still in the archives did not bother the Chronicler. Done with his rewriting, he would perhaps have loaned the scroll to a few like-minded friends within what must have been a very small community of interested readers among the elite of Yehud. Eventually, the scroll was deposited in the temple library, and he returned to the bureaucratic tasks that paid his bills. He was not out to *erase* history; the scrolls that he copied and revised continued to be available for consultation. Those who wanted to consult the official archives thus had their choice of versions. For the vast majority of residents of Yehud, these written versions would hardly have mattered. Their primary contact with their history remained through oral stories. The scrolls were for the use of government officials and the very small circle of scribes.

Throughout the fourth century, the Judean elite of Jerusalem were slowly and organically creating for themselves a new identity. This was an identity that centered on the worship of the God of Israel—alone—in the temple of Jerusalem. Their distinctive customs were attributed to their founder figure, Moses. They wanted to see themselves as continuous with the ancient kingdom of Judah, and asserted this identity by the use of Hebrew and the updating of history. If to this identity there were sectarian challenges based on genealogical purity, their traces no longer survive in our written sources. Most likely, though, the seeds of sectarianism planted by Ezra and Nehemiah lay dormant. After all, Jerusalem was a small city of limited resources whose elite would largely have known each other. In such a community, there would have been enormous pressure to suppress or negotiate serious disagreements.

This developing sense of identity was a local phenomenon. Just how local we can begin to see from an extraordinary cache of papyri that was unearthed about a century ago. These papyri relate to the Jewish garrison whose members lived on a small island in the Nile River called Elephantine. Like those in Jerusalem, they worshipped YHWH and they observed some of the same customs, such as the holiday of Passover. This, however, is largely where the similarities stop. They had their own temple, priests, and sacrifices. They, like the earlier Israelites and Judahites, acknowledged the existence of other deities in private contexts. They used the language and script of Aramaic rather than Hebrew. They show no signs of having any familiarity with the Pentateuch or any other of the writings being developed in Jerusalem at this time. And they show no signs of having been troubled by any of these differences.

Judeans had arrived in Elephantine—a strategic island at the southern edge of Egypt's border—by the fifth century BCE. They may have arrived there as refugees after the fall of Jerusalem in 586 BCE, but more probably they came later as Persian mercenaries. Their job was both to deter external threats and to project Persian power in order to lessen the possibility of revolt by the native Egyptians.

Elephantine was the site of large-scale archaeological excavations at the end of the nineteenth and beginning of the twentieth century. The island had been thickly settled in antiquity, and the Judean garrison was but part of a diverse and teeming populace. The papyri from the Judean garrison, preserved due to the dry climate, emerged onto the gray antiquities market while the excavations were taking place; there is thus no reliable information about where they were found. The caches for the most part consisted of three archives, each of which contained about a dozen documents. Two of the archives are legal records of individual families and consist primarily of marriage contracts and sale records. One appears to be an archive of official communal correspondence.[15]

The Judeans of Elephantine were devoted to their ancestral god, Yah. This, in any case, is the form of God's name that they used in many of their names. Unlike contemporary theophoric Jewish names in Yehud and Babylonia, the Elephantine names never used "el" as God's name. Names might end (for example, Benaiyah, meaning "Yah built") or begin (Yehotal, "Yah is (my) dew") with the name, but in either case they reflect a parent's attempt to evoke divine protection.

The Judeans of Elephantine were devoted to Yah, the God of Israel. But this does not mean that they couldn't hedge their bets. One would expect that the oaths recorded in the legal documents of the community should be made "by the life of Yahu or Yah, the God." And, indeed, several say exactly that. But these very same Jews also make oaths by the life of other beings, such as Sati the goddess or by Anathyahu or Herembethel. According to a collection list, Jews gave monetary donations not only to Yahu, the God of Israel, but also to Eshembethel and Anathbethel, Aramean deities. Worship of the God of Israel was not seen as incompatible with some kind of devotion to other deities as well.[16]

The Judeans of Elephantine worshipped the God of Israel in the way that they thought was most fitting: they built a temple to YHWH and offered sacrifices. They, in fact, seem to be completely unaware that this is in any way problematic. Thus, when their temple was destroyed by rioting Egyptians in 410 BCE, they did not hesitate to turn to their brethren in Jerusalem for help in rebuilding it. We have a copy of the letter that the commander of the garrison and the Judean priests of Elephantine sent to Bagohi, the governor of Yehud. After telling the history of the temple (which dates back to 525 BCE) and describing its beauty, Jedaniah relates that since they no longer had the ability to offer sacrifices, they have been in constant mourning from the time of its destruction, wearing sackcloth and fasting, "the wives of ours as widow(s) are made; (with) oil (we) do not anoint (ourselves), and wine do not drink." These classic acts of mourning were meant to propitiate their god, to cause the "Lord of Heaven" to take pity on them and to give them the opportunity and resources that they needed to rebuild the temple.[17]

At this point in the letter Jedaniah suddenly reveals that this was actually following up on an earlier request sent shortly after the temple's destruction. "A letter we sent (to) our lord, and to Jehohanan the High Priest and his colleagues the priests who are in Jerusalem, and to Ostanes the brother of Anani and the nobles of the Jews. A letter they did not send us."[18] The Judeans of Elephantine appealed to the Jerusalem priests, nobles, and authorities for help in reconstructing their own temple and nobody bothered to reply to them. If the Jerusalem priests had hoped to send a subtle message to Jedaniah, he apparently didn't get it. For good measure he also sent a copy of his follow-up letter to "Delaiah and Shelemiah sons of Sanballat governor of Samaria." If the Jerusalem nobles wouldn't help him, maybe the sons of Nehemiah's old nemesis would. Jedaniah's request to Bagohi, the governor of Yehud, is modest but specific:

> Now, your servants Jedaniah and his colleagues and the Jews,
> all (of them) citizens of Elephantine, thus say: If to our lord it is
> good, take thought of that Temple to (re)build (it) since they do
> not let us (re)build it. Regard your obligees and your friends who
> are here in Egypt. May a letter from you be sent to them about
> the Temple of YHW the God to (re)build it in Elephantine the
> fortress just as it had been built formerly. And the meal-offering
> and the incense and the burnt-offering they will offer on the altar
> of YHW the God in our name and we shall pray for you at all
> times—we and our wives and our children and the Jews, all (of
> them) who are here. If thus they do until that Temple be (re)built,
> a merit you will have before YHW the God of Heaven more
> than a person who will offer him burnt-offerings and sacrifices
> (whose) worth is as the worth of silver, 1 thousand talents and
> about gold.[19]

Jedaniah asked only for a letter of recommendation. He felt that if Bagohi wrote to the current Persian authorities in Elephantine he might be allowed to rebuild the temple and reinstate the incense, meal, and animal sacrifices.

We possess only the copy of the letter that we assume was sent to Jerusalem. If there was a reply, it did not survive. Quite possibly, though, this time too there was no reply. The Jerusalem authorities continued to have no reason to support the rebuilding of the temple of Yahu in Elephantine, and we possess no evidence in the rest of the archive from Elephantine that the temple ever was rebuilt.

The fact that Jedaniah and his colleagues had no qualms about approaching the Jerusalem priesthood for support in rebuilding their temple indicates that they did not, apparently, know the Pentateuch as it survives today. This is the only plausible explanation as to how Jedaniah and his colleagues could have expected a positive response from Jerusalem. Even Deuteronomy, which probably had existed in more or less its present form since the seventh century BCE and which contains some of the harshest criticisms of worship outside of Jerusalem, was unknown to them. Deuteronomy, though, was known in Jerusalem. At the same time, perhaps the Jerusalem priests were still uncertain about how far they could push their own authority. Thus, instead of telling the Elephantine Jews that they must not rebuild the temple, they ignored the issue and hoped that it might go away on its own.

Another letter from the communal archive points in the same direction. This was sent in 419 BCE from "your brother Hananiah" to "Jedaniah and his colleagues [at] the Jewish garrison." Known as the "Passover letter," it is a relatively straightforward summary of the laws of Passover. Hananiah tells them to keep the "festival of the unleavened bread" from the fifteenth of Nisan for seven days, to the twenty-first of the month. They should not eat any unleavened items, including beer, from sunset on the fourteenth day of Nisan until sunset on the twenty-first. They should not work on the first and last day of the festival.[20]

This letter may have simply been a reminder of the approaching festival and its rules. It may, though, also have been notice of a new holiday with a set of regulations that would have been unknown to the Elephantine community. The community may well have observed the Passover festival, the one-day sacrificial holiday, but not the Feast of Unleavened Bread described by Hananiah. In today's Bible, the two festivals have been combined into one, but the Judeans in Elephantine were apparently either unaware of that or didn't care. When Hananiah tried to justify his authority to prescribe this observance, he pointed not to tradition or a written text but to the "authority of the king."

Nor did these Jews turn to the Pentateuch to help guide their legal practices. Their extant personal archives consist largely of loan, sale, and marriage contracts. They are, for all intents and purposes, formally identical to contracts that were being drawn up by non-Jewish scribes in the region. They did not use any distinctive scribal formulas or substantive law. There is no evidence that they knew the "law of Moses" or any other form of what we might term "Jewish" law.[21] Personal letters too are indistinguishable from what we might expect from non-Judeans.

Like the author of Chronicles, they were also not concerned with what we would call "intermarriage." Intermarriages within this community occurred in both directions, with Jewish men marrying Egyptian women and vice versa.[22] The idea that Jews should remain genealogically pure, as advocated by Ezra, would have seemed as odd to them as it does to us.

In the fourth century, the Pentateuch appears still to have been in formation. Deuteronomy had long existed and survived, and Ezra and Nehemiah possessed scrolls that contain materials that we attribute to the P (and H) source. Nehemiah contains a historical narrative connected to a scroll similar to the JE source. The pieces all seem present in fourth-century Yehud. Given the evidence from Elephantine (not to mention the internal evidence of the Bible itself), these texts were not yet accepted as normative, and the authority that they possessed—literary or academic, mainly—was limited to a small Jerusalem elite. Were they, though, part of a single whole? Had the Pentateuch as such—which we clearly see for the first time only around 200 BCE—yet come into being?

Whatever scholarly debate exists about the documentary hypothesis pales against the debates about why, when, and where the final version of the Pentateuch was produced. It is hard to talk here about a scholarly consensus, although in recent years several scholars have made renewed arguments that the Pentateuch was redacted in Persia, whether under Persian auspices as "law of the king" or as an internal response to the loss of statehood and an attempt to create a national consciousness among the displaced Israelites. Who would have done the actual work of redaction in these reconstructions is left rather fuzzy.[23]

The story of Chronicles suggests another possibility. In the fourth century BCE, scribes were active in Jerusalem. If not an actual theocracy, Yehud's government had strong priestly influence. Throughout the fourth century, there were local revolts against the Persians; the destruction of the Jewish temple on Elephantine was a sign of local Egyptian dislike of Persians more than Jews per se. Jews had little reason to join these revolts, but they may have provoked the ruling elite to consider more seriously what it would mean to live in an independent state with no seed of David to rule them.

It would make sense for the Pentateuch to take form in this context. Sometime in the fourth century BCE, some scroll of earlier material needed copying. This might well have been a scroll of JE, the ancient stories of Israel's origins. The scribe, though, was a priest, a member of the elite at a time when priestly authority and aspirations were high. As with the Chronicler's revision of the Deuteronomistic history, this priestly scribe revised the copy in line with his own times. He thus included the ancient P source and updated the resulting narrative as he thought appropriate. As with Chronicles, these scrolls were not meant to be promulgated as a "public" document; they arose incidentally from the need to copy an old scroll. Unlike Chronicles, however, the old scrolls upon which the revisions were based have been lost to history. Before that happened, however, the scrolls of the books of the Pentateuch coexisted with, not replaced, the scrolls that contained its sources. Only much later, when they were elevated as the authoritative constitution of the Jews and the will of their God, would the other scrolls crumble to dust from neglect.

To the extent that any of these scrolls had any authority, it was quite limited. There were still, to our knowledge, no means of public dissemination. Most people did not read and there were no regular public recitations of these texts. The small scribal class would have known, copied, and revised many of them as part of their training and duties. These scrolls would have been concentrated in the temple library, although it is likely that other copies too circulated among both the scribes and other members of the literate (and wealthy) elite. The sense of status and éclat given to writing that was found in the last years of the kingdom of Judah had been lost. It would take many more years, and the fall of Persia, for that to return to Jerusalem.

Part II

6 The Dawn of Hellenism: Judea, 350–175 BCE

It took Alexander the Great less than a decade to dismantle the Persian Empire. Born in 356 BCE in Macedonia and given the best Greek education that money could buy (Aristotle was his tutor), Alexander began his military campaigns shortly after his father, King Phillip II, was assassinated. By 332 he had broken the Persian army and moved down into Syria, the Levant, and Egypt. From Egypt, Alexander took his army east into Babylonia and Persia proper. After defeating the last Persian king, Darius III, Alexander moved further east in 327 into India. Following a mostly successful but exhausting campaign, Alexander returned to Babylonia, where he died of illness in 323.

Alexander's conquest changed the shape of the Levant. He never had time to knit his empire together into a single bureaucratic entity; upon his death his generals and followers (known as the Diadochoi) split it into individual fiefdoms and quickly began to fight each other. They shared, however, a superior sense of their own Greekness, or, as it came to be known, Hellenism. Hellenism is a loose designation for a fluid package of institutions, texts, ideas, language, art and architecture, and practices that had their roots in classical Greece. Native populations conquered by Alexander adapted different parts of this package according to their own sensibilities. Accordingly, Hellenism in one of Alexander's conquered provinces might look quite different from its appearance in another.

Judea, the new Greek name given to the old Persian province of Yehud, was a buffer zone between the two new kingdoms founded by two of Alexander's successors, Ptolemy and Seleucus. The Ptolemies established

themselves in the rich province of Egypt; the Seleucids in the sprawling area of modern-day Syria, Iraq, and Iran. Judea ended up primarily under control of the Ptolemies throughout the third century, although this was hotly contested by the Seleucids. Finally, in 200 BCE, the Seleucids managed to wrest control of the province for themselves.

The Ptolemies had established certain basic Hellenistic institutions. Only with the end of more than a century of political and military uncertainty did Judeans begin to engage in a more sustained way with these institutions and the ideas and values that accompanied them. The result was a sudden economic and cultural explosion in Jerusalem in particular that generated a new class of literary elite. These elite not only copied and revised old texts but also generated entirely new ones, in both traditional and novel genres. Three of these new texts—Ecclesiastes (Kohelet), Ecclesiasticus (Ben Sira), and 1 Enoch—exhibit very different responses to this shifting landscape. Each gives us insight into the different roles that texts were beginning to play in second-century Judea.

Although the Seleucids and Ptolemies would go to war five times over the provinces of Judea and Samaria, throughout most of the century these provinces were firmly under Ptolemaic control. The Ptolemies organized their landholding in this area into a single administrative province that they called Syria. Syria was then subdivided into subgovernments, which included Samaria and Judea. While a Ptolemaic appointee ran the province (with other officials in charge of subregions), it appears that much of the local governance remained in the hands of local aristocrats.

While the Ptolemies were largely content to stay out of local politics, they were hands on when it came to money. Judea alone was required to pay five hundred kilograms a year of silver to Egypt in tribute. The money was raised through a tax system that was so elaborate it makes the American tax code look simple. The Ptolemies taxed land, produce, salt, commerce, services, and eventually people. A papyrus known as the "Revenue Laws," issued around 259 BCE by Ptolemy II Philadelphus, specifies in great (but now fragmentary) detail the various taxes and their mode of collection.[1] The Ptolemies relied on "tax farmers" to deliver the tax revenues. These tax farmers were private individuals who bid for the right to collect the revenues of an area; they were entitled to keep any surplus that they collected. Unsurprisingly, the tax farmer was reviled throughout antiquity.

The Ptolemies had an economic as well as a strategic interest in their new province of Syria. More productive land areas were given directly to favored Ptolemaic officials in Egypt who administered the land from afar while enjoying its revenues. A Ptolemaic finance minister named Apollonius, for example, was given large swaths of land in Judea. According to papyri, he sent his agent Zenon on several trips to check up on these estates. Zenon's letters tell of his business, mainly official, while he was there between 260 and 258 BCE.[2] By this time the Ptolemies had solidified their centralized economic control of the region.

Alexander's conquest, and more significantly the spread of Ptolemaic control throughout the area, brought heightened awareness of the "Greeks" to Judeans, especially those in the highlands. Prior to the third century, Judeans, particularly those who lived closer to the coastal regions, had had contact with Greek merchants and mercenaries. Their land, language, and culture, though, were of little interest to Judeans— they were foreigners, like all others. This slowly began to change in the third century as the Ptolemies established garrison towns of Macedonians at strategic points throughout their province of Syria. The main line of Ptolemaic settlements stretched up the Jordan valley, with a particularly important hub at Beit Shean.[3] Beit Shean is located about thirty kilometers south of the Sea of Galilee and by the third century BCE had been occupied (sporadically) for more than a millennium. The Ptolemies established an autonomous Greek city on the site called Scythopolis.

The "Greeks," as the Ptolemies styled themselves, brought many new things to Syria, but none was more important than the Greek city, or polis. The polis was the primary political institution of the Hellenistic world. Each polis had its own constitution with its own rights of semi-autonomous self-governance; a resident's primary loyalty was to his or her own polis.[4] The boundaries of a polis usually stretched out into a city's dependent lands. The residents of these more outlying areas would depend on the polis to buy their agricultural products and the like, and they would be able to retreat into the walls of the polis for shelter should danger strike.

For a city to gain the status of a polis, it had to first successfully petition the imperial authorities. Most cities in and around Syria desired and vied for this status, for the polis had the right to extensive (but limited) self-governance and on occasions the right to mint its own currency (according, of course, to the Ptolemaic standards). Frequently the status also came with tax advantages.

Although modeled on democratic Athens, the Hellenistic polis—as with Athens itself—was hardly what we would call a democracy. Participation in the governance of the polis was limited to adult male citizens. Even becoming a citizen of a polis was not automatic or consistent throughout the Ptolemaic kingdom. In general, though, the male children of citizens who were educated in the gymnasium were eligible.

The gymnasium was the most important institution within a polis. The Hellenistic gymnasium integrated the teaching of academics, sports, and warfare. For the earlier Greeks of Athens, this latter training in war was perhaps most important; there the point was to train citizen-warriors. By the Hellenistic period, though, which saw the rise of professional armies, the gymnasium de-emphasized this aspect. The gymnasium was as much a site of acculturation as it was anything else, a place where boys would learn Greek and the various skills and manners that would be expected of them as citizens of the polis. At some point, it seems, they would be enrolled on a written list as citizens of the polis.

Gymnasium comes from the Greek root meaning "naked" and refers to the peculiar custom of Greek men to exercise in the nude. Judeans certainly found this odd, but so too did the Romans and, we can assume, many others. For most Judeans, far more problematic would have been the religious rites and sacrifices that were part of the normal routine of life in the gymnasium. Many Judeans would have been unwilling to offer sacrifices to Greek gods. This, in turn, would have made them less welcome in the gymnasium, if it would even think to accept them in the first place.[5]

If the gymnasium was the basic political institution of the Hellenistic polis, the theater was the principal cultural and civic one. The polis's theater would host shows and assemblies and would be the city's central gathering place. Frequently, the shows involved dramatic productions drawn, again, from ancient Greek models. Although actors were generally looked down upon in the Hellenistic world, the dramas that they facilitated were central to the cultural identity of their audiences.

The dramas, of course, were in Greek. Greek was the new lingua franca, the language of government and of international commerce that replaced Aramaic. Greek speakers, and readers, also had access to a world of new literature and ideas, from Homer to Aristotle and beyond.

Despite the legal, commercial, and intellectual doors that knowledge of Greek opened, through the third century most Judeans were apparently content to stay with Aramaic, with knowledge of Greek in Judea largely confined to the Ptolemaic settlements. Most Jews in Judea, living in villages and making their living from agriculture, did not bother learning Greek. The tax collectors and local scribes mediated between them and Ptolemaic authorities as needed.

For those who wanted to take full advantage of this new world, however, knowledge of at least some Greek was necessary. In Judea, this might most vividly be seen in the city of Marisa (Maresha), an Idumaean city located about twenty kilometers west of modern-day Hebron in southern Israel. By the mid-third century the Idumaeans had established a vibrant Greek city along a vital trade route between Ptolemaic Egypt and the Levant. While Idumaeans continued to use Aramaic for some matters, the inscriptions from Maresha—even graffiti outside of the city limits—are in Greek and use Greek names. Whether or not it was a polis in a formal legal sense, Maresha was for all intents and purposes a Greek city.[6]

While some Greek ideas and institutions probably reached Jerusalem under the Ptolemies, they found a real foothold only under the Seleucids. A final series of battles between the two dynasties took place between 201 and 198 BCE, and at its end Egypt had permanently lost "Syria" to its rival, led by Antiochus III, also known as Antiochus the Great.

From the point of view of most Judeans, the change of regimes probably did not matter much. Like the Ptolemies before him, Antiochus III quickly reasserted the Judeans' right to limited self-governance, provided that they delivered their taxes, remained peaceful, and gave whatever aid they were called upon to give. And as the Ptolemies earlier had in the interests of continuity maintained official Persian institutions and re-appointed Persian officials in their new province in Syria, so too did Antiochus III maintain much of the Ptolemaic infrastructure in the newly named province of Coele-Syria.[7]

With the Ptolemies weakened but still posing a potential threat and the newly expansionist Roman army encroaching on his northern territories, Antiochus III had every reason to keep the Judeans loyal. According to Josephus, Antiochus issued an edict shortly after his conquest. Lauding the Judeans for their support of him, he gave a generous gift to the temple and ordered that it be repaired forthwith. He issued tax exemptions on the materials used to construct the temple as well as to official and temple functionaries: members of the "senate," priests, scribes, and singers did not have to pay taxes, and the population as a whole had a three-year tax reprieve in order to rebuild from the hostilities. As was also customary, he guaranteed to the Judeans the right to live by their ancestral laws, a provision he also included in another edict dealing with some Jews in Asia Minor.[8] In his decrees Antiochus supported the Jerusalem temple.

Antiochus's interest in promoting his own piety through support of the temple was consistent with his actions throughout his kingdom. Antiochus III both supported existing temples in his kingdom and appointed overseers of "sacred precincts," one of whose duties it was to ensure the proper functioning of the temples.[9] Through support of local temples Antiochus could gain at least some goodwill of those he conquered as well as position himself as a pious ruler, which was an important element of imperial propaganda. Plus, it would not have hurt to have as many gods on his side as he could muster.

Jerusalem—by far the largest settlement in Judea—appears to have suffered little damage during the war between the Ptolemies and Seleucids and underwent little immediate political change. According to Josephus, Antiochus actually gave the city and surrounding provinces back to the reigning Ptolemy ruler (Ptolemy Epiphanes) as dowry for his daughter, with whom he contracted a diplomatic marriage. Nevertheless, Antiochus clearly was in ultimate control, and his tax policies supported the upper classes of the city. New municipal construction began in Jerusalem and the city expanded.[10]

These were boom years in Jerusalem. New money, tax exemptions, and building generated prosperity. Prosperity brought new immigrants and ideas to the city, among which was the Greek model of education. Prior to 200 BCE, the technical skills of reading and writing literary texts (as opposed, for example, to rudimentary literacy that would have been more widespread) in Jerusalem were largely concentrated in the hands of the priests. The heavily centralized Ptolemaic bureaucracy had weakened the power of the local notables, and thus their need (as under the Persians) to maintain their own administrative centers. This, in turn, would have led both to a decrease in the number of scribes and a weakening of the literary culture of the city. There was little place for "intellectuals" in Jerusalem in the mid-third century.[11]

The Greek cities, with their gymnasia, put a value on the distinctive form of education that they termed *paideia*. This training consisted of both literacy and acquaintance with a broad range of texts and topics, similar to what we might term a "liberal education." The gymnasium and its training generated a culture of respect around knowledge and those who mastered and taught it. Those who desired to go beyond the basic gymnasium education and join the community of intellectuals would, money and time permitting (not small matters), study with a philosopher. The most well known and successful of these philosophers usually followed one of the accepted schools (for example, Epicureans) and might run his own academy. For those who wanted to stay local, however, other, lesser-known philosophers could be found in many cities.[12]

In 200 BCE Jerusalem was not officially incorporated as a polis and did not have a gymnasium—yet. The Hellenistic educational ethos, however, did begin to penetrate into the city. The increasing prosperity of the city led to an increase in the number of men (probably mostly priests) who would have had the financial means to turn to a life of study. They would be aware of the status that elites from other cities gave to a certain form of education. Itinerant philosophers or trips to nearby Scythopolis would have introduced the basics of paideia to a small, elite, and growing group of men. The problem, however, was that without a gymnasium education, good Greek, and solid knowledge of the Greek classics, they could never hope to advance very far. So they did the best they could, combining the ethos of paideia and some basic ideas that they were able to pick up with content that they knew from their own culture and upbringing.

Three surviving literary works open a window into how this new ethos and set of ideas resonated in early second-century Jerusalem. The author of Ecclesiastes more or less accepted a simplified version of Epicureanism, casting it in a beautiful and poetic Hebrew. Ecclesiastes had no use for tradition of any kind. A contemporary of his, Jesus ben Sira, was alarmed by Ecclesiastes and pushed back. He responded with a Hebrew book known as Ecclesiasticus, written by and for the priestly establishment. Ben Sira attempted to make the case that the traditional books already embodied the new Greek ethos. The third work we will discuss looks very different from the other two. Originally written in Aramaic, 1 Enoch (or more accurately a section of this book) is an account of a mythical figure's trip to heaven and the divinely authored tablets with which he returned. For this author, books are important—just not the books that one might suppose.

"The words of Kohelet, the son of David, king in Jerusalem" (Ecclesiastes 1:1) begins the book of Ecclesiastes. Based on this verse and a later one that identifies the author as "king of Jerusalem" (v. 12), later Jewish and Christian traditions would come to identify the author of this book as King Solomon. This attribution, however, has long been shown to be a fiction. The author's identity is in fact far murkier. Perhaps the best that we can say is that he was a "sage" who adopted the persona of a king in this work for literary purposes.[13]

The author's Hebrew name, Kohelet, might also provide some thin information about him. Kohelet is not a proper noun, but in this case is probably best translated as "Assembler" or "Teacher." Toward the very end of the book, the author writes, "Besides being wise, Kohelet also taught the people knowledge, weighing and studying and arranging many proverbs. Kohelet sought to find pleasing words, and he wrote words of truth plainly. The sayings of the wise are like goads, and like nails firmly fixed are the collected sayings that are given by one shepherd. Of anything beyond these, my child, beware. Of making many books there is no end, and much study is a weariness of the flesh" (12:9–12). In this epilogue, the author is portrayed as a public sage, a man who delivers maxims orally. His social position would have been similar to that of a contemporary Greek philosopher.[14]

It is not just his social position that aligns him with Greek philosophy. With the exception of a single line at the book's end, Kohelet's message is almost unremittingly bleak, with a message so obvious that even my eight-year-old daughter, unprompted, summed it up to me as "Life stinks and then you die." Ecclesiastes' favorite word is *hevel*, wind or vapor, often translated as vanity. All is like vapor, elusive and immaterial. Money, labor, even wisdom—all vapor, bringing inevitable grief that culminates in death (1:17–18, 4:4). The only response to the human condition is enjoyment: "Go, eat your bread in gladness and drink your wine in joy; for your action was long ago approved by God. Let your clothes always be freshly washed, and your head never lack ointment. Enjoy happiness with a woman you love all the fleeting days of life that have been granted to you under the sun—all your fleeting days. For that alone is what you can get out of life and out of the means you acquire under the sun. . . . For there is no action, no reasoning, no learning, no wisdom in Sheol, where you are going" (9:7–10). God is around, but only abstractly. God has preordained everything, but seems to no longer be involved in the world, all the more so in the flow of history or individual justice. Our end is in Sheol, the shadowy place where one goes after death, with no judgment or afterlife. "Sometimes an upright man is requited according to the conduct of the scoundrel; and sometimes the scoundrel is requited according to the conduct of the upright," the author complains (8:14). In the end, we all die. More vapor.

Ecclesiastes is not entirely consistent theologically. On the one hand, God has preordained all. On the other, however, God can get angry and punish individuals. God, like a king, is thus to be feared and approached only warily. You should watch your language, particularly when it comes to vows to God that you might not be able to fulfill, "else God may be angered by your talk and destroy your possessions" (5:5). Even approaching the temple to offer sacrifices should be done carefully and with moderation. "Discerning" or "heeding" is better than mindless offerings, undoubtedly in part because it keeps one at a safer distance from God (4:17).

Ecclesiastes' God never rewards humans for their actions. One must carefully acknowledge God's power to avoid destruction, but there is no place in this theology for a personal God or one who grants trivial requests or prayers. Aside from the very last lines of the book and perhaps very elliptically the statement that God prefers "discernment" or "heeding" (of what is not specified), there is no mention of the fact that "reverence" of God might mean observing God's commandments. Nor is there any mention of Israel's unique historical experience. The book is addressed to all humans, not only the Judeans. In all of these features the book strongly parallels Hellenistic "popular philosophy," in which Epicureanism in particular played an important role.[15]

Another peculiar aspect of Ecclesiastes is that it shows no unambiguous awareness of the Pentateuch or other earlier written documents. The book, full of pithy maxims based on observation of nature, is in the tradition of earlier wisdom literature such as is now found in Proverbs, but the genre was common throughout the region and there is no reason to assume that the author drew particularly on earlier Israelite literature. He knows of the Jerusalem temple from its existence, not from any text (8:10). His stock of trade was proverbs, not the intense study of the many books that weary him. If he knew the Torah and other Israelite writings—as one might expect from a "sage"—it is not at all apparent.

To Elias Bickerman, a modern scholar, "Koheleth is Job who failed the test." The author, Bickerman argues, was a "devout Jew" who became disillusioned with God's justice, "alone in a world foreign to him." This foreign world was that of Greek ideas, an "age of enlightenment." As a child of this age of inquiry, the author of Ecclesiastes addressed the same questions as contemporary Hellenistic philosophers: What is the purpose of life? What is a proper use of one's wealth?[16]

This, of course, is only a question that the wealthy would bother to ask. Kohelet is troubled by the excessive wealth that he sees around him (and might very well possess himself; see 2:9), but not in the way that some of the biblical prophets were. He never advises his readers to use their wealth for the public good or support of the poor. His problem is not social injustice but that his readers are consumed with worrying about their wealth. Kohelet tells us that with his abundance of time, "I put my mind to studying, exploring, and seeking wisdom and reason for things" (7:25). Kohelet, I think was less a "devout Jew" than a wealthy Jewish man for whom the snippets of Hellenistic philosophy he somehow picked up resonated. He had clearly received a good education in Hebrew, which he used to express these sentiments.

Unlike almost all of the other texts discussed until now, Ecclesiastes does not appear to have been written within any kind of institutional framework. The author might well have been a scribe (although he never makes this claim), but this was a work for him and his circle. It was not the kind of writing that we would expect to have found its way into the temple library. At some point in its circulation, a copyist dampened the book's radical claim by adding two verses to the end: "The end of the matter; all has been heard. Fear God, and keep his commandments; for that is the whole duty of everyone. For God will bring every deed into judgment, including every secret thing, whether good or evil" (12:13–14).[17] These verses go against the entire argument of the book, but they were apparently effective. They, together with the book's mistaken attribution to Solomon, were enough to give it a wider circulation and, perhaps, to make possible its deposit in the temple library.

Kohelet had no need for tradition or the authority of written texts. Experience grounded in the natural world was authoritative enough. Not everyone in Jerusalem would have agreed with him, though. At least one of his contemporaries, Jesus ben Sira, decidedly didn't. Jesus ben Sira, also known as Ben Sira or Ecclesiasticus, was a scribe who saw the new Hellenistic ideas through the lens of the texts with which he was trained.

The book of Ben Sira was originally written in Hebrew and then translated into Greek by his grandson in 117 BCE. This Greek version entered the Apocrypha, a collection of originally Jewish books to which several Christian groups give canonical authority. Only in the late nineteenth century did versions of the original Hebrew text surface, first in the Cairo Geniza (a repository of discarded Jewish medieval manuscripts) and then among the Dead Sea Scrolls.[18]

Ben Sira does not easily fit into a single social type. Indeed, we shouldn't expect him to. Jerusalem was a small city, and when Antiochus the Great mentioned in his proclamations the social classes of senators, priests, scribes, singers, and others, it is reasonable to assume that many of these individuals at least knew each other, and some fell within more than one of these designations. Ben Sira was a great supporter of the priesthood and may well have been a priest himself. "With all your soul fear the Lord, and revere his priests," he says. "With all your might love your Maker, and do not neglect his ministers. Fear the Lord and honor the priest, and give him his portion, as you have been commanded: the first fruits, the guild offering, the gift of the shoulders, the sacrifice of sanctification, and the first fruits of the holy things" (Ecclesiasticus 7:29–31). He lavishly praises the high priest Simon, "the pride of his people," a figure who stood directly in the line of Israel's sacred history. Ben Sira witnessed Simon's presiding over the temple service: "How glorious he was, surrounded by the people, as he came out of the house of the curtain" (50:5). He goes on to compare Simon to a morning star, a full moon, the sun, a rainbow, flowers, and fire, among other things. In addition to cutting a good figure, Simon built walls in the city and created a vast water cistern. While his hero Simon was a priest descended from the line of Zadok, Ben Sira supported all priests from the line of Pinhas (Phineas), Aaron's son.[19]

Ben Sira, though, was also a scribe and sage. "Draw near to me, you who are uneducated, and lodge in the house of instruction," he says (51:23). While he commends all laborers and artisans, without whom "no city can be inhabited" (38:32), his heart is with the wealthy scribe: "The wisdom of the scribe depends on the opportunity of leisure; only the one who has little business can become wise. How can one become wise who handles the plow, and who glories in the shaft of a goad, who drives oxen and is occupied with their work, and whose talk is about bulls?" (38:24–25). He then expands this idea into a full paean for the one who "devotes himself to the study of the law of the Most High":

He seeks out the wisdom of all the ancients, and is concerned with
   prophecies;
he preserves the sayings of the famous and penetrates the subtleties of
   parables;
he seeks out the hidden meanings of proverbs and is at home with the
   obscurities of parables.

He serves among the great and appears before rulers;
he travels in foreign lands and learns what is good and evil in the human lot.

He sets his heart to rise early to seek the Lord who made him, and to petition the Most High;
he opens his mouth in prayer and asks pardon for his sins.

If the great Lord is willing, he will be filled with the spirit of understanding;
he will put forth words of wisdom of his own and give thanks to the Lord in prayer.

The Lord will direct his counsel and knowledge, as he meditates on his mysteries.

He will show the wisdom of what he has learned, and will glory in the law of the Lord's covenant.

Many will praise his understanding; it will never be blotted out.

His memory will not disappear, and his name will live through all generations.

Nations will speak of his wisdom, and the congregation will proclaim his praise.

If he lives long, he will leave a name greater than a thousand, and if he goes to rest, it is enough for him.   (38:34–39:11)

Ben Sira's vision of the scribe/sage's role and place in society differs radically from that of Ecclesiastes. Ecclesiastes gains knowledge from experience. Ben Sira, though, finds knowledge in the elucidation of traditions such as "wisdom," "prophecies," and "parables." Ben Sira's knowledge is academic, primarily a function of interpretation of and meditation on texts rewarded with a healthy dose of God's grace. Like Ecclesiastes, Ben

Sira thinks that God should be revered, but he more pointedly defines reverence as prayer and sacrifices. Such acts must also be accompanied by good deeds and general adherence to the law of God (35:1–2).

Ben Sira knew well many of the texts that would become part of the Bible. As a relatively wealthy man (or even boy) well connected to the temple establishment, his familiarity with them is not surprising. What is surprising is that he almost never mentions the physical existence of such texts, nor does he explicitly cite from them. Chapters 44–49 "sing the praises of famous men, our ancestors in their generations" (44:1). He begins with Enoch and ends with Nehemiah before very quickly moving to praise of his hero Simon, the son of Onias, thus insinuating that he too was part of Israel's sacred history. The praise of "famous men" directly parallels what is found in the Bible. In other passages too he seems to be drawing on stories that he may have read.[20]

The only place where he mentions the existence of a specific written text occurs in praise of wisdom: "All this is the book of the Most High God, the law that Moses commanded us as an inheritance for the congregations of Jacob" (24:23). In this passage he equates a personified wisdom with this law. The passage domesticates and parochializes wisdom. This idea, though, is soon dropped.[21] Ben Sira is ultimately not interested in arguing for the authority of this book. His interest, rather, is in asserting that all knowledge and wisdom that appear foreign really aren't. His is a strategy for appropriating Hellenistic ideas and packaging them as native.

Like Kohelet, Ben Sira was familiar with these new ideas. Some scholars have argued that he actually read some Hellenistic authors, although this is far from conclusive.[22] Whether he was exposed to such ideas through texts or conversation, he was attracted to them. There are parallels in his book to the writings of Greek (especially the sixth-century BCE Greek poet Theognis) and Egyptian authors. It was not only wisdom in the abstract that Ben Sira sought to appropriate but also specific instances that appealed to him. Unlike Kohelet, he found a base for them in his ancestral writings.

These differences between Kohelet and Ben Sira might not be accidental. It is possible that Ben Sira knew and was subtly responding to Kohelet. Ben Sira clearly and definitively rejects Kohelet's vision of an amoral world. "The one who keeps the law preserves himself, and the one who trusts the Lord will not suffer loss" (32:24). God knows our sins and will punish us for them (17:15–32). Ben Sira and Kohelet emerged from more or less the same social conditions in Jerusalem. Both were wealthy and learned. Each laid claim to wisdom and each seemed to have nurtured a circle of disciples. Both wrote in Hebrew to those within their class. Jerusalem was small and its elite class of literati smaller. It does not seem unlikely to me that they would have known each other.[23]

Ben Sira might also give us an indirect glimpse of how scribes were trained at this time. Ben Sira knew and drew upon oral traditions and texts. These texts—which would have included many of the texts that became part of the Bible—appear to have been part of Ben Sira's training. They had earned by that time a certain literary authority. Hence, Ben Sira drew upon them not as definitive and normative sources but as literary resources to deploy in order to raise the literary standing of his work in the eyes of the other literate elite. Although this was a common practice of Hellenistic writers at the time, it was also not an uncommon practice among earlier scribes. By the early second century Ben Sira and his establishment circle had a sense of the books that they should master. This was a fluid and very specific kind of authority.[24]

Like the book of Ecclesiastes, the book of Ecclesiasticus was not written as a public, official, or authoritative text. Neither makes any pretense of being anything other than a book of advice written by an individual in a specific historical context. They thus both stand in sharp contrast with yet another book written around the same time, probably in Jerusalem or its environs, known today as 1 Enoch.

The book of 1 Enoch, as it is now known, is a compilation of a few different texts from different periods, all of which coalesce around a single figure (much like the book of Isaiah combines the work of different prophets). The fullest version that we possess exists only in Ethoipic (Ge'ez), the language of the Christian monastery where the medieval manuscript was located. While there are fragments of 1 Enoch in Greek and Latin, the Aramaic fragments found among the Dead Sea Scrolls strongly suggest that this was the original language of the work. Although Jews eventually lost interest in this book, some Christians con-

Figure 5: Fragment of 4Q201, a copy of 1 Enoch. (Photo Shai Halevi, Spectral Image, Courtesy of the Israel Antiquities Authority)

tinued to translate and read it, occasionally emending it in the course of its transmission. Today the book can be most easily found in a scholarly collection known as the Pseudepigrapha.[25] First compiled and named in the modern period, the Pseudepigrapha collects "falsely attributed" works that date to antiquity and are not part of the contemporary standard canons (fig. 5).

The figure of Enoch is first mentioned in the first genealogy of Adam's line in the book of Genesis. In the middle of a formulaic list of who lived, how long they lived, and whom they fathered (there are few women in this list), Enoch appears: "When Enoch had lived for sixty-five years, he became the father of Methuselah. Enoch walked with God after the birth of Methuselah for three hundred years, and had other sons and daughters. Thus all the days of Enoch were three hundred and sixty-five years. Enoch walked with God; then he was no more, because God took him" (Genesis 5:21–24). There are several puzzling features about these verses. What does it mean that Enoch "walked with God"? Is there any significance to the number 365, which makes his end premature relative to the others in this list? Did Enoch actually die? These are the questions around which later writers structured this literature.

1 Enoch opens with Enoch introducing his revelation: "This is a holy vision from the heavens which the angels showed me: and I heard from them everything and I understood. I look not for this generation but for the distant one that is coming. I speak about the elect ones and concerning them."[26] Enoch, it turned out, did not simply sit around here on earth and receive angelic messages. He himself ascended to heaven (the interpretation of the biblical phrase "walked with God") and toured, receiving his revelations in images as well as words. He thus receives a divine "revelation"—the literal meaning of the Greek root for "apocalypse." 1 Enoch (and other books) are thus sometimes referred to as apocalypses, not necessarily because of any "end of the world" prophecies but because they record disclosures from the divine.

Theodicy, the explanation of how God can allow humans to suffer unjustly, is a major theme of 1 Enoch. During his ascent, the reason for unjust suffering is made clear to him: there are independent malevolent forces at work in the world, produced by the bastard mating of the divine with the human. In primordial times fallen angels took human wives and taught them magic and other destructive arts. The angel Azazel, for example, was said to have taught people how to make weapons of war, and women how to beautify themselves so that they could seduce men.[27] These offspring of fallen angels—not God and not fate—cause all that is evil in the world, whether through seducing humans or direct intervention.

A second important theme in 1 Enoch is the calendar. Enoch—a man whose life on earth was reported to have been 365 years—is shown that a solar 364-day calendar was part of the cosmic order. This was almost certainly a polemic against the Jerusalem priests' use of a lunar 354-day calendar.[28] The calendar will be a continuing sore point in priestly circles for the next three centuries.

Like Ben Sira, the author(s) of 1 Enoch knows and draws from several of the texts that would become biblical, but gives them little explicit authority. It is possible that they had a similar scribal training. This would dovetail with other similarities between the two books to suggest a common social milieu for two works that might seem on the surface to be very different.[29]

In the earlier prophetic books, the divine communication via the prophets is oral. The prophetic oracles and admonitions are in most cases recorded into writing transparently, and in the cases where a scribe is mentioned (for example, in Jeremiah), he is incidental to the actual revelation. In 1 Enoch, however, writing becomes an essential part of the oracular process. After touring the heavens, Enoch is admonished: "'Look, Enoch, at these heavenly tablets, and read what is written on them, and learn every individual fact.' And I looked at everything on the heavenly tablets, and I read everything that was written, and I learned everything. And I read the book and everything that was written in it—all the deeds of men and all the sons of flesh that will be upon the earth until the generations of eternity. And then I blessed the great Lord." Enoch's multisensory experience in heaven ends with a written account of all of history and future events. A slightly later composition (incorporated into 1 Enoch) has Enoch consulting these heavenly tablets in order to divine the future fate of individuals.[30]

1 Enoch cannot exactly be read as a text that "authorizes" an actual set of heavenly tablets in the way that Esther authorizes Purim or that the Letter of Aristeas would come to authorize the Greek translation of the Pentateuch. The tablets are not central to the narrative and it is difficult to imagine what they might actually look like. Nor can 1 Enoch be read as reflecting the specific knowledge of the tablets. The reference is more abstract and conceptual. We should know that individual fate is divinely predetermined, indelibly written but accessible only by means of a special revelation.[31]

Unlike Kohelet and Ben Sira, the original language of 1 Enoch was Aramaic, the common or vernacular language of the time. This is in a way surprising. Especially Kohelet, but also Ben Sira to some degree, are collections of maxims that probably also were recited in an oral context, whereas 1 Enoch's contents are more abstruse and esoteric. Might the difference in language indicate that they emerged from different social strata or geographical locations? Or might the change in language signal a different function or audience?

One possibility is that the works written in Hebrew really were intended for the private reading of a scribal elite. Responding to the new ideas that they were encountering and building on the earlier Hebrew works to which they had access, they began to forge a new intellectual ethos and culture that for very practical reasons did not require mastery of Greek. I Enoch was certainly not meant for the masses, but with its concern for the temple and the cultic calendar (even if it was at odds with the one in use), it was written by and for a priestly elite. While the priests and scribes worked in close proximity to each other and sometimes overlapped, not all priests would have had good command of Hebrew.

A collection of texts known as the Aramaic Testament of Levi (known from the Dead Sea Scrolls) provides support for this reconstruction. This very fragmentary text valorizes Levi, the progenitor of the priests. It adopts a solar calendar and locates the detailed regulations for the cult in Levi's last words rather than in a written text or Mosaic revelation. Like I Enoch, this text was written in Aramaic by and for priests and demonstrates a similar disregard for the normative authority of earlier texts.[32]

There is yet one other piece of evidence to briefly consider, the book of Tobit. Now found, like Ben Sira, in the Catholic Apocrypha, it is an engaging and moralistic story of a Jewish family's attempt to assure its continuity, set at the time of the Persian conquest of the Babylonians (late sixth century BCE). Although several scholars have argued that Tobit was originally composed in Aramaic between 225 and 175 BCE, there is still little certainty.[33]

The author of Tobit, like Ben Sira, knows and appropriates earlier texts that are now part of the Bible.[34] Moreover, though, the author actually cites from these texts. In separate passages he recalls prophecies of Amos (Tobit 2:6) and Nahum (14:4) and vaguely references "the prophets" (v. 5). The written oracles of ancient written prophecies carried a weight that legal writings had yet to acquire.

It had taken more than a century since the conquest of Alexander the Great, but by 175 BCE Jerusalem finally encountered Hellenism. Even in the meager extant literature from this time we can see different responses.

Kohelet responded enthusiastically. He was entirely sympathetic to the popular Hellenistic philosophical ideas he encountered, expressing them in a new Hebrew idiom. The priestly reaction, represented by 1 Enoch and the Aramaic Testament of Levi, was more guarded but far from hostile. Whatever specific elements in their writings may or may not have come from this encounter with Hellenism, it led to priests beginning to write texts in their vernacular language and to consider the possibility of "heavenly tablets." Ben Sira stood somewhere between these two points. Unlike Kohelet and the author of 1 Enoch, who assigned no direct authority to earlier texts, he experimented with developing a Hellenistic ethos with Hebrew texts. For him, the link to the written past was important.

It would be another several decades until "Hellenism" actually acquired a name. The scribes and priests of Jerusalem slowly began to encounter discrete new ideas and either appropriated them or didn't. There was no sense that these new ideas—as a package—presented a problem or challenge.[35] Later, after the revolt of the Maccabees, ancient authors would look back at this time as a clash of civilizations. I do not think that Kohelet, Ben Sira, or the priests of the time would have shared that perspective.

Ideas and texts are one thing, institutions another. Like most sizable cities in this part of the world, Jerusalem was gradually moving toward becoming a polis. This would raise not abstract issues of ideas and culture but very tangible ones of power and money. These were the issues that led to the revolt of the Maccabees.

7 The Maccabean Revolt: Judea, 175–135 BCE

Today, there are three popular versions of the story of the Jewish holiday of Hanukkah. The narrative that is dominant in the United States sees the clash between the forces of Antiochus IV Epiphanes, the Seleucid king who assumed power in 175 BCE, and the Jews of Jerusalem as a warning story of assimilation. The evil king, aided by evil Jews, wanted to eradicate Judaism and replace it with Hellenism. The brave Maccabee brothers rose up in outrage and defeated them. The narrative most commonly known in Israel recasts the events of the Maccabean revolt as a nationalistic story of the Jews gaining their autonomy from the Seleucids. A third narrative, now dominant in more religious Jewish circles, by and large ignores the historical meaning and causes of the revolt and focuses instead on the miracle that God performed during the purification and rededication of the temple (that is, allowing one day's worth of pure oil to last for eight days) after Judah Maccabee recaptured it from the Seleucids.[1]

Each of these three dominant narratives (parts of which are often combined in popular retellings) draws on historical sources. The nationalist narrative derives primarily from 1 Maccabees, a sober and authoritative court history of the Hasmoneans, the descendents of the Maccabees, written about fifty years after the events of the revolt. The assimilationist narrative follows the book of 2 Maccabees, written around the same time, which survives today only as a version abridged for use in the Diaspora. Both of these works today are part of the Catholic Apocrypha. The third narrative (the miraculous one) derives from a legend found in the Talmud that dates from a much later time. Each of these sources, of course, has its own reasons for presenting the revolt in the way that it does.

What all of these narratives, modern and ancient, either neglect to mention or attempt to hide is that the primary cause of the events that led to the Maccabean revolt was a power struggle among elite Jerusalem families. It was, in other words, a civil war caused by competition for power and money. The events were further complicated by internal struggles within some of these families as well as by what was in retrospect the ill-advised reaction of Antiochus IV, who mistook an internal power struggle for a revolt against him.

The smoke finally cleared around 135 BCE with the ascension of the Hasmonean John Hyrcanus to the throne. Hyrcanus and his descendents, though, could never quite overcome the venal circumstances that led to their claim to power. The older families who lost power due to the revolt still existed and struggled to assert their power in the new regime. This struggle would lead to the formation of two proto-political parties, the Pharisees and Sadducees, around the time of Hyrcanus, and to a seismic shift in the role played by writings that were thought to be sacred. To understand how and why that happened, though, we must first go back to the Maccabean revolt and its aftermath.

The events that led up to the Maccabean revolt began as a family feud.[2] A man named Onias III was the high priest. He was the son of the high priest Simon who had been so fulsomely praised by Ben Sira, and his family had occupied this post for many years, perhaps going back to the restoration of the second temple in 520 BCE. As high priest, Onias III wielded a tremendous amount of power and wealth. "But a man named Simon, of the tribe of Benjamin, who had been made captain of the temple, had a disagreement with the high priest about the administration of the city market" (2 Maccabees 3:4). It is a scene reminiscent of an episode of the *Sopranos*. Simon apparently thought that Onias was not properly sharing his power and lucre with his closest and most deserving underlings. So began a competition between these families that would lead to the ruin of the temple.

The competition, though, was also internal. Onais III's own brother Jason deposed him by bribing the new Seleucid king, Antiochus IV. Once in power, Jason had high ambitions. Jason petitioned Antiochus IV for permission to turn Jerusalem into a polis—a semiautonomous Greek city—and rename it Antioch. It was a natural request, and it was granted. Jerusalem had been slowly coming into contact with and adapting elements of the Hellenistic ethos without any sense of unease. Jason must have been reflecting the desire of many to elevate the standing of the city and to establish some of the key institutions of the traditional polis, especially the gymnasium (1 Maccabees 1:11–15; 2 Maccabees 4:11–17). Later historians would point to the establishment of a gymnasium in Jerusalem as a grave offense, but it is difficult to follow the logic of these attacks. At the time, most would have welcomed it.[3]

The problem was not the change of status and the establishment of a gymnasium but the continuing competition between Jason's (and Onias III's) family and Simon's, now continued by Simon's brothers, Menelaus and Lysimachus. The two families competed for support from Antiochus IV, with each trying to outbid the other with unrealistic offers of gold. These negotiations ultimately led to the execution of Onias III and unrest in Jerusalem (2 Maccabees 4:32–38). The unrest was magnified by increasing knowledge that Menelaus and Lysimachus, who then held the post, were looting the temple's treasury to make good on their promises to Antiochus IV.

In 168 BCE, Antiochus IV made the mistake of attacking Egypt. For whatever reason, Jason, who had been living in exile, attacked Jerusalem in order to regain his high priesthood. Antiochus, who had just been rebuffed by the Romans (the new emerging geopolitical power in the region), misunderstood this civil conflict as revolt against him.[4] Antiochus launched his own savage attack on the city. The author of 2 Maccabees claims that forty thousand were killed and another forty thousand were sold into slavery (5:11–26). The numbers must be wildly exaggerated, but they reflect the deep trauma left by the attack.

Although Antiochus was understandably upset at both what he saw as a rebellion and the nonappearance of the money that Menelaus and Lysimachus had promised him, his response continues to puzzle modern historians. According to 2 Maccabees, Antiochus "sent an Athenian senator to compel the Jews to forsake the laws of their ancestors and no longer to live by the laws of God; also to pollute the temple in Jerusalem and to call it the temple of Olympian Zeus" (6:1–2). This was followed by persecutions of personal religious freedoms (as we might call it): "On the monthly celebration of the king's birthday," 2 Maccabees relates, "the Jews were taken, under bitter constraint, to partake of the sacrifices; and when a festival of Dionysus was celebrated, they were compelled to wear wreaths of ivy and to walk in the procession in honor of Dionysus" (6:7). Judeans, we are told, in both Jerusalem and surrounding Greek cities were killed for observing the Sabbath and for circumcising their children (2 Maccabees 6:6, 10; 1 Maccabees 1:60–61).

Such actions are almost unprecedented in the ancient world. They were bad for loyalty and bad for tax revenues. Assuming that the report is, at least in a general way, accurate, how are we to account for Antiochus's actions? According to 1 Maccabees, these persecutions were part of Antiochus's broader policy, in which "all should be one people, and that all should give up their particular customs" (1 Maccabees 1:41–42). In this telling, Judeans (and then, only the ones in the area that Antiochus thought was under revolt) are singled out because they refused to do so. This seems not particularly likely, but scholars still do not have a satisfying answer as to Antiochus's motivations.[5]

These persecutions, along with the mess made in Jerusalem by the two feuding families, provided an opening for a third family led by Mattathias. A priest from a distinguished although not high-priestly line, he had moved from Jerusalem to Modi'in, a town about halfway between Jerusalem and modern Tel Aviv (1 Maccabees 2:1). With his sons, Mattathias began a guerilla campaign, killing Seleucid officials and Jewish collaborators alike. On his death, his son Judah, who would later gain the nickname "Maccabeus," or "hammer," took control of the loosely organized campaign. After a year of fighting he somewhat improbably succeeded in taking back the Jerusalem temple.[6]

Judah's first act was to appoint unblemished priests to resanctify the temple. This turned out to be a bit tricky. The altar had been desecrated by the "abomination of desolation" (we remain not entirely sure what this was) set up by the Seleucids, but the stones were still holy. In the end, Judah decided to destroy the altar and store the stones "until a prophet should come to tell what to do with them." He then rebuilt a new altar on that site from different stones (1 Maccabees 4:46). They restored the temple implements and then, on the twenty-fifth day of the Hebrew month of Kislev in 164 BCE, they offered the first animal sacrifices in the restored temple. "[Judah] and his brothers and all the assembly of Israel determined that every year at that season the days of dedication of the altar should be observed with joy and gladness for eight days, beginning with the twenty-fifth day of the month of Kislev" (4:59). The holiday of Hanukkah—literally, "dedication"—was established to mark the sanctification of a temple whose sanctity, even according to the Hasmonean supporter who wrote 1 Maccabees, was a little questionable.

Judah's position was hardly secure. He faced continued pressure from the Seleucids as well as competition from local Judeans. According to 1 Maccabees, Judah rebuffed the attempts of two Judean military leaders to ally with him (5:61–62). We do not know if these leaders had any connections to the former leading families of Jerusalem, but their attempt to forge an alliance replays a familiar dynamic and is a harbinger of the future tensions between the Hasmoneans and others who thought that they deserved to share some of their power and wealth.

These competing families—called "renegades" by the later Hasmonean court historian—pop more clearly into view in 160 BCE, when Judah fell in continuing battle against the Seleucids. Under the leadership of another high priest, Alcimus, they succeeded in taking control of Jerusalem. Alcimus, though, died of natural causes only a year later (1 Maccabees 9:23–56).

Among the groups that supported Judah and his brothers against Alcimus and the old establishment was the same circle of somewhat disaffected priests who had produced the earlier Enoch composition and the Aramaic Testament of Levi. Both of these texts, in addition to showing concern for matters of interests to priests, were written in Aramaic, followed (polemically, in the case of the Enoch material) a solar calendar, demonstrated familiarity with older texts but did not cite them for authority, and had an interest in writing. These priests (or those who were close to them) may never have fit comfortably within the temple establishment, but surely their position was further weakened with the power shifts launched by the struggle between Onias III and Simon. In Judah, though, they placed high hope.

This is the same group that likely authored two short and opaque compositions that we can date with an unusual degree of precision. Both laud Judah as a kind of messianic savior while seeming unaware of his death, allowing us to date them between 164–160 BCE. Both were written in Aramaic, demonstrated familiarity with older texts, and have an explicit interest in the authority of writing. One is what scholars refer to as the "Animal Apocalypse" and is now found in 1 Enoch. The other is embedded in the biblical book of Daniel.

The Animal Apocalypse is framed as a vision given to Enoch. The vision is a biblical history that stretches from the very time of creation that draws on without explicitly citing the Pentateuch and early prophets, much like Ben Sira does. Bizarrely, though, it changes all the characters to animals. For example, in its concise recapitulation of the story of how Joseph and his brothers ended up in Egypt and their descendents were oppressed, the Animal Apocalypse states: "When those twelve sheep [Jacob's sons] had grown up, they handed over one of themselves to the wild asses, and those wild asses, in turn, handed that sheep over to the wolves [Egyptians], and that sheep grew up in the midst of the wolves. And the ram [Jacob] led forth the eleven sheep to dwell with it, and to pasture with it in the midst of the wolves. And they multiplied and became many flocks of sheep. And the wolves began to fear them and oppress them."[7] On the one hand, the use of animals seems to make the story more esoteric, although on the other almost all the identities are transparent.

The Animal Apocalypse's history ends with the triumph of Judah Maccabee. In the midst of telling how the Seleucids (the "ravens") were attacking the Jews (the "lambs"), the vision relates that "a great horn sprouted on one of those sheep."[8] With the help of the "Lord of sheep," the great horn went on to empower the other sheep and gain victory over the ravens and other noxious beasts.

The vision is clearly sympathetic to Judah Maccabee. As it celebrates his victories but does not mention his death, we can be relatively certain that it was written very shortly before 160 BCE. The author opposes the current temple establishment, but his more general stance toward and relationship with the temple and its priests is a bit more obscure.[9]

As with the earlier Enochic author who suggested that there were "heavenly tablets," this one too supposes that there are documents written in heaven that detail the fates of individuals and communities. "Every excess and destruction that is done by the shepherds, write down," the Lord of sheep commands his angelic scribe.[10] All will eventually receive judgment.

The visions that are now found as chapters 7–12 in the biblical book of Daniel are in many respects similar to the Animal Apocalypse and date from the same short period of time.[11] These chapters relate several visions that Daniel, the mythic prophet in captivity in Babylonia, received about future events. Like the Animal Apocalypse, these visions contain lightly veiled allusions to the events of the Maccabean revolt, in fact also at times using the animal imagery contained in that Apocalypse.

The first vision in this series was recorded in Aramaic very shortly before the Maccabean revolt. Using the image of four great beasts, the vision tells of the progression of the empires of Babylon, Media, Persia, and Greece. The author's real interest is in this fourth beast, "terrifying and dreadful and exceedingly strong" (Daniel 7:7). This beast sprouts several horns (representing the successors of Alexander the Great). In the midst of these horns, another small one pushes its way in and began to speak arrogantly, making "war with the holy ones" (v. 21). Daniel asks for an explanation of the vision and is told about this small horn, which clearly represents Antiochus IV: "He shall speak words against the Most High, shall wear out the holy ones of the Most High, and shall attempt to change the sacred seasons and the law; and they shall be given into his power for a time, two times, and a half a time" (v. 25). This vision accuses Antiochus of blasphemy and religious persecution, which is predicted to last three and a half years.

A second vision (in Hebrew) was recorded shortly after this one. Again, there is a vision of empires represented by beasts that culminates with a small horn (8:9). "Even against the prince of the host it acted arrogantly; it took the regular burnt offering away from him and overthrew the place of his sanctuary" (v. 11). This vision refers to the desecration of the temple. Since the vision incorrectly predicts how long the temple will remain defiled, we can be relatively confident that it was written shortly after the event.¹² A couple of chapters later Daniel is given a third, more direct and specific vision of Antiochus IV's military campaigns and violation of the temple (11–12). This vision too incorrectly predicts the time that the temple will remain desecrated and the circumstances by which Antiochus dies.

Like the author of the Animal Apocalypse, this writer asserted that there was a heavenly book that predicted all future time (7:10; 10:21; 12:4). This writer, though, also explicitly engaged with earlier writings. Daniel declares, "I, Daniel, perceived in the books the number of years that, according to the word of the Lord to the prophet Jeremiah, must be fulfilled for the devastation of Jerusalem, namely, seventy years" (9:2). The reference is to Jeremiah's prophecy that the first temple will lie in ruins for seventy years before being restored (Jeremiah 25:11–12, 29:10). Daniel fasts and prays to God that although the destruction of Jerusalem was a just reward for their sins and was foretold "just as it is written in the law of Moses" (Daniel 9:13), "let your face shine upon your desolated sanctuary" (v. 17).¹³

The angel Gabriel appears in answer to Daniel's prayer. He explains that Daniel has misunderstood Jeremiah. Jeremiah actually meant seventy *weeks* of years, that is, 490 (70 times 7) years (v. 24). The last of those weeks began with the death of Onias III (in 171 BCE). Antiochus IV, Gabriel explains to Daniel, "shall make a strong covenant with many for one week, and for half of the week he shall make sacrifice and offering cease; and in their place shall be an abomination that desolates, until the decreed end is poured out on the desolator" (v. 27). The reference is to Antiochus's desecration of the temple and the author's hope that God will avenge it.

This author, then, cited both a written copy of the "law of Moses" and Jeremiah as authoritative texts. The kind of authority, though, like that of the other heavenly books, is specifically *oracular*. Much as the author of Jeremiah had read Deutero-Isaiah, the author of 2 Chronicles had read Jeremiah, and Tobit had read Amos, the author of this vision understands the real authoritative value of divinely inspired texts as containing true predictions of the future. The predictions, though, were by no means transparent. Some remained the preserve of heaven, ensconced in the sealed book entrusted to Daniel (12:4). Others needed continuing divine inspiration to interpret, as Gabriel had for Jeremiah's oracle. The written oracles, even when available, needed a secret key to unlock.

The author of Daniel (and of the Animal Apocalypse) thought that he possessed that key. He identifies himself with the group of the "wise." At the time of the persecutions, he writes, "The wise among the people shall give understanding to many; for some days, however, they shall fall by sword and flame, and suffer captivity and plunder. When they fall victim, they shall receive a little help, and many shall join them insincerely. Some of the wise shall fall, so that they may be refined, purified, and cleansed, until the time of the end, for there is still an interval until the time appointed" (11:33–35).

Some scholars have connected this group of the "wise" to the Hasideans. The Hasideans are mentioned very briefly in 1 and 2 Maccabees. These sources portray the Hasideans as "mighty warriors of Israel" who defended the law and attacked the "renegades" (1 Maccabees 2:42–48; 2 Maccabees 14:6). Later they are said to have mistakenly trusted Alcimus, who murdered a number of them (1 Maccabees 7:13–18). This is all we know of the Hasideans and as other scholars have argued, a connection between them and the "wise" of Daniel is almost entirely speculative.[14]

I would be very surprised if the authors of the Animal Apocalypse and the Daniel visions did not know each other or at least travel in similar circles.[15] To know for certain from the small fragments that we possess is impossible, but the author of the Daniel visions—or perhaps, if there were multiple authors, just the author of Daniel 9—had more scribal training or connections than the author of the Animal Apocalypse. Only here do we find specific earlier texts invoked for authority in a vision written in Hebrew. The Daniel visions are more cautious about the Maccabees than the Animal Apocalypse (in Daniel, deliverance will come directly from God, not from Judah Maccabee), but they shared a general approach and set of interests. Other, more fragmentary texts that were found among the Dead Sea Scrolls may well have either been produced by or just known to this group.[16]

The "wise," as a loosely organized group, may have survived the persecutions, the Maccabean revolt, and the subsequent years of shifting political ground that lasted until 135 BCE. They appear, after all, to have been in a safe enough location that during the persecution they could write. Moreover, the writings themselves survived not merely as accidental finds of papyri but as texts that were copied multiple times by those close to the center of power. The remnants of this group, or at least their ideas, would emerge again in the late second century BCE, this time linked to a new movement called the Sadducees.

For the seven years after Alcimus's death, there was no clear Jewish ruler in Judea. By 152 BCE, though, one of Judah's brothers, Jonathan, gained the favor of the new Seleucid king and was appointed both "king's friend" and "high priest." These titles, to which "governor" was added two years later, indicate that Jonathan owed his throne to the Seleucids. The Maccabean revolt had quickly led to an accommodation with the far stronger Seleucids. Even that relationship, though, could not save him from assassination (12:48).

Simon, another of Judah's brothers, replaced Jonathan and was confirmed as a "king's friend." The author of 1 Maccabees regards this as a critical moment. In 142 BCE, he writes, "the yoke of the Gentiles was removed from Israel, and the people began to write in their documents and contracts, 'In the first year of Simon the great high priest and commander and leader of the Jews'" (13:41–42). The people confirmed his rule on a lengthy inscription made on bronze tablets, placed on a monument on Mt. Zion, confirming Simon's rule. "All the people agreed to grant Simon the right to act in accordance with these decisions. So Simon accepted and agreed to be high priest, to be commander and ethnarch of the Jews and priests, and to be protector of them all" (14:46–47). Archaeologists have yet to find such a set of tablets.[17]

By 135 BCE, Simon was old and had begun to turn over his throne to his two oldest sons, Judah and John. It appears that not everyone agreed with the succession. Simon's own son-in-law and commander of the plain of Jericho tricked and murdered him and two of his sons. A third son, John, survived. He would soon take control, avenge his family's enemies, and attempt to put the Hasmonean dynasty on surer footing.

Over the four decades since the rise of Antiochus IV to the confirmation of John Hyrcanus Jerusalem had changed. Hyrcanus had first and foremost to defend his legitimacy. The Maccabee brothers may have been seen as heroes and liberators—which is certainly how they portrayed themselves—but they were not from the line of Onias III. Even the despised high priest Alcimus appears to have had a better genealogical claim than the Hasmoneans. Rich and well-established families, whether they had been allied with Onias III and Jason or with Simon, Menelaus, and Lysimachus, were now out of power and waiting for an opportunity to regain it in the new regime.

Hyrcanus also faced a secondary set of problems. The public cult at the temple had been disrupted and, it was feared, had been corrupted. Hasmonean propaganda repeatedly argued that despite the temple's looting and desecration by the Seleucids, Judah's purification and rededication in 164 BCE was efficacious; he really was able to remove the Seleucid impurities and restore pure worship to the God of Israel. The temple, the Hasmoneans assured, was returned to its old state of purity.

Purity was important in antiquity. Ritual purity was seen primarily as a state or condition into which people routinely came and went. It was hard to live normally for very long without unavoidably becoming impure. Contact with a dead human body or graveyard, some kinds of animals (such as reptiles), semen, and menstrual blood all created impurity. Ritual impurity was also seen as contagious; touching an impure person could make you impure. Whereas becoming impure was effortless (even touching a garment used by a woman during her period could impart impurity), getting out of impurity—becoming ritually pure—did require a modest effort. There were different levels of impurity (contact with a human corpse was most severe), and each had somewhat different requirements for purification. Most, though, required the passage of time followed by immersion in water.

Many, probably most, residents of Jerusalem took ritual purity seriously. Later, Jerusalem would come to have scores of "step-pools," small pools dug deeply into the rock that contain steps to enter into them.[18] We assume that male Jews desiring to become ritually pure, especially before entering the temple, would first use the pools to immerse themselves. Women who finished their menstrual cycle would also immerse in these pools prior to resuming sexual relations.

They took purity seriously because God demanded it, particularly when entering his house. To enter into the presence of God while ritually impure meant angering God, and to anger God was to risk bringing God's wrath down not only on you but also on all of Israel. Sacrifices that were performed or eaten by priests who were ritually impure were seen as abominable, offerings that would anger rather than appease the God of Israel. The temple had to be an "impurity-free zone."

But was the temple now, under John Hyrcanus, pure? 1 Maccabees addressed this concern directly when it asserted that Judah put aside the original stones of the altar, just to be on the safe side. This, though, would have been just the tip of the iceberg. The specific rules of purity were handed down from priest to son; there is no evidence that they consulted written sources, such as the scroll of Leviticus, for guidance. With the turmoil at the temple and the change of priestly families who held charge, this chain of knowledge broke. The priests on the outside looking in must have been upset with what they would have seen as critically flawed purity practices.

John Hyrcanus had his hands full.

8 The Holy Books:
Judea, 135–104 BCE

The Hasmonean claim to legitimacy was tenuous. They were priests, but not of the right line. Their family had successfully fought the Seleucids, but they achieved something more akin to vassal status than true self-autonomy. They saved their compatriots from persecution, but by the reign of John Hyrcanus (135–104 BCE) that was already well in the past. They maintained power only with the tacit permission of the Seleucid king and Rome and, through their appropriation of the high priesthood, by their de facto control of the Jerusalem temple.

As high priests, the power of the Hasmoneans depended on their control of the Jerusalem temple. And it was precisely here that they were most vulnerable. From one direction they had to fight off the charge that, being from an inferior priestly genealogy, they did not deserve to inherit the post held by Onias III. From the other direction they faced the problem of whether Judah and his successors had properly purified the temple when they recaptured it from the Seleucids.

Opposition to Hasmonean rule would slowly crystallize around these issues of priestly legitimacy and the purity of the temple. There had always been Jewish opposition to the Hasmoneans, as even the biased Hasmonean court histories (especially 1 Maccabees) make clear. As the Hasmoneans solidified their hold on the temple and other organs of the state, promoting their own supporters over the "old guard," such opposition grew. An entire group of aristocratic families, the supporters of Onias and his family who may have held power and lucrative positions for centuries, now found themselves on the losing side.

The Hasmoneans also needed these old aristocratic families. They had built up a large patronage network throughout Judea upon which the smooth governance of the state depended. Yet the position of these old aristocratic families was hardly secure. By supporting the losing side in the Maccabean revolt—one that the Maccabees had succeeded in labeling renegades—they lost not only political power but also popular support. And, of course, the Hasmoneans had little reason to trust them.

At the very beginning of the Hasmonean reign, the established aristocratic families were in no position to oppose the new leaders. Over the next few decades, though, they did begin to loosely organize into a political faction, or sect. Later writers would refer to this group as the Pharisees, whether or not they actually used this name to refer to themselves. Soon they would be opposed by another group called the Sadducees. It would be the Sadducees who, in their attempt to argue against the established customs of the old aristocracy and priests, developed the notion that authoritative texts, or scripture, had normative authority that should guide religious practice.

The established aristocracy, who derived much of its political power from its control of the Jerusalem temple, never needed texts to justify its authority. It relied on traditional customs and knowledge that was passed down orally and in practice. Indeed, in Jerusalem prior to the Hasmonean rule, the older important written texts were largely library texts, written in Hebrew (the language of the intelligentsia) and accessible only to a small and rarefied group of priestly and scribal elite that granted academic and prophetic importance to these texts. They were studied, copied, and engaged as part of a proper education (or paideia), or consulted for ancient oracles. No one would have thought to appeal to them for proper temple practice or to justify one's authority or political position.

The Sadducees who would come to oppose the Pharisees also had a place in the Jerusalem temple, but a lesser one. They emerged from the group of learned priests (and those in their circles) who had begun to compose texts in the vernacular language, Aramaic. These texts were also oracular; they contained divine messages concerning the future. They emphasized the role and authority of writing in the divine realm, positing the existence of heavenly tablets and divine books that told the future and of a perfect cosmic order that involved a solar calendar. They claimed that there were secret books and secret keys to them delivered from divine revelation. These priests probably never constituted a very large fraction of the temple priesthood. They lost power during the period of the Maccabean revolt but they, unlike the aristocratic families, supported the Maccabees. After the Maccabees won, they expected to be rewarded with positions of authority.

John Hyrcanus was naturally sympathetic to this group of priests who had earlier given support to his family. Also catalyzing others (especially priests) who sought power in the new regime, these priests used their own and other earlier writings against the old aristocracy. They thereby began to change the very status and authority of these writings, adding to them legal and political (normative) authority. The battle for political power was tied to the battle over texts and the meaning and authority given to them. Nobody at the time could possibly have predicted this political struggle would spawn a slow and organic process that would ultimately lead to the idea that the Bible had far-reaching normative authority.

John Hyrcanus began his reign in 135 BCE after the assassination of his father, Simon. His first concern, quite understandably, was to secure his own political position. Fortunately for him, infighting among his Seleucid overlords made this relatively easy. With the Seleucids weakened and having freshly negotiated a treaty with Rome, Hyrcanus launched military campaigns in order to expand his territory and settle some old scores.

His first campaign was in the north, conquering Samaria and destroying its temple at Mt. Gerizim in the city of Shechem. The temple, which was associated with the old kingdom of Israel (although, of course, that earlier temple had been destroyed centuries earlier), had long been an irritant to those in Jerusalem. By that time, however, it may also have become an irritant to many of those who lived in the region. Many "Samaritans," who worshipped the same God as their Judean neighbors to the south, may thus have welcomed Hyrcanus and his destruction of the temple. This helps to explain why, with the exception of Shechem itself, archaeologists have found very little evidence of military conquest from this time in the region. For Hyrcanus, Samaria presented itself as an easy and natural first target, with a population that could be easily integrated into his kingdom.[1]

With Samaria subdued, Hyrcanus turned to his south. The Idumaeans lived in the area around modern-day Be'er Sheva. They appear to have been a distinct people who settled, beginning in the fourth century BCE, in the area that used to be inhabited by the ancient Edomites. Mostly agricultural workers and speakers of an Aramaic dialect, they began to adopt Greek in some of their larger cities, primarily as a result of settlement by Greek speakers.[2] We do not know how much contact this population had with that of Judea at this time, but it is clear that they worshipped different gods, including the Greek pantheon and Qos, the ancient Edomite god.

Hyrcanus attacked and apparently easily subdued Idumaea. "After subduing all the Idumaeans," the Jewish historian Josephus relates, "Hyrcanus permitted them to remain in their country so long as they had themselves circumcised and were willing to observe the laws of the Jews. And so, out of attachment to the land of their fathers, they submitted to circumcision and to making their manner of life conform in all other respects to that of the Jews. And from that time on they have continued to be Jews."[3] Hyrcanus, according to Josephus, did no such thing to the Samaritans.

Josephus's report, which at first blush appears to suggest that the Idumaeans were forcibly "converted," is best taken as a dramatic summary of a much more complex process. Some of the Idumaeans, particularly in areas that put up stiff resistance, might well have been given such a stark choice. Others may have themselves seen the advantages of joining the Judeans. I doubt that there was any official mechanism for checking to see whether a particular family had uncircumcised males or worshipped Greek gods in the privacy of their homes. Whether the semi-integration of the Idumaeans to the Judeans came from Hyrcanus, from the Idumaeans themselves, or from some combination (the most likely scenario, in my opinion), the result was a merging of identities.[4]

Hyrcanus was confronted with the same problem that the kingdom of Israel had centuries before. He was trying to knit together a coherent

kingdom out of diverse groups of ethnic communities. The Idumaeans had their own customs, gods, ruling institutions, and identity. They,
like the Judeans, constituted a distinctive ethnos. After conquering them,
Hyrcanus, following the usual practice, could have simply allowed the
Idumaeans to maintain their own ethnic identity. Following the logic of
Ezra and Nehemiah, he could have defined the Judeans not only as an
ethnicity, but also as a kind of genealogically pure race, thus even further
rejecting the notion that anyone from another ethnicity could "become"
a Judean. Hyrcanus, though, chose not to do that.

Instead, he created a way to become a Judean that was only loosely
connected to ethnic identity. Not very much was required. Men had
to be circumcised and the Idumaeans as a group had to conform to
Judean norms or mores, whatever exactly that meant at the time. Note
that at this time there is no notice of the other major components of
what would become the conversion rituals discussed by the rabbis of
the fourth century CE: no ritual immersion and no study or knowledge
of texts. To "be" a Judean meant some combination of being born to
Judean parents, worshipping the God of Israel, and living according to
"traditional" practices. How each of these components was weighted no
doubt varied widely by family and community. This was not particularly
difficult for the Idumaeans; they continued to identify as Judeans until
well after the Hasmonean reign ended.[5]

Hyrcanus chose to absorb the Idumaeans, to "make" them Judeans, at
least for the purposes of appearance. To be Judean in this case meant to
follow similar practices, not simply to be born to Judean parents. It was
a loose, permeable conception of ethnicity that would not have been favored by the Sadducees, with their emphasis on genealogical purity. But
then, John Hyrcanus had not yet become a Sadducee.

According to Josephus, the Jewish historian writing in Rome in the
late first century CE, John Hyrcanus began his reign as a "disciple" of
the Pharisees but ultimately broke with them and allied himself with the
Sadducees. This is the first time in any surviving account that the Pharisees and Sadducees appear as historical actors.[6] Who were they? Where
did they come from?

In his colorful account of Hyrcanus's break with the Pharisees (a dramatic story of a banquet at which a cantankerous Pharisee essentially accuses Hyrcanus's mother of being a whore), Josephus makes several comments about these groups. He calls them Jewish "schools" and writes about them: "The Pharisees had passed on to the people certain regulations handed down by former generations and not recorded in the laws of Moses, for which reason they are rejected by the Sadducaean group, who hold that only those regulations should be considered valid which were written down (in scripture), and that those which had been handed down by former generations need not be observed. And concerning these matters the two parties came to have controversies and serious differences, the Sadducees having the confidence of the wealthy alone but no following among the populace, while the Pharisees have the support of the masses."[7]

Josephus's discussion of the Pharisees and Sadducees, and this passage in particular, has generated an enormous quantity of scholarly discussion. The central problem is whether to understand this account as an accurate reflection of the situation at the time of Hyrcanus; as the opinion of one of Josephus's historical sources; as a retrojection of what Josephus or his source knew about the Pharisees and Sadducees of his day back into the past; or as an attempt by Josephus to advance the fortunes of the Pharisees in his own day. Our picture of the historical origins of the Pharisees depends entirely on our evaluation of Josephus.[8]

One way through this thicket of possibilities is to focus on what Josephus identifies as the primary difference between Pharisees and Sadducees: the refusal of the Sadducees to accept legal traditions that are not contained in writings that they regard as authoritative. By the first century CE the Pharisees and Sadducees had changed somewhat, with the Pharisees achieving the wider influence that Josephus insinuates they possessed in the time of Hyrcanus. In the late second century BCE, though, the two groups appear in his account as competing, loosely organized political parties.[9]

If we use this as our starting point, then the following scenario begins to emerge. A position that gives authority to unwritten but continuing practices is essentially support of the status quo. It is a position that justifies traditional power structures and in this case would best be identified as the old aristocracy, which Hyrcanus both needs but is deeply suspicious of. The aristocracy is not exactly a well-bounded "party" that requires some kind of membership, but a number of wealthier, connected families that have overlapping interests. This is the group that Josephus calls the "Pharisees."

Against them, though, was another, more radical group that insisted that customs—and here the reference is almost certainly to proper practices in the temple—must follow the guidelines of written texts.[10] This group challenged the status quo and sought to wrest power from established authorities. I propose that the members of this loose group, whom Josephus calls the "Sadducees," were linked (exactly how and to what degree is unclear) to those who had earlier produced the writings in 1 Enoch, the Aramaic Testament of Levi, and the Daniel oracles. These texts all elevate the authority of writing. More important, at least some of these authors had actively supported the Maccabees. John Hyrcanus would have trusted them more than the older families and given them some position of influence in his court. At some point, probably in a more deliberate and calculated fashion than described by Josephus, Hyrcanus allowed these Sadducees to abrogate the Pharisaic temple practices and institute their own.

We do not know if the "Pharisees" or the "Sadducees" actually called themselves by these names at this time. Nor is there a clear consensus about the meaning of these names.[11] Simply for ease of reference I will continue here to refer to these political alliances as Pharisees and Sadducees.

The Sadducees had gained influence within Hyrcanus's court at a good time. Hyrcanus had solidified his political position both internally and externally, having significantly expanded his borders and brought a period of prosperity to Judea. Secure in their position, the Sadducees began to bring their particular commitment to the authority of written, divinely revealed texts to the Hasmonean court. They were, however, far from a uniform lot. In this formative period we can make out three different approaches to these texts. One approach, represented in 1 Maccabees, was that of an official court historian who attempted, in a somewhat halting and tentative way, to portray his employers as defenders of the "holy books." A second approach, found in a composition known as the Temple Scroll (which was found among the Dead Sea Scrolls), was to entirely rewrite earlier texts with the goal of creating a normative (if perhaps utopian) guide to proper practices connected to the temple and cult. The third and most radical approach argued that the laws and practices of the cult sprang not simply from random revealed words of God but were woven into the very fabric of nature. This is reflected in a book known as Jubilees. Josephus, I believe, would have called each of these approaches "Sadducean," despite the fact that there are tensions between them. It would, however, take another twenty-five years for these tensions to erupt into open dispute.

Toward the end of John Hyrcanus's reign, someone close to him set out to justify his reign by writing a court history, now known as 1 Maccabees. Written originally in Hebrew (although today it survives only in a Greek translation), 1 Maccabees argues that the traditional holders of priestly power in Jerusalem effectively gave up their right to serve in the temple with their infighting and abandonment of traditional ways of life, which in turn led to religious persecution and the temple's desecration. Only the Maccabees were able to put an end to the persecutions and retake the temple. Thus only the Maccabees and their descendents, confirmed by popular acclamation in Simon's time (140 BCE), have gained the right to the high priesthood.[12]

The author of 1 Maccabees believes that the strongest argument for Hasmonean legitimacy was the Hasmoneans' role in undoing the damage done by their predecessors. He does not appear to regard any argument from texts to be powerful, and might in fact have felt that his patron would not be particularly impressed by such arguments. Nevertheless, he clearly knew some of these texts and tried to integrate his commitment to them into his tract. He connected, for example, the Maccabean family patriarch, Mattathias, back to David and Phinehas, great leaders of Israel. Many of his readers would have known such stories at least in oral form.[13]

A more subtle and telling way in which the author reveals his commitment to these books is in adding yet another claim for Hasmonean leadership: the Hasmoneans protected the holy books. 1 Maccabees reports that in addition to defiling the temple, the Seleucids destroyed the "books of the law" and "anyone found possessing the book of the covenant . . . was condemned to death by decree of the king" (1 Maccabees 1:56–57). This curious detail is not found in the longer report of persecutions in 2 Maccabees and is likely to be the author's own invention. A later letter cited by 1 Maccabees also mentions the existence of "holy books" (12:9).

This is the first time that the term "holy books" appears in a text from Judea and in a text originally written in Hebrew. The term also appears about this time in Greek texts from outside of Judea and it is possible that the author of 1 Maccabees imported the concept from there. Whether or not this is the case, though, the author here makes a significant leap. The books/scrolls have become "holy." In both Greek (*hagia*) and the presumed Hebrew original (*kadosh*), the term implies a connection with the temple and priesthood. Such a connection also implies a certain level of common inaccessibility; a "holy" thing is one set apart due to its sanctity. Because this is the only (originally) Hebrew attestation of the term from this time and place, such connections cannot be pushed too far. The very use of the term, however, reflects the increasing value that the author, and presumably his wider circle, attributed to these works.[14]

What were these holy books? In one passage, Judah consulted "the book of the law" before going into battle, inquiring "into those matters about which the Gentiles consulted the likeness of their gods" (3:48). The authority of the "book of the law" here is prophetic or oracular, not normative.[15] Building on this traditional authority of some of these scrolls as authentic prophecies, this author is making a tentative claim that identifies these books as national or ethnic symbols. They are so important that the evil Antiochus, desiring to destroy Judean identity, must prohibit them. The Hasmoneans are to be commended for venerating and preserving them, but this alone would have been seen then as a weak argument for Hasmonean legitimacy.

The author of 1 Maccabees, I suggest, was a Sadducee. Writing in John Hyrcanus's court at a time when the Sadducees had increased influence, this author was committed to the authority of texts but was also uncertain how far he could promote them. This well reflects the general context in which he lived. His fellow Sadducees too were groping for a sense of normative textual authority. Two different but far stronger claims that emerged from this same time are reflected in two texts known as the Temple Scroll and Jubilees.

The Temple Scroll is known only from its discovery among the Dead Sea Scrolls. One copy is among the longest and best preserved of all of the scrolls, but smaller fragments of other copies were found as well. While the handwriting on the copies is generally dated to the mid-first century BCE and later, there is wide scholarly agreement that the original composition was made around the time of John Hyrcanus.[16]

The scroll reads much like the book of Deuteronomy, although it harmonizes it with other texts. The most prominent difference, though, is that unlike Deuteronomy, the Temple Scroll is written in the first person of God. For example, whereas one biblical verse begins, "When a man makes a vow to the Lord" (Numbers 30:2), the Temple Scroll records the same rule as "When a man makes a vow *to me*."[17] Moses, who plays such a large role, especially in Deuteronomy, does not appear at all in the Temple Scroll.

There are other features that set the Temple Scroll apart from Deuteronomy. Deuteronomy contains a hodgepodge of laws whose sequence follows no discernible sequence. The Temple Scroll organizes these laws into three coherent themes. Most of the scroll deals with the temple and its (ideal) construction. In these sections the author drew heavily from the descriptions of an ideal temple found in the book of Ezekiel. The second theme is the calendar, especially as it relates to the liturgical year. Like 1 Enoch, the Temple Scroll assumes a 364-day solar year. The third theme is purity, of both the priests and the temple itself. A final section attempts to make some order of the many laws in Deuteronomy that cannot be easily grouped, with most dealing with personal law and the relation of individuals to the state.

The Temple Scroll prescribes a temple that is almost unimaginably large located within a city that is itself to remain ritually pure. This is not the temple and Jerusalem as they existed at the time. While there may be an element of critique of contemporary practice in this description, it is also more than a little utopian: the Temple Scroll's vision of the temple is in fact unrealizable. The scroll is thus better read as a wistful fantasy than a critique of current practice.[18]

The Temple Scroll's author believes that the written law, administered by priests, should stand at the center of the ideal state. In one extensive passage, the author revised Deuteronomy 17:18–20, which says that a king should have a scroll of the law made and that he should keep it with him as a guide to proper behavior. According to the Temple Scroll, though, this law—which has been transformed to self-referentially refer to the Temple Scroll—is to serve as a normative guide not only for the king but also for his priestly *council*, which the Temple Scroll invents: "And the twelve leaders of his people (shall be) with him, and of the priests twelve, and of the Levites twelve. They shall sit together with him for judgment, and (declare the decisions of) the law, that his heart may not be lifted up above them, and that he may not do anything by any counsel apart from them."[19]

This same passage appears to offer a subtle critique of practice in his own day. It states that the king was to muster troops whose primary function was to serve as a bodyguard. In the author's imagination, this army protects the ruler from shame and defilement lest he fall into enemy hands. The king is a symbol for all of Israel and therefore must be kept pure. The passage, scholars have argued, is a critique of John Hyrcanus's own mustering of troops.[20]

The king is important, but not so important that he operates above the divinely ordained political order. The king is actually subject to the laws as understood by the council of thirty-six, on which priests and Levites are overrepresented. In Deuteronomy, the purpose of keeping the law with him is to keep him humble among all Israelites. In the Temple Scroll, it is the council—of which he appears to be little more than a figurehead—that keeps him in his place. They were the truly legitimate leaders of the people.[21]

While I have emphasized here the differences between the Temple Scroll and Deuteronomy, it would be a mistake to think that the author of the Temple Scroll simply took a fixed text of Deuteronomy and rewrote it according to his own needs. The author knew and drew on many texts that would find their way into the Bible. Many of these texts, though, were still fluid. Among the Dead Sea Scrolls there were several substantial fragments of what scholars have termed "reworked Penta-teuch" manuscripts that originally date to around this period. These texts seem to be updated (in ways both minor and major) copies of earlier texts. The author of the Temple Scroll may have drawn on texts like these. The Temple Scroll is but one (albeit extreme) example of a wider phe-nomenon taking place at the time in which scribes were freely engaging with older texts.[22]

The author of the Temple Scroll was thus a learned man (presumably) who had scribal training in Hebrew and was part (however loosely) of a circle whose members were deeply engaged with texts that they thought were authoritative. The author of the Temple Scroll, despite its utopian elements, appears to have thought that his composition had more than scribal authority. Almost all of the fragments of the Temple Scroll write out the tetragrammaton, God's four-letter name, a practice that is pri-marily limited to scrolls of biblical texts. This was composed as a norma-tive text that was connected directly to God; it could hardly have been more "holy." It pushed the logic of 1 Maccabees significantly further.

I suggest that we see the author of this text as a radical Sadducee. He was loosely allied with the other Sadducees who held important posi-tions in Hyrcanus's court and shared their developing commitment to texts as sources of authority against the Pharisaic "traditions." This au-thor, though, was not entirely satisfied with Hyrcanus and the cult. Many Sadducees, such as the author of 1 Maccabees, were in his eyes perhaps too cautious in flexing their new power in order to reform the cult ac-cording to these texts. With its not entirely subtle critique of Hyrcanus and his fellow Sadducees, the Temple Scroll, we imagine, was quietly circulated to like-minded scribes and priests. Certainly he would have been called to account had it found its way into the hands of those more loyal to Hyrcanus.

A book that is known today as Jubilees also demonstrates both the flu-idity of texts and the ways in which Sadducees were experimenting with textual authority. Jubilees makes a claim to authority that is very different from that of the Temple Scroll, but one that is no less bold: God's laws have already been established as part of primal history.

Complete copies of this book are known only in Ethiopic translation (they were found in manuscripts in monasteries in Ethiopia), but many Hebrew fragments of the book were found among the Dead Sea Scrolls. The original language of composition was Hebrew.[23]

The book of Jubilees was a composite work. There was an original core to the book that probably dates from sometime in the early to mid-second century BCE, around the time of the composition of parts of 1 Enoch, Daniel, and the Aramaic Testament of Levi. It underwent a later revision, however, that could have occurred around the time of John Hyrcanus. This revision gave it its distinctive ideology that linked it more closely to concerns that I have been calling Sadducean.[24]

Just as the Temple Scroll closely tracks Deuteronomy, Jubilees (with the exception of the very beginning) closely tracks Genesis. The composition, which is structured around the story of the patriarchs, Abraham, Isaac, and Jacob, has an obsessive interest in dates and chronologies. This interest is clearly linked to the author's more general polemic for the solar, or 364-day, calendar also found in 1 Enoch, the Aramaic Testament of Levi, and the Temple Scroll.

For the author of Jubilees, this calendar was written into the very fabric of the universe. This 364-day calendar is theoretically elegant; it amounts to 52, 7-day weeks exactly, with the days of the week remaining on their monthly dates for eternity. The lunar calendar, apparently being used in the temple, is by contrast an abomination. "And there will be those who will examine the moon diligently," the author fulminates, "because it will corrupt the appointed times and it will advance from year to year ten days." This mistaken calendar will get everything wrong. It "make[s] a day of testimony a reproach and a profane day a festival, and they will mix up everything, a holy day as profaned and a profane one for a holy day."[25]

This is not the only feature that links Jubilees to these other Sadducean works. The book shows heightened concern for writing. Moses is thus instructed to write God's words, "both what (was) in the beginning and what will occur (in the future)," which echoes the idea that texts contain divinely given predictions of the future. "Heavenly tablets" frequently appear throughout Jubilees, often serving a variety of functions.

The author is also deeply conversant with previous texts, drawing upon and reworking them.[26]

The author of Jubilees—or better here, its reviser—links the heavenly tablets to the Pentateuch (in the varying forms that he knew them) and gave these texts a normative authority that was rooted in the original divine plan.

Jubilees' treatment of the Sabbath exemplifies this approach. The author links the Sabbath not only to the creation of the world—as is also seen in Genesis 2:3—but also to the practice of the angels themselves. The angel tells Moses that God created the Sabbath so that the angelic beings might keep it with him. A sanctified people would then join the angels in keeping the Sabbath, refraining from twenty-two specific kinds of work activities. Observance of the Sabbath is made into a cosmic event.[27]

In its final form, Jubilees goes much further than any of the other texts examined thus far in assigning normative authority to a text. The text, though, is a heavenly one that in turn mirrors the cosmic reality of the angels. It, like that of the Temple Scroll, springs from the divine realm, but whereas the Temple Scroll is the revealed word of God, Jubilees positions itself as a reflection of a supernal reality.

In 150 BCE, Judeans ascribed to a variety of ancient texts with differing levels of mainly prophetic (oracular) and scribal, or literary, authority. What they by and large lacked was normative authority. Aside from a marginal group of priests, this didn't seem to trouble anyone. The authority of scripture took a back seat to the authority of custom and, in the temple, the traditions of the established priests.

This changed under Hasmonean rule. The Hasmonean rulers themselves did not make the change as much as they created the conditions that allowed it to happen. Loosely organized political parties, the Pharisees and the Sadducees, emerged and began to compete for power within the Hasmonean court. The Pharisees represented more of the "old guard" than the Sadducees; they sought to justify the status quo. The Sadducees were the upstarts, and to justify their own authority against established customs they used texts to which they assigned divine authority. Texts, of course, had previously been used for political means: Josiah's use of Hezekiah's scroll or Ezra's public reading of the scroll of Moses, for example. This time, however, the attempt picked up some traction, particularly in a Sadducean or Sadducean-leaning group.

This group, though, was itself diverse. There were Sadducees who were close to John Hyrcanus and who composed his court histories. And then there were Sadducees who thought that Hyrcanus did not go far enough. We can imagine—and here we must imagine, for we lack any direct evidence—a group of relatively young, well-educated, upwardly mobile priests who were attracted to a more ideologically pure and radical set of ideas than their elders. They were certainly not ready to break away into their own school or sect, but the seed had been sown.[28]

This group, which produced the Temple Scroll and perhaps was responsible for revising Jubilees, was led by a man whom the Dead Sea Scrolls mysteriously call the "Teacher of Righteousness." According to one later, cryptic account, God "raised for them a Teacher of Righteousness to guide them in the way of His heart. And he made known to latter generations that which God had done to the latter generation, the congregation of traitors, to those who had departed from the way." Who was this "Teacher"? The scrolls offer only tantalizing (and perhaps tendentious) scraps of information. The Teacher was in conflict with a certain "Wicked Priest" who opposed the Teacher's calendar, "the law which he [the Teacher] sent to him [the Wicked Priest]," and the Teacher's council.[29] A "Liar" and "Scoffer" are also mentioned in the scrolls as being opposed to the Teacher, but it is not clear if they are the same person and/ or to be identified with the "Wicked Priest."

In addition to these notices, we possess a group of hymns that many scholars believe were written by the Teacher of Righteousness or those close to him. These hymns, like the historical notices, are tantalizingly vague—in most of them, the writer thanks God for saving him from persecution and giving him knowledge. "Thou hast placed me, O my God, among the branches of the Council of Holiness," he writes in one hymn. "Thou hast [established my mouth] in Thy Covenant, and my tongue is like that of Thy disciples." In several other places the hymnist also mentions the "Council" as devoted to the true knowledge of and service to God.[30]

It is tempting to tie this repeated connection between the Teacher and the Council back to the idealized council found in the Temple Scroll. The Teacher either formed a Council of upstart Sadducean ideologues, or they had their own loose and not very effective organization until the charismatic Teacher appeared. Perhaps—to take a further speculative leap—the Teacher even authored the Temple Scroll.

Scholars have sometimes tended to see in these sources a binary battle between Sadducees and Pharisees. But the political landscape was far more dynamic than that, and it is likely that there were significant disagreements within those groups outsiders called "Pharisees" and "Sadducees." The Teacher led a Sadducean group in an administration controlled by Sadducees, and yet despite this common umbrella they came to view each other with mutual antipathy. The "Wicked Priest" need not be a Pharisee or an actual Hasmonean ruler, as some scholars have argued, but another Sadducee in the court of John Hyrcanus. As a result of this internal conflict, the group might then have begun to think of itself as a separate "remnant" that was not quite ready to formally break away. Its members were beginning to write codes of conduct that would unite them and give them a coherent self-identity without having to relinquish their perks as officers of the court and temple. It would be another two decades until the group decided that enough was enough, and retired to the Judean desert.

For aristocratic circles in the late second and early first centuries, then, "scripture"—its meaning, its text, and its authority—was in play. The Sadducean claims could not simply be ignored, for much was potentially at stake, including the legitimacy of the Hasmoneans and control of the temple. The Pharisees and others who sought power would eventually have to develop and mobilize their own understandings of scripture. Scrolls like the Temple Scroll and Jubilees were harbingers of the struggle that was about to take place among the upper levels of the Jerusalem aristocracy.[31]

Did this growing prominence of the written text spill outside of these circles, though? The answer, surprisingly, is no. Ordinary, nonaristocratic (and nonsectarian) Judeans at this time left behind nothing that testifies to any relationship at all with these texts. Moreover, there is no evidence that Judeans at this time regularly read the Torah in public, as they would later come to do. There is, in fact, not even evidence for the existence of synagogues in Judea from this time. Most Judeans would have known many traditional stories about the patriarchs, the Exodus, King David, and the like, but their knowledge would have come from oral recitations. The scrolls that contained written versions of these stories had limited circulation among the elite. When the author of 1 Maccabees created the detail of Antiochus's decree against owning a scroll of Torah, he wrote as a member of the elite and for those of his own class. To the extent that most nonelite Jews had political leanings (if they did at all), they would probably have been toward the Pharisees, who were religiously conservative.

The situation was different in Alexandria. There, around 250 BCE, a few decades before the Jerusalem scribes Kohelet and Ben Sira were creating new kinds of Hebrew writings, some of the older Hebrew scrolls were translated into Greek. Over the next century these scrolls would assume an increasing cultural importance for the Jews of Egypt and then other locations outside of Judea. So while most Judeans were content to continue the customs of their ancestors with a marginal regard for "scripture," the Jews of Alexandria were experiencing a religious renaissance sparked by the Greek translation of the Pentateuch, known as the Septuagint.

9 The Septuagint:
Alexandria, Third Century BCE–
First Century CE

To Philo, the Jewish philosopher writing in Alexandria in the first century BCE to first century CE, the Greek translation of the Hebrew Bible, which would become known as the Septuagint, was perfect. The Greek translators were not translators at all "but . . . prophets and priests of the mysteries, whose sincerity and singleness of thought has enabled them to go hand in hand with the purest of spirits, the spirit of Moses."[1]

Philo's rapturous praise of the Greek translation was overblown but it also reflects the critical role that this document had come to play in his own Jewish community. Philo devoted his own life to studying and writing about this text, but he was far from alone. He lived and worked within a Jewish intellectual community for which these texts were central. Just as the Greek intellectual elite in Alexandria engaged Homer and the Greek classics, so would Jewish intellectuals engage, critique, and generate written and cultural productions from "their" ancestral texts. By the first century CE, these Jewish cultural productions had succeeded in popularizing the Septuagint (at least some of it, in some form). Around the same time, quite possibly as a result of the increasing importance being given to these Greek translations, Jews for the first time began to read them publicly in some regular fashion on the Sabbath in their synagogues. The Septuagint became a holy book that Alexandrian Jews saw as central to their identity and relationship to their God, even if they largely ignored its normative authority.

This was a far from predictable development. The Judahite refugees from the sixth century BCE, the Judean mercenaries at Elephantine in the fourth century BCE, and even the Judean refugees who fled Jerusalem at the time of the Maccabees would have possessed or known little more than a smattering of the texts that would come to constitute the Septuagint. How, then, did these texts come to be translated into Greek? And how and why would they become so important to the Jewish community in Egypt?

In John Hyrcanus's Jerusalem court in the late second century BCE, the rise of the authority of texts was inextricably linked to politics and power. This, however, was not the case in Egypt. The story of how the Jews in Egypt came to assign authority to these ancient texts is a very different one than what happened in Judea, although the two stories briefly intersect at points. Eventually, they would merge.

The Ptolemies, the dynasty that inherited Egypt after Alexander the Great died in 323 BCE, soon became aware of the Jews. The presence within Egypt itself of Jewish communities, the descendents of earlier refugees from Judah and Persian mercenaries, would barely have registered—they were but one of a jumble of ethnic groups whose distinctive identities would have been of little interest to the new Greek (as they liked to style themselves) rulers. Of more concern to them were the residents of Judea whose territory they ruled. Who were these people? How might they best be administered so that they provided the most amount of revenue with the least amount of trouble?[2]

Prior to the Ptolemies, and despite previous (although limited) commerce between the Greeks and the residents of Yehud and Samaria, Greek writers had barely mentioned these places or their residents. In Greek eyes, they, like other non-Greeks, were simply barbarians, a lot that was generally indistinguishable from each other, with the exception of their mortal enemies, the Persians.

Soon after the conquest of Alexander, though, this began to change. Greek writers began to develop ethnographies. The Macedonians now needed to know something about the many diverse peoples they ruled, and ethnographies met the needs of their expanding empire. At the same time, though, these new ethnographers were often genuinely curious about their subjects, and like writers in all times and places they could hardly pass up an opportunity to spin good yarns about exotic peoples that would increase their own fame.[3]

The father of Hellenistic ethnography was Hecataeus of Abdera. A Greek working for Alexander's general and successor, Ptolemy I Soter (367–283 BCE), Hecataeus wrote a comprehensive account of the Egyptians. Part history that drew on historical documents, part ethnography that would be useful to ruling authorities, and part vivid imagination, Hecataeus's *Aegyptiaca* influenced generations of later Greek ethnographers. *Aegyptiaca* contains an excursus on the Judeans, whom he identifies as a distinct polity centered in Jerusalem ("Hieroslyma") and ruled primarily by priests.

In Hecataeus's account, the Judeans began as a group that was expelled from Egypt on account of its deviant religious practices, which in turn had led Egyptians to neglect their own gods, who became angry with them. Moses, the leader of this expelled group, established a distinctive set of religious practices for the Judeans that included worship of the heavens. After building the temple, Moses "established the offices and rites for the divinity, codified and arranged the things relating to the *politeia* . . . [and] appointed [priests] to be the judges of the greatest disputes, and entrusted to them the guardianship of the laws and customs."[4]

The Greek word *politeia* does not have a very good English translation. "Constitution" comes close, but its range of meanings is wider than what we normally mean by the term. It is better thought of as encompassing the full range of an ethnic group's distinctive practices, political and otherwise. In this excursus on the Judeans, Hecataeus thus set out to describe their politeia, the distinctive ways in which they lived and ordered their lives.[5]

Hecataeus was aware of, and maybe consulted, a written source that he believed to contain the Judean politeia. He writes, "At the end of their laws there is even appended the statement: 'These are the words that Moses heard from God and declares unto the Jews.'" How he would have had access to such a document is unclear; most likely it would have been mediated through a local Jewish informant. More puzzling is the identity of the source itself. The closest parallel in our Bible is the sentence, "These are the commandments that the Lord gave Moses for the Israelite people on Mount Sinai" (Leviticus 27:34). The source might then be just Leviticus, whence he should have been able to have derived nearly all of the details in his account. If this is correct, it is unclear whether Hecataeus or his informant would have updated the language to include the word "Jews." In any case, he never calls this text "holy," although perhaps not coincidentally (in the minds of later readers) he is the first writer in Greek to use the term "holy book," applying it to Egyptian texts.[6]

Hecataeus was not interested in the Judeans for their own sake. *Aegyptiaca* was about the Egyptians, and his interest in the Judeans only went as far as they impinged on his primary story. The primary source of his excursus was a scroll that had made its way from Jerusalem to Egypt and was, apparently, brought to his attention by an informant (the owner of the scroll?) who could translate it into, or at least summarize its contents in, Greek. More than this is impossible to know. Hecataeus, however, crucially, if elusively, asserted that a written scroll described the Judean politeia. I think that this assertion would have surprised nearly all Judeans at that time, whether they were living in Jerusalem or Egypt. It was a detail that a later sharp-eyed official in the court of one of Ptolemy I's successors would notice.

Ptolemy I Soter founded Alexandria and moved his capital there from the traditional Egyptian capital of Memphis. In a public relations coup, he managed to obtain (or at least convince people that he did so) the body of Alexander the Great himself, interring him in his new administrative center. Built on a harbor on the Mediterranean on the western edge of the Nile Delta, Alexandria quickly grew into a thriving and prosperous city, the nerve center of the intensively bureaucratized Ptolemaic Empire. By the time Ptolemy II (283–246 BCE) assumed power, Alexandria was already the governmental, economic, and military center of his kingdom. By the time he left, it was also the cultural center. Ptolemy II established a new and ambitious academy and library that would soon find fame throughout the ancient world. Ptolemy II gave Athens, still a vibrant intellectual center, a run for its money.[7]

The Library of Alexandria was a museum, research library, university, and temple (devoted to the god Serapis) all rolled into one. It was a royal initiative that may have begun under Ptolemy I but that expanded dramatically during the reign of his son. Through the third century BCE, the Library of Alexandria became the first universal library. Its director was charged with collecting all written human knowledge worth saving. This meant producing copies (mostly on papyrus), cataloguing, and storing vast numbers of scrolls. The Library achieved renown even in its early days, and it attracted Greek intellectuals who cultivated students and developed a lively academic culture.[8]

According to the later account of the Letter of Aristeas (written in Greek in the late first century BCE), it was the director of the Library of Alexandria who commissioned a translation of the Pentateuch into Greek. His reason, according to this account, was simple, if vague: "Information has reached me that the lawbooks of the Jews are worth translation and inclusion in your royal library," he says to the king.[9] It was human knowledge, and thus merited inclusion in the Library. Unlike most of the other texts included, however, these "lawbooks," the Letter of Aristeas carefully notes, also needed to be translated into Greek.

The Letter of Aristeas, of course, has its own agenda, and the author had a bit of a hyperactive imagination. As a result of this, many scholars consider the entire story to be a myth. The Jews themselves, they argue, translated the Torah into Greek for their own purposes, whether liturgical or as a "means of exhibiting Jewish pride and self-confidence."[10] The translation was made by Jewish intellectuals who wished to fit into the emerging academic culture.

While this is one possible scenario, the possibility that the Pentateuch really was translated through the initiative of the Library should not be dismissed out of hand. The Library did seem on occasion to commission or at least include in it translations of foreign books, although this was far from a frequent occurrence. Royal authorities, for example, translated a legal guide used by Egyptian priests into Greek, presumably for their own legal reference.[11]

In contrast to a translation of a book of Egyptian priests, which was intended to help the Ptolemies domestically, the Greek translation of the Pentateuch was driven primarily by foreign policy. While the Ptolemies would not have noticed the Jews who lived in Egypt, they were very much aware of those who lived in Judea, over whose land they ruled through most of the century. The Ptolemies, of course, sought to gain maximum economic benefit from Judea. Large tracts of land in Judea were given to favored Ptolemaic officials, who would then send agents to administer their holdings and send them their revenues. Masters at creating bureaucracy, the Ptolemies imposed their own complex taxes and customs throughout Judea.[12]

Ptolemaic authorities would naturally have wanted to know about the politeia of their subjects. One way to acquire this knowledge would have been to commission a Greek ethnography of them. It is possible that they did exactly this, although no trace of such a tract survives. At the same time, however, they knew from the influential Hecataeus that the Judeans already possessed a written form of their politeia. Thus alerted, they ordered its translation into Greek, not quite realizing at the time that by Greek standards, the Judean Pentateuch did not quite look like either a classic description of a politeia or a law book. Once a translation was made, it could then have found its way into the Library.

This course of events, although largely speculative, helps to account for both the account in the Letter of Aristeas and the peculiar features of the translation itself. According to the Letter of Aristeas, the royal authorities sent to the high priest in Judea for translators, and he sent seventy-two elders. (It was after an alternative version of this myth that says that there were seventy translators that this translation would be named the Septuagint.) A scenario like this is plausible. There is no evidence that the Jews of Egypt had their own scrolls of these books at this time, certainly not public ones. When Ptolemy II's administrators sought a copy of the law of the Jews, they might naturally turn to the priests of Jerusalem—who, after all, worked for them. Given another ancient tradition in which Ptolemy II invites Athenian sages to his court, it is not inconceivable that the Jerusalem priests sent not only the scroll but its translators as well.[13]

The peculiar features of the Greek of the Septuagint are consistent with this scenario. Translations can be more or less literal; the closer they stick to the terminology and syntax of the original language of their source, the odder the translation sounds in its new language. A more fluent translation that reads well in the new language, on the other hand, hides the feel, complexity, and occasional problems of the language of the original text. The Greek translation of the Pentateuch is highly literal, to the point where it might, in places, hardly resemble Greek.[14]

The reason that this is so was not because the translators made a deliberate choice to make the underlying Hebrew text visible in the Greek. Rather, it was because their Greek was not very good. This is what we might expect from a translator (or more than one) from Jerusalem in the mid-third century BCE, well before Greek was eagerly adopted by the Jewish elite. These translators knew enough Greek to get by. They knew enough vocabulary to know when they encountered potential theological problems. The translators, for example, coined a Greek word to translate the Hebrew term for "altar" rather than use the existing Greek word, which would have suggested "pagan" sacrifice. Occasionally the translator downplayed biblical anthropomorphisms, perhaps as a reaction to representations of Greek gods. On the whole, though, they had problems with writing Greek like a native Greek speaker.[15]

The Greek translation of the Pentateuch was an academic and administrative initiative. It was probably a disappointment to those who commissioned it. The Letter of Aristeas is likely correct that a copy was deposited in the Library of Alexandria, but even there it attracted little attention.

Yet beginning in the late second century some Jewish intellectuals in Alexandria began to see the Septuagint as an ancient and foundational text that they could treat in much the same way that their non-Jewish contemporaries did Homer. It was given literary authority. The Greek translation of the Pentateuch led to Greek translations of other biblical books and, more important, to the flourishing of an innovative and extensive Jewish literature based on it.

One unexpected result of the crisis in Jerusalem in 170 BCE was the development of a strong Jewish intellectual class in Alexandria. These new intellectuals, refugees from Judea and their children, would help to transform the Septuagint from a reference book for royal authorities into the foundation of intellectual life for Jews in the Greek-speaking world.

The Maccabean revolt and the power shake-up in Jerusalem in the mid-second century sent a stream of refugees fleeing to Egypt. Many of these refugees were, of course, peasants. Others, however, belonged to the elite and educated classes. Having allied with the losing side, or simply unable to stomach the uncertainty, they fled for their lives. With the Seleucids all around, their only good option was south, into Egypt.

One group of Judean elite, led by the high priests driven out between 170 and 162 BCE, settled together in Egypt in a place known as Leontopolis.

When the high priest, Onias III or his son, Onias IV, and his retinue arrived in Egypt, the principle of "the enemy of my enemy is my friend" was operative: Onias's family was no friend of the Seleucids, the Ptolemies' archenemy. King Ptolemy VI rewarded Onias with a large tract of land, on which he built a new Jewish temple that would stand until 73 CE.[16]

No remains of this temple have yet been unearthed, but scholars are relatively certain that they have identified the area of the settlement. Many ancient epitaphs, about half of which contain presumably Judean names, were found at a site known as Tell el-Yehoudieh. The inscriptions are entirely in Greek and use the Egyptian calendar; one refers explicitly to the place as the "land of Onias." Other than the names, however, there is nothing distinctively Jewish about the inscriptions or the site. This refugee settlement may have functioned like the much earlier one of Elephantine, with a temple and full sacrificial system.[17]

Another group of refugees found its way to Alexandria. Among these refugees were the intellectual elite of Judea, those who might not have had (at least before they fled) the spectacular wealth of a high priest or the estates of the old landed aristocracy but whose skills allowed them a greater degree of mobility. Sometime in the mid-second century BCE, they or their children organized an administrative structure known in Greek as a *politeuma*.

A politeuma (plural, *politeumata*) was a community within the Greek city that took responsibility (with the support of the municipal or local authorities) for administering itself in limited ways. Scholars still do not fully understand how this political structure functioned, but a recently published archive from another community in Egypt, in Heracleopolis, attests to the presence of a Judean politeuma there. Membership in the politeuma appears to have been optional, and the organization's primary power was its ability to adjudicate judicial matters between its members. At Heracleopolis there is scant evidence that they turned to any older written texts such as the Pentateuch for legal guidance.[18]

In the mid-second century BCE, the Jews of Alexandria too created a politeuma. Like the one at Heracleopolis, it is likely that it served as a voluntary association within which its members agreed to settle their judicial disputes. There was also undoubtedly a social dimension to the organization, and perhaps its leaders also served some role in dealing with the Alexandrian municipal authorities. Later, the Greek historian Strabo would be struck by the Alexandrian Jewish community: "In Egypt, for example, territory has been set apart for a Jewish settlement, and in Alexandria a great part of the city has been allocated to this nation. And an ethnarch of their own has been installed, who governs the people and adjudicates suits and supervised contracts and ordinances, just as if he were the head of a sovereign state." Strabo undoubtedly exaggerated the power of the "ethnarch." As in Heracleopolis, there is little evidence that the Alexandrian politeuma consulted the Pentateuch or followed any distinctive law based on it.[19]

The Jewish politeuma (like the other politeumata in Egypt at this time) provided an alternative civic structure. As a voluntary organization, the psychological benefits it offered may have been as attractive as the limited practical one. Like the Egyptians, Jews were not eligible for enrollment as Alexandrian citizens. This put them at a legal and economic disadvantage to the "Greek" citizens of Alexandria. Practically, there was not much that they could do about that in the Ptolemaic period. Joining the local politeuma, however, with its "citizenlike" terminology and organization, might have taken some of the emotional sting out of the exclusion.

Particularly as their comfort in Alexandria increased, another way that they sought the respect and prestige that they desired was through intellectual involvement. One of the primary paths to prestige in the Hellenistic world was education, and the basis of that education was Homer. Not only was Homer a central text in the gymnasium (attended by all Greek male citizens of Alexandria), it was also used to teach children. For Jewish intellectuals, Homer's worldview, with its assumptions about the gods and their interactions, would have presented a challenge to engaging in this world. So just as they had turned to the politeuma as a substitute for true civic involvement, so too they would turn to the Septuagint in order to create an intellectual culture in which they could display their erudition and compete for prestige.[20]

The world of the Jewish intellectuals in Alexandria in the second century BCE is almost entirely lost to us. Yet the few stray fragments of their writings that did survive reveal a lively, increasingly confident engagement with the Greek Pentateuch and the Alexandrian intellectual world from which they were excluded.

The very first evidence that we possess for appropriation of the Greek translation of the Pentateuch by Jewish intellectuals comes from a man named Demetrios, a Jewish "chronographer" who attempted to reconcile the various dates and genealogies in the Septuagint.[21]

In attempting to engage the Septuagint critically in this way, Demetrios also inserted himself into a vibrant intellectual discourse, if in a peculiar way. On the one hand, he can be seen as one of a number of "oriental historians" from the region who similarly attempted to derive historical lists from their native myths, with the point primarily to set the record straight. On the other, though, he was also tapping into a style and technique of engaging ancient texts that was active in Alexandria at that time. Demetrios was appropriating the kind of intellectual inquiry that was being applied to Homer and instead applying it to the Greek translation of the Pentateuch. Unfortunately, we know nothing more about Demetrios's background and life.[22]

Aristobulus wrote in a more philosophical vein than Demetrios. Much as the anthropomorphisms in Homer made his contemporaries uncomfortable, the Septuagint's divine anthropomorphisms, he felt, needed to be understood in a different way. He explains, for example, that the biblical verse "God brought you out of Egypt with a mighty hand" (Exodus 13:9) refers not to God's actual hand—for God has no hands!—but to "the power of God. For it is possible for people speaking metaphorically to consider that the entire strength of human beings and their active powers are in their hands." His attempt to prove that the Sabbath (and the notion that the tireless God "rested" on it, as stated in the Pentateuch) was philosophically reasonable even invoked Homer and Hesiod. Elsewhere he states that Plato had taken many of his ideas from a Greek version of the Bible that had preceded the Septuagint.[23]

Artapanus was another shadowy Jewish figure, probably writing in Alexandria a few decades after Demetrios. Artapanus's writings were of a type altogether different from those of Demetrios, but they similarly engage the Greek Pentateuch and show signs of being produced in and for an intellectual milieu. Artapanus aggressively rewrote the biblical story of Moses to make his hero a universal cultural and intellectual exemplar, not a giver of particularistic laws. He was, for example, the inventor of "boats and devices for stone construction and the Egyptian arms and the implements for drawing water and for warfare, and philosophy." This is the voice of one educated Jew writing a fun, learned, and proud work for other educated Jews. Most interesting, while Artapanus can be read without any prior knowledge of the Pentateuch, those who did have such knowledge would have been able to better appreciate his creativity. They would have felt "in the know."[24]

These three authors all engaged the Pentateuch. In the mid–second century BCE, though, the state and status of older Jewish texts, and even the Pentateuch itself, was still in flux. We can see this in the prologue that an ancient editor added to the book we now call 2 Maccabees. Originally written by a certain Jason of Cyrene, 2 Maccabees was edited (to make it a more exciting and enjoyable read, according to its editor) in 143 BCE. We do not know where the editor lived, but it could well have been in Alexandria. In his introduction, he discusses his sources: "The same things are reported in the records and in the memoirs of Nehemiah, and also that he founded a library and collected the books about the kings and prophets, and the writings of David, and letters of kings about votive offerings. In the same way Judah also collected all the books that had been lost on account of the war that had come upon us, and they are in our possession. So if you have need of them, send people to get them for you" (2 Maccabees 2:13–15).

The author of this letter mentions different collections of books of national importance. By evoking Nehemiah as the founder of this library he gives them authority. Judah is then by extension cast as a Nehemiah redux. But while the books are clearly marked as important, they are not called "holy." The author and redactor of 2 Maccabees both had a notion of important and authoritative texts, but it was by no means firm.[25]

By the end of the century, as we can see in the Letter of Aristeas, this has begun to change. The Letter of Aristeas is hardly a "letter" in the conventional sense; it is a tract written in Greek in the genre of a letter but meant to be read by a wide audience. Narrated by a fictional non-Jewish official in Ptolemy's court named Aristeas, the tract alleges to tell the story of the Greek translation of the Torah.

The Letter of Aristeas is structured as a narrative. It begins with King Ptolemy II Philadelphus, together with Demetrius of Phalerum, the head of the Library of Alexandria, commissioning a Greek translation of the "law books" of the Jews. They sent to the high priest in Jerusalem for the text and translators. When the seventy-two translators finished, their work was read aloud, and the leaders arose afterward and said, "Inasmuch as the translation has been well and piously made and is in every respect accurate, it is right that it should remain in its present form and that no revision of any sort take place."[26] The story clearly functions as a "charter myth" for one particular Greek translation of these books.[27]

This basic plot, however, takes up relatively little space. Most of the tract is devoted to conversations between the translators and their Greek hosts in Alexandria prior to their actual work of translation. These occasionally tedious conversations each attempt to prove, much like Aristobulus, that the Jewish writings are rational. In one extended passage, for example, the king asks the translators about the proper conduct of the king. "In conclusion," the king finally exclaimed, "the greatest blessings have accrued to me by your coming here, for I have profited greatly by the doctrine which you have grounded for me with reference to kingship."[28] Curiously, throughout this conversation the translators neither actually cited the Pentateuch (which actually says very little about kingship) nor offered any advice that can be particularly identified as anything other than good Greco-Roman virtues. The point of the exchange seems to be to enhance the standing of the translators and only then by extension that of the translation itself.

Other passages attempt to give reasons for some of the Pentateuch's more obscure prescriptions. For example, it explains the laws of prohibiting the consumption of certain animals symbolically: certain birds like raptors are forbidden in order to inculcate in us values of gentleness rather than of rampant and unjust violence.[29] The author never dismisses the nonsymbolic, literal prohibition, but claims that in addition to this the real import is to be found behind the practices. There are rational reasons for these restrictions, even if the Septuagint itself does not say what they are.

The main thrust of the Letter of Aristeas is to authorize a *particular* Greek translation of the Pentateuch. By the time the Letter was written, probably in the late second century BCE, there were different Greek translations in circulation. This is hardly surprising. Changes inevitably entered the copies, and copies of copies, of the original translation, and more recent translations (by the Judeans who had left Jerusalem?) also might have well been made. The increased Jewish engagement with the text would have increased the demand for further copies.

The strategy that the Letter takes to prove this, however, is innovative and significant: it claims that *this* Greek translation is *a perfect, holy text*. In his argument to the king for the resources to make the translation, Demetrius of Phalerum states that "these books too, in an emended form, should be given a place in your library, for their legislation is most philosophical and flawless, inasmuch as it is divine." A curse was laid on anyone who altered the text in any way whatsoever, "so that the work might be preserved imperishable and unchanging always."[30]

The decision (of at least one author!) to fix a specific text at this moment fits well into the general intellectual environment of Alexandria. Greek scholars created a discipline of textual studies that sought to reconcile the various versions of Homer then current, and then to bring that text in line with contemporary values. The language of the Letter demonstrates full awareness of the methods of this new Homeric scholarship. The Letter of Aristeas occasionally uses technical terms similar to those used by the Alexandrian scholars of Homer. Its author modeled the Septuagint's project on the Homeric project, thus hoping to tap into the prestige that accompanied the latter.[31]

In appropriating this essentially scholastic model of textual authority, though, the author of the Letter of Aristeas made two innovative claims. The first is that the Pentateuch was a collection of "laws," or perhaps better, ancestral customs. I suspect that the author was here grasping for a term to describe the Pentateuch taken as a whole as it does not easily fit into a recognizable Greek genre. One of the Letter's major claims is that this book is a perfect, rational source of philosophy, despite the fact that no one with even a minimum acquaintance with Greek philosophical texts would have labeled the Pentateuch as such. Although the Septuagint did not serve as an operative legal code for Jews in Alexandria, the author of the Letter of Aristeas, searching for some description of a genre to call it, uncomfortably settled on the genre of law.

The Letter's second claim is that the Pentateuch constitutes a single book, and that this book comes from God. The author seems here, as when he labels the Pentateuch as a collection of laws, to be a bit unsure.

Committed to understanding this translation as being from God, he elsewhere claims it to be a collection of divine oracles. The claim of divine authorship is, I believe, less the expression of a communally shared, deep and profoundly held belief than it is the articulation of a vaguer sentiment that helps to support the author's claim. It is a claim that could also have been drawn from Egyptian notions of a "holy" book.[32]

What does not appear to be vague, however, is the author's incidental mention of the Pentateuch as a single book. Similarly, in the prologue to his translation into Greek of Ecclesiasticus (or Ben Sira) from the Hebrew, the author's grandson (probably a contemporary of the author of the Letter of Aristeas) repeatedly mentions "the Law and the Prophets and the other books of our ancestors." By the end of the second century BCE, then, it would appear that the three basic divisions of our Hebrew Bible or Old Testament had been established. How and why this was done must be a matter of some speculation, but it could have emerged from the way in which the individual scrolls were categorized in the Library of Alexandria. Some evidence suggests that a system was developed within the Library in which shelves were labeled by subject. If this was the case, then the Greek translations of Hebrew texts might have been deposited into one of these three shelves, or simply grouped together in the catalogue. This could explain where both the author of the Letter of Aristeas and the translator of Ecclesiasticus derived their understanding of the Pentateuch as a single, unified work.[33]

The Letter of Aristeas was influential. Both the Jewish philosopher Philo (first century BCE–first century CE) and the Jewish historian Josephus (first century CE) knew and drew from it. By Philo's time an annual festival was held in Alexandria to celebrate the translation. It is possible, albeit speculative, that the claims that first emerged in Alexandria made their way to the Sadducees in Jerusalem, who under John Hyrcanus began to develop the normative authority of the Pentateuch in particular. What is clear is that Alexandrian Jews, far more than those in Jerusalem, turned to the Greek translation(s?) of the Pentateuch as a cultural and intellectual touchstone.[34]

By the first century BCE, in Alexandria (and perhaps throughout Egypt) Jewish knowledge of the Greek translation of the Pentateuch was pervasive. Two mechanisms, the theater (along with other popular cultural productions) and the synagogue, enabled this diffusion of knowledge. By the end of the century, as the writings of Philo demonstrate, the Greek-speaking Jews of Alexandria, and likely beyond, saw the Pentateuch as a holy and vitally important book.

We have seen that Jewish chronographers, philosophers, and historians in Alexandria all directly engaged and drew upon the Greek translation of the Pentateuch. So too, though, did playwrights and other producers of more popular culture. There is some evidence that plays that were based on the Septuagint were written (and probably performed). These would have served as one path by which knowledge of it trickled down to the Jewish community at large.[35]

The increasing public knowledge of this text, along with its growing authority and status among the cultural elite, led to its recitation in the synagogue. Synagogues, more commonly termed "prayer halls," had existed in Egypt since the mid-third century BCE. We have almost no information about what actually occurred in these places, but the name suggests that they were indeed places of prayer. By the first century BCE, though, it is clear that they were also being used for the reading and study of the Pentateuch. According to Philo, "The Jews every seventh day occupy themselves with the philosophy of their fathers, dedicating that time to the acquiring of knowledge and the study of the truths of nature. For what are our places of prayer throughout the cities but schools of prudence and courage and temperance and justice and also of piety, holiness and every virtue by which duties to God and men are discerned and rightly performed?"[36]

Elsewhere Philo also discusses two small Jewish groups that study regularly. Every Sabbath the Essenes sit in synagogues and listen to a reading from the books and their exposition. Another group, the Therapeutae, similarly read the "holy writings," which Philo identifies with the "ancestral philosophy," presumably also on the Sabbath. The Therapeutae are known only from Philo; some scholars have doubted their actual existence. Philo describes them as an isolated group whose members devote themselves to study and prayer. They embody the quest for perfection through study (in contrast to the Essenes, who seek perfection through their practices). The "holy writings" and their allegorical interpretation stood at the center of their praxis.[37]

While these groups were exceptional, and Philo himself has a strong agenda, this nevertheless suggests that Jews engaging in this activity would essentially have been positioning themselves—to themselves and to each other—as cultured Greeks, engaged in the learned study of their holy, perfect, ancestral philosophy. Reading and studying the text in synagogue became a way for a less-educated populace to see itself as participating in a high-status activity. (As we will see later, this dynamic also helps to explain how Gentiles came to become acquainted with Jewish scriptures.) Consequently, increasing numbers of Jews became familiar with these texts and their contents.[38]

Philo provides additional support for the claim that the Pentateuch was gaining status as a source of all truth, even after we recognize that Philo was undoubtedly exceptional. Philo's large corpus—preserved by later church fathers such as Gregory of Nyssa, who drew upon him—reveals little about his life. Living from approximately 30 BCE to 42 CE, he was well educated and came from an affluent and well-connected family; his brother Alexander served as a Roman tax official and ran his own prosperous business on the side, and Alexander's son Tiberius Julius Alexander rose to become praetorian prefect in Rome.[39]

Philo's surviving works deeply engage the Septuagint, predominantly the Pentateuch. One group of writings constitutes an "allegorical commentary" on the first half or so of the book of Genesis. A second group of writings, called "the exposition of the law," goes over some of the same ground as the "allegorical commentary" but focuses on the early biblical figures as embodiments of the divine law, and then deals with the actual law codes. A much smaller number of works might be categorized as historical, philosophical, and *questiones*, a genre written in a question-and-answer format.[40] The questions are about the meaning of biblical texts.

In his allegorical commentary, Philo largely follows the contours developed by earlier Jewish-Greek writers such as Aristobulus, smoothing out issues in the text so that they conform to modern sensibilities while at the same time asserting its ultimate superiority. One example of his allegorical approach can be seen in his treatment of the statement in Genesis that "God brought a trance upon Adam, and he fell asleep; and He took one of his sides" (Genesis 2:21). Philo writes, "These words in their literal sense are of the nature of a myth. For how could anyone admit that a woman, or a human being at all, came into existence out of a man's side?" Philo goes on to explain the *real* allegorical meaning of the biblical verse, which he reads as a statement on the human condition, not as a statement of historical fact.[41]

Throughout the "exposition of the law" Philo goes to great lengths to show that both "the Law" and Moses, its giver, are in every way perfect. Retelling the story from the Letter of Aristeas, Philo states that each scribe arrived at exactly the same translation, "as though dictated to each by an invisible prompter." The laws themselves "seek to attain to the harmony of the universe and are in agreement with the principles of eternal nature." Philo's esteem for Moses is so high that it is possible that he held him to be semidivine, or at least implied as much.[42]

Philo, however, was not simply an interpreter and apologist. He was very much a "philosopher," which in his day meant wrestling with the fundamental question of the meaning of life. Philo's project was both to show how the perfect, divine law addressed this basic question and, more important, to develop an answer to it. Philo's answer is quite subtle, and perhaps could even resonate in our own world.[43]

Philo understood the human soul to be made of three interdependent parts. One part is the mind (reason), one is the "spirited part" (the emotions), and the third is the appetites. Given our human condition, our task, according to Philo, is to suppress the spirit and appetites—which together form the "irrational" part of the soul—so that "mind" or rational intellect can flourish. The "perfect" man can cut out "the seat of anger entirely from the wrangling soul," thus coming more into harmony with the world.[44] Because few of us—really none of us—can actually do this (although Moses did), we must be content to be in the stage of "progress," in which we strive for that goal. The Pentateuch is God's gift to us, a sign of his benevolence. Studying and engaging it helps us to suppress the irrational part of our soul and achieve human flourishing. Philo has made the Septuagint into the written expression of the very laws of nature, a perfect reflection of all truth given by the deity through the semidivine lawgiver, Moses.

The Septuagint began as a relatively small-scale administrative exercise. In the middle of the third century BCE, some administrative office of Ptolemy's court wanted to know more about the politeia, the general organization and way of life, of the new Judean subjects. Officials sent to Jerusalem and received in return some scrolls and help in translating them. The new Greek scrolls were neither very readable nor influential, and they were filed away.

About a century later, though, a new Jewish intelligentsia in Alexandria would dust off these scrolls and build a vibrant intellectual culture around them. They did so in order to participate in the flourishing academic world around them when both their religious scruples and their very status as Judeans (and not "Greeks") were barriers. Unable to join this world fully, they attempted to create a parallel one in which they could show to themselves and each other (and perhaps, they may have dreamed, even to the Greeks) their intellectual prowess. The process they put into motion was pushed much further by the claims of the Letter of Aristeas, which added divine authority to their foundational text, and then, at the turn of the era, by Philo, who equated the text with the law of nature. These understandings of the text trickled down by means of performances and readings in the theater and synagogue, allowing less-educated Jews too to participate and compete for prestige in this cultural arena.[45]

This historical trajectory intersected only glancingly with what was happening in Judea. Jerusalem supplied the original scrolls, and the Sadducees may have drawn on some of the ideas developed in Alexandria for their own evolving understanding of their authority. Different stakes were involved, though. In Alexandria, the stakes were culture and prestige. In Jerusalem, the authority of texts was drawn into a high-stakes and sometimes fatal struggle for power and money. The story of how the Bible became holy is really two different stories, one that took place in Alexandria (and from there spread to other Greek-speaking Jewish communities) and one that took place in Jerusalem. We will now return to Jerusalem, to the end of the reign of John Hyrcanus in 104 BCE and the steep decline of the Hasmonean dynasty, to pick up that story.

IO The Sadducees and the Dead Sea Scrolls: Judea, 104–103 BCE

At the end of the second century BCE, the Sadducees found themselves at the center of power in Jerusalem, influential in the royal court of John Hyrcanus and in control of the temple. To a large extent, this "party"— best thought of as a loose coalition of the former supporters of the Maccabees who were fighting the entrenched interests of the older aristocratic families—continued to play an important political role for the next century.

The Sadducees, like the older aristocratic families from this period that we know of as the Pharisees, did not constitute a very coherent group. They shared a political commitment to the Hasmoneans and an ideological commitment to the normative authority of texts. This commitment could be rather weak, as it was for the more politically minded court author of 1 Maccabees, or it could be more extreme, as shown in the book of Jubilees. As long as they held power, these differences could be minimized. Only when the Pharisees finally succeeded in displacing the Sadducees almost forty years after the death of John Hyrcanus, though, did the divisions openly erupt. One group, splitting from the others, moved to the Judean desert, where they established a settlement in Qumran and authored many of the texts that we know as the Dead Sea Scrolls. Over time, left alone by Herod, they would develop an increasingly idiosyncratic worldview.

The Dead Sea Scrolls constitute, by far, the best evidence that we have from this period for the evolution of textual authority and the development of the Bible in Judea. Evaluating this evidence, though, is complicated by the very fact that the group at Qumran was on the fringes, self-consciously having set itself apart (quite literally) from the temple and wider Judean society. Nevertheless, the Dead Sea Scrolls, even if not fully representative, clearly show the way in which textual and political authority developed in tandem with each other, and how that convergence decisively shaped the future attitude to sacred scripture.

To understand the development of the normative authority of the Bible, we must turn to the Dead Sea Scrolls and the community that produced them. In order to understand this community, we first need to return to the power struggles of the Hasmonean court. It was from here, during the second century BCE, that the Sadducean followers of the Teacher of Righteousness finally decided that they could no longer endure the status quo and decamped for Qumran, a small inhospitable hill on the shores of the Dead Sea (fig. 6).

John Hyrcanus died in 104 BCE and was soon succeeded, in 103 BCE, by his son Alexander Janneaus. The Sadducees had established themselves as influential in Hyrcanus's court, and Janneaus was apparently content with allowing them to continue this position in his own.

The Sadducees were able to maintain and even strengthen their position in large measure due to the behavior of their opponents, the Pharisees. Early in Janneaus's reign, the Pharisees, perhaps sensing an opportunity to return to power, engineered a revolt against him. Janneaus suppressed the revolt savagely and crucified six thousand Pharisees.[1] After that incident, the Pharisees never had a hope of regaining influence in Janneaus's court. Their revolt also most probably strengthened Sadducean influence in both the court and the temple. Janneaus reigned until 76 BCE, and his long and successful reign gave the Sadducees time to get used to their powerful position. It must, then, have come as something of a shock when Janneaus's wife displaced them.

Janneaus bequeathed his kingdom to Alexandra Salome (ruled 76–67 BCE). According to Josephus, on his deathbed he advised his wife that in order to rule the nation successfully she needed the support of the Pharisees. Whether the report is accurate or not, Alexandra did shift her allegiance, and it was to the great disadvantage of the Sadducees. The newly empowered Pharisees may have had the reputation of being "the most pious of all the others," but their actual activities when in power

Figure 6: Overview of Qumran, looking over the Dead Sea. (Courtesy of Albatross Aerial Photography)

were decidedly murderous. With the new queen's permission, they killed all of those who had been involved with Janneaus's earlier brutal suppression of the Pharisees and their supporters.[2]

Left to their own desires, the Pharisees might well have wiped out Alexander Janneaus's former Sadducean advisors. These people of "rank," though, appealed to Alexandra's son Aristobulus II, who intervened with his mother on their behalf. Their lives spared, they were exiled from the court and "dispersed about the country."[3]

Alexandra Salome appointed her other son, John Hyrcanus (II), as high priest, and it was up to him to institute the appropriate changes in the temple that the Pharisees demanded. Having wielded power for almost three generations, the Sadducees suddenly found themselves out in the cold. This loss of power allowed the long-simmering tensions within the group to erupt. The members of one small group of Sadducees, a segment of those who subscribed to the teachings of the Teacher of Righteousness, decided that the time had come, now that they had less to lose, to finally break with the temple and its hierarchy. They decamped for a small abandoned settlement in the Judean desert, located on a small hilltop overlooking the Dead Sea. The settlement would be known as Qumran, and its residents would, over time, collect, copy, and write the texts that we know as the Dead Sea Scrolls.

The story of the discovery of the Dead Sea Scrolls is by now well known. In 1948, two bored Bedouin shepherds were tossing rocks into caves when they heard pottery break. They investigated and discovered jars inside of which were scrolls. The cave would later be called Cave 1, and their find—which included what is still one of the largest extant scrolls, the Isaiah Scroll—set off a race among shepherds, antiquity hunters, and archaeologists to discover others. A total of eleven caves containing scrolls were located, with the vast majority of the texts found in caves that were just outside of the ancient settlement of Qumran. About forty kilometers east of Jerusalem, Qumran is a stark site overlooking the Dead Sea. The site contains extensive remains, and is a major league baseball throw from the largest caches of Dead Sea Scrolls, found in caves that were hollowed out of the soft limestone. Archaeologists logically presumed a connection between the settlement and the scrolls and excavated the site itself.[4]

The story of the control and publication of the scrolls is equally colorful. Qumran was under Jordanian control until 1967, and the Jordanians entrusted excavations of the site to a French team led by Catholic priests. They quickly published the scrolls that were easiest to decipher and placed most of the originals in the Rockefeller Museum in East Jerusalem. Publication soon slowed, and in 1967 the Israelis took both Qumran and East Jerusalem from the Jordanians, throwing into limbo not only the project team but also the legal status of the scrolls themselves. For many complicated reasons, publication of the scrolls lagged until the 1990s when photographs of all of the scrolls were made public, igniting a flurry of scholarly activity. Today, almost all of the scrolls have been published.

Publishing the scrolls was no minor feat. "Scrolls" is a bit of a misnomer. Aside from comparatively few nearly complete scrolls (all, ironically, among the first discovered by the shepherds in Cave 1), the bulk of the "scrolls" are actually fragments of parchment. There are tens of thousands of such fragments; they were often found jumbled up on a cave floor. These fragments range significantly in size, together comprising between nine hundred and one thousand discrete texts. Recognizing the task of sorting these delicate, sometimes nearly illegible fragments into discrete texts and then reconstructing that text with significant pieces missing goes a long way toward explaining why the publication of the scrolls took so long.

The term "Dead Sea Scrolls" actually masks the great diversity among this collection of texts. Some of these scrolls originated in a single distinctive group or sect. These scrolls share technical terminology, linguistic features, and a worldview, and these are the scrolls that might be said to reflect a community at odds with the establishment. Most of the scrolls, though, originated in other Jewish circles. The same group that wrote these "sectarian" texts clearly did not write the many biblical texts (including the very few written in Greek!) found among the scrolls. Several other scrolls, like Jubilees and the Temple Scroll, were created by the Sadducean group that spawned the sect rather than the later members of the sect. The community in Qumran read widely over time, and as its members solidified their own self-identity, they increasingly began to author distinctive texts of their own.

The group of disaffected Sadducees that retired to Qumran in the days of John Hyrcanus II did not spontaneously appear. While their prehistory is murky—partly the result of the state of the surviving evidence and partly the result of their own annoying (to historians) lack of interest in what we would call history—it is clear that they had one that went back to the time of the Teacher of Righteousness. If, as I suggested, the Teacher lived in the time of John Hyrcanus I at the end of the second century BCE, that would mean at least some of his followers had, over the next forty years or so, formed themselves into a coherent group.

We know from both the Dead Sea Scrolls and an extraordinary find in the Cairo Geniza (a collection of worn Hebrew manuscripts that date from the Middle Ages and that were deposited in the attic of a synagogue in Cairo) that the community possessed two rule books. One of these books (more accurately, of course, scrolls) is addressed to an organized group whose members live within a larger society. This document, known as the Damascus Document, assumes that its members will adhere to a specific set of ritual laws; be part of a distinctive, well-ordered, and hierarchical "Congregation"; and also live among and have commerce with those outside of the Congregation. The second collection of rules, known as the Community Rule, uses a different terminology for the group and assumes no contact between its members and outsiders (fig. 7). There is a great deal of overlap between the specific precepts of both of these collections.[5]

Multiple copies of both rule documents were found, and it is likely that they both existed in multiple versions, perhaps even circulating at the same time. The earliest fragments appear to date from the late second to early first century BCE. They thus appear to describe a community, or

Figure 7: Fragment of 4Q258, the Community Rule. (Photo Shai Halevi, Spectral Image, Courtesy of the Israel Antiquities Authority)

maybe even a group of closely related communities, that was developing a distinctive identity. In terms of ritual practice, the members of this community would have been almost indistinguishable from other Jews. They kept the Sabbath, followed purity regulations, and participated in activities at the temple. What would have distinguished them were their obligations and obedience to their group and their beliefs, both theological and historical.[6]

At some point the group members began to see themselves as a remnant with whom God had made a new covenant and who, if they remained obedient, were destined to see God's ultimate salvation. At the moment, however, they lived in "Damascus," a maddeningly obscure reference that might be a synonym simply for the metaphorical wilderness in which they lived prior to salvation. In this unredeemed state their primary task was to follow God's rules, as revealed from earlier authoritative texts and their interpretation.[7]

Indeed, these written, normatively authoritative texts—which we can here call scripture—were at the center of this community's religious life. Their earliest writings quote texts for proof of both specific beliefs and laws. One passage, that is admittedly hard to date, states that "where the ten are, there shall never lack a man among them who shall study the Law continually, day and night, concerning the right conduct of a man with his companion. And the Congregation shall watch in community for a third of every night of the year, to read the Book and to study the Law and to bless together." The community thus made the study of the "Law" and the "Book" an integral part of its communal ritual practice. Community members, who must have been drawn from literate (although most likely not the very top social and economic) classes, themselves probably possessed various scrolls that they regarded as scriptural. A large number of the "biblical" texts found among the Dead Sea Scrolls appear to have predated the establishment of the community at Qumran and were most likely brought there by its occupants.[8]

At Qumran, on a plateau on the shores of the Dead Sea, this group constructed a fairly elaborate complex of industrial installations, storerooms, and a water system. The water system is quite remarkable, designed to channel the water from the one or two flash floods that the region might receive annually into giant cisterns and pools for use the rest of the year. The builders of these installations arrived with access to technical expertise, labor, and capital.[9]

We do not know why they chose Qumran. Perhaps they wanted to finally live in a true rather than just metaphorical wilderness. Despite its harsh climate, the location may have also been less inaccessible than we might imagine. There was a bustling trade across the Dead Sea and the oasis of Ein Gedi, along with its extensive agricultural settlements, was not far away. Rather than offering isolation, maybe Qumran was appealing because it allowed its residents to live together, according to their own organizational rules, while remaining in commercial contact with outsiders. It is unlikely that the community could have ever been self-sufficient.

In one remarkable document, the newly separated community members at Qumran address the fundamental question of why they decided to create their own sectarian enclave. The document, known to scholars today as the Halakhic Letter, was written in Hebrew and found in multiple copies among the Dead Sea Scrolls. While it has the form of a letter, it is possible that this was just a literary convention, and that it was meant to circulate only within the community in order to strengthen the group's self-identity. In any case, the author writes:

> And you know that we have separated from the mass of the people . . . and from mingling with them in these matters and from being in contact with them in these matters. And you know that no treachery or lie or evil is found in our hands. . . . And furthermore we have written to you that you should understand the Book of Moses and the Books of the Prophets and David and all the events of every age. . . . Remember the kings of Israel and understand their works that each of them who feared the Torah was saved from troubles, and to those who were seekers of Law, their iniquities were pardoned. Remember David, that he was a man of piety, and that he was also saved from many troubles and pardoned. We have also written to you concerning some of the observances of the Law, which we think are beneficial to you and

your people. For we have noticed that prudence and knowledge of the Law are with you.[10]

The "you" of the letter is written in the singular (in Hebrew a different word would be used for "you" in the plural) and appears to be a ruler. He should remember David as a model and watch out for his people. The "we" rhetorically position themselves as concerned outsiders, reassuring the addressee that he need only to follow the "observances of the Law," as "we" understand them, to receive divine benevolence. Here was a ruler whom the authors thought could be reasoned with.

The early part of the Halakhic Letter details the practices to which the group objects. They predominantly concern very specific, technical issues of ritual purity, the conduct of the priests, and other issues relating to the sacrificial service at the temple. It is likely that another section of the same document provided a description of the 364-day solar calendar, presumably in opposition to the lunar calendar then in use.

The Halakhic Letter would fit well with the reign of John Hyrcanus II, perhaps even when his mother still reigned. Those who composed the Halakhic Letter, a Sadducean group, not only found themselves losing power to the resurgent Pharisees but were sincerely alarmed at the reforms that were being made in temple practices—reforms that, incidentally, may well have served to reverse the changes that the Sadducees had themselves introduced over the last forty years. They withdrew to Qumran out of some combination of prudence (they had already witnessed a purge under Alexandra, and perhaps left during that period) and religious conviction. They also felt, though, that their fall might be temporary and that they would be able to convince John Hyrcanus II to abandon the "new" Pharisaic practices.[11]

The author's argument is explicitly scriptural. The author invokes three or four categories of authoritative writings: the book of Moses, the books of the Prophets, the books of David, and "all the events of every age." Presumably, the first three more or less correspond to the Pentateuch, the section of the Hebrew Bible known as the Prophets, and the book of Psalms (perhaps along with some other texts that in today's Jewish Bible are known together as the Writings). The fourth division might be referring to books like 1 Enoch and Jubilees, which claim the existence of heavenly tablets that contain history and destiny. The author's argument to the ruler is that their rules conform to these writings and therefore should be followed. John Hyrcanus II may or may not have shared the Halakhic Letter's claim that these texts had normative authority, but clearly by this time it was a reasonable one to make. Throughout the Halakhic Letter the author refers and alludes to "scripture," even if the references are sometimes rather loose.[12] In a confrontation between accepted practice and scripture, the Halakhic Letter argues, scripture wins.

The evocation of these three (or arguably four) categories of authoritative writings points to the value that this Sadducean group placed on scripture. This value, which dated back to the time of the Teacher of Righteousness under John Hyrcanus I, is also reflected in the many "biblical" texts found among the Dead Sea Scrolls. The community had a clear notion that there were authoritative texts or scripture, but a fluid notion of what falls within this category. Fragments of all of the books (except Esther) of today's Jewish Bible are among the Dead Sea Scrolls, often in multiple copies. The sectarians clearly assigned an important status to these books, although, perhaps surprisingly to us, they seem to have been relatively untroubled by the fluidity of the texts. That is, copies of the same books are often (usually slightly) different from each other as well as the text in today's Bible, which was fixed only in the early Middle Ages (and is known as the Masoretic Text). The biblical texts found at Qumran, although authoritative, often differed, even if only slightly, from each other and the Masoretic Text.[13]

Those in the sect at Qumran had a loose but not closed canon. They brought with them from the temple, acquired, and created many texts that are not part of today's Bible. These texts too were thought to be divinely inspired and to have authority. They reflect the sect's idea that God continued to reveal his will in the world. For this sect, God's presence was real and immediate and opened the possibility of new interpretations of old scriptural texts as well as the production of entirely new authoritative texts.[14]

I realize that to those who think that the Essenes, not the Sadducees, wrote the Dead Sea Scrolls this reconstruction might be surprising. The identification of the scrolls with the Essenes goes back to the very beginning of their publication and continues to have many supporters. There are, in fact, reasonably strong arguments in its favor. Josephus and Philo describe the beliefs and practices of the Essenes (a term that never appears in the scrolls themselves), which line up with much of what we find in the scrolls. Another classical author, Pliny, moreover locates an Essene settlement in the area of Qumran. It is thus not unreasonable to think that many of those writing in the first century CE knew the community at Qumran as "Essenes," who were certainly distinct from the mainstream Sadducees whom they also would have known at that time.[15]

Just because these later authors may have known that Qumran community as Essenes, though, does not mean that they originated under that title. Scholars have increasingly recognized that the specific legal positions found in the scrolls are similar to those that the rabbis later explicitly credit to the Sadducees, and the idea that the group at Qumran had connections to the Sadducees, at least in its formation and early years, has gained scholarly support over the last two decades. If this is correct—and I believe that it is—how did they come to be known as Essenes?

Josephus does not tell us how the Essenes originated, but a few incidental references suggest that they began as a loose group associated with prophecy and fortune-telling. Judas, the first Essene mentioned by Josephus, lived in 103 BCE and "had never been known to speak falsely in his prophecies."[16] Josephus never describes the Essenes as engaged in political activity, like the Pharisees and Sadducees. Whether they even had a name for themselves or saw themselves as any kind of unified group at this time is doubtful.

I think that at some point in the late first century BCE or the first century CE, the breakaway Sadducean group at Qumran, with its strong belief in continuing prophecy, was identified by outsiders as "Essene," which also distinguished it from the "real" Sadducees, who continued to play a political role.

Yet whether or not this reconstruction is correct, there is not much at stake in the question of whether the authors of the Dead Sea Scrolls are Essenes. The evidence of the scrolls themselves overwhelm the very little we know of the Essenes and their origins from classical authors such as Josephus and Pliny. The scrolls are important not because they tell us something about the Essenes but because they provide a window into a single Jewish community from antiquity. Arguably, no writings from this period by actual Pharisees or Sadducees of this time survive. Whether we call the authors of the Dead Sea Scrolls "Essenes" or "sons of light" and members of "the renewed covenant"—as they call themselves in their texts—the scrolls reveal the inner dynamics of how and why at least one Judean group increasingly turned to written texts as a source of authority.

John Hyrcanus II, the last of the Hasmonean rulers, was apparently not among them. He never abandoned the Pharisees, although it may not have been in their best interest to remain with him. After Hyrcanus II's mother, Alexandra, died in 67 BCE, he and his brother struggled bitterly to succeed her. In 63 BCE, they invited Rome to Jerusalem to adjudicate their dispute. This was the beginning of the end for the Hasmoneans and would set the stage for the ascension of Herod the Great to the throne and the resurgence of the Sadducees.

Herod did not trust very many people, but aside from members of his family he might have trusted the Pharisees least of all. During Herod's long, prosperous, and largely successful rule he marginalized the Pharisees and allowed the Sadducees some, if still limited, influence in the temple. The reason that he did this had nothing to do with theoretical issues about the authority of texts or beliefs, but everything, once again, to do with politics and money.

Antipater, Herod's father, paved his path to power. Antipater had served John Hyrcanus II as a trusted advisor, although he clearly used this position to advance his own and his family's power. Sensing that the Hasmonean dynasty was imploding, he created personal ties with the Roman authorities. These paid off in 40 BCE when, with the Hasmoneans in complete disarray, Rome appointed Herod as king. It took Herod another three years to gain control of Judea. He was not truly secure, though, until Octavian—known as the Roman emperor Augustus—confirmed his rule in 30 BCE, which must have come as a great relief since he had earlier been an ally of his rival, Marc Antony. He would rule another twenty-six years, dying in 4 BCE.

For most of his reign he kept his territories peaceful and prosperous, pursuing bandits with vigor. He engaged in a massive building program that included not only the creation of several new fortresses and palaces but extensive renovation of entire cities such as Caesarea. He reshaped the topography of Jerusalem through his extensive building, which included creating the very hill on which his magnificent new temple would rest, a building project so ambitious that it continued for more than fifty years after Herod's death.[17]

Even in antiquity, building on this scale was expensive. The renovations of the temple alone required thousands of workers, skilled and unskilled, over a long period of time. Herod paid for these projects out of "his own" income, which is to say the taxes he collected from the populace along with the revenues from his own vast and productive estates granted to him by Rome. Herod's decision to "invest" much of this income in public works, a strategy perhaps derived from Augustus's own extensive public works program in Rome, had a number of far-reaching ramifications. One of them, not very coincidentally, was to redistribute wealth from the rural landholding aristocracy—the class traditionally associated with the Pharisees—to the new urban elites. Herod's building was not only about building or glory—it was very much about punishing those whom he mistrusted (and who had earlier backed John Hyrcanus II) and rewarding his supporters.[18]

We can reconstruct these economic ramifications by tracing the flow of capital. Much of Herod's tax income came from the wealthy landholders. By using this money to build cities, he in effect gave it to the urban workers. These workers would live more or less on a subsistence level, and thus have to spend most of their earnings in the cities on basic needs. This would enrich the urban elite who controlled the markets and local centers of production. At the same time, since many workers were moving to the cities, labor for the rural landholders would become scarcer and more expensive.

Herod also undermined the rural aristocracy more subtly. His building program throughout his kingdom and a carefully calibrated tax policy supplied him with a surplus that he sometimes used directly to support the rural poor, bypassing the landholders. In the face of a famine in 25/24 BCE, Herod spent a significant amount of his own money (even melting down palace ornaments) to buy grain from Egypt to feed the populace, which "made such a powerful impression upon the Jews and [was] so much talked about by other nations, that the old hatreds which had been aroused by his altering some of the customs and royal practices were completely eradicated throughout the entire nation." A few years later Herod eased the tax burden by one-third in consideration of a decreased harvest.[19]

Herod was deeply suspicious of the old rural aristocracy, but he also needed it. Under a system that Rome had put into place before Herod came to power, Judea was divided into districts, each of which was governed by these families. In trying to balance his suspicion and need of them, he cultivated a base of power among cities outside of Judea in order to counterbalance some of these internal threats. He also ruthlessly suppressed internal dissent. In one extraordinary passage, Josephus claims that Herod enacted a program that could describe many modern totalitarian states: "No meeting of citizens was permitted, nor were walking together or being together permitted, and all their movements were observed. Those who were caught were punished severely, and many were taken, either openly or secretly, to the fortress of Hyrcania and there put to death. Both in the city and on the open roads there were men who spied upon those who met together. . . . As for the rest of the populace, he demanded that they submit to taking an oath of loyalty, and he compelled them to make a sworn declaration that they would maintain a friendly attitude to his rule."[20]

The oath was at least in part directed toward the Pharisees, the party of the old aristocracy. According to Josephus, the Pharisees refused to take the oath of loyalty. The only group that was exempt from taking the oath was, curiously, the Essenes.[21]

There are other signs that Herod's relationship with the Pharisees was tense, if not simply hostile. When Herod discovered that the Pharisees were making inroads among women of his court, he had the responsible parties killed. Later, as Herod lay dying in 4 BCE, two "sophists," who had reputations as experts in the ancestral laws, encouraged their followers to rip down and dismantle the golden eagle that Herod had erected over the gate of the temple. Herod, though, still had enough fight and ferocity in him that he quickly ordered the execution of all those involved. Josephus never explicitly calls this group Pharisaic, but the terminology that he uses in this account strongly suggests it. Moreover, the leaders are said to have encouraged their followers by saying that the souls of those who die performing such religious acts attain "immortality and an eternally abiding sense of felicity." The idea of the survival of the soul is reported as a distinctively Pharisaic belief.[22]

The sources do not explicitly state that the Sadducees regained power under Herod, but it is hard for me to imagine that they were not able to take advantage of Herod's hostility to the Pharisees. They were natural partners in Herod's promotion of the new urban elite. They had legitimacy earned during their years of temple leadership, and Herod may have seen them as useful allies.

This is not to say that the Sadducees gained much political power under Herod. Herod was suspicious of any potential base of opposition, which would have included the Sadducees and the Jerusalem priesthood (groups that overlapped but were not identical). He thus quickly assumed the power to appoint the high priest, traditionally a hereditary office. During Herod's reign there were seven high priests, with five serving for a year or less.[23] Many of these appointees were from outside Judea; the longest serving, Jesus, son of Phiabi, was most likely from Leontopolis in Egypt. Without a local power base, these high priests were easily controlled by Herod. The priests and Sadducees are not identical, of course, but it is easy to imagine that Herod's support of the Sadducees within the temple establishment helped him to further neutralize any potential political threats.

Even if they had had the opportunity—which is highly unlikely—the residents of Qumran would have had little interest in rejoining the Sadducees, who had now found limited favor in Herod's court. Over the last several decades they had formed their own distinctive identity based in part on their alienation from the temple. They came to see themselves as part of a larger cosmic drama in which they were the "sons of light" who would fight on the side of the angels against the forces of evil. They knew this because it was revealed to them in the ancient written oracles.[24]

The Qumran community assigned various kinds of authority to a large and growing number of texts. Their liturgical texts, for example, often drew on, reworked, spliced together, and alluded to passages from their "scriptures" while almost never referring to them as such. The authors of these liturgies were deeply steeped in these earlier texts and used them for inspiration while feeling free to modify them as necessary. Similarly, the authors of texts that scholars often refer to as "reworked Bible" simply retold stories that they knew from earlier texts in their own words and with their own agendas. They felt no reason to mark the distinction between what was "really" scripture and where they intervened in it.[25]

Despite this fluidity, the community gradually began to consider it important to preserve the integrity of some of these texts. This is most evident in a class of texts known as the *pesher* texts. *Pesher* literally means "interpretation," more specifically in this context, the real hidden meaning of a short selection of scripture. Revealed revelation is found on the surface of the text; it is the simple or plain meaning of the texts. The very same texts, though, also were thought to contain hidden meanings, accessible only to those inspired by God. Of course, one of these inspired interpreters was the Teacher of Righteousness. While the prophet Habbakuk wrote down words without understanding their full meaning, to the Teacher of Righteousness, "God made known all the mysteries of the words of His servants the prophets." The Teacher of Righteousness was not the only recipient of these mysteries. Knowledge of the end was given to the "Priest [in whose heart] God set [understanding] that he might interpret all the words of His servants the Prophets, through whom He foretold all that would happen to His people and [His land]." Joining the sect entitled a member to learn the "hidden" meaning of scripture, which he swore not to reveal to any outsiders.[26]

The extant pesharim, which survive only in fragmentary form, are usually arranged as running commentaries on prophetic books, such as Isaiah, Habbakuk, Micah, and Hosea. The pesher on Psalms interprets selected verses rather than proceeding through the book verse by verse. Although there is no pesher dedicated solely to any books from the Pentateuch, the same technique of inspired interpretation is sometimes applied in other scrolls to verses from the Pentateuch.[27]

The pesher literature illustrates a particular approach to a specific kind of text. The authors of this literature, who believed that they lived at a critical moment in the unfolding of the divine plan, knew that the entire plan existed in written form on the "heavenly tablets" mentioned in the older literature of 1 Enoch and Jubilees. They assimilated this idea to the prophets and other texts (such as sections of the Pentateuch) that they thought were oracular. The prophetic texts were increasingly seen as holding the key, when read correctly, to all of history, past and future. As such, the ancient oracle—not just its surface message but also its secret meaning, encoded in its precise language—must be preserved exactly. This is why the pesher literature formally differentiates the oracle from its interpretation. Despite the fact that the interpretation itself was thought to be divinely inspired, it still remained secondary to the original divine words of the prophetic oracle. The importance of authentic written prophecy to the community is reflected in the distribution of the biblical manuscripts found among the Dead Sea Scrolls: manuscripts of Psalms and Isaiah are two of the three most represented biblical manuscripts in this corpus.[28]

The commitment that the group had to locating prophecies that continue to be relevant in written texts is highlighted by contrasting it to a recent archaeological find known as the Gabriel Revelation. This is an ink inscription on a piece of limestone that appears to date from the time of Herod. Although fragmentary, it appears to record a direct contemporary prophecy given through the angel Gabriel. The pesher literature eschews this model of prophecy. Continuing revelation might be needed to interpret the oracle, but the oracle had already, long ago, been given.[29]

The pesher literature reads into the earlier scripture references to both the recent past and the imminent future. It mentions Rome but no identifiable historical events after 31 BCE, thus pointing to a date of composition in the early Herodian period. This dating corresponds perfectly with another phenomenon seen in the scrolls: the addition of clearly indicated

Figure 8: Fragment of 4Q41, a copy of Deuteronomy (containing the Ten Commandments). (Photo Shai Halevi, Spectral Image, Courtesy of the Israel Antiquities Authority)

citations of authoritative texts to the rules contained in the Community Rule. While this text was originally composed in the late second century BCE, copies made during the Herodian period sometimes add textual citations in order to provide justifications.[30]

At the same time, the group was increasingly paying attention to the actual physical scrolls of texts that it regarded as authoritative. In a fascinating and technical discussion of the scribal practices seen in the Dead Sea Scrolls, Emanuel Tov, a scholar at Hebrew University, has identified what he calls "*de luxe*" editions. These scrolls are written on only one side of a leather sheet in a relatively large script and using wide margins. Among these editions, which were produced only after 50 BCE, copies of books that are now part of the Hebrew Bible predominate.[31] The object, not just content, of authoritative texts is gaining status (fig. 8).

Qumran was a small, highly isolated settlement. Whatever was happening there, the more important question is whether other, less elite Judeans were also becoming more aware of and ascribing more authority to written texts. I think that the answer is that they were, and the primary institution through which this was happening was the synagogue.

Part III

II Jesus and the Synagogue: Judea and Galilee, 4 BCE–30 CE

Herod had utterly transformed Jerusalem from a respectable but sleepy provincial capital into a world-class city and economic juggernaut. His building projects, which were so massive that they would continue for decades after his death, reshaped even the topography of the city. Dominated by a glittering temple built on top of a newly created artificial platform, Jerusalem expanded rapidly to support the vast numbers of workers and skilled artisans that flooded into the city. This, though, was just the start. Pilgrims, who before might never have had any desire to make the long and difficult trip to the temple, also began to stream into the city in large numbers.

Among the economic beneficiaries of this boom were the priests. Archaeologists have discovered several of the large and luxurious mansions that occupied much of what is known as the "Upper City" of Jerusalem, directly west of the temple mount. Their floors were paved with intricate mosaics and their walls covered with elaborate frescoes that were regularly redone in order to stay up with the latest style. They contained a variety of expensive imported goods that testify to the wealth of their owners, who did not even have to descend into the valley that separated them from the temple mount: they traversed a special bridge on their way to the temple that allowed them to look down on the teeming and crowded bustle of the pilgrim trade (fig. 9).[1]

These rich priests were not all Sadducees, and not all Sadducees were priests. But under Herod many of these priests, even shorn of any real political power, would have loosely shared a set of beliefs and commitments

Figure 9: Reconstruction of palatial mansion found in the Upper City of Jerusalem. (Courtesy of Ritmeyer Archaeological Design)

that we can call Sadducean. Certainly, those priests whose sympathies leaned more Pharisaic would have kept a low profile. To the extent that they were able, these rich Sadducean priests would have tried to shape the temple rituals and calendar according to their scriptures, as they understood them. While their very status as priests, both biologically and functionally, gave them a great degree of status, they still relied on scripture as a source of authority, especially useful against the claims of traditional practices made by the Pharisees.

These rich Sadducees had limited power and ability to spread this commitment to the authority of scripture. In the first century BCE, few people in Jerusalem outside of elite circles had more than vague knowledge of the texts in the temple library. This, however, began to change in the early first century CE. The new pilgrims, especially those from Egypt and other Greek-speaking locations, brought with them the idea of the synagogue as a place for the public reading of scripture. This was an idea that the Sadducees liked and to the limited extent that they were able (primarily through their wealth) began to adopt. They did not need, though, to establish any centralized program in order to spread the institution throughout Judea. As today, the aspiring classes sought to emulate the wealthy, to the extent that their wallets allowed. If the rich and powerful Jerusalem priests preferred a certain kind of pottery and imported wine, why shouldn't we? If they believed in the authority of a certain body of texts, shouldn't we? This process worked slowly and unevenly, but eventually would bring these texts out of their libraries and into the public light. Synagogues began to spread throughout Judea and Galilee, and with them an increasing awareness of scripture.

This was the environment in which Jesus lived. A couple of decades after his death, some of his followers would come to link his life to scripture, particularly read (as in the Dead Sea Scrolls) as oracles. Jesus himself, though, had a much looser knowledge of and connection to scripture. Growing up in Galilee, which remained dominated by the older rural families that Herod had suppressed (and that were sympathetic to the Pharisees), Jesus engaged with (and was sometimes critical of) practices justified on the basis of *tradition* rather than text. Jesus, in fact, might in many ways be understood as a Pharisee, a stance that made things even more difficult for him when he came before the authorities in Jerusalem.

In the decades between Herod's and Jesus's deaths, the Sadducees continued to occupy positions of power and prestige in Jerusalem and largely overshadowed the Pharisees. In Galilee, on the other hand, the fledgling rich and aristocratic families were more sympathetic to the Pharisees. To understand how this happened, and thus to understand how, consequently, scripture began to move outside of its rarefied circles, we must first untangle the political mess that Herod left upon his death.

Herod left scores of wives and children with competing agendas who did not trust each other; a sister, Salome, whose meddling wreaked havoc on everything she touched (at least as portrayed by Josephus); and opposition parties, long suppressed, waiting for an opportunity to strike. One son, Archelaus, managed Herod's funeral and immediately claimed the throne, only to face riots at the temple during Passover. He ruthlessly suppressed them and then quickly tried to outrace his brother Antipas to

Rome, where both sought confirmation from Augustus as the new king. As they waited in Rome for a decision from Augustus, Judea erupted in riots that the Roman authorities quickly put down.

Archelaus and Antipas were not the only parties from Judea in Rome who were competing for Augustus's favor. Josephus elliptically refers to another group that he calls only "the Judeans." These Judeans were opposed to the continuation of any Herodian rule: Herod, they claimed, had wrought destruction, plundered property, killed nobility, taxed heavily, and perpetrated a general variety of humiliating outrages.[2] It is likely that these "Judeans" were in fact the older aristocratic families that Herod had suppressed. They would most likely have been allied with the Pharisees, a fact that Josephus (if he knew) might not have wanted to mention, given their pleas that Rome take direct charge of administering the country. Although they were unsuccessful at this juncture, the incident shows them to have been sufficiently organized and powerful to play a continuing role in Judean affairs.

Augustus gave something to everybody. He divided Herod's former territory into three districts, each to be administered by a different son of Herod: Archelaus was given Judea, Samaria, and Idumaea; Antipas received Galilee and Peraea; and Phillip received some lesser territories. As a concession to the old aristocracy, Archelaus was given the title "ethnarch" rather than "king," although Augustus held out the possibility in the future that he could regain the monarchic title.[3]

Archelaus lasted ten years before the old aristocracy was able to depose him. The aristocrats complained to Augustus about his rule and this time he listened, exiling Archelaus in 6 CE to Gaul and confiscating his estates. From this time on, the provinces of Judea, Samaria, and Idumaea were put directly under the administration of the Roman governor of Syria. The Romans sold Archelaus's (that is, Herod's former royal) estates, presumably to the Judean aristocracy. The political transition must have thus resulted in a tidy profit for Rome. The Romans (as Herod had earlier done) also took the prerogative of appointing the Jewish high priests. Antipas and Phillip were allowed to continue to rule their respective territories.[4]

In addition to selling Archelaus's estates, the Roman administrators of Judea, Samaria, and Idumaea registered all private lands for the purposes of tax collection. This led to a minor insurrection. According to Josephus, the insurrection was led by a certain Judas, who came from either Galilee or a region nearby to Judea.[5] He was accompanied by Saddok, identified as a Pharisee. According to Josephus, this was packaged as an ideological revolt against Roman rule, especially as manifested in the need to pay tribute. This ideology was tied either to the desire for national autonomy as a value in its own right or to the need to recognize only God as Judea's legitimate ruler. In any case, the Romans quickly suppressed the revolt.

Antipas may have had a hand in this revolt. Antipas, probably supported by the local elite, controlled Galilee. Like his father, he engaged in monumental building projects, strengthening regional centers such as Sepphoris. Certainly, the direct Roman administration of Judea and the registration of land would have made Antipas and his cohort uneasy. Judas, with loose support from the Pharisees—who were allied with this old order—might have been sent, supported, or encouraged to test Roman resolve. The Romans passed.

By the early first century CE, most Jews who lived in larger cities outside of Judea would probably have had far greater knowledge of scripture than those who lived in Jerusalem. Some encountered the Septuagint as part of their education; many others would have heard it recited and discussed in synagogues. In both cases, they would have heard it in Greek, their native language. Outside of the political and literary elite, though, most Jews in Jerusalem and throughout Judea more generally would have had far less exposure. They would have encountered only a small smattering of scripture in the temple, and synagogues had not yet been established there. And even in the cases where they might encounter these scrolls, most of them, who knew Aramaic rather than Hebrew, would have had difficulty making sense of them. With the support of the Sadducees, this would begin to change.

Even after 6 CE, the Romans left the administration of the temple and its sacrificial cult to the Jerusalem priests. The high priest would certainly have been a Roman lackey, but he would not have interfered much with the temple's daily routine. For their part, the priests, whatever their ideological leanings or desires, would have been severely constrained in their ability to make any changes. The Roman authorities as well as the wealthier priests would have frowned on any activities that could cause disruption or unrest.

Changes that were not potentially disruptive, however, could be made. Such changes were also made possible by the architectural changes that Herod made to the temple; there were new spaces that did not bear the constraints of traditional practices. Traditionally, the sacrificial service itself had always been performed in silence. While this continued to be the case in Herod's temple, there also begins to arise at this time a verbal liturgy that was connected to the sacrifices but that took place in a different part of the temple.[6]

According to later rabbinic texts, two verbal ceremonies would accompany the twice-daily sacrifices. One of these ceremonies was the singing of specific hymns, conducted in public after the sacrifice was burned on the altar. This public recitation of hymns at the temple had apparently long been customary and to some extent accounts for the collection known as Psalms. These hymns, many of which were quite ancient, gained an added veneer of holiness through their use in this context.[7]

More remarkably, however, prior to the public hymnal singing there was a smaller private liturgy for the officiating priests only. According to an early rabbinic text, after killing and butchering the sacrifice, the priests would retreat into the "Hall of Hewn Stones" outside of the ritual precincts. Here, they would bless God, read four short scriptural passages, and then ask God to protect the people. The four passages they would read (the verb specifically implies that they read from a written text) included the Ten Commandments (perhaps the version from Deuteronomy, as it was physically located close to the next reading); the Shema (Deuteronomy 6:4 and probably the passage that follows); Deuteronomy 11:13 and the following paragraph, which specifies communal rewards for following God's commandments; and Numbers 15:37, on God's redemption of Israel and commanding them to wear fringes on their garments.[8]

If this description is a more or less accurate account of practice in the temple, it would reflect an attempt by the priests to infuse scripture and its recitation into the temple cult. On the one hand, this would have been a somewhat radical move to tie the otherwise silent cult to the verbal recitation of written texts. On the other hand, though, it was relatively safe: a few short passages of scripture, recited privately by richer and more educated priests on the fringes of the temple, would not have been considered particularly problematic, even if it caused a short delay in completing the sacrifice.

The same impulse that led to the introduction of this new scriptural reading in the temple was also behind the establishment of synagogues in Jerusalem. Synagogues—whether we use the term to refer to a dedicated physical place or just an ad hoc group of Jews engaged in either prayer or the teaching of religious texts or practices—are first attested in Egypt in the third century BCE. By the first century BCE the institution had spread through the Greek-speaking world and had come to be a dedicated space where the Septuagint was read and expounded, primarily on the Sabbath. Synagogues are completely unattested in Judea prior to the late first century BCE or early first century CE.[9]

The first evidence for the existence of a synagogue in Judea or Galilee comes not from literary mention or archaeological remains but from an ancient inscription found in Jerusalem, disconnected from any physical structure. This large and beautiful Greek inscription was probably engraved in the first century BCE–first century CE. It reads: "Theodotus son of Vettenos, priest and archisynagogos, son of an archisynagogos, grandson of an archisynagogos, built this synagogue for the reading of the Law and the teaching of the commandments, and the guest-house and the (other) rooms and water installations (?) for the lodging of those who are in need of it from abroad, which (the synagogue) his forefathers, the elders and Simonides founded."[10]

The inscription commemorates the "building" of a previously "founded" synagogue. The distinction between these two activities is unclear. One scholar, pointing also to the fact that Theodotus's father bears a Latin name, Vettenos, and that such names were rarely found among Jews from Judea, suggests that Theodotus's family founded and led (indicated by the title "archisynagogos," literally, "head of the synagogue") a synagogue community elsewhere. Theodotus then moved to Jerusalem, perhaps with members of this community, and established a building for them.[11]

The implications of this interpretation of the inscription are significant. It would link one of the earliest synagogues known from Judea to a Jewish priest from outside of Judea. Put differently, and with all the caution necessary in interpreting a single object that reached us through happenstance, it suggests that the synagogue could have been imported from outside of Judea.

Theodotus's synagogue may or (more likely) may not have been the first synagogue in Jerusalem or Judea, but it was part of a larger phenomenon. Herod imported priests from abroad in order to help run the Jerusalem temple without presenting any danger to his own authority. These priests were almost certainly familiar with the synagogue from their homes. In order to make themselves, their families, and their entourage more comfortable, those of means might then have built synagogues in Jerusalem.

Upon acclimating to the temple culture in Jerusalem, though, these priests also would have come into contact with the Sadducean promotion of the authority of the text. The building of a place in which to read and teach "the Law"—the Torah—would have appealed to these Sadducees. Far from serving as a replacement for the temple (as some scholars have claimed), the synagogue thus emerged as an extension of it that helped to extend the authority of one of its dominant groups. The idea came from outside of Judea, but it took root due to the specific conditions of Jerusalem in the first century BCE.

Rabbinic sources might provide an echo of this early link between the Jerusalem priests and the synagogue. They report that priests and Levites were divided into "courses," groups that would take turns serving in the Jerusalem temple. Each of the twenty-four courses also had associated with it a *ma'amad* of Israelites, Jews who were neither priests nor Levites. When a course went up to serve in the Jerusalem temple, the rabbis report, their associated ma'amad would "gather in their cities and read in the works of creation," which is explained as the very beginning of the book of Genesis.[12] We don't know the extent to which this was actually done, but it might point to a priestly/Sadducean attempt to link their authority and service in the temple to both the Pentateuch and the natural order—the same kind of link found in the book of Jubilees.

The Sadducees, though, did not have the means, authority, or organization necessary to spread synagogues throughout Judea. Instead, we must imagine that their slow and halting diffusion through the first century CE

Figure 10: Remains of the synagogue at Gamla. (Copyright www.HolyLandPhotos.org. Used by permission)

was not the result of imposition but of imitation. Local elite would see or learn of synagogues in Jerusalem, and would then, money, means, and personal and communal ideology permitting, desire their own. Fortunately for modern archaeologists, this process of diffusion from a central location led also to relative consistency among these otherwise unmarked and largely unadorned structures. With some variation, they tended to be square or rectangular rooms with benches built into the sides and two rows of supporting pillars. Many also have water installations that seem designed for ritual immersions connected to them, perhaps suggesting another connection to the priests (fig. 10).[13]

Despite the synagogue's connection to the Sadducees and the priesthood, the rural elite, even with their Pharisaic leanings, appropriated it. Largely, I suspect, this was a matter of prestige; they and other residents who visited Jerusalem would have learned of such structures and came to saw them as status markers that could be built at relatively modest cost. Whether they also used the building for "reading of the Law and the teaching of the commandments," as the Theodotus inscription declares, is unknown but not impossible. Part of the appropriation of synagogues may have involved the appropriation of scripture and its interpretation as well, this time by the Pharisees. Ultimately, the Pharisees would gain prestige as expert interpreters of the law. Perhaps here, at the beginning of their appropriation of the synagogue in Galilee, is where they got their start.

This explanation of the development of the synagogue in first century CE Judea and throughout Galilee helps us to better understand the activities of Jesus and his followers and, ultimately, the emergence of Christianity. Drilling underneath the complex historical sources at our disposal, however, to discover the "real" historical Jesus is not as straightforward a task as one might think.

We can be relatively certain that there was an actual historical figure named Jesus, that he spent most of his life in Galilee, and that he was crucified by the Romans. Here the later accounts that would enter the New Testament agree among themselves and receive some corroboration from Josephus. For more precise information, however, we must rely almost entirely on the New Testament Gospels.

The New Testament contains four "Gospels" that are essentially chronological narratives of Jesus's life. These books—Mark, Matthew, Luke, and John—were written decades after Jesus's death. They were probably written in Greek (although it is not impossible that one or more were first written in Aramaic), and their final redactors (like Paul) may well have never met Jesus, or in fact even lived in Judea. Three of these Gospels, Matthew, Mark, and Luke, contain many parallels and are thus termed the "synoptic Gospels." These many parallels are thought to come from shared sources. Mark was apparently written first, and then Matthew and Luke drew upon it as well as an earlier source containing sayings of Jesus that scholars have termed Q. John, probably written at the beginning of the second century CE, has a very different narrative than the synoptic Gospels and does not use Q or Mark.

These four Gospels each press a thick but somewhat different agenda. Thus, like many of the other historical sources we have encountered, they cannot be read as transparent accounts of the events that they purport to describe. The question is whether we can pare away the later interpretations and agendas to arrive at a clearer picture of Jesus. Many scholars over a very long time have attempted to do this. The results of this scholarship have been rather modest but significant, revealing at least the general contours of Jesus's life.[14]

Jesus was raised as a Jew in a traditional Galilean village. As such, the ancestral practices of his ancestors—such as traditional food laws and observance of the Sabbath—would have been part and parcel of his life. He was unlikely to have received much of a formal education, and his knowledge of scripture would have been acquired through occasional attendance at the synagogue and perhaps the teachings of local Pharisees. It would thus have been ad hoc, aural, and disjointed. Nevertheless, scripture and the lessons associated with it clearly intrigued him.[15]

All of the Gospel sources strongly portray Jesus as a teacher. Sometimes, especially to the apostles, Jesus teaches with parables, with no reference to scripture. Frequently, though, Jesus teaches by citing and explaining scripture. "Jesus went through Galilee," Matthew states, "teaching in their synagogues and proclaiming the good news of the kingdom and curing every disease and every sickness among the people" (Matthew 4:23).

How and what did Jesus "teach"? One of the best examples of what "teaching" meant at this time, both for Jesus and other contemporary Jews, might be the Sermon on the Mount. After a short set of blessings, Jesus launches into a series of teachings on enigmatic laws found in the Pentateuch. "You have heard that it was said, 'You shall not commit adultery,'" Jesus says. But this is far from an obvious law: what, after all, constitutes "adultery"? Here, as elsewhere in the sermon, Jesus opts for a maximalist interpretation: "But I say to you that everyone who looks at a woman with lust has already committed adultery with her in his heart" (Matthew 5:27–28). While this particular interpretation may have been novel, the act of reading and explaining the meaning of a scriptural passage wasn't.

The Sermon on the Mount might constitute our best evidence for what exactly happened in a synagogue in first-century CE Galilee (even though this sermon, of course, was taught outside). In this sermon, Jesus never introduces the verse that he explains with, "You read in the Torah." Instead, he uses the phrase, "You have heard it said" or "You have heard that it was said to those of ancient times." This points to the ad hoc way in which his audience would have known scripture. They did not read it; even if they had access to it, most could not read! They would have been familiar with these texts only to the extent that they had heard them. This knowledge would have come from "teachers" like Jesus, who inside and outside the synagogue would have read verses and explained them.[16]

Another Gospel account shows how ad hoc even this knowledge could be. According to Luke, Jesus entered a synagogue in Nazareth and "stood up to read." He was given a scroll of Isaiah, and read three non-sequential verses, and then sat down and explained them (Luke 4:16–22). The choice of reading Isaiah, no less this passage in Isaiah, appears to have been entirely random, not part of any regular lectionary cycle. This, in fact, is an important feature of Luke's story: scripture plays an oracular function here, giving further divine authority to Jesus. If you were an ordinary Jew in antiquity who knew scripture only from such citations, your knowledge would have been spotty indeed. Jesus, as a curious commoner, might have gone slightly beyond this level of knowledge, but not by much. Outside of this account in Luke, Jesus is nowhere portrayed as actually reading a text.[17]

It was as a teacher dealing with the explication of traditional customs, and to a lesser extent with scriptures, that he came into contact with the Pharisees. With the Sadducees more or less secure in Jerusalem at this time, Herod the Great's son Antipas, in control of Galilee during the time of Jesus, appears to have been sympathetic to the Pharisees. Politically, this made sense: the Pharisees had been allied with the older, aristocratic families who had found refuge in Galilee. Pharisaic teachers, who specialized in interpreting ancient customs, would have been active throughout Galilee. Perhaps Jesus learned from and studied with them. Whether he did or not, however, his own teaching activity would have brought him into conflict with these teachers.[18]

The Gospels clearly have a negative view of the Pharisees. Yet a close reading of their account of Jesus's life reveals a Jesus far more intertwined with the Pharisees than the later sources might care to admit. He works entirely within the framework of "the Law," that is, ancestral customs. His disputes about Jewish customs focus on specific, usually relatively technical, points. In some cases, as in the Sermon on the Mount, he opts for strict interpretations, whereas in others (for example, healing on the Sabbath in Mark 3:1–5), he prefers a more lenient position. "Do not think that I have come to abolish the law or the prophets," Jesus says. "I have come not to abolish but to fulfill. For truly I tell you, until heaven and earth pass away, not one letter, not one stroke of a letter, will pass from the law until all is accomplished" (Matthew 5:17–18). This is entirely consistent with his instruction to his disciples that they "go nowhere among the Gentiles, and enter no town of the Samaritans, but go rather to the lost sheep of the house of Israel" (Mark 10:5–6). Jesus never questioned his own identity as a Jew.

At the same time, he was an independent thinker, and the quarrels that the Gospels record him as having with the Pharisees all revolve around relatively small and technical points of practice. The Pharisees challenged Jesus when his disciples picked grain and he healed a man on the Sabbath (Matthew 12:1–21). They insisted that he provide a public sign of his religious authority (vv. 38–45). They accused him of transgressing the "ancestral traditions" (15:1–20). These are the kinds of quarrels that occur among those allied with the same group, not between opposing groups. As long as he was in Galilee, the Sadducees did not harass him. This makes sense: they lacked much presence in Galilee and Jesus's occasional use of scripture against the Pharisees might also have made them somewhat sympathetic to him. That, of course, changed when he took his message south to Jerusalem.

Jesus would not have been seen as simply another Pharisaic teacher. He was born into a religious landscape that was dotted with healers, wonder-workers, and prophets, with whom he is often identified. We are told that Jesus was impressed by John the Baptist (and John the Baptist by Jesus!), an itinerant prophet who gathered a large enough group of followers to come to the attention of Antipas, who put him to death. Like other similarly executed wandering prophets mentioned by Josephus, John posed a threat, however minor in reality, to the political order.[19]

Jesus was seen, and perhaps saw himself, as a wonder-worker, healer, and prophet in addition to teacher. One chapter in the Gospel of Mark neatly contains all of these depictions. At the beginning of Mark 8, Jesus multiplies bread and fish in order to feed a large crowd. He then travels to Bethsaida, where he heals a blind man. Then, after Peter informs him that he is thought to be a prophet but that he, Peter, thinks that he is the messiah, God's anointed one, Jesus foresees his end. Other Jews in Galilee would certainly have seen Jesus as unusual but not unique—they were used to seeing prophets, healers, and wonder-workers (Mark 5:4, 15–16).[20]

Sometime in the late second or early third decade of the first century CE, Jesus and some of his followers visited Jerusalem. This visit, of course, precipitated a series of events that ended approximately six weeks later with his crucifixion. Whether or not this was intended (or, from a religious perspective, destined), Jesus's visit and ultimate execution must be seen within the distinctive political context of Judea and Jerusalem.

Judea's political trajectory had followed a different course than Galilee's. From 6 to 66 CE the Romans directly ruled Judea. From the perspective of Roman imperial administration, Judea was one of only a few areas that were not governed by men of senatorial rank. The Roman administrator was called a *procurator* or *praefectus*, who answered to the governor of Syria. During these six decades, fourteen men served as procurators/prefects of Judea, with terms ranging from one to eleven years.[21]

The position of procurator/prefect often culminated the career of a Roman "knight," a man of the "equestrian" order. Augustus had reformed and formalized the Roman hierarchy, limiting this order to those who had both the right descent and who met a wealth threshold. The knights held many important positions within the Roman administration, although they were strictly distinguished from the much smaller and more rarefied men of the "senatorial" order. A knight in imperial service might be expected to assist in administrative and military roles before ascending to a position of significant responsibility. Procurators received salaries, but they could significantly increase their income from dealings in the areas that they administered. While they were free to take advantage of their office for personal gain, there was a limit to what was tolerated: activities that led to riots or otherwise destabilized the area could bring unwanted attention from Rome and result in exile or worse.

In Judea, as in other Roman territories that held the same status, the prefect had military, judicial, and administrative authority. The prefect of Judea had somewhere in the neighborhood of six cohorts (each of five hundred troops) of auxiliary soldiers under his command, several of which maintained small garrisons. These troops were more for keeping the peace and enabling Roman administration to run smoothly than they were to deter outside attacks or suppress serious rebellions. The prefect was ultimately responsible for the administration of the Roman court system in Judea, and was the only one in the province who could authorize a death sentence. From the perspective of Rome, though, the most important function of the prefect was to keep the taxes flowing and the domestic situation stable. Fiscal issues, such as the minting of local coinage, also fell under the authority of the prefect. The prefect of Judea was resident in Caesarea, although during Passover he took up residence in Jerusalem in order to make sure that the crowds stayed under control.

Of all the Roman administrators of Judea, the most well known, by far, is Pontius Pilate. Very little is known of Pilate's life prior to his being appointed prefect of Judea in 26 CE. Pilate—whose service as prefect is attested by an ancient inscription found in Caesarea—of course gained infamy for his role in the crucifixion of Jesus. Josephus and Philo as well as the Gospels all contain depictions of Pilate, none of which are positive. Pilate promoted the imperial cult throughout Judea in order to project Roman visibility and power. He served as prefect of Judea for a decade and it is unlikely that he would have had much memory of the single decision to crucify Jesus—it was all in an ordinary day's work.[22]

For the most part, the Romans left the day-to-day administration of their provinces in the hands of trusted local elites. In Judea, there were only three thousand second-rate troops on the ground, and while the threat of Roman power in the form of the legions was crucial to keeping control of the local population, it lurked well in the background. One sign of the lack of real Roman presence outside of Caesarea, the seat of the Roman administration of Judea, is the almost complete absence of inscriptions written in Latin from this period or the attestation of Latin names. Throughout the centuries of Roman rule over Judea, Latin in fact never penetrated to the Judean interior. Aramaic and Greek were the colloquial, administrative, and legal languages in Judea under Roman administration. Local institutions functioned more or less autonomously.

These local institutions were primarily judicial and administrative. We know less than we would like about both, but particularly about the Judean judicial institutions. Civil cases were usually judged through arbitration: the sides would agree on a respected party to adjudicate their claims and, if necessary, read their contracts. The position of "judge" in this respect was ad hoc rather than official, although the resulting decision would, through the arbitration decision, be binding and enforceable by administrative authorities, who could use Roman troops to assure compliance.[23] The "law" depended more on common sense and precedents than on statute. Disputants were also free to take their case to the Roman administration, although the time, effort, and uncertain outcome involved in this process would have usually made this seem unattractive.

Individual cities in Judea maintained councils. These councils, composed of the local elite, would appoint the officials who ensured the regular functioning of the city. Some of the city councils were given permission by the Romans to mint their own bronze coins. The council would ultimately be responsible for keeping the city in good repair; administrating the fiscal affairs of the city, especially the marketplace; collecting the taxes due to Rome; and keeping order through the capture and punishment of criminals. There is, again, no evidence of a regular sitting court that would judge felons. The most serious cases would be turned over to Roman authorities while presumably improvised courts would deal with lesser ones.

The Sanhedrin, mentioned in the Gospels and later rabbinic sources, should be seen in this context. It was not a standing court, and even less a national legislative body. It was instead an improvised council or court, convened for a particular reason and dissolved thereafter. This was the kind of court that would "try" and condemn Jesus.[24]

While there was no governing national body (aside from the Romans) in Judea, the institutions in Jerusalem carried some weight. The temple and priesthood remained important both symbolically and economically. The city council in Jerusalem did not have authority outside the city's limits, but especially to the extent that it conveyed the authority of priests (many of whom were wealthy and presumably would have either been members of it or exerted influence on it), it could exert a more subtle influence outside of its official limits.

Roman power, then, was hardly the blunt instrument that is sometimes imagined. Not only were Judeans largely left to govern themselves, it was in fact vitally important to Rome that they do so. They were free to worship in the temple (even though the large gatherings at Passover made Roman authorities nervous) and to conduct whatever religious rites that they wished, as long as they did not impinge upon others. For the most part, this arrangement worked through the first half of the first century CE—except, as in the case of Jesus, when it didn't.

Jesus went to Jerusalem to stir up trouble. On arriving in the city he first scouted out the temple. He returned the next day to overturn the tables of the "moneychangers and the seats of those who sold doves," accusing them of theft (Mark 11:15–17). The charge was by no means obvious. Only a single currency was accepted in the temple, so money-changers were necessary. Similarly, people bought doves before entering the temple so they could sacrifice them—bringing one's own doves on a pilgrimage would have been cumbersome. The reason for his action is obscure. Was Jesus protesting their business practices? Did he want them to move further away from the temple? Or was he, through his actions, indicating God's displeasure with the temple and forecasting that it, like the tables, would be overthrown? Modern scholars are unsure, and it may have been that those who witnessed the act in antiquity were as well. In any event, it made the temple authorities most unhappy.[25]

After directly confronting Jesus, the temple authorities are said to have "sent to him some Pharisees and Herodians"—that is, some of those associated with Herod Antipas in Galilee—"to trap him in what he said" (Mark 12:13).[26] If this, or something like it, really happened (the sources conflict about who initiated what), it was an understandable and clever move on the part of the authorities: they sent to Jesus those with whom he would have been familiar, and who would have been familiar with him. The attempt was unsuccessful, thus setting the stage for another confrontation.

That confrontation was the arrest, trial, and execution of Jesus. The synoptic Gospels all tell a similar story. The temple authorities—at this point Pharisees and Sadducees drop out of the story completely—arrested Jesus and tried him. Finding him guilty of the vague charge of blasphemy, they brought him to the Roman procurator Pontius Pilate. As was the Roman practice, Pilate was in Jerusalem with his retinue over the Passover holiday to keep a close watch on the crowds. Pilate reluctantly confirmed the sentence and had his soldiers carry out the crucifixion.

Jesus had had relatively little contact with the Sadducees. They too debated him in Jerusalem, but his final fatal encounter was with the priests, not the Sadducees (Matthew 22:23–33). Curiously, in this encounter Jesus confirms his belief in angels and resurrection, both of which Josephus indicates are signal Pharisaic beliefs.

Jesus died as he was born and lived, as a Jew. He confirmed the value of most of the "ancestral customs" of the Jews—it is not very difficult to see him as a participant in an intra-Pharisaic debate that revolved not around the value and authority of the customs themselves but about their correct understanding. The Gospel texts themselves are unclear about how much scripture Jesus knew, and whence he knew it. The Gospels do show Jesus "teaching," which seems to mean citing a few verses of scripture and explaining them. Yet when Jesus communicates with his disciples, he much prefers to use actions and parables rather than scripture and its interpretation; scripture per se appeared to have played a marginal role in his religious life. The authors of the Gospels, following Paul, would reframe Jesus's life around his fulfillment of scriptural prophecies, but it is likely that Jesus—even if he saw himself as God's anointed (a much-debated point in New Testament scholarship)—never quite framed his own life in that way.

By the time Jesus died, around 30 CE, scripture was emerging as a powerful presence in Jewish life in Judea and Galilee. Citing a text carried authority, even among the Pharisees. Most people would have had access to these texts only through their oral recitation and explanation by a "teacher," who himself (or herself?) may have been reciting from memory.

Scribes were the one class that would have had access to written versions of such texts. Scribes, however, also would have been occupied primarily with the preparation of more ordinary documents (legal contracts and depositions, for example). They, like everyone else, needed to make a living, and we can presume that they would usually copy such texts for patrons who could pay for them. We have no evidence from this time that local communities would pay them for a scriptural scroll or other communally owned scripture; Qumran, an exceptional community, is the exception with the Dead Sea Scrolls. Accordingly, most synagogues would not possess their own copies of these scrolls, and to the extent that they made them available they would be brought by their owners—undoubtedly members of the educated elite.

"Scripture" is a vague term. While we can be relatively sure that most Jews in Judea and Galilee would have ascribed authority to most if not all of the books included in the Jewish Bible, the limits of scripture—both *what* "counts" and *how* it counts—were still fuzzy. Jesus's death would begin a process that would help both Jews and those who would soon call themselves Christians to answer both questions.

12 Paul: Jerusalem and Abroad, 37–66 CE

Jesus's death must have caused quite a stir. Even if the Gospel accounts of his public trial, humiliating parade through the streets of Jerusalem, and slow and painful death on the cross overlooking Jerusalem are greatly exaggerated—as they most likely are—it was still not every day that the Romans executed an apocalyptic prophet. Jerusalem, full of pilgrims who had come for Passover, throbbed with activity. Sensing the heightened anxiety of the Roman troops, people must have asked, "Who was that man? What did he do?"[1]

Whatever answers they received, most would quickly have forgotten him. They packed up, went back to their homes, and resumed their usual routines. Roman executions of such characters were not common occurrences, but they weren't entirely rare either. In their eyes, Jesus was just another rabble-rouser who, unlike the others, happened to be executed in a particularly public forum.

Not everybody, though, forgot him. His family and closest followers, whom Roman authorities did not consider to be threatening, began to work out the implications of his death. Convinced that he was neither a charlatan nor any ordinary wonder-worker or prophet but that instead he was connected far more closely with God, they began to organize themselves into a community of Jews who believed that Jesus was the anointed one, the messiah, the Christ.

Had it not been for Paul, a Jew whose only glancing contact with the fleshly Jesus could possibly have been as a young member of that Jerusalem crowd who witnessed his death, even Jesus's loyal family and followers would have soon faded away, leaving just a trace of a memory. Paul did not simply spread the news and message of Jesus to the Gentiles. He created the message. This message, which at its heart asserts that God sent Jesus to die as an atonement for all of our sins, would prove over time to be extraordinarily attractive.[2]

Paul was among the first to see the meaning of Jesus's life and death through the lens of scripture. Like many Jews of his time, he understood scripture primarily as a collection of divine oracles. Jesus, he thought, fulfilled their predictions. This was a message that resonated differently in different communities: a Jerusalem Jew, such as Paul, understood the authority of scripture somewhat differently from a Jew in Rome, or from the Gentile who might occasionally show up at a synagogue on the Sabbath. Paul lived a life that was betwixt and between Jerusalem and the Greek-speaking world, Jew and Gentile. His letters offer a fascinating case study of how different communities at that time knew or did not know scripture, and the kind of authority that they gave to these written texts.

If not actually born in Jerusalem (although I suspect that he was), Paul apparently spent his formative years there. Both his knowledge of scripture and the way in which he understood its authority are, in fact, best seen as emerging from first-century Jerusalem. In many ways, Paul was an idiosyncratic thinker, but his patchy knowledge of scripture and the oracular authority that he assigned to it were typical products of a Jerusalem education.[3]

Paul's Jerusalem had briefly experienced a kind of "Sadducean renaissance" under the rule of King Agrippa, in 41–43 CE. Marcus Julius Agrippa, a descendent of Herod the Great, was appointed by the Romans. Despite his short and relatively ineffectual reign, both Josephus and the later rabbis remember him fondly. Agrippa is credited with both taking an active and well-meaning (if sometimes counterproductive) interest in Jewish communities outside of his kingdom and maintaining a generally beneficent and pious disposition. Agrippa's territory included both Judea and Galilee, and when he died of natural causes in 43, a unified Judea would pass back to direct Roman control.[4]

Agrippa may not have actively patronized the Sadducees, but most likely he neglected them benignly and allowed them to retain their important positions within the temple. His grandfather Herod had supported them and he might have counted on their continuing support for his family. They appear to have used their position to expand their influence, at least within Jerusalem.[5]

In Paul's Jerusalem, the Sadducees constituted a sizeable proportion of the rich elite. We might expect that in addition to providing their children with a proper Greek education, they also would have hired tutors to teach them how to read and understand Hebrew scriptures. They would have continued to patronize synagogues as institutions for the public reading of these texts as well. Although perhaps fanciful, a rabbinic tradition that Agrippa read portions of the book of Deuteronomy in public is telling. Under Sadducean influence, the soft power of scripture permeated Jerusalem. According to Josephus, in 48 CE the desecration of a scroll of the law by a Roman soldier led to riots. These scriptures had, at least in some places, achieved an important symbolic weight.[6]

Paul appears to have received an education that would have been typical for a relatively well-off Jewish child in Jerusalem. His letters demonstrate that he had a reasonable education in reading and writing Greek as well as some basic knowledge of Greek philosophy. He knew Aramaic and had access to scripture in Hebrew. It is easier to explain these traits within the context of a relatively well-off Jerusalem family than in that of Asia Minor, where there would have been little reason or opportunity to learn Aramaic.[7]

As an adolescent or young adult, Paul was attracted to the Pharisees. Whether or not he really did study with Rabban Gamaliel (Acts 22:3), "becoming" a Pharisee would primarily have meant studying in a small group with a teacher. He claims that he "advanced in Judaism beyond many among my people of the same age, for I was far more zealous for the traditions of my ancestors" (Galatians 1:14). This would fit with what we presume would be a Pharisaic emphasis on ancestral traditions.

Today, we might call Paul a religious searcher. Not satisfied with the Sadducean ethos in which he was raised, he turned to the Pharisees. This, however, proved also to be insufficient. Paul is vague about how he became acquainted with the early followers of Jesus, implying that it came about through a combination of persecuting them on behalf of the

Pharisees (Galatians 1:13) and his vision of Jesus. This is primarily for rhetorical flourish; I suspect the truth was more prosaic. After Jesus's death, his brother James and his disciple Peter were at the head of a loosely organized group that claimed that Jesus was "both Lord and Messiah" (Acts 2:36). This group was for all intents and purposes ethnically Judean and did not question the necessity of keeping the ancestral customs. In fact, there was among them a significant number of Pharisees (15:5). Given the earlier connections (despite the hostilities) between Jesus and the Pharisees, this is perhaps less surprising than it first appears. These early believers in Jesus might be seen as a Pharisaic offshoot. Paul may well have found his way to them through his experimentation with the Pharisees.[8]

It is very difficult to recover much of anything about this early group. So let us imagine, for a moment, what it might have been like to be a Jew in first-century Jerusalem who believed that Jesus was the Christ. On the one hand, in most respects you would have seen yourself and been seen by others as any other Jew. You would have continued to think of yourself as part of the community of Israel; you continued to share in the same history as your parents and grandparents. Your outward religious practices would have remained more or less the same as well. You continued to observe the same food laws, honor the Sabbath, and circumcise your sons much as your nonbelieving neighbors. At this time the total number of "Christ-believers" was miniscule and almost all had grown up in traditional, Jewish families that did not believe that the messiah had yet come. Relations with your family may have been strained, but it is likely that they continued.

On the other hand, you held a belief that put you at odds with your family and neighbors and, more important, you belonged to a new community that had organized around this belief. The term the "Jerusalem church," sometimes used by scholars, implies a level of organization and grandiosity that certainly did not yet exist. Yet there was a small group, led by James, Jesus's brother, Peter, and others who personally knew Jesus. Its members assembled in somebody's house. Whatever they did during these meetings, they would have been trying to figure out exactly what it meant to be a Christ-believer. If we are to believe the account in Acts, these early followers of Jesus were the first to frame the meaning of Jesus's life and death in terms of scripture. The disciple Peter is said to have claimed that Jesus was foretold in the scriptural oracles (Acts 2–3).[9]

This was a community in formation. Its members would have looked to the other contemporary Jewish groups—the Pharisees, Sadducees, and Essenes—for models of how to create a community based on belief. The problem, though, was that they were not Pharisees, Sadducees, or Essenes, all groups with a place in the social order. They were, instead, a small group of probably middle- or lower-class folk who venerated a man who had deliberately provoked the temple authorities and was then executed by Rome for treason. As long as they stayed quiet and minded their own business, they could reasonably expect to be left alone. Should they somehow emerge into the public light, though, they might expect a chilly or hostile reaction (Acts 7).

This was the group that Paul found in Jerusalem. He did not stay with it long, however. The author of Acts, who treats Paul as his hero and model, claims that shortly after joining them Paul so vigorously pressed their case in public that the "brothers" sent him far away to Tarsus (his purported birthplace) for his own safety (9:30). It is just as likely that they did not particularly trust him (9:26). So whether this was his first trip to Tarsus or a return home, Paul found himself at the beginning of his mission to the Gentiles.

Paul understood himself as having been called to "proclaim him to the Gentiles" (Galatians 1:16). How, though, would he do this? Where would he have found Gentiles who were receptive to his message? One answer is suggested by the author of Acts, who portrays Paul as frequently preaching in local synagogues. To understand why Paul would have done this, we must first step back to consider the nature of the Jewish communities outside of Judea and Egypt.

By Paul's time, Jewish communities had been established in most of the major cities in the eastern Mediterranean. These communities often maintained some kind of officially recognized organization. The Romans generally granted to these Jewish communities the right to practice their ancestral laws, which usually meant that they were exempt from participating in the civic or the Roman cults and could avoid activities that would have caused them to desecrate the Sabbath. By and large they did not hold Roman citizenship and thus also occupied an anomalous place in the civic order.[10] These communities also maintained synagogues. We have very little evidence about what took place in these synagogues, but by this time we can safely assume that some scriptural reading, probably on the Sabbath, was a common practice.

The public communal reading of these ancient and holy scrolls would have had two distinctive resonances within the context of the Greco-Roman city. The first was wealth, culture, and intelligence. The Romans had already developed the idea that owning, reading, and giving books (still in the form of scrolls) were signs of culture. Roman aristocrats used books as status symbols. Gradually, reflection on texts also became a philosophical activity. Whereas in the past philosophy had been largely an oral practice, in the Roman period it increasingly acquired a textual focus. Philosophers and their circles not only wrote tracts but also studied or reflected upon them as part of the very practice of philosophy. Texts and their study thus came to signal intelligence.[11]

By the Roman period, Jews had already long acquired the reputation of being "a people of philosophers." This designation first arose in the Hellenistic period, when a Greek ethnographer observed that Jews did not worship physical representations of the gods. In this ethnographer's eyes, this looked very much like a "philosophical religion," as other Greek writers imagined it. Over time, the idea that the Jews were "philosophers" became a stereotype, and eventually even some Jews began to understand themselves this way. The reason for the designation, though, changed. For Jews like Philo, the reason that they were philosophical was because they had and studied a text that was in accord with the laws of nature and from which they could learn how to live the philosophically good life.[12]

Many synagogue attendees in the first century CE, Jew and Gentile, must have understood the reading and teaching of these ancient texts in Greek translation as a philosophical activity. In their minds (and perhaps in real life), this was a status-enhancing activity. They could now feel themselves striving toward the rich aristocrats they envied. They could never hope to attain their wealth and the time, education, and ownership of texts that it enabled, but they could view themselves as moving into the same orbit.

The public reading of the ancient Jewish scriptures would also have had a second and very different resonance. The Romans, unlike the Greeks, knew of "holy" oracles from the gods delivered in written form. One collection of such oracles was known as the Sibylline Books and was stored in a Roman temple, where priests would consult the books at particularly critical moments. For Romans, the concept of divinely revealed oracles was also connected to mystery and the exotic East. Books—such as, in Plutarch's telling, the "sacred books" of a mythological figure that contained "mysteries" so powerful that they needed to be buried with their author—had power.[13]

So while some might have understood the public reading of scripture in the synagogue as a philosophical exercise, others would have been more attracted by the cryptic, oracular passages that they saw as tapping into something sacred, mysterious, and exotic. In this understanding, the synagogue would have been closer to one of the foreign mystery cults that were gaining popularity throughout the Roman world than to a gathering of intellectuals.

We do not know how many Gentiles were attracted to Jewish synagogues in first-century Greco-Roman cities, but we can be sure that they existed. Whatever else attracted them to the synagogue, it is likely that the reading of scripture—whether understood as a status-enhancing philosophical text or as a mysterious source of oriental wisdom—was a powerful draw. Some of our sources call these Gentiles "God-fearers," although we do not know whether they would have called themselves this, or if indeed they referred to themselves in any distinctive way at this time.[14]

This is why Paul often appears to have stopped at the local synagogue when entering a new city. It was where he thought that the Gentiles who would be most receptive to his message would be. As a knowledgeable Jew visiting from Judea, he probably would have found it relatively easy to convince the synagogue elders to allow him to speak once, although after they heard what he had to say it is unlikely that he would have been invited back. He certainly would not have minded if some Jews were convinced by his message of Christ, but he was really targeting the Gentiles, who had enough familiarity and respect for scripture to make his scripturally based message comprehensible. Once he had a small core nucleus of people who were at least intrigued by his message, he could try to tap their families and networks to expand the community of believers.

The communities, or "churches," that Paul set up in the course of his travels were mostly composed of middle-class, urban strivers and seekers. Just as some of their members had once attended (and maybe continued to attend) the synagogue or a mystery cult, they now attended meetings of this new voluntary organization of "brothers" and "sisters." Paul spent some time working with them in order to teach them the basic components of his message and to establish distinctly "Christian" practices, although both theology and ritual were works in progress. It is thus hardly surprising that when Paul left them—and he never stayed long in any one community—they soon became unsure of themselves. Paul may also have helped to establish authoritative community leaders to resolve some of the community's inevitable problems, questions, and disputes, but they too had received limited training. And so, when the issue became too difficult for them to solve, they wrote to their founder and perhaps the only Christian they knew: Paul.[15]

When the members of one of Paul's communities found themselves at an impasse, they would write to Paul. We know neither how many such letters Paul received nor whether he responded to them all, but clearly he did to at least some. All that remains of Paul's writings are a few of his letters that had been preserved by their recipients. To our knowledge, he never wrote any narrative or systematic tracts explaining his thought.

The communal problems that provoked a letter to Paul were of different types, although they are all somewhat predictable. In Corinth, for example, the rise of new charismatic leaders was dividing the community. "Each of you," Paul recounts, "says 'I belong to Paul,' or 'I belong to Apollos,' or 'I belong to Cephas,' or 'I belong to Christ'" (1 Corinthians 1:12). Paul goes on in this case to clarify that he actually baptized very few of them and exhorts them to behave as a single community. The community was troubled not only by the confusing rise of new charismatic figures but also by very practical questions that it could not figure out how to solve. The two problems are connected. These communities were not sure how to solve such practical issues without recourse to charismatic authority. It was precisely because Paul was seen by these communities as having ultimate charismatic authority that they preserved and venerated his letters of response back to them. Undoubtedly many other communities to which he wrote looked by then to other charismatic authorities, and thus did not believe that Paul's letters to them were worth preserving.

Paul's letters are reactive. The problems they had to address forced him to confront a mounting series of new questions and issues, from the theological to the practical. His most theologically dense letter, to the Roman community, wrestles with the problem of the relationship between both Jews and Gentiles to God's covenant, as revealed in the sacred writings. The letter has spawned an immense corpus of scholarship, largely because Paul is not entirely clear about how to answer this question: he seems to be working it out as he goes along. The letters are thus shaped both by Paul's need to develop answers to some very thorny problems quickly (the community, after all, is waiting for an answer) and by his desire to tailor the language and style of the letter in order to be effective in that particular community. In one passage he admits that he forms his thoughts and actions in order to achieve his goals: "To the Jews I became as a Jew, in order to win Jews. To those under the law I became as one under the law (though I myself am not under the law) so that I might win those under the law. To those outside the law I became as one outside the law (though I am not free from God's law but am under Christ's law) so that I might win those outside the law. To the weak I became weak, so that I might win the weak. I have become all things to all people, that I might by all means save some" (1 Corinthians 9:20–21). Paul did not intend to write his letters for posterity, nor did he see them as polished theological tracts. They were instrumental, written and sent in order to solve specific local problems.[16]

This is the context within which we need to consider Paul's use of scripture in his letters. Paul had learned scripture and had come to recognize Jesus as the fulfillment of the scriptural prophecies. This was a way of reading an ancient revealed text that grew out of a Judean background but that also resonated in the Greek cities of the Roman Mediterranean. When Paul uses scripture in his letters, only in part can it be seen as an abstract theological reflection. Primarily its use must be seen as rhetorical; he cites scripture because he thinks that it will prove his point to his audience. For this, we must assume an audience that has already come to accept in some way the authority of scripture, at least as oracular. A community that contained Jews and/or Gentiles who had developed an attachment to Jewish scriptures would thus be the likely recipients of such a rhetorical strategy.

Paul's instrumental and rhetorical use of scripture, and his awareness of his audience, can be seen by contrasting two of his letters, 1 Thessalonians and Galatians. Thessalonica is located in Greece on the Aegean Sea and was a politically and economically important city, briefly serving as a Roman provincial capital. According to Acts, despite receiving an unusually hostile reaction in the synagogue, Paul succeeded in persuading "a great many of the devout Greeks and not a few of the leading women" to join him (17:1–9). While this account, like all the other accounts in Acts, is historically suspect, it implies that the community that Paul founded in Thessalonica was largely Gentile.

Indeed, Paul's subsequent letter to the Thessalonians contains a remarkable feature: it is the only one of Paul's surviving letters not to quote scripture a single time. Paul's letter emphasizes the authority of the Holy Spirit for this community. When Paul turns in the letter to address the problem that may have originally caused the Thessalonians to write him—a matter involving fornication—he justifies his instructions to them as coming not from scripture but "through the Lord Jesus" (4:2). Near the end of the letter he vaguely alludes to the "words of the prophets," but this appears to be intentionally vague (5:20). This community had less invested in Jewish scriptures so Paul felt no need to cite them for justification.[17]

Galatians, though, takes an entirely different rhetorical strategy. The problem in Galatia—a large province in Asia Minor—was one of both authority and traditional practice. Some members of the Galatian community had been arguing for the necessity of following traditional Jewish practices, most notably circumcision. The argument was apparently being made from scripture. Paul begins his response with a full-throated, even apoplectic, defense of his own authority: "The gospel that was proclaimed by me is not of human origin; for I did not receive it from a human source, nor was I taught it, but I received it through a revelation of Jesus Christ" (Galatians 1:11–12). Paul then makes his (somewhat convoluted) case that Gentiles should not circumcise themselves. He is not content, though, simply to make his case on the basis of his own authority. At several points he invokes and interprets scripture; if his opponents are using scripture successfully, he can hardly ignore it. At the same time, though, some of his interpretations are so strained that he seems to be counting on the fact that his audience gives authority to scripture but does not actually know it well enough to take apart his arguments.[18]

Although Paul uses scripture in a variety of ways, he most commonly cites it for its oracular authority. This is reflected in the books that he most commonly cites. He quotes most frequently from Isaiah and Psalms, and a few (for example, Joshua and Ecclesiastes) he ignores completely. This preference for Isaiah and Psalms is not accidental. They are the two best-represented texts among the Dead Sea Scrolls, and both were seen as containing true divine oracles. One of Paul's favorite strategies is to cite a passage from one of these books and to claim that the prophecy has been fulfilled.[19]

The oracular use of these texts would have been familiar to Paul from Jerusalem. The authors of the Dead Sea Scrolls frequently do this, and while we cannot presume that he had any direct contact with them, that method of interpretation might well have been incorporated into his training in scripture. Texts seen as oracular, though, may also have circulated outside of more learned circles. Such texts could well have been seen as possessing special numinous power. They would have been used by ritual specialists. If a person wanted to know what he or she should do in a particular situation, to thank God for the healing of a sick child or a good harvest, or to request the same—he or she might visit such a local specialist, a ritual expert. In response to the request, these experts consulted, wrote, or recited texts (undoubtedly for a fee). "Authentic" oracles were ideal texts for such activity. The ritual expert consulted his (or maybe her) books; the client heard the words that were recited; the words became more familiar and made their way into the "street." Oracular texts in particular thus circulated in small passages out of all context, and it would mainly be through this circulation that many Jews in Jerusalem would have known books like Isaiah and Psalms.[20]

The oral circulation of these oracular texts points to another distinctive feature of Paul's use of scripture. It is often said that Paul knows scripture through the Septuagint. This, however, turns out not exactly to be the case. Although Paul's letters have been copied for centuries, and his scriptural citations have been "corrected" to be more in line with the official church version, the Septuagint, they still contain a surprising number of scriptural citations that either agree with the Hebrew version (as it now exists) or represent no known version at all. Scholars have labeled this "pluriformity." How can we explain this?[21]

Unlike some popular portrayals of Paul that date from the Renaissance, Paul almost certainly did not write his letters in his study with scrolls open all around him so he could find just the right citations and quote them accurately. Instead, he quoted from the memory of texts that he might well have known primarily, or only, orally. He learned some of these texts in Hebrew, and others in Greek. The precise wording of the texts in these cases was less important than their general sense. He assumed that his audience too would not be overly concerned with the specific wording. Once they arrived at their destinations, these letters would have been read aloud to their communities (1 Thessalonians 5:27). Few listeners would have heard a verse, thought that it conflicted with a version of the verse that they knew, and then gone to consult the appropriate written text to check. "Scripture" primarily circulated in oral form.

Paul appears to have established few communities that we can consider purely "Gentile." Most of his communities seemed to have contained some mixture of ethnic Jews, Gentile sympathizers, and perhaps some Gentiles who were less familiar with Jewish scriptures or even not at all. These communities would serve as a start. Paul clearly saw them as base communities that would both actively reach out to and passively attract local Gentiles. They were apparently relatively successful.

Yet the very success of these communities also created some very serious practical problems. The Jews in these communities took for granted practices like circumcision and observance of some food taboos. The increasing number of Gentiles who joined the small communities—many of which were so small that all their members could fit together into a private house—raised pointed questions about whether it continued to be necessary to observe these practices. This created friction in the communities, and their members, in the midst of their fractious debate, wrote to Paul to resolve their disputes. Paul responded in his letters, offering guidance and attempting to clarify his thinking on these issues. (Whether he succeeded in clarifying matters or simply confusing things even more must remain an open question.) He calibrated his use of scripture according to the composition of the community, hoping to have the maximum impact.

From our perspective it is sometimes hard to imagine just how strange most of the Bible is and how Gentiles in antiquity would have read it. By the time Paul was writing, most Jews in both Judea and the Diaspora thought that the books that would constitute the Jewish Bible were holy. They took the authority of these texts for granted. A Gentile who came to these communities without having first encountered scripture in a synagogue, though, did not share such an assumption. To such a person, a disconnected citation of an oracle from men named "Isaiah" or "David" meant little or nothing.

Paul cited scriptural texts in his letters because he assumed that his audience—Greek-speaking, primarily Jewish, believers in Christ—would find them convincing. Had he been writing to fellow compatriots in Judea at this time, I suspect that he would instead have made vaguer references to ancestral laws and customs. Despite the spread of scriptural knowledge and authority throughout Judea, it still had lagged behind the status and diffusion of Greek translations among Greek-speaking Jews abroad. His upbringing in Jerusalem had given him sufficient scriptural knowledge to address this audience, but that knowledge came largely from exposure to an oracular, oral culture. This is why Paul's letters seem odd when seen against Greek writings by Jews at this time. All other such writings are either narratives that might track or draw on scripture in some way (for example, Josephus) or are, like those of Philo, expositions of extended passages. None are independent arguments that cite isolated scriptural verses for support.

We do not know if Paul's audiences would have understood or been swayed by what would have seemed to them his odd use of scripture. It may well have been Paul's charisma that gave him authority in these communities rather than his intellectual virtuosity. If so, it would not have been Paul's use of scripture that convinced them of his argument, but the fact that Paul uses scripture to convince them of the latter's authority and relevance for understanding the meaning of Jesus's death. To many, particularly Gentile, believers in Jesus at this time, the relevance of Jewish scriptures for understanding the meaning of Jesus's life and death was by no means obvious.

Paul lived the last years of his life in Rome. Whether he was in prison or not during those years in the early 60s, and whether he was executed or died a natural death, he was at least spared the experience of watching his native land descend into increasing turmoil and, ultimately, a crushingly destructive war with Rome.[22]

Had he lived to see it, Paul, I suspect, would have been shaken by the destruction of the Jerusalem temple in 70 CE. It is true that Paul's own relationship with the Jewish community had been rocky, and some of his letters at least flirt with a theological stance of "supersessionism," the idea that God established a new covenant through Christ that superseded or replaced the old one with Israel. Nevertheless, the community of Israel, the Jews, continued to maintain a privileged place in the divine economy. Even after the coming of Christ, Paul writes, "the adoption, the glory, the covenants, the giving of the law, the worship, and the promises" continued to belong to the Israelites (Romans 9:4). The temple service, or "the worship," continued to have theological meaning.[23] The temple's destruction would create a considerable theological problem, and an opportunity, for both Jews and Christians.

13 The Gospels: Judea, 66–100 CE

Paul died just a few years before the outbreak of the revolt in Judea, often called the Jewish War. The revolt against Rome, which began in 66 CE and ended for all practical purposes four years later in 70 CE with the destruction of the Jerusalem temple, reconfigured the religious landscape. For many Jews, it raised uncomfortable practical and theological questions about the continuing relationship between God and Israel. Without a temple and its sacrifices, how could they, as a people, continue to properly serve the God of Israel? Even worse, could the destruction of God's house mean that God had abandoned them?

Paul, like other Jews of his time, might himself have argued that the destruction of the temple resulted from God's displeasure with his people, not his abandonment of them. Israel had sinned, particularly in rejecting Christ, and God had punished it. The Jews, though, still remained an important part of the divine plan.

Not all Christ-believers, though, took this stance. For many, it was stunning confirmation of what they had slowly begun to suspect from their reading of scripture. God had now rejected the old Israel, forming a new covenant with them. The destruction of the temple and the rejection of the Jews was the culmination of the scriptural prophecies. To the four writers of the books that would become the canonical Gospels—Mark, Matthew, Luke, and John—the destruction of the temple was a clarion call.

These authors all sought to make sense of Jesus's life and death. Like Paul, they were familiar with and assumed the authority of earlier scriptures. They found in these books oracles and prophecies, predictions that they applied to Jesus. Unlike Paul, however, they wrote narratives that focused primarily on Jesus's life rather than practical, ad hoc letters with theological musings largely connected to the meaning of Jesus's death.

Jesus, from all that we can tell, did not particularly link his own life to scripture. He knew at least bits and pieces of scripture, but he, like the Pharisees, was more engaged with traditional practice. It would be Paul and then the authors of the canonical Gospels that would tightly tie Jesus to scripture. At that time it was by no means obvious that scripture should be used to interpret the meaning of Jesus's life. Other writers, such as those who wrote the so-called Gnostic literature and the Christian Apocrypha, made different decisions.

The early Christ-believers faced a central problem: the messiah had been born, lived, and died, and yet nothing appeared to have changed. Intellectually, of course, there were ways around this critical problem, but many would have been bothered by the fact that the redeemed world looked exactly like the unredeemed world. They were waiting for a cataclysmic event to confirm their beliefs, and in the Jewish revolt of 66 CE many of them got it. Let me first briefly sketch the events that led to this revolt and then show how the authors who wrote what would become the canonical Gospels responded to them.

After King Agrippa died in 43 CE, the Romans began to administer Judea directly. They appointed a series of procurators, many of whom were far more interested in enriching themselves than in governing effectively. Not only did the economic situation decline under their rule, but so too did the relationships between Jews and Greeks in the mixed cities of Judea. To add to the instability of the situation, the Jewish elite themselves were competing for power.[1]

"The war opened," Josephus writes, "in the twelfth year of the principate of Nero," with an incident that occurred in Caesarea around May 66 CE. It began as a conflict over the land adjoining a synagogue. In the course of this conflict, some of the "Greeks" of Caesarea erected a small altar at the entrance to the synagogue on the Sabbath. The Jews considered this "an outrage upon their laws and desecration." The conflict escalated into a fight and the Jews "snatched up [their copies] of the laws" and retreated to a suburb of the city.[2] We do not know the precise contents of these scrolls, but we can presume that by this time scrolls of scripture could be commonly found in synagogues throughout Judea.

The conflict quickly spread, mushrooming into a full-blown revolt against Rome that never had a chance. The Roman army quickly restored order, with the remaining rebels holing up in Jerusalem and, when the city walls were breached, the temple. In the course of the rebels' final stand, in 70 CE, the temple was set ablaze—it is unclear if the fire was intentionally set. The Romans sacked what was left and brought their booty and prisoners back to Rome to celebrate a triumph for the commanding general, Titus. The triumph is famously commemorated on the arch erected for the occasion, which still stands in Rome.[3]

The practical impact of the temple's destruction would have varied widely. For the residents of Jerusalem and its suburbs, whose economic and religious lives revolved around it, it would have been devastating. At further distances, however, the impact lessened. Jews from Galilee, such as Jesus, might have been to the temple only a few times in their lives, and those in the more far-flung Jewish communities along the Mediterranean or in Persia may never have seen it at all. For them, the temple's significance was largely symbolic and theological. They, along with local Jews, might have asked (as their ancestors did after the destruction of the first temple) whether the God of Israel had been defeated or if he had allowed his house on earth to be destroyed, and why. These theological questions precipitated by the revolt were pressing in the last decades of the first century CE. They form the intellectual context in which the four Gospels that would eventually enter into the New Testament canon took shape.

Mark, the earliest of the canonical Gospels, was most likely written around the outbreak of the revolt. Mark (as, for reasons of convenience, I will call the author of this tract, who was certainly not a disciple of Jesus and probably had a different name altogether) most likely had an education similar to that of Paul. In fact, of all the Gospel writers, Mark most resembles Paul, even though he appears not to have been familiar with his letters. He had a deep knowledge of scriptures and used them both as oracular texts that predicted the coming of Jesus and as a literary model on which to structure his own narrative of Jesus's life. The importance of scripture for Mark is indicated in the very first verses of the Gospel, in the only direct citation of scripture that he does not attribute to a character in the narrative: "In the beginning of the good news of Jesus Christ, the Son of God. As it is written in the prophet Isaiah, 'See, I am sending my messenger ahead of you, who will prepare your way; the voice of one crying out in the wilderness: "Prepare the way of the Lord, make his paths straight"'" (Mark 1:1–3). For Mark, this scriptural citation (Isaiah 40:3) may not only indicate the theme of his story but also signal his understanding of the purpose of his own community. They were to prepare the way for the coming eschaton.[4]

Mark reinforces this theme with repeated allusions to scripture, most of which are used, like the passage from Isaiah, in order to frame Jesus as the fulfillment of scriptural prophecies. Such allusions are particularly dense in Mark's account of Jesus's arrest and death, although they can be rather subtle. Mark's goal with these allusions appears to be to provide a second level of meaning to those, like him, who understand the scriptural context (Mark 14–16).[5]

Also like Paul, Mark's citation of scripture seems to draw from Greek and Hebrew versions. This pluriformity of scriptural citations indicates that he, like Paul, was working from memory, which was shaped by a jumbled pastiche of passages that he had heard. Yet the author Mark did not only hear, he also apparently read. In one passage, Mark has Jesus rebuke the Sadducees by citing a scriptural passage, prefacing the citation with the words "Have you not *read* in the book of Moses" (12:26). Elsewhere too Mark attributes this formula to Jesus (2:25, 12:10). Mark was assuming here an environment in which reading a written text was a possibility.

Mark does one thing that Paul never does: he puts scripture in Jesus's mouth. Paul almost always directly quotes scripture in order to prove that Jesus "fulfills" the scriptural prophecy. Mark apparently knew of stories that were circulating about Jesus. In retelling them, though, he added the scriptural citations, transforming Jesus into a citer of scripture. The scripture-citing Jesus of Mark and the other Gospels is thus not an accurate representation of the historical Jesus. He is the creation of later writers who have come to see Jesus through scripture, and who believed that Jesus himself either would have or should have done so as well.[6]

The Gospel of Mark was probably intended for a Gentile audience. Mark knew that those in his audience would have little or no direct knowledge of scripture, and to the extent that they did, they would have been less receptive to its authority. He may himself have seen the importance of scripture for understanding Jesus, but he limited himself to allusions and literary citations. In part he probably could not help himself, as much of his own literary training may have come in the form of scriptural study. In part he was also hoping that like-minded individuals would also read his tract and better relate to his own understanding. It was a tract that could thus be read on two levels.

Not addressed to any particular community and written in an easy-to-read narrative form, Mark's Gospel circulated among the small communities of Christ-believers. While the name Mark was not yet attached to the Gospel, it would have quickly gained authority through its correct "prophecies" concerning the destruction of the Jerusalem temple—the destruction confirmed the (perhaps post facto) prediction and thus enhanced its prestige (Mark 13:9–14). Like Paul's letters, it was read aloud within the communities among which it circulated.[7] Mark's Gospel thus existed in both written and oral form, and while some scribes aimed for fidelity as they made copies for further circulation, others sought to improve on the story as a result of the feedback that they would have received from those listening to the public recitations. This is the context that generated two later Gospels, Matthew and Luke, although each of these authors revised Mark in very different ways.

To many early communities of Christ-believers, Mark would not have been very satisfying. Mark begins his story of Jesus's life in the middle, with his baptism by John the Baptist when he was, we presume, an adolescent or young adult. He ends it abruptly with Jesus's appearance, after he was entombed, to Mary Magdalene, Mary the mother of James, and Salome. Mark's style is choppy throughout and lacks the drama and adventure of the Hellenistic novels that were circulating at the time. So it is not a surprise that not long after Mark began to be read aloud within these communities another educated Jew would decide to rewrite an improved version. This author, whose work was the Gospel of Matthew, we will call Matthew, although like Mark he was certainly never a disciple of Jesus.[8]

Mark's opening with Jesus's baptism must have raised questions for his audience. Where did this man come from? Who were his parents? Earlier scriptural accounts with which they might have been familiar in at least some form tell of the births of great prophets and heroes such as Samuel and Sampson. What about Jesus? Matthew's concise but powerful narrative answers this question while at the same time framing Jesus's life, far more than Mark did, as a fulfillment of biblical prophecies. Beginning with a genealogical account that moves from Abraham to David to Joseph, the father of Jesus, Matthew positions Jesus as the rightful heir of God's promises to both Abraham and David. Joseph, though he serves only a minor role in the Gospel, has a vitally necessary one: he allows for this line of descent to be traced through the fathers. Matthew invents (or perhaps picks up on a legend he heard) the now-famous story of Jesus's birth from the virgin Mary. Then, as today, it makes for a compelling story.

Mark's listeners would also have been disappointed by the ending. Mark ends with a very brief account of Jesus's resurrection. Matthew expands this, adding a rousing story of the risen Jesus appearing to his disciples and instructing them to "make disciples in all nations" (28:19). Later scribes, acquainted with Matthew, were in fact so dissatisfied with the ending to Mark that they appended a new one more in line with Matthew.[9]

Matthew also repeatedly heightened the drama of Mark's story, mostly at the expense of the Jews. For example, he adds to the Mark narrative a long passage in which Jesus condemns scribes and Pharisees for hypocrisy (23:1–36). In Mark, when the crowd, urged by the high priests, asks Pilate not to release Jesus, Mark succinctly says that "Pilate, wishing to satisfy the crowd, released Barabbas for them" (15:15). Matthew, telling the same story, reports that "when Pilate saw that he could do nothing, but rather that a riot was beginning, he took some water and washed his hands before the crowd, saying, 'I am innocent of this man's blood; see to it yourselves.' Then the people as a whole answered, 'his blood be on us and on our children!'" (27:24–25). It was Matthew's flair for the dramatic that made his version of the Passion narrative among the more widely popular for many centuries afterward.

When rewriting Mark, though, Matthew sought not only to spice it up. He also was concerned to set the record straight. He had come across a collection of sayings of Jesus. This collection probably existed in written form, but it may also have circulated orally. Scholars today label this hypothetical source—we have no direct evidence for its existence—Q, from the German *Quelle*, or source. Noticing that Mark did not include these Jesus sayings in his narrative, Matthew added them in order to provide a fuller, more authoritative narrative, although he did not hesitate to make changes in order to better fit his message.[10]

Matthew appears to have been an educated Jew writing for ethnically Jewish Christ-believers. Scholars understand his seemingly anti-Jewish tendency as the result of his community's "especially vigorous debate" with the other Jews. That is, the polemics are targeted internally rather than externally. His use of scripture too points to a Jewish audience, or at least one for whom the authority of scripture and its key to understanding Jesus's life is taken for granted.[11]

Matthew's use of scripture is like Mark on steroids. Matthew cites almost every one of the scriptural passages found in Mark, and then quite a few more, attributing most to Jesus himself. Jesus is the one who cites and interprets scripture. Matthew, like Paul and Mark, locates the value of scripture in its prophecies, which Jesus has come to fulfill. He simply extends this much further than his predecessors.[12]

Mark and Matthew appear to have had similar backgrounds as ethnic Jews who had received intensive training in scripture, probably as children. They thus shared the conception of scripture, popular in Judea at that time, as a set of divine prophecies. Their actual citation and use of scripture in their writings, though, was to some extent determined by their intended audiences. Matthew, writing for a Jewish audience, thus created a much tighter link between Jesus and scripture than did either Mark or Paul.

Mark proved unsatisfying not only to the author of Matthew but also to the author of Luke. Luke wrote around 80 CE, with the express intention of setting the record straight about Jesus's life.[13]

Luke's improvements of Mark were similar to those of Matthew. He added an infancy narrative at the beginning. Luke weaved the story of John the Baptist's birth into that of Jesus's, intertwining their stories to make clear the divine role that John would play in prophesying the coming of Jesus. Luke also added a scene (absent from Matthew) of the infant Jesus at the Jerusalem temple, where an exceptionally righteous man (Simon) and a prophetess (Anna) foretell his greatness (2:25–38). Luke sought even more than Matthew to heighten Jesus's miraculous nature.

Also like Matthew, Luke added an epilogue to Jesus's death. In this account, Jesus appears to the disciples on the road to Emmaus (24:13–35). He tells his disciples, who do not recognize him, how he had been killed and had risen. "Then, beginning with Moses and all the prophets, he interpreted to them the things about himself in all the scriptures" (v. 27). The disciples later describe this act of interpretation as "opening" scripture (v. 32). After Jesus proves that it is really he in the flesh (which he does by eating a piece of fish), he says "that everything written about me in the law of Moses, the prophets, and the psalms must be fulfilled. Then he opened their minds to understand the scriptures" (vv. 44–45). Luke thus positions Jesus not just as the fulfillment of scriptures but as the very key to their understanding: Jesus himself unlocks their true, secret meaning. This goes beyond Matthew. For Matthew, scriptural prophecies refer to Jesus; scripture and Jesus are distinct from each other. For Luke, scripture and Jesus are more complexly intertwined.[14]

Luke targeted a different audience than Matthew. He was not speaking to Jews who would have taken for granted the authority of scripture. Nor was he speaking, like Mark or Paul in 1 Thessalonians, to a Gentile audience that would have been mystified by claims based on scripture. Instead, his audience, like that of some of Paul's letters, is those Gentiles who had some familiarity with scripture already and who were open to learning more, but who needed a guide. This is the community of "God-fearers," as he calls them.

Luke was also, as far as we can tell, the author of the book of Acts. This book focuses on the history of the early Christ-believers from the death of Jesus until Paul is summoned to Rome, focusing mainly on Paul. Early in the book he includes the story of the "Ethiopian eunuch," which I believe is directed at this audience of God-fearers. The story is strategically placed after the accounts of Paul's failure to convince his fellow Jews that Jesus is the messiah. At that point, Luke switches scenes. He now tells a story of the apostle Philip who comes across the eunuch (a high but unspecified government official) while he was returning home after worshipping in the temple. We never learn if this Ethiopian eunuch is Jewish or not, and if the latter, how and why he was at the temple. Nor do we ever learn why it is that he happened to be reading a scroll of Isaiah when Philip found him, especially as he has no idea how to read it (Acts 8: 26–40). This strange character, according to Luke, quickly submitted to baptism at Philip's urging, and at that point Philip magically disappeared. Not clearly indicated as either Jew or Gentile, the temple-worshipping, Isaiah-reading Ethiopian eunuch signaled for Luke the transition to a new mission. Now Luke turns his attention to Paul and the mission to the Gentiles. The story is one of the ways in which Luke, as an author, reached out to try to make a connection to his audience of scripture-reading Gentiles, who must have felt themselves as unmoored and in between as the Ethiopian eunuch.

To these Gentiles, Luke is saying that Jesus is their key to understanding scripture. This was a message that some Jews might well accept, but it was really aimed at those who came to scripture from the outside and found it puzzling. It may have been a small audience, but it was a distinctive one. It would also generate a dual message. On the one hand, scripture gave proof that Jesus was the true messiah. On the other hand, Jesus gave authority to scripture. This, as we will shortly see, would become a critical dialectical issue among early Christians.

For Luke, scripture played another important role. One of the attractions that Jesus had, especially (but not only) for Gentiles, was his possession of supernatural powers. The stories of his use of these powers rather than the citations of scripture would have had much more impact on Luke's audience. Yet, as Luke recognized, the line between this kind of belief and belief in other contemporary "magicians" was thin. One of his stories, about the magician Simon who became a believer in Jesus, is meant to address precisely this point (Acts 8:9–13). Jesus is not just any ordinary magician. We know this because scripture has told us so.

The Gospel of John is a different story altogether. John used neither Mark nor Q in his tract—we do not know if that was because he did not know them or he chose to ignore them. He was probably writing to a Jewish audience in the late first century CE.[15]

John is generally recognized as the most theological of all of the Gospels. It is John, and only John, that directly identifies Jesus as "the Word became flesh" (1:14). John is far more explicit than Mark and Matthew about the meaning of Jesus's life. In one passage, John has Jesus explain the relationship between him and his "Father," God, an issue that remains critical among modern Christian theologians (5:20–24).

How, though, does the author "know" this? Whereas the other Gospel writers tend to support their assertions about Jesus with references to scripture, the author of John does not. Matthew assumes that his audience accepts the authority of scripture and then uses it to prove his claims about Jesus. John, on the other hand, simply assumes that his audience accepts Jesus. He is writing in order to strengthen the faith of a community that has already accepted the Gospel's basic tenets, although probably in a less articulate and more inchoate form.[16]

Scripture thus was secondary for John, subsumed to the message. He is clearly comfortable with it, alluding to it frequently. He tends to quote from the Septuagint, although he uses the Hebrew version when it better suits his needs. His use of the scripture, especially when seen against Paul and the synoptic Gospels, is quite distinctive.[17]

John employs scripture aggressively. Using a conventional set of citations that derive mainly from "the Bible of the Early Church," the author of John in effect wields these verses to show that Jews are blind to their own authoritative texts. Scripture is used here less to convince the Gospel's readers that Jesus is their fulfillment (after all, they already accept Jesus's divinity) than to emphasize and explain Jewish blindness.[18]

John has long been recognized as both the most Jewish and anti-Jewish of all the canonical Gospels. The Gospel goes well beyond accusing the Jews of blindness. In Matthew, the chief priests and elders of the Jews prosecuted Jesus before Pilate (27:11–14). John's account is far more elaborate and takes place in front of "the Jews" (18:28–19:16). In one particularly noxious passage Jesus accuses the Jews who will not accept him as having Satan as a father (8:44). "The Jews" agreed that "anyone who confessed Jesus to be the Messiah would be put out of the synagogue" (9:28). The Jews—not just their leaders—actively persecute Jesus and his followers.

John emerges from a community that was pushed over the edge. The "vigorous debate" between Jewish groups had in John's audience become openly hostile. Excluded from the Jewish community, these Christ-believers would have been pushed into a kind of no-man's land. John responded by lashing out and declaring them to be the new Israel, the real people of the covenant. Scripture, though, was strongly associated with the Jews and their synagogues. The author of John is not ready to abandon scripture altogether, but he does displace its importance in favor of Jesus as the prime vehicle of God's revelation. Scripture was still relevant, but now theologically less so.[19]

For the first four centuries of its existence, "Christianity," as it came to be known, was still trying to find its legs. The communities of Christ-believers were remarkably diverse, as we might expect from such a loosely organized group. Mark, Matthew, Luke, and John reveal only a sliver of that diversity. These Gospels circulated separately and the reception that they received in different communities varied according to the needs and sensitivities of each. A community whose members had strong Jewish associations, for example, might be attracted to Matthew. With Matthew in hand, there would be no need for Mark or Luke, and John would have been off-putting. The more distant a community was from the Jewish community—or the more hostility that it felt toward it—the more it might be attracted to John. Mixed communities of Jews and Gentiles in which the latter felt drawn to the synagogue and its scriptures might have gravitated to Luke. Unsurprisingly, from surviving manuscript evidence it appears that Mark, the least developed of the Gospels, circulated far less widely than the others.[20]

Yet many other communities, perhaps even most of them, may never have been exposed to these four Gospels. Instead, they may have seen one of the many other retellings of the story of Jesus and his early followers. These "gospels" and other writings—excluded from the canonical New Testament—are known to us today through isolated quotations in other texts that did survive, manuscripts and, most important, the Nag Hammadi finds in Egypt. They show an extensive Christian literary culture in the first centuries of this era.

In scope and importance for the study of ancient religion, the finds in Nag Hammadi rival those of Qumran. In 1945, a set of codices written in Coptic (a form of late Egyptian written in a modified Greek alphabet) was discovered in Nag Hammadi in Upper Egypt.[21] These Coptic writings were, for the most part, translations of ancient Greek Christian texts. They contain a variety of different kinds of texts, from the Gospel of Thomas—a story of Jesus's life told through the eyes of his disciple Thomas—to writings of Valentinus and his school, the Gnostic heretics, as they were known to Christian Orthodox writers.

The Nag Hammadi documents complement a large corpus of early Christian literature that survived in other forms, mostly as forgotten manuscripts. Together, this "apocryphal" Christian literature, like the tracts that eventually became part of the New Testament, fall into four genres. Mark, Matthew, Luke, John, and Thomas are all "gospels"; they tell the story of Jesus's life. Thomas was perhaps the most popular of all of the gospels that were not canonized, but there were many more. There are gospels attributed to Peter, Mary, Philip, Judas, and James, as well as fragments of many other gospels too incomplete to assign.[22] We do not know the context in which these gospels were produced, but it is not a stretch to imagine that many emerged out of an oral culture of storytelling. Stories and sayings were told and retold, improved upon in response to the reaction of the listeners, and at random points in this process put into writing. As with the Gospels that would become canonical, these other gospels gained varying amounts of authority—or none at all—within local Christian communities based on community sensibility.

A second popular genre of Christian writing was acts. Like Luke's Acts of the Apostles, acts were narratives of events that occurred (mostly) to Christian heroes and holy people after Jesus's death. We have acts of John, Paul, Thecla, Andrew Thomas, Peter, and even Pilate.[23] These were often rousingly good stories (the Acts of Thecla, with its depictions of the naked Thecla in the amphitheater before being martyred, was particularly popular) that revealed God's saving power.

The third popular genre was the epistle. The New Testament contains, in addition to Paul's genuine epistles, several others that were most likely written by others but were attributed to Paul.[24] While the New Testament contains several other epistles as well (such as Hebrews, James, and 1 and 2 Peter), scores more existed, such as 1 and 2 Clement and the Letter of Barnabas. Although these texts are structured as letters, many of them were not actually written to be sent to particular communities.

The epistle, like the novel, was a popular ancient literary genre, written to be circulated more widely. Some of these letters gained status within particular communities because they were believed to have really been written by Paul or other holy figures. Others would have gained status because additionally (or perhaps even with doubts about their authenticity) their content resonated with the community.

The fourth, vaguer genre is that of visions and revelatory texts, such as the canonical book of Revelation. We know of a large number of such Christian texts, including the Shepherd of Hermas and the apocalypses of Peter and Paul. This is the same genre as books such as 1 Enoch and 4 Ezra, usually revelations by divine beings to the author concerning the future.

Most of these writings are difficult to date with much precision, and several of them were undoubtedly written after the first century or early second century CE. Taken together, however, they point to a nascent and burgeoning Christian literary culture. The second-generation Christian community contained more Gentiles, often educated, than in Paul's day. These "cultural producers" engaged previous Christian literature, stories, and ideas, in the process creating new literary works. These literary works may or may not have circulated widely, and they may or may not have found audiences willing to grant them authority. The gospel of the Hebrews, known only because it is mentioned and cited in snippets by several later church fathers, did appear to have some authority in at least one community. Whether, however, texts like the Paraphrase of Shem—a revelatory text known only from the Nag Hammadi discoveries that reports that the winds "received in their womb foam from the penis of the demons" to produce barren wives and sterile husbands—ever gained traction is an open question.[25]

This large body of early Christian literature also demonstrates that Christians vigorously debated, implicitly and explicitly, the continued relevance of earlier authoritative texts. Christians were well represented on the extremes. Some Christians asserted that since the coming of Jesus all earlier texts ceased to have any authority. Other Christian groups asserted not only that the Jewish scriptures remained relevant (the position shared by all the canonical Gospels) but that its laws remained authoritative. And then, of course, there were many more nuanced positions in the middle.

Many of the noncanonical Christian writings from this time simply ignored Jewish scriptures. The Gospel of Thomas, for example, is more of a collection of sayings of Jesus than a narrative story, but unlike the canonical Gospels, in Thomas Jesus never actually cites a scriptural verse. The extant fragment of the gospel of Peter contains the story of Jesus's crucifixion and burial that is similar to the narratives in the canonical Gospels, but unlike them it does not contain any notice that the acts fulfilled biblical prophecies. The "Infancy Gospel of Thomas"—a popular collection of stories of Jesus's childhood—describes Joseph's attempt to educate Jesus, which of course failed because Jesus was already all-wise, amazing his teachers with his knowledge. That knowledge, however, is never described as scriptural. He was to be educated in letters but he reveals their true, symbolic meaning. Even when he is depicted picking up a book, that book is not described as scriptural.[26] It is as if earlier authoritative texts did not exist. So too, characters in the acts do not cite scripture (as they do in Acts of the Apostles), and scriptural citations are entirely absent from many of the epistles.

On the other extreme, though, were those believers in Jesus who, more in the mold of the authors of the (not yet) canonical Gospels, believed in the divinity and authority of the Hebrew Bible. Some of these groups even went a step further. Building on their understanding of the apostle Peter (and against Paul) and what he represented, they argued that the laws of scripture remained in effect, even after the coming of Jesus. Later church fathers were particularly hostile to one such group that they called the Ebionites.[27]

While Ebionite writings survive only as a few sporadic quotations by church fathers, another set of writings known today as the Pseudo-Clementines probably generally reflects their approach. Scripture and its law remained relevant to their authors. While these authors primarily used Peter as their mouthpiece, one letter, labeled 3 Corinthians, has Paul defend the authority of the prophets of the Jewish scriptures. Another letter, attributed to Barnabas, vigorously attacks the Jewish misunderstanding of their own scriptures while at the same time asserting their continuing importance.[28]

Some of the Nag Hammadi texts take a stance between these two extremes. Although they almost never directly cite scripture, they do frequently allude to it. Their myths are themselves rewritings of those of the book of Genesis, usually (but not always) without acknowledgment. We are still not sure if these allusions meant that the author wanted his or her audience to understand the writing against the "base text," or whether he or she was hoping not to get caught. One tract develops a complex understanding of Jewish scriptures as an admixture of truly good divine (albeit from a secondary divinity) revelation and corruption.[29] In any case, though, scripture was not so diminished as to be ignored.

The end of the first century CE was awash in Christian texts. Whatever their authors intended, though, these texts were rarely seen as "scripture" by the communities that read them.

Many of these texts would have been circulated primarily through impromptu public readings. When Paul sent a letter to a community, he expected that it would be read aloud. "And when this letter has been read among you," the author writes, "have it read also in the church of the Laodiceans; and see that you read also the letter from Laodicea" (Colossians 4:16). The role of the public reading of the letter seems to be less a matter of worship than of public (surrogate) teaching and instruction. Only a bit later was a more regular institutionalized public reading of Christian texts (or anything at all, for that matter) established.[30]

We can imagine that some Christian communities at this time occasionally read aloud from public letters or gospels that arrived or that they particularly liked. Such a practice was probably more common among those who were familiar with the regular readings of scripture in Jewish synagogues; the public reading of texts within a worship service would have seemed quite odd to a Gentile who had no previous exposure to such a practice. Wealthier members, of course, could purchase and read such literature on their own. Particularly learned and abstruse texts, like those of the Gnostics, were intended more for private (or classroom?) study than for liturgical function. They helped to unlock the key to salvation, but they were not themselves agents of salvation.

By the end of the first century CE all Christians would believe that Christ and his acts on earth constituted the key to salvation. What function, then, did texts serve? Did they have authority, and if so, of what kind? This was a question that would come to divide Christian communities. Early Jewish writers, such as Paul and the authors of the canonical Gospels, assumed the prophetic authority of scripture. They frequently wrote to Jewish communities of Christ-believers that would have shared this assumption. To the extent that they would have considered the author to himself have prophetic authority, they may have accepted the new writing as also authoritative, thus also confirming the authority of the texts that he cites (2 Peter 3:15–16). Mainly, though, these texts were read as stories conveying important messages.

A somewhat different dynamic was present in Christian communities that were largely or entirely Gentile. For many Gentiles, both the Jewish scriptures and the texts that cited them had little meaning or authority. They were readily attracted to the message of Jesus and salvation but did not see the need to put it in the context of this much older story of God's covenant with Israel. They created and read alternative accounts of Jesus's life that stood independently of Jewish scriptures. These were texts meant to teach and edify. They too were not, at this stage, seen as authoritative.

Other Gentile communities, though, did not dismiss these earlier texts, however puzzling they appeared. Some may have been attracted by the content of some of these texts. John, for example, appears to have been widely read in antiquity, probably because it told a good, powerful story with a message that resonated with its audience, which did not need to know or accept the Jewish scriptures to understand the message or argument. Yet the fact that John *does* contain scripture is not irrelevant. Once a community began to assign authority to a text like John, it would soon have to wrestle with the status of the scriptural texts that the author regarded as authoritative.

The early Christian focus on the message or lesson of the text had two powerful implications, especially when seen against contemporary Jewish practice. The first was on the practice of interpretation. Put simply, it hardly needed to exist. As long as these Christian tracts were read as stories and lessons and not as authoritative texts, they did not lend themselves to the kind of detailed attention to language that characterized the writings of some contemporary Jewish authors, like Paul himself. The second implication was the treatment of the text as a physical object. By the second half of the first century, the "scroll of the Law" was seen by Jews as a symbol; a Roman ripping up such a scroll could lead to a riot.

The actual content of the scroll was almost secondary. Early Christians, though, did not appear to value their "religious" texts, as physical objects, any more than any other texts. A copy of one of Paul's letters or a gospel, for example, might be read aloud in a church or studied privately, but the physical scroll was treated and stored like any "secular" text. The message mattered, not the precise words with which it was written or the scroll on which it was inscribed.

These were not mere theoretical or academic issues. They cut to the heart of nascent Christian practice. Did texts have authority? If so, which texts, and what kind of authority? Christians would spend the next century arguing bitterly about these issues, ultimately arriving at a set of answers that would shape not only their own communities but the Jewish ones as well.

14 Early Christians: Rome and Egypt, 100–200 CE

If you were a Christian in the early second century who lived in a relatively isolated, low-profile house church in a city somewhere in the Roman Empire—just an ordinary, middle-class believer with perhaps some basic literacy skills—it might never have occurred to you that the Christian world was full of different, sometimes contradictory texts. Even if that fact somehow came to your attention—maybe a visiting Christian from another community brought with him such a conflicting text— you would probably have taken it in stride. After all, why shouldn't there be other texts?

If, however, you were a member of the learned elite—perhaps a well-off, well-educated Gentile who converted to Christianity—the situation might begin to make you a little uneasy. Having access to written scrolls of the various documents, you might begin to notice that they didn't all cohere. You might notice, for example, that the gospels (both those that would become canonical and those that wouldn't) that tell the story of Jesus's life differ in small and large ways. You would certainly notice that Mark and John do not mention anything about Jesus's birth and that the accounts in Matthew and Luke contain discrepancies. As you probed deeper, all kinds of small contradictions would appear. In one of the miracle stories in Matthew, a man beseeched Jesus concerning his dead daughter, who in the version in Luke is not yet dead (Matthew 9:18; Luke 8:42). Small differences, to be sure, but these are the kinds of differences that you would have been trained to flag as problems. As they piled up they became increasingly difficult to explain.

Small textual differences would probably not have disturbed you as much as doctrinal ones. As an elite man (and the rare woman) educated in the Roman Empire, whether in a primarily Greek or Latin city, you learned philosophy and were taught that ideas should be systematic and coherent. The scriptural texts you were reading were neither. As a new Christian, you were drawn to the religion due to the power of its ideas, and if you believed that Christ was entirely a divine being it might disturb you to discover that according to some of these texts he actually walked, talked, ate, suffered, and died like a human.

You might have also been concerned about the production of new revelatory texts. Christians, like Jews, continued to produce texts that recounted direct divine revelations. The Shepherd of Hermas, for example, was a collection of Christian visions from the second century CE that was extremely popular among Christians in Egypt at this time. A revelatory text requires that you trust the author, who almost always hid behind a pseudonym. To the extent that new writings were independent of previous texts and stories, they also presented a potential threat to established authority.

Now imagine that as a literate, educated, sincere new Christian you did not live in some far-flung city somewhere in the Roman Empire but in Rome itself. Rome was the pulsing, teeming epicenter of the world, a kind of New York, Paris, Washington, and London rolled into one. It was large and populous, swollen with the booty of its conquests, both material and human. Despite the political spasms through most of the first century, the city had developed a vibrant intellectual culture by the early second, displacing both Athens and Alexandria in reputation. Many of these Roman intellectuals were originally "imported," which is a polite way of saying that they were either brought as captives, mainly from the Greek East, or as political hostages. Once in Rome, they often found patrons among the Roman aristocratic families (or even the imperial court). Many others flocked to Rome looking both for riches and intellectual stimulation. There they would join fellow travelers from near and far.[1]

In such a large city, not all of them would meet, but through the tight social networks many would. They would gather on occasion to trade ideas and perform their latest works in declamations, the Roman equivalent of literary salons. In these forums they not only enjoyed each other's company but also competed to maintain the support of their (hopefully delighted) patrons, their prestige, and their place in the pecking order.

In the second century the number of Jewish and Christian intellectuals in Rome increased dramatically. They arrived there for many of the same reasons that everyone else did. The Jewish intellectual in Rome about whom we know the most, Josephus, was brought as a captive but was patronized by the emperor and allowed to write in comfort. Christian intellectuals, such as Justin (later surnamed Martyr) and Marcion, began to arrive from the Greek East simply because that is where an intellectual from the Greek East went in order to be in the thick of things, despite the dangers that faced outspoken Christians at that time. These Jews and Christians, playing and working within a distinctively Roman intellectual environment, were forced to confront difficult questions and to articulate answers that could stand up to the critical scrutiny of their peers. Which texts are important or authoritative, and which are just mere amusements? These are the kinds of intellectual questions that emerged from this social and intellectual environment and that gave birth to the notion of the biblical canon.

Prior to 100 CE, as we have seen, Jews often categorized their scriptures on the basis of their purported authors. The books that constitute the Pentateuch were known as the law of Moses, with other books being lumped together with the books of the prophets or David. We do not know precisely which Jews thought which books went into which category. The Temple Scroll, for example, may have been seen as part of the "law of Moses" by some. It is not at all clear how these categories would have worked for many of the books that became part of the Hebrew Bible. Books such as Judges had long been part of the Deuteronomistic history, but did not really fall into the category of the "law of Moses." Ezra and Nehemiah were not prophets, and a variety of other texts, such as Ruth and Esther, would have been equally difficult to pigeonhole. Moreover, where would books such as 1 Enoch and Jubilees fit, for those who ascribed authority to them? These questions may have concerned a few particularly punctilious intellectuals, but most Jews would not have given them much thought.

So too, I doubt that most Jews would have given much thought to whether particular texts were "really" scripture or not. If you heard the public recitation from a scroll of oracles or stories that were ascribed to a revered prophet whose name you recognized, as long as the contents did not overtly challenge your preconceptions of what should be in such a text, why doubt its authenticity? There was not very much at stake. This is why prior to the second century CE, nobody thought to create a "closed canon," a definitive list of specific books that should be considered "scripture."

The notion that Jews had a closed canon of scripture is first found in the writings of Josephus. The Jews, he confidently states, ascribe authority to only twenty-two books. There is, however, less to this statement than meets the eye. As we shall shortly see, this is not a description of a well-known and accepted Jewish canon. It is, rather, the somewhat wishful thinking of a Jewish intellectual.

Josephus's assertion that Jews ascribe authority to a limited number of books appears in only a single place. In the 90s, in the comfort of his Roman villa, Josephus had written *Jewish Antiquities*, a massive history that traces the history of the Jews from the beginning of time to the present. He followed this up quickly with an apologetic tract against a Greek Alexandrian intellectual named Apion. Apion had earlier written a tract attacking the Jews, which we know only through Josephus's response to it. In it, Apion asserted that since only later Greek historians noticed the Jews, they must be a relatively recent people. The Jews did not have the ancient and storied past that Josephus claimed for them.[2]

Josephus responds to this, as well as Apion's many other critiques, in a two-book tract called *Against Apion*. The Greek historians, he argues, were themselves so full of contradictions that they could not be trusted. By contrast, the Jews, and more specifically the priests, had kept scrupulous records. "We," unlike the Greek historians, he claims, "do not possess myriads of inconsistent books, conflicting with each other. Our books, those which are justly accredited, are but two and twenty, and contain the record of all time." He then classifies these books. The first five are the books of Moses, consisting of "the traditional history from the birth of man down to the death of the lawgiver." The next thirteen books are from the prophets. The last four books "contain hymns to God and precepts for the conduct of human life." But the real proof of the fidelity of these books is the reverence in which Jews have held them: "For, although such long ages have now passed, no one has ventured either to add, or to remove, or to alter a syllable; and it is an instinct with every Jew, from the day of his birth, to regard them as the decrees of God, to abide by them, and, if need be, cheerfully to die for them. Time and again ere now the sight has been witnessed of prisoners enduring tortures and death in every form in the theatres, rather than utter a single word against the laws and the allied documents."[3]

The core of Josephus's argument is that Jewish scripture was so carefully preserved that it must be an authentic record of the past. It must therefore be taken more seriously than the Greek historians cited by Apion.

Josephus's assertion that the Jews have only these twenty-two books is not exactly a fiction, but it is also not exactly the whole truth. In Rome, Josephus would have been exposed to a more limited set of Jewish "scriptures" than he had encountered in Judea. By the second century, these scriptures would have been the Greek translations of the books that more or less would end up in the Jewish Bible. He would have been familiar with all or most of these books (or at least their purported authors) from Judea, although he also knew of others to which he or others ascribed different levels of authority.[4]

But an implicit collection of texts to which most Jews would have ascribed authority is not really a canon, and that is not in any case what Josephus is after here. His point is not that Jews had a canon, only that unlike the Greeks they did not have contradictory histories (although given biblical inconsistency, this also is not entirely true). Josephus is engaging in a bit of "canon formation" for his own rhetorical purposes. He certainly adds another rhetorical flourish at the end of the passage: while Jews did sacrifice themselves rather than contravene the divine laws (as they understood them), it is unlikely that they also suffered death for the "allied documents," which is itself a term "rather awkwardly tacked on here," as one scholar notes.[5]

I would like to suggest that Josephus's concept of scripture in fact developed specifically in Rome. This does not mean that Josephus did not learn scripture in Jerusalem; he certainly did. In his autobiography,

Josephus relates that he so excelled at his education that when he was fourteen the chief priests and elders used to come to consult him about particulars of the "laws." Josephus's education was probably similar to his contemporary Paul's. He learned to read and write Hebrew and Greek. Even his own bragging, though, does not necessarily indicate that he excelled in the study of scripture per se. His knowledge of the laws derived from some combination of traditional practices and scripture. He tells us that after trying out the different Jewish schools of thought, he decided to govern his life according to the Pharisees, which might indicate that he put more stock in tradition than scripture.[6]

Josephus's earliest composition, when he was fresh in Rome, exhibits limited interest in and knowledge of scripture. Explaining why he begins his account with the first revolt against Rome in the second century BCE, he writes that "many Jews before me have accurately recorded the history of our ancestors, and . . . these records have been translated by certain Greeks into their native tongue without serious error." His reference here is to the writings of earlier Jewish historians, not to the history told in scripture. This stands in contrast to *Jewish Antiquities*, written after a couple of decades in Rome, in which he uses scripture as historical sources. In short passages throughout *Jewish War* he evokes scripture, but he never cites it explicitly, as we might expect in a work claimed to have been written primarily for a Jewish audience. When Josephus relates the biblical story of Abraham in *Jewish War*, he attributes it not to scripture but to the inhabitants of Hebron. Josephus has internalized certain scriptural stories, but he shows little evidence of engaging with the written text of scripture in any systematic way. In one passage, he treats it like a collection of oracles, which would have been in line with the way that most Jerusalem Jews in the first century would have seen it.[7]

Now it is entirely possible that this is merely due to the genre and particular purpose of *Jewish War*, but it does stand in sharp contrast to his later work, *Jewish Antiquities*, written after he was well settled in Rome. Most of this work is a summary of the biblical narrative, smoothed and molded, of course, according to his needs. Throughout this work Josephus demonstrates a much sharper awareness of the "holy writings." He portrays Moses as the ideal lawgiver, much as Philo had done. Despite what I believe to be the importance of the Greek translations of scripture for his own understanding, he reflects a patriotic streak by calling them secondary to the Hebrew original. In his prologue to *Jewish Antiquities* he claims that he had meant to tell this history in *Jewish War*, but his insecurity about writing in Greek at the time kept him from doing so; as his preface to *Jewish War* shows, this is a bald lie.[8] He was at best ambivalent about considering scripture a historical source.

Josephus relates that on the fall of the temple Titus gave him a gift of "holy books."[9] This is the term that Josephus uses most frequently in his later works to refer to scriptures, and it is possible that this was the first time that he had possessed a copy of them. Over the next two decades Josephus worked his way through them systematically and within the context of the larger Roman intellectual circles in which he traveled. Josephus's notion of authoritative scriptures evolved and grew as a response to his participation in these circles.

Justin Martyr, like Josephus, wrestled with the issue of Jewish scriptural authority. The problem that he was trying to address, however, was different. Josephus wanted to prove that Jewish scriptures provided a more accurate account of the past than did the contradictory Greek histories. Justin, though, could not care less about the historical accuracy of scripture. He, instead, saw scripture—and here he quite specifically means the Septuagint—as a collection of authentic divine oracles that foretold the coming of Christ and thus should have a place in Christian life.

In contrast to Josephus, Justin Martyr arrived in Rome a free man. Justin was born around 100 CE (around the time Josephus died) in Nabulus, a thriving city in Samaria, into a Gentile family of some means. As befitting a boy in his station, he received a traditional Greek education but abandoned his philosophical studies to become a Christian. He soon made his way to Rome, where he taught and wrote until around 165 CE when, legend has it, he was executed by the Romans.[10]

Justin attributes his conversion to Christianity to his encounter with Jewish scriptures. Originally he had been attracted to philosophy and studied with philosophers from different schools. Each of these experiences, he tells us, was unsatisfying: one demanded money, another had no interest in the deity, a third demanded that he learn music, astronomy, and geometry before he would teach him. Eventually, he met "an old man" who converted him to Christianity, convincing him that the purest truth was to be found in the (Hebrew) prophets, who spoke under the influence of the Holy Spirit. The account is undoubtedly tendentious, but it may well reflect the impact that these strange scriptural books, as taught by Christians, would have had on a young, educated, Gentile seeker like Justin.[11]

Justin's Rome was a dangerous place for a Christian. Through the first half of the second century CE, Roman authorities took an increasingly dim view of Christians. For the most part, ordinary, run-of-the-mill, poor, illiterate Christians were of little concern to the authorities. More troubling were the Romans from good, wealthy, and educated families who rejected traditional pious practices. These practices, mainly those that centered on participation in public ceremonies and sacrifices, served several functions: they kept the gods on Rome's side, they reinforced the bond between Romans and their ancestors, and they showed loyalty to the emperor. Like Jews, Christians felt that these public events were idolatrous and forbidden to them. By this time, Romans well understood and respected the Jewish avoidance of these activities, even if they thought them ridiculous. When their own sons and daughters began to reject them, though, they were not as understanding. A "Christian," in the eyes of the Romans, was essentially a traitorous Roman.

Since there were relatively few Christians in the Roman Empire in the second century, Roman authorities never bothered to frame a coherent legal response to this challenge. They maintained a vague "Don't ask, don't tell" policy throughout the empire. The government as such did not pursue Christians, although individuals could charge others with being Christians, a charge that Roman authorities had to take seriously. When denounced, Christians were given ample opportunities to recant. In a famous letter to the emperor Trajan around 111 CE, a Roman governor, Pliny, expresses confusion about how to handle the Christians. He decided that having accused Christians make a token offering before an image of Trajan and curse Jesus would be sufficient to clear them. Trajan agreed with his approach, adding that anonymous denunciations of Christians should be ignored.[12]

Even so, Justin was outraged. He proceeded to write two tracts, now called *1* and *2 Apology*, that attempted to explain to the Roman authorities why they were mistaken to persecute Christians. Like many such tracts from antiquity, these were written more for an already Christian audience than for their putative recipients, the Roman emperor Antoninus Pius (*1 Apology*) and the Roman Senate (*2 Apology*). Nevertheless, the structure and language of their arguments show that Justin also had a non-Christian, non-Jewish audience in mind. His main arguments are logical and factual, attempting to show that Christians are not who the Romans think they are. In pressing his factual case, Justin reveals his knowledge of scripture without actually making an argument from it. Responding to the accusation that Christians evade taxes, for example, Justin states that "everywhere we, more readily than all men, endeavour to pay to those appointed by you the taxes both ordinary and extraordinary," proving this by citing Jesus's statement, "Render therefore to Caesar the things that are Caesar's, and to God the things that are God's."[13] Justin appeals to Jesus, not scripture, as an authority of Christian practice and belief. Justin understood that his Roman readers would have no understanding of scripture and would certainly not regard it as authoritative.

Yet ultimately he could not resist dragging scripture into his argument. Although there was no real need to do this, he had been so taken with the accounts of the gospels and the letters of Paul that he felt that he could not omit the connection between the Christian and the Jewish stories. He also realized, though, that arguing that Jesus fulfilled earlier scriptural prophecies would be meaningless to an audience that did not know them or accept their authority. So he explains his understanding of the books to his Roman audience.

Justin explains Jewish scripture as oracles delivered by God's prophets that have been carefully preserved by the ruling kings. These kings thus created "their own Hebrew library." Drawing now on the story in the Letter of Aristeas, Justin states that these books were sent to Ptolemy at his request, along with translators. They were translated into Greek and faithfully preserved through royal patronage in Alexandria. "They are also in the possession of all Jews throughout the world," he concludes, "but they, though they read, do not understand what is said, but count us foes and enemies."[14]

Justin's explanation of Jewish scripture to the Romans is rather more clever than his grasp of Jewish history (in his account, it is Herod who sent the books to Ptolemy II). He presents scripture as the writings of the Hebrew prophets, carefully guarded by Gentile monarchs. Here was an explanation that Romans could easily understand. It is the same one that attracted Gentiles into the synagogues to hear the readings from these scrolls. These were ancient prophecies, analogous to the Sibylline books that the Romans kept in the Temple of Apollo on the Palatine, where priests guarded and consulted them at the behest of the government. Since the Romans, however, had destroyed the Jewish temple, Justin needed to create another unbroken chain of reliable transmission. That chain, according to Justin, could be found in the Septuagint, not the Hebrew Bible preserved by the Jews. He cites a number of these scriptural prophecies in *1 Apology*, but his Roman audience undoubtedly found them odd: in *2 Apology* he did not once cite scripture.[15]

Justin's contact with scripture had led to his own conversion and he was eager to share his newfound insights with other potential converts. One tract, *Dialogue with Trypho*, ostensibly describes an encounter that he had with a Jew. The vast bulk of the tract consists of Justin battering the Jew Trypho with scriptural citations that, he claims, foretell the coming of Christ. Justin cites from many of the books that would become part of the Jewish Bible, but also included one book, the Wisdom of Solomon, that did not. Trypho remains unconvinced. But Trypho specifically and the Jews generally were not the audience for this tract. It was really written for Gentiles who, like Justin himself, might be attracted by the mystery and force of these ancient and exotic prophecies.[16]

Justin knew that the Jews had a more or less stable set of books that they regarded as divinely revealed and authoritative and claimed that those books were also important for Christians. Indeed, he declared them now Christian books, given over to the Christians on account of Jewish unbelief.[17]

Justin, then, made a strong case to the Gentile Christians of Rome in the mid-second century CE that Jewish scriptures (in Greek translation) were authentic divine oracles that foretold the coming of Christ. Perhaps curiously, he has little interest in Christian texts. Justin seems to know of at least some of the gospels, which he calls "memoirs of apostles," but these play a relatively minor role for him.[18]

They also didn't play much of a role in the lives of most ordinary Christians. Justin provides one of the first descriptions of what Christians would do on Sunday, the Lord's Day. "And on the day called Sunday," Justin Martyr writes, "all who live in cities or in the country gather together to one place, and the memoirs of the apostles or the writings of the prophets are read, as long as time permits." The reading was followed by a sermon, prayer, the Eucharist, and a collection for the poor. It is those latter activities more than the reading that formed the core of Christian service. That is, the *fact* of Christ and his salvation, in which believers could participate via the Eucharist and collection, mattered far more than his words or words about him. There is no testimony from this time that Christians educated their children in scripture, and there is no Christian art from the time that would have (secondarily) exposed Christians to the stories of scripture.[19]

Justin was in Rome at the same time as Marcion, whom he disapprovingly mentions by name.[20] During his time in Rome, Marcion engaged in his own process of "canon formation" in which he attempted to determine which of the many Christian texts then in circulation were genuinely authentic. His conclusions, which entirely excluded Jewish scriptures, would have enraged Justin.

Marcion was born in Asia Minor around 100 CE, the same time as Justin. He was a rich Gentile merchant who decided to use his vast wealth in Rome to further his understanding of Christianity. Marcion knew and rejected Jewish scripture not just as irrelevant for Christians but as the work of a lesser God. Jesus was the revelation, not scripture. Marcion claimed to take his inspiration from Paul, particularly his letter to the Galatians (which was by now circulating between Christian communities as an authoritative text, although not, apparently, for Justin).[21]

Marcion's reliance on Paul, though, created a problem: Paul himself accepted Jewish scriptures as authoritative! In Marcion's thinking this could not have been right. His solution was that the passages in Paul that suggest that he accepted scripture were actually forged—the real Paul did no such thing.[22]

Marcion was troubled by the chaotic state of Christian scripture. Which ones were truly authoritative? To Marcion, those Christian books that relied heavily on Jewish scriptures by definition could not be considered authentic. He settled on a "canon" consisting only of Paul's letters—with the offending parts removed—and a version of Luke's Gospel that had similarly been brought into conformance with Marcion's beliefs. This was in many respects the first attempt to create a Christian "canon."

In creating his short list of authoritative Christian books, though, Marcion did not exactly create a "canon" as we usually understand the word. Marcion was engaged in an intellectual activity that was common to his time; Roman intellectuals too were sorting and classifying "authentic" texts. This was not far from Josephus's own act of "canon formation" fifty years earlier. Marcion's activities, like those of later Christian writers, may also have been intended to help build a community. Marcion established a network of independent churches, and he may have seen this new "canon" as one feature that could help it establish an independent identity.[23]

Josephus, Justin, and Marcion, although all immigrants to Rome, participated in its intellectual culture, in which books played an important part. All were concerned with establishing which books were truly authoritative and in resolving the problems that they saw in them; they approached this task less as religious leaders than as intellectuals. So too did Justin's student, Tatian, also an immigrant to Rome. He harmonized the four Gospels—the now canonical Gospels of Matthew, Mark, Luke, and John—into a single narrative that was probably originally written in Syriac. This work was known as the Diatessaron. The Diatessaron would have made Justin proud; it was the kind of monumental scholarly work that was valued at the time. It became popular, especially in the eastern Roman provinces, but eventually lost out to Irenaeus's establishment of a "four-Gospel" canon.

Marcion set into motion an attempt by Christian intellectuals to determine the role that scripture—Jewish and Christian—should play in the life of their community. In the second century CE, the main figure in this emerging battle was Irenaeus.

Irenaeus was born in Asia Minor in the mid-second century CE. He made his way to Lyons, a thriving Greek city, where he proselytized the Gauls. Little is known of his education or background, or whether he spent any time in Rome on his way to Lyons—some surviving letters indicate that he was at least informed of some of the happenings in Rome at this time.[24] Irenaeus left a significant and lasting impact on the church, but not due to his relatively negligible success among the Gauls.

Irenaeus made his mark as a "heresiologist." Although he was living in the West, his attention seemed focused primarily on his native Asia Minor. He had heard that one particular school of Christian thought, that of Valentinus, was gaining adherents. Valentinus himself was, much like Josephus, a Greek-speaking immigrant to Rome in the early second century. He created a complex and sophisticated theology that in some ways resembled Marcion's. At least as elaborated by his disciples, Valentinus's system involved a sharp break between matter and the spiritual. The task of the true Christian was to engage in intellectual activity ("gnosis") that would lead to true knowledge of the spiritual Christ.[25] While for many Christians Valentinus's system was not radically different from others, it outraged Irenaeus, who responded to it with his massive tract, *Against the Heresies*.

Against the Heresies seeks to explain exactly where the Valentinians, among other contemporary Christian groups, went wrong. In the course of these discussions he eventually arrives at "scripture." On this matter, Irenaeus has two problems with the Valentinians, Marcion, and their ilk. The first was that they believed that true salvation comes from knowledge that is external to any traditional source. The initiate relies on the charismatic authority of the teacher rather than a text or the (developing notion of an) apostolic tradition. For Irenaeus, this cavalier approach to tradition and authority could only lead to heresy.

Irenaeus's other problem centered precisely on the unsettled authority of both Christian scripture in general and the specific writings in particular. On the one hand, Irenaeus castigates Marcion for rejecting texts that Irenaeus thinks are truly authoritative. On the other hand, he is appalled at the Valentinians, who "publish writings of their own composition, and boast of possessing more gospels than there are."[26] To Irenaeus it is clear that there are four, and only four, authoritative Gospels. John, Luke, Matthew, and Mark (curiously, in that order) are the canonical Gospels, the Christian authoritative scripture that supplements the Septuagint.[27] He cites as authoritative many of the books that would become part of the canonical New Testament throughout his writing but does not include them as part of a canonical list, as he does these four Gospels. This leads one to suspect that Irenaeus did not set out to create a New Testament canon. His assertion of the four Gospels as authoritative was a kind of reactive afterthought, an issue that he felt he needed to deal with in the context of much more important theological issues that needed to be addressed. This is comparable to how Josephus dealt with the issue of historical truth. The assertion of canonical books was, for both, incidental and meant to serve a larger rhetorical purpose.

By the end of the second century CE, Christian communities still did not have a united or clear understanding of whether and how scripture—both the Septuagint and the newer Christian writings—should play a role in their faith. Justin and Irenaeus had similar positions that scholars today frequently term "proto-Orthodox." They accepted the authority of the Septuagint (as testimony to the coming of Christ) and a limited number of more recent texts written (they thought) by Paul and the apostles. Marcion, Valentinus, and to some extent even Tatian held different positions.

Through the end of the second century, there really was no "Christian church." There were churches, local, often small, groups of Christians who most often did not have a dedicated building. There was no central institution for educating or certifying the leaders of these churches. Local communities made their own choices in such matters. They did not exist in isolation from each other, though. Both letters and people circulated between the local churches, bringing ideas and texts. They thus formed a loose network that would ultimately begin to harden into a more hierarchical structure centered in Rome. That hardening, though, would not occur until the fourth century.

In the second century it was still very much a local decision whether to assign authority to Jewish scriptures; to accept individual Christian letters, gospels, and revelations as authoritative; to use Marcion's canon, Tatian's gospel, or nothing at all; and to read or not to read from any of these works in public worship services. Communal decisions were often informed by communication with other communities; the pressure to find common ground with other small, like-minded groups also played a role in decisions. This is how "schools" like the Valentinians could spread, and why in Irenaeus's thinking they were a potent threat.

Men like Justin, Marcion, Tatian, Valentinus, and Ireneaus were intellectuals engaged in a largely academic exchange of ideas. They (or their students) wrote for each other and other disciples. Their ideas would filter down into actual communal practices, but they (except, perhaps, for Marcion) were not writing for the general community of Christians. One indication of the gap that existed between this intellectual Christian elite and ordinary Christians can be found in their approach to the actual book of "scripture."

Despite their many disagreements, all the Christian elite I have discussed had a concept of "sacred" scripture. They never discuss the very practical ramifications, though, of what that means in a material sense. Are the books of these sacred scriptures to be prepared and treated just like any other texts? Can I or should I read it in the bathroom? When it begins to decay, should I simply throw it in the trash?

It turns out that for at least many Christian communities in Egypt from this time, whatever they *thought* of the holiness of these texts, they treated them in a rather ordinary way. The copies of early Christian manuscripts from around the second century CE were utilitarian. They were generally on papyrus rather than the more expensive and durable parchment. They lack the signs both of being written by a professional scribe and of being intended for public recitation. For example, the Greek texts found in Egypt were written with no spaces between words, unlike the marked texts that were used for public recitation. Most of these texts appear to have been personal copies made by the owners for their own reading. They are indistinguishable from the non-Christian Greek texts found in the same area.[28]

Despite their resemblance to these other texts, they do have one distinguishing characteristic: they are written in codex rather than scroll form. The codex offered significant technical advantages over the scroll. Because both sides of the page could be used, it was more economical than the scroll and was generally less bulky and easier to transport. One scholar has suggested that the fact that they were easy to hide made them more attractive to Christians when they were being persecuted. Christians disagreed about many things, but they almost uniformly adopted the codex. Although Greeks, Romans, and Jews continued to use scrolls, nearly all Christian manuscripts from antiquity were written on codices.[29]

In addition to the technical advantages of the codex, it may also have reflected a more popular approach to written text, even when it was "sacred." All of the great classical literature of the era was written on scrolls. The very object of the scroll, even on papyrus, had a certain cachet; scrolls were important objects that could be given as gifts. More utilitarian documents, such as informal letters and receipts, were not written in scrolls but on sheets of papyri. By adopting the form of utilitarian documents rather than that of traditional literary works Christians were also implicitly asserting that the *text* was less important than the *message*; the only function of the text was to convey the message. The written word per se was to be subsumed to the "good news" of Christ and the spirit.

The physical aspects of the text, then, had only secondary (if any) importance. The physical words on a page were just that, devoid of any special status. In fact, almost all the surviving ancient papyri of early Christian texts were found in the ancient *garbage dump* of Oxyrynchus, Egypt.[30] Christians disposed of these texts just as they did their other refuse. The rabbis would proceed in almost a directly opposite direction.

15 The Rabbis:
Judea, 100–220 CE

To the inhabitants of Rome in the early second century CE, Judea must have seemed very far away. Three decades after the destruction of the temple there were still, it is true, a few reminders of the Roman conquest of the stubborn province. An inscription at the entrance to the Coliseum reminded the streams of spectators that the emperor Titus had funded its construction from the booty he took from Jerusalem. Small coinage that circulated widely displayed an image of a Roman soldier standing over a mourning woman who personified the defeated province of Judea (fig. 11). Many slaves brought thirty years earlier from Judea, and their descendents, lived in Rome and once in a while might have been seen as living reminders of the conquest. By now, though, the memory of the revolt had largely calcified into brittle patriotic slogans that few Romans would have noticed. Judea was just another captured and distant Roman province, one among scores.[1]

To the residents of Judea, though, Rome was overwhelmingly present. The land continued to bear the scars of the revolt. Jerusalem was full of burned ruins and the areas around it deforested, the lumber having been used by the Roman army during their siege. Villages from Galilee to Masada were destroyed and lay abandoned. The Roman army set up camps in strategic locations and proudly announced its presence. Roman troops would have been frequent visitors to many of the major urban centers throughout Judea. Many Judeans would have still remembered the family members they had lost during the revolt, whether to death or capture. All Judeans were required to remit a special tax, the *fiscus iudaicus*, to pay for their own suppression. The proceeds of this tax went

Figure 11: Rendering of Roman "Judaea capta" coin, personifying the conquest of Rome over Judea.

to the Temple of Jupiter in Rome, a humiliating reminder of their God's powerlessness. Judeans were allowed to resume their lives free of excessive Roman interference or persecution, but many would have regularly experienced humiliations small and large reminding them of what had been lost.

These humiliations must have played at least some part in catalyzing another Judean revolt some sixty years after the destruction of the temple. So too, apparently, did the linking of this revolt and its leaders to the ancient scriptural oracles. A man born as Shimon bar Kosiba became known to at least some of his supporters as Bar Kokhba, the "son of the star." He was to bring freedom and honor to the Judeans, maybe even as God's anointed. The Bar Kokhba revolt, however, was doomed to failure. It took only three years for Rome to efficiently and ruthlessly suppress it.

In the aftermath of this revolt and the devastation that it caused to Judea, many Judeans (at least those who worshipped the God of Israel) headed north to Galilee. Galilee would develop into an area of vibrant Jewish settlement that would flourish over the next several centuries. It was in this environment that the rabbinic movement took shape. "Movement" may in fact be something of a misnomer. Starting a bit after 70, small disciple circles, consisting of Pharisees and Sadducees, among others, began to form. There was some contact between these circles but little real organization. They were a self-styled intellectual elite, with little reach or even desire to reach outside of their individual circles.

Over the course of the second century, these circles would find a common meeting place in the court of a rich patron, the Gamaliel family. The Gamaliels were important not because of their learning but because of their money and influence, which ultimately resulted in some kind of official standing vis-à-vis the Roman authorities. It was here that the Pharisees and Sadducees were finally forced to find common ground and essentially dissolve their own identities in favor of a common "rabbinic" identity.

To this emerging coalition, the status of scripture loomed as an important issue. Was it to remain largely secondary to established traditions, or was it to be the primary and driving force of law and practice? The result was a compromise that looked like a Sadducean victory: scripture won. If it was a victory, though, it was a pyrrhic one. The text was objectified, almost fetishized. Phrases, words, and letters were ripped out of their context for creative interpretation. The text and even the parchment on which it was written became sacrosanct and untouchable, like a snow globe to be admired and cherished. Real power—the power to interpret and deploy the text—was put in the hands of those with the unwritten customs, the Pharisees. If the early Christians chose the message over the text, the early rabbis chose the text over the message.

The Romans saw the defeat of Judea and the destruction of the Jerusalem temple as a defeat not only of the Jews but also of their god. The authors of the canonical New Testament Gospels understood it as the prophetically predicted abandonment of Israel by its God. There is little question that some Jews, theologically shaken, agreed. To them, the God of Israel was tested and found wanting.[2]

To other Jews, though, the destruction of the temple presented less of a theological challenge. Josephus understood the destruction of the temple as God's punishment of Israel for its sins, a traditional explanation that can be found as early as Deuteronomy. "The Deity has fled from the holy places," he writes, "and taken His stand on the side of those with whom you are now at war."[3] Josephus thus disarmed the potential argument that

God was himself defeated by Rome and its own gods. Just as God used Nebuchadnezzar as an agent to punish Israel for its sins in times past, now he was using the Romans.

Probably a decade or two after Josephus wrote these words, a scribe in Judea wrote a tract in Hebrew that, like Josephus, understood the destruction of the temple in traditional theological terms, as a temporary punishment for Israel's sins. At the same time, though, this tract, which we today call 4 Ezra, shows that the Sadducean understanding of scripture as connected to the "heavenly tablets" remained alive and well decades after the temple's destruction. The author of 4 Ezra, in fact, goes beyond these earlier assertions that there existed, somewhere up there, a set of heavenly tablets upon which were inscribed all of human history, past and present. This author instead identifies these tablets with scripture. Jewish scripture contains two levels of meaning. There is the surface, or literal meaning of the text, and then the more important concealed meaning, accessible only to a proper ritual expert.

The author of this tract is a scribe who took on the persona of the biblical Ezra. His choice of this pseudonym, rather than, for example, Enoch or one of the patriarchs, was hardly accidental. Ezra was the archetypal scribe, and this more recent author wanted to anchor his own reflections to scribal authority and tradition. For this author, Ezra, and by extension the author himself, inherited Moses's claim to authority.[4]

Since 4 Ezra is set at the time of the original Ezra (ca. 458 BCE), it uses the destruction of the first Jerusalem temple as a literary device to address the problems raised by the second destruction. Ezra admits that his community has been far from perfect in their observance of the law. But the Gentiles do no better! Why should Israel be punished?

His answer is not particularly original. God's ways are inscrutable and the just will be properly rewarded in the world to come. Ezra seems content with this answer.[5] It is not, in the end, a very sophisticated or satisfying answer to a very troubling theological problem.

The destruction of the temple also provided an opportunity for the author to reflect on the nature of the revelation. At the end of the book, God commands Ezra to take five scribes and many writing tablets with him into a field, where for forty days they will fast and receive dictation from God: "And the Most High gave understanding to the five men, and by turns they wrote what was dictated, in characters which they did not know. They sat forty days, and wrote during the daytime, and ate their bread at night. As for me, I spoke in the daytime and was not silent at night. So during the forty days ninety-four books were written. And when the forty days were ended, the Most High spoke to me, saying, 'Make public the twenty-four books that you wrote first and let the worthy and the unworthy read them; but keep the seventy that were written last, in order to give them to the wise among your people. For in them is the spring of understanding, the fountain of wisdom, and the river of knowledge.'"[6]

For the author, according to this passage, there were two types of written revelation. The first type consists of the "twenty-four books." While earlier authors had asserted the existence of these two different kinds (revealed and concealed) of revelation, none had so explicitly connected the "revealed" revelation to the "twenty-four books." These books are, presumably, the contents of the Hebrew Bible as it more or less exists today.[7] These (and the other) books are written in the "strange characters" of the new Aramaic script, used to this day in Torah scrolls. The author wants to emphasize that since the scribes did not understand what they were writing they could not change the contents. The publicly accessible books, though, are only the tip of the iceberg of God's revelation. The bulk of this revelation is written in the seventy books, accessible only to the wise, which contain the true "river of knowledge."

The author of 4 Ezra saw scripture as holy and authoritative, but he had an expansive understanding of "scripture." He already knew about and accepted the "twenty-four books," although he ascribed them to Ezra rather than Moses. For him, however, this was merely a starting point, the lowest level of access to scripture. Most of God's revelation—and the most important part of it—was "hidden" in books available only to the elite. In these books were not the "traditions" of the Pharisees but the hidden knowledge found in 1 Enoch, Jubilees, and the Dead Sea Scrolls.

The author of 4 Ezra used the destruction of the temple as an opportunity to reaffirm this tradition of a hidden written revelation. The destruction was not a sign of God's abnegation of his covenant with Israel, but was instead an opportunity for God to renew that covenant with a new revelation, even if the new revelation was similar to the former one. This new revelation was closely tied to Ezra, the *scribe*, and to contemporary scribes. 4 Ezra wisely concedes that the "public" revelation is now out of scribal hands; one no longer needs scribes to access this text. By the second century CE, the "twenty-four books" circulated widely enough that a claim that scribes controlled access to them would have been met with skepticism. 4 Ezra responded to this situation by devaluing the worth of these public books. They may be God's revelation but they are the smaller and inferior part of it; the really important part of the revelation is contained in the hidden books controlled by scribes. It is there that one can find the insight and knowledge that explains God's plan.

These are not just any scribes, though. They are scribes who have access to the hidden wisdom. The ability to access such knowledge seems to result more from oracular revelation than technical skill. As in the cases of earlier (pre-)Sadducean texts such as 1 Enoch and Jubilees, it is left unclear how one can gain access to this hidden revelation. What is reasonably clear, though, is that the answer is not simply education. One needs somehow to gain from the divine realm the key to this greater revelation. It is a Sadducean perspective that has turned inward, reinforcing and hardening its stance toward both the authority of the text and the need for an inspired interpretation that is not interpretation at all but just revelation of that which already exists. It is a stance that the Pharisees would oppose.

Following the destruction of Jerusalem and the devastation of Judea, the surviving intellectual elite, consisting of scribes, Sadducees, and Pharisees (among others), scattered. According to later rabbinic accounts, several of them coalesced into a small community at Yavneh (or Jamnia), outside of modern Tel Aviv. Whether this account is true or not (or, as I think likely, has a kernel of truth), the scattered elite and their children would not have much time to settle and restore their standings before the Bar Kokhba revolt displaced them once again.[8]

The first "rabbis" slowly emerged in the period between 70 and 132 CE. They were the few local, landholding elites who had the wealth and education that would enable them to devote a significant amount of time to learning and teaching. They gathered disciples. Over time, some of these disciple circles began to form a loose network based on a common intellectual project. To the extent that these rabbis exercised authority, they did so as wealthy individuals who were respected within their communities for a variety of reasons, most of which would have had little connection specifically to their title as rabbi.

These men (they were all men) had previously been attracted to both Pharisaic and Sadducean schools of thought. Some, following Pharisaic practice, based their teachings more on "traditional" practices. These practices might also have run in their families. Others, following a Sadducean approach, based their teachings more directly on authoritative texts. By this time, though, the distinction had become fuzzy. Pharisees had incorporated text-based authority into their thinking, and Sadducees by now had their own traditions to which they gave authority. Individual "rabbis" may have emerged from different movements, but the movements themselves had in practice drawn closer to each other.

Over the six decades from 70 to 130 CE, some of these disciple circles began to coalesce into new "schools" of thought that increasingly superseded the old Pharisaic and Sadducean schools even while maintaining their distinctive approaches to the authority of scripture. By 130, these two approaches began to crystallize around two disciple circles, one led by Rabbi Ishmael and the other by Rabbi Akiva.[9] Rabbi Ishmael's approach bore a strong relationship to that of the Sadducees: scripture was seen as the authoritative guide to proper practice. Rabbi Akiva's approach was Pharisaic: tradition took precedence, even when it seemed to conflict with scripture. The small and scattered rabbinic disciple circles that sought to form larger networks (some probably had no such desire) identified themselves with either Ishmael or Akiva and their distinctive approaches. These circles were shattered with the outbreak of a fresh revolt in Judea.

In 132 CE, war broke out again in Palestine. The cause of this new revolt against Rome is obscure, but we do know that it was led by a man named Shimon bar Kosiba and centered in the area around the Dead Sea. For three years, Bar Kosiba gave Rome a run for its money. Although he never managed to take Jerusalem, he minted his own coinage on which he proclaimed the "freedom of Israel"; proclaimed himself to be the *nasi*, or supreme ruler, of Israel; and inspired uprisings against Rome throughout the region.[10] Like the revolt of 66–70, though, this one too never had a chance. Once the Roman forces organized and bored down, the rebels retreated to caves in the Judean desert from which they were ultimately smoked. Because the caves are hard to access and the climate is dry, however, they left caches of documents, undisturbed until modern archaeologists (and looters) unearthed them. Some of these documents even bear the signature of Bar Kosiba himself.

If Bar Kosiba had any knowledge of scripture or gave to it any authority, he does not demonstrate it in his documents. Nor do these documents show any awareness of the rabbis. Bar Kosiba was scrupulous (however he understood this) about observance of the Sabbath, the Feast of Tabernacles (Sukkot), and perhaps tithing. He never cites scripture for authority, though, and uses no distinctive phrases to evoke it. Similarly, the surviving contracts and other documents of ordinary Jews who were swept up in the revolt and forced to flee to the caves demonstrate no awareness of scripture, the rabbis, or their emerging law.[11]

According to later rabbinic tradition, however, Bar Kosiba did have one strong connection to scripture: he (or his followers) claimed that he was the messiah, the fulfillment of the scriptural oracle of Balaam: "A *star* shall come out of Jacob, and a scepter shall rise out of Israel" (Numbers 24:17). Bar Kokhba ("son of a *star*") was seen as the prophesied messiah. The power of the oracular understanding of scripture, applied a century earlier to Jesus, was still strong. Whether Bar Kokhba understood himself in these terms is unclear, although perhaps his use of Hebrew in his documents and coins, which suggest a nationalistic agenda, is slight evidence that he did.[12]

Rome crushed this revolt, perhaps even more savagely than it did the one of 66 CE. The Judeans had now earned for themselves a reputation for rebelliousness and Rome set out to ensure that the second revolt would be the last. The emperor Hadrian renamed Jerusalem Aelia Capitolina. The Romans erected temples and statues of their gods in the new colony and prohibited Jews from living there. At the same time, the Romans initiated some form of religious persecution. Roman sources are almost silent on this issue. Rabbinic sources, however, create a vivid and searing picture of Roman persecution. According to one Talmudic legend, the Romans outlawed the study of Torah and, when Rabbi Akiva ignored the ban and taught Torah in public, the Romans cruelly executed him. Another tradition mentions the execution of Rabbi Ishmael and Rabbi Shimon, attributing the reason for their deaths to their own minor sins.[13]

These rabbinic accounts say more about the concerns and values of their authors than they do about the actual events of 132–135 CE that they claim to describe. Here again, though, there may be a kernel of truth. It is certainly not impossible that in the course of the war and its aftermath several important rabbis, including Rabbi Akiva and Rabbi Ishmael, lost their lives.[14]

Roman sources do not mention the rabbis or religious persecution, but they do note that wide swaths of Judea were destroyed in the aftermath of the revolt and that many were killed.[15] As a result, Jewish settlement moved northward and concentrated especially in Galilee. Prior to the Bar Kokhba revolt there is little evidence of the presence of rabbis in Galilee; they were primarily active in Judea. After the revolt they, like many of their Judean compatriots, fled north.

The refugees from Judea streamed into both existing and new settlements in Galilee. Where they chose to settle was determined by a complex combination of available housing, work, and personal connections. Rabbis too settled throughout Galilee. They had to rebuild their communities, attract new followers and students, and with the disintegration of the circles that had formed around Akiva and Ishmael had to figure out new ways of organizing themselves.[16]

By the mid- to late second century CE, a rabbinic leader emerged. Rabbinic sources call him the nasi, often translated as "prince," the same title taken by Bar Kokhba. We do not know whether the first holders of this title took it for themselves or whether it was a term applied to them by their followers, but it implies a level of wide prestige and authority that they almost certainly did not enjoy.

Members of the Gamaliel family, an old Pharisaic line, were the first to assume this title. Their distinguished lineage and maybe even genuine learning could have contributed to their rise to leadership among the rabbis. A more likely factor, however, was their money, which they used to patronize the rabbis. In return, they demanded from the rabbis—sometimes successfully, sometimes less so—a certain level of authority and prestige. The rabbis who were drawn to the Gamaliel estate formed a kind of unofficial court led by the nasi. When the Gamaliels moved—from Usha to Shefaram to Beit Shearim and then in the third century to Sepphoris—so too did their coterie of rabbis. Some rabbis, attracted by the wealth, prestige, concentration of other rabbis, and potential job opportunities controlled by the nasi, were attracted to his court. Some would have settled nearby; others might have paid regular visits. Other rabbis, though, remained distant or even hostile to the Gamaliels' attempt to exert control over them. The Gamaliels benefited by gaining the support of a group of relatively well-educated followers. In the third century they were able to parlay this support into Roman recognition of them as the "patriarchs" of the Jews.[17]

It was within the court of the nasi that the rabbis struck a "grand coalition." Although the Gamaliels had formerly aligned themselves with the Pharisees and still maintained Pharisaic leanings, they recognized that in order to broaden their base of support among the rabbis they had to adopt a more inclusive stance. Individual rabbis might be more sympathetic to traditionally Pharisaic or Sadducean approaches, but they as a whole were no longer Pharisees or Sadducees. They were to see themselves as all part of the same "school." It was in the interest of both the Gamaliels and the rabbis they patronized to create a framework that could accommodate disagreements without fracturing into sects.[18]

The success of this coalition can be seen at precisely the moment when the Gamaliels attempted to overreach. The first of the Gamaliels to achieve Roman recognition was Rabbi Judah, at the beginning of the third century. Perhaps inspired by his new relationship with Rome and the financial opportunities that opened up to him and his followers, Rabbi Judah the nasi (also called "the Prince" or "the Patriarch") set out to collect and codify the traditions of the ancestors—which now also included the traditions of previous rabbis. The result was the Mishnah. In style, it was a "Pharisaic" document that was organized by topic (rather than any order found in or dictated by scripture). By rarely quoting scripture as a source of its normative law, it implicitly claimed its authority from tradition. Rabbis, fully aware of the perks that could flow from close ties with the nasi, quickly hailed it, even as they subtly sought to undermine its authority.[19] By the early third century, scripture had become too important for the rabbis to ignore. They did not want to alienate the powerful patriarch, but they also did not hesitate to analyze each sentence and clause of the Mishnah in order to "discover" its underlying scriptural authority.

Through the third century the story of the rabbis and the nasi is very much a story about them, not about the wider Jewish community. Individual rabbis had followers who would consult them about a variety of matters, but they did not by and large exercise communal religious leadership. Some rabbis achieved positions of judicial authority in their villages and cities (where they are more frequently found toward the beginning of the third century) by virtue of their ability, status, wealth, and connections, not as rabbis per se. Similarly, until Rabbi Judah's time (and to an even greater extent after) the Gamaliels were climbers who aspired to wide communal authority, not leaders who exercised it.[20]

The Mishnah was in a sense a desperate last gasp of the Pharisaic rabbis. The rabbis, of course, would continue to use and regard as authoritative traditions that they received, whether they stretched back into the (imagined) hoary past or simply back a generation to their teacher or teacher's teacher. The "Oral Law"—the nonscriptural traditions that generations passed down—was an important part of rabbinic thinking. From the third century on, though, the center of rabbinic veneration and piety was scripture or, in their parlance, Torah.

The rabbis had an expansive understanding of "Torah." For these rabbis, "Torah" meant the divine will, how it is that God wants his people to behave. A little earlier the author of 4 Ezra had essentially claimed that God continued to make his knowledge and will known through continuing revelation. This view was hardly unique; many Jews continued to subscribe to some notion of continuing prophecy. In one sense the rabbis rejected this belief: direct prophetic revelation had ceased. In another sense, however, they modified it. All divine knowledge and the seeds for God's continuing revelation were seen to be in scripture. Now the interpreter of scripture, not the prophet, would reveal God's will, and would do so not through inspiration or God's direct revelation but instead through the mastery of a skill. The text was seen as pregnant with meaning. The interpreter had no independent authority by virtue of title (like the priest) or of inspiration (like the prophet). The validity of his interpretations was determined entirely by the skill that he (as usual, almost always a he) was thought to bring to the text.

One of the overwhelmingly prominent characteristics of rabbinic literature is the way it formally marks scriptural passages. Like the pesher literature from the Dead Sea Scrolls, Paul's letters, and many of the gospels, rabbinic literature clearly distinguishes between a citation of scripture and its interpretation. Citation formulas such as "as it is written" or "as it is said" pervade almost every rabbinic text (except the Mishnah and a kind of companion volume, the Tosefta, where they appear infrequently). In the vast majority of cases they introduce direct scriptural quotations. Scripture is kept strictly separate from its interpretation, unlike earlier works like the book of Jubilees or the history of Artapanus or even Josephus's retelling of the biblical stories.

Paul and the authors of the pesher literature and gospels primarily mined scripture for its oracles and prophecies. While the rabbis, like these authors, formally divided the citation of scripture from its interpretation, the use to which they put these divisions fundamentally differed from these earlier authors. The rabbis almost never used scriptural verses to verify or announce prophecies. Although at this stage they were probably still not reacting directly to Christian claims, they adopted a different approach to scripture. For the rabbis, it was not a collection of oracles but the source of all true knowledge. It was not just a historical record of God's revelation but the very place at which God continued to reveal his will to his people.

The rabbis thus saw scripture as "omnisignificant."[21] The text of scripture at its very finest detail encapsulated the divine message. This approach to scripture caused the rabbis to be attentive not only to the surface or obvious message of scriptural passages but also to the clauses and very words used. A seeming redundancy, contradiction, or spelling mistake in the Hebrew text cannot be what it seems; it must instead be an integral part of the divine revelation that signals us to interpret it. The rabbis understand God as the perfect author of a perfect text. It is our job to understand how a text that does not seem perfect really is.

The assumption that all of scripture is perfect in its very language is at the heart of the rabbinic genre of Midrash. *Midrash* is a term that today is sometimes applied to any kind of explanation or interpretation of scripture. For the rabbis, though, it was a very specific kind of interpretation focused on the wording of the Hebrew text and springing from the assumption that even textual peculiarities were divinely placed.

What, though, "counts" as scripture? Midrash requires a very strong assumption that the base text is divine. Without this assumption, there would be no reason to assume that the text was omnisignificant.

By this time there was an implicit canon. Greek-speaking Jews outside of Palestine probably had a somewhat better notion of which books "counted" as divinely inspired than their Palestinian compatriots, but by this time there was a largely shared consensus about most of the texts. The rabbis never directly confront the issue of canon, of which books are considered "inside" and "outside" scripture. Yet they cite as authoritative proof-texts verses from every book of the present Jewish Bible, and almost none from books that are outside of that Bible. It was within this corpus that all of divine knowledge was to be found.[22]

But was there also divine knowledge to be found, as the Pharisees had maintained, outside of these texts in traditions and living practices? For many rabbis—and their primary patron, Rabbi Judah—the answer was clearly affirmative. To some degree, the tension between rabbis through the early third century simply continued that which earlier existed between the Pharisees and Sadducees. At the same time, however, the rabbis began to develop an inchoate position between these two extremes that, like a modern political compromise, was not entirely consistent but contained enough wiggle room to allow most parties to claim victory.

In short, the rabbinic approach made two almost contradictory claims. On the one hand, they claimed that all divine knowledge was found in "Torah," which they defined to include both scripture and the received traditions. On the other hand, though, they treated scripture—both as text and as written object—in a special way. The rabbis went to great pains to preserve the distinctiveness of written scripture from nonscriptural traditions, although they remained somewhat vague about the *authority* of these distinctive realms.

The rabbinic approach to liturgy highlights this tension. In the first century CE a liturgy took place at the Jerusalem temple. It was relatively short, secondary to offering the sacrifice, and consisted almost entirely of the recitation of biblical passages and verses. This was consistent with the position of the Sadducees. Outside of the temple prayer was neither fixed nor required. Within Judea and Galilee Jews undoubtedly prayed in the few and scattered synagogues; in communal assemblies called to address such threats as drought; and during private events such as weddings. Whatever prayers recited at these events, though, were customary or ad hoc rather than required and followed no fixed text.[23]

In the late second and early third centuries the rabbis sought to set some broad contours for the requirements and contents of prayer. They required individuals to pray at least twice (and according to some opinions three times) daily. They declared that certain prayers and blessings must contain very specific verbal formulas.[24]

These blessings, the rabbis clearly state, might be inspired by or draw upon scripture, but they were not to contain extended passages of scripture. Blessings, for the rabbis, needed to be distinct from scripture. Even the language and form of prayer must maintain a separation between prayer and the recitation of scripture.[25]

Prayer and the recitation of scripture constituted distinct activities within the rabbinic liturgy. Early rabbinic texts state that the Torah— here they mean the Pentateuch alone—was to be read aloud as part of the public worship service on Saturday, Monday, and Thursday mornings as well as Saturday afternoons. They suggest that from week to week (or in some cases from recitation to recitation) the reading be sequential, but a fixed lectionary had not yet been set. Slightly later rabbinic sources show that for Palestinians it would take around three and a half years to complete the reading of the entire Pentateuch, but there could be wide variations between individual synagogues.[26]

One of the most prominent visual markers of the distinctiveness of scripture was the production and use of the written scroll itself. Whatever precise form prayer took in antiquity, it was almost entirely oral. When people gathered to pray, they appointed a leader. The leader recited aloud the prayers that he either memorized or created. There was no written text of the prayers to consult or against which to check the leader.

The production of a written scroll for the reading of the Torah was visually significant. The scroll was itself produced, stored, and cared for according to a strict ritual. Unlike the Christian codices, the scroll (and not merely its content) mattered.

The rabbis carefully and clearly established the scroll of the Torah as a sacred object. The Torah scroll sits at the top of their hierarchy of holiness. They specify the hierarchy as: Torah, other holy writings, wrappings for these scrolls, ark to house these writings, and synagogue to house the ark. Money earned from the sale of anything lower on the hierarchy can be used to buy something further up on the list, but not the reverse. Ideally, the Torah scroll is too holy to sell.[27]

The Torah's holiness is also somewhat strangely expressed in the rabbinic insistence that the scroll—indeed, even fragments of a scroll of Torah—"defiles the hands." While the exact force of this statement, and the reason why something holy should convey ritual impurity, remains obscure, the general idea is clear: scrolls that contain texts that are considered "holy" have a distinctive status. This naturally leads to further rabbinic reflection on which scrolls "count" as holy. Ben Sira and "all books written from then onward do not defile the hands," according to one opinion, apparently using the date of composition as a criterion. Although they mention the name of God, "the Gospels and the books of the heretics" too do not defile the hands.[28]

From a modern perspective (and perhaps even an ancient one), this discussion seems to make the primary issue—which texts are holy and why—secondary, and the secondary issue—the purity effects of those scrolls—primary. For the rabbis, however, it was the very *materiality* of the claim to holiness that was most important. "Holiness" for them was not a question of status and authority but a very practical one about how to treat scrolls. Scrolls that "defile the hands" are ones that must be treated carefully and with respect; they are not to be handled as everyday objects.

Alongside the special treatment that they gave to the scrolls of scripture, the rabbis pursued another strategy intended to both privilege and, paradoxically, thereby marginalize scripture. This relates to their broad understanding of "Torah" and the role that orality plays in its transmission.

The rabbis developed a notion that not only scripture but also non-scriptural "traditions" were all to be considered "Torah" and of divine origin. In the third and fourth centuries they more fully articulated this understanding into a theory of the "Oral Torah" and the "Written Torah," both of which were given to Moses at the moment of revelation on Mt. Sinai.[29] "Written Torah" was simply scripture. "Oral Torah" constituted the nonscriptural traditions and ongoing dialogue and debate. In rabbinic thought, this theory of an Oral and Written Torah always carried with it some degree of tension. On the one hand, both Torahs presumably originated with God and had equal authority. At the same time, the rabbis subtly acknowledged that their own deductions and pronouncements, although part of the Oral Torah, had less authority than the Written Torah. The two Torahs both were and were not one.

Just as the rabbis fiercely insisted on the materiality and the very "writtenness" of the Written Torah, so too did they fight to keep the Oral Torah oral. The Oral Torah, according to repeated rabbinic strictures, is not to be written down. Students might keep personal notes of the teachings of their masters, but the traditions themselves were to be transmitted orally and by memory. The Mishnah itself—a good-sized text that I like to think of as a snapshot of Oral Torah at a specific moment and place—appears to have been transmitted orally. Professionals called in Aramaic *tannaim* (singular, *tanna*), literally "reciters," would memorize and make known to rabbis the "authoritative" version of traditions.[30] Later, the term evolved to include all of the rabbis who dated from around Rabbi Judah's time and earlier, but the oral nature of the Oral Law was not lost, and was in fact accompanied by prohibitions against committing it to writing.

Incredibly, the rabbis appear to have largely observed the prohibition against writing down the "oral" traditions up until the early Middle Ages, when finally the Talmud was committed to writing.[31] This was a practice to which they clearly gave thought. In one Talmudic story, one rabbi scolds another for reading aloud to a congregation from a book that contained some kind of extrascriptural teaching. "Matters that were said orally [must be given] orally, and matters that were said in writing [must be given] in writing!" he tells him.[32] By reading from the book he has confused the "oral" and "written" realms.

Students memorized and passed along the traditions and laws that they knew. In limited exchanges with other small rabbinic circles they would have been aware of different and competing traditions, but not until the increased institutionalization of the rabbis around the eighth century CE did they have to reckon with such a sprawling set of materials that their desire to preserve it in writing overcame their scruples.[33]

In the second and third century, though, the rabbinic insistence on the orality of Oral Law extended far beyond prohibitions on writing certain texts. It developed into a culture. The rabbinic world, like that of many of the Greek and Roman philosophers current at that time, was an oral one. Not only was the daily work of learning, study, and the production of new knowledge done orally, but an oral culture led to the extension of "Torah" beyond "traditions."[34] The rabbinic teacher came to be thought of as literally embodying Torah knowledge; the student must be attentive to both his words and his actions, however seemingly mundane. True, divine knowledge was passed down by means of the teacher-student relationship, not words on a page.

Here, then, is the paradox. On the one hand, the rabbis promoted the orality of their own teaching in order to protect the sanctity and privileged position of the Written Torah. The rabbis had no problems with the writing of ordinary documents and texts that could not be confused with scripture. Texts that did or could be seen as having some divine authority, however, they insisted were to remain oral. The Written and Oral Torahs may have come from the same place, but there was to be a strict division between them.

On the other hand, this very protection of scripture isolates and marginalizes it—the scroll becomes a precious reference book and object of veneration rather than a living document. Scripture thus *loses* importance to the oral traditions and the give-and-take that accompanies them. Rabbis traffic and make their reputation in the Oral Torah, not the written one. Not surprisingly, with the Written Torah safely off to the side, the rabbis slowly but surely began to assign increasing holiness to the Oral Torah. Ultimately, the rabbis begin to treat the Oral Torah much as they do the Written Torah by applying the same interpretive techniques to both.[35]

This double-faced rabbinic approach to the Written Torah also finds expression in their attitude toward biblical translations, or *targumim* (singular, *targum*). Aramaic translations of parts of the Bible were found among the Dead Sea Scrolls. The fact that such translations existed is not surprising. Jews in Judea and Galilee had been increasingly using Aramaic as their common language since the fifth century BCE. To the vast majority of Jews, the Hebrew of scripture would have been almost incomprehensible. The targumim make scripture accessible.

But to whom and in what context? Aramaic translations of scripture might have circulated for personal use; this is most likely how the owners of the Dead Sea Scroll fragments used their copies. Written translations might also have been used for the public readings in the few synagogues active in Judea and Galilee in the first and second centuries CE. Communal practices of translation must have varied widely. So too would the translations that they used, with some communities perhaps employing experts to translate on the fly. As synagogues became more popular in Galilee, increasing numbers of Jews would have known scripture primarily or only through these translations.

These translations posed two very different problems for the rabbis. First, since they were not uniform, and since every translation is by necessity also an interpretation, the targumim worked to multiply scripture, as it were. Different synagogue communities would know different versions of scripture. Even if the rabbis could not point to anything objectionable in particular targumim, the very fact that they fostered diverse understandings of scripture was troubling to them. Second, there was a blurry line between targumim and scripture itself. Were written Aramaic texts of scripture to be treated as scripture?

The rabbis never developed a clear answer to this question. Different translations circulated (both orally and in writing), and at least through the third century CE the rabbis never attempted to authorize any particular one, as the Letter of Aristeas had done for the Septuagint Greek translation. Several centuries later the Byzantine emperor Justinian noted with consternation that Jews were using several different Greek translations of scripture and he legislated that this must stop: the Greek-speaking Jews were from that time forth to use only the one authentic translation, which for this Christian emperor was of course the Septuagint. Justinian could not care less which Aramaic translation the Jews were using.[36]

The rabbis solved the second problem by proclaiming that targumim in fact should not be written.[37] They created an elaborate ritual involving the public reading of the Torah and its translation: after each verse of the Torah was read, a different person translated it into Aramaic, specifically not consulting a written text. Written Aramaic versions of scripture did exist, of course, and whether many people would have followed this rabbinic ruling is an open question.[38] These versions may contain the same textual meaning as scripture, but they are not to be confused with it. Scripture had become the authoritative text par excellence.

Finally, after more than three centuries of wrangling over the authority of scripture, the Sadducees posthumously won. They may no longer have been an identifiable group, but the authority of the Jewish Bible was largely secure. Its words were seen as divine and containing all possible knowledge. The scrolls were venerated as material objects. Religious power, in this new rabbinic understanding, was to pass from those who claimed that "tradition" was on their side—which included, as always in such cases, those who benefited under the status quo—to the experts in scripture. Scripture was the definitive source of authority.

Or was it? The "Pharisaic-leaning" rabbis—those that continued to ascribe authority to traditional sayings and practices—revalued nearly every element of this victory. Torah was the definitive source of authority, but Torah went beyond written scripture to include these traditions. Written scripture was paramount but also had become secondary to the Oral Torah. A written text stood as the symbolic heart of what was essentially an oral culture.

Like all compromises, this one was hardly perfect. The rabbis of late antiquity never fully articulated a theory of how the Written and Oral Torahs related to each other. They ignored many of the problems and inconsistencies of this inchoate scheme. But then again, as those of us who have had to negotiate compromises at work and home know well, some things are best left unsaid in order to avoid conflict. During the Karaite controversy in the early Middle Ages the tensions inherent in this compromise would erupt. For now, though, it was good enough.

Epilogue

In the third century CE, "the Bible" as we know it still did not exist. There was, to our knowledge, no single codex or composition that combined all or most of the writings that comprise either the Jewish Bible (Old Testament) or the New Testament, and all the more so both together. By this time most Jews and Christians considered most of the writings that would become part of our Bible(s) as "holy" and authoritative, in one way or another. It would take another several centuries, though, for the canonical Bible to emerge.

Christians were the first to develop a formal canon. In 367 CE, Athanasius, bishop of Alexandria, enumerated the precise list of books in the Old and New Testaments that (right-believing) Christians should consider holy. The church ultimately made these books the "official" Bible. But with its historic emphasis on message over text, the church also struggled with the issue of ascribing authority to a particular text and its translations. The result of this tension was that Christians ultimately adopted different versions of the Bible. For instance, in the fifth century CE Jerome translated the Bible into Latin in an edition known as the Vulgate. This was adopted as the official Bible of the Latin-speaking (Roman Catholic) church. The Greek-speaking Christians in the eastern Mediterranean, though, continued to use the Greek texts of the biblical books including, for their Old Testament, the Septuagint. Moving a little further east, those who spoke Syriac, a dialect of Aramaic, translated the Greek text (and probably the Hebrew of the Old Testament) into their language, creating a version of the Bible known as the Peshitta. Other editions and translations soon followed. These Bibles were quite similar in content, but they also contained many textual and interpretive differences. Today, of course, this diversity continues even in the varying authority for different Christian groups of English translations such as the King James Version and the Standard Revised Version.

It took Jews longer to formalize their text and canon, most likely because no one felt a pressing need to do so. For Christians in the fourth and fifth centuries (as we also saw for the second century), the issue of text and canon was connected to issues of heresy, and with the increasing Christianization of Byzantium, heresy also became a matter of state. A "heresy" was a legal status that could have serious consequences. Jewish "heresies," though, were not labeled and regulated by the state. Throughout late antiquity the rabbis did occasionally talk about the status of this book or that, but they were content to work with an implicit canon. There was more diversity among other Jews (as late as the sixth century some synagogues read the Torah in Greek), but to our knowledge Jews did not standardize their canon.

Despite the rabbinic insistence on the importance of the very text of the Bible, Jews would not come to a final consensus about a standard Hebrew text until the eleventh century CE. It was only then that Maimonides, a towering and revered intellectual figure in his time, declared that one particular text—that of the Aleppo Codex—was to be considered the standard. To this day, for most Jews translations of the Bible, or *Tanak*, are considered secondary to this official Hebrew version.

Jewish and Christian approaches to the authority of the Bible came closer together beginning in the early third century CE. With their authorized texts and translations, Christian churches moved closer to the earlier rabbinic view of the primacy of text over message. The Bible itself, as a book, grew to be an important religious item to be illustrated, protected, and revered, not casually discarded. Rabbis, on the other hand, increasingly began to pay attention to the message of the Bible, as the Jews of Alexandria had done long before. Today both Jewish and Christian approaches to the Bible are much more similar than they were in the third century CE.

Throughout this book I have focused on the varying and shifting kinds of authority that people gave to the texts that were made (and not made) biblical. These models of authority and their historical trajectories, more than the Bible itself, constitute the Bible's powerful and enduring legacy. Each of the three modes of authority—literary, oracular, and normative—took distinct if crisscrossing paths, but they all end in the same place: the formation not only of textual culture but also of communities that are based on texts. Many of us are members of more than one such community, and each can be traced back to one of these modes of authority. Literary authority has given rise to communities of writers and readers; oracular authority to religion; and normative authority to nations. Reflecting on these modes of textual authority and the communities that they continue to generate leads to a much deeper awareness and understanding of a critical feature of our own culture that we take for granted.

The literary authority that we have seen throughout antiquity remains very much with us today. Writers are in conversation with each other. Academic theorists have many more precise terms to describe the nature of the relationships between literary texts (allusion, influence, echo, and intertextuality, for examples), but at bottom they all reflect the same dynamic. Writers are made, not born. They, like the scribes we have repeatedly seen throughout this book, are trained through education. They learn their craft by reading, imitating, and writing for audiences of other writers. They have read a similar implicit canon of texts. They talk to each other, exchange ideas, and read each other's work. They may be formally organized in reading groups, workshops, or academic units or not, but they form a loose community held together not just by the act of writing but by specific, if changing, texts that they engage and rework.

Writers today come in many types, far more than there were in antiquity, with its limited access to education, time, and the necessary physical materials. Whether we write fictional stories, books of history, newspaper or magazine articles, user manuals, legal briefs, or even office memos, and whether we do this writing professionally or just for fun, we participate in a similar dynamic. In each case we have learned how to do such writing from models that we then imitate more closely at first, less so as our skill and comfort grow. Even a mundane office memo might contain a sly and subtle reference to some earlier text, the bored author's wink at the reader to signal his or her independence and creativity. Writing is not, and never was, simply about the transmission of information.

Through most of antiquity, there was a significant overlap between communities of writers and communities of readers. Those with the skills to read also had the skills to write similar kinds of texts. In our world, though, there is a much larger gap between these communities. Most readers of fiction, for example, do not write fiction. Readers, though, also form communities, however tenuous, weak, and shifting they may be. They may gather physically in book groups, virtually in an online discussion of an essay, or around the coffee machine in the office to discuss a business or sports story. Words create communities.

Texts do not naturally give rise to reading communities. It is a reading community that gives authority to the texts. In the social and cultural world in which many of us live, we are members of many groups that are held together by a large variety of forces, including common interests, family or ethnic ties, beliefs, and pragmatism. Yet a surprising number of these groups, both professional and social, anchor themselves to the production or consumption of written words.

If the literary authority of texts is very much with us today, their oracular authority, unsurprisingly, is not. In antiquity, people assigned oracular authority to texts that they believed contained divinely given messages, particularly about the future. This is the primary sense in which the Bible was thought "holy"; it was a book of oracles. Today, many people continue to read the Bible (or other books) in this sense, analyzing its words for messages about what will happen or seeking direction in what we (as a community or as individuals) should do in a particular situation.

In the circles in which I travel, few read the Bible or any other text this way. For those who see the Bible as a human rather than divine work (a view that has developed powerfully from the time of the Enlightenment), it obviously makes no sense to mine it for otherworldly messages. Yet despite the rejection of the divine status of the text, this oracular mode of authority continues to exert a powerful force, albeit in a different form. Oracular authority venerates a text but uses that text to assign power, prestige, and authority to its interpreters.

This is the kind of thinking that has led to the formation of most of the world's major religions. The text(s) that stand at the center of these institutions and organizations are in a sense secondary to the community of interpreters. The rabbis largely ceased to read the Bible as oracular, but

they did claim that they possessed the skills to unpack the true meaning of the divine text. For Christians, the authority to interpret the true
meaning of scripture created a major crisis that led to the Reformation
and the development of Protestantism. Muslims and Hindus each appeal
to their holy texts, and their leaders base their claims to authority at least
in part on their ability to interpret them "correctly."

The base text, though, need not be seen as holy in order to create interpretive communities. A company organized around a text (say, a mission
statement) or a group fighting about the meaning of some document is
at its core an interpretive community, the fruit of "oracular thinking." In
such communities or groups, conflict often arises out of interpretive issues: who has the authority to interpret the text in question, and whence
does that authority arise? Does one ascend to a position of interpretive authority because the group believes that he or she possesses some
kind of charismatic insight (like the Teacher of Righteousness and Paul);
other forms of capital that the interpreter will bestow upon the group's
members (like the nasi); or intellectual skill or firepower (like, perhaps,
Philo and the Alexandrian Jewish elite who preceded him)? Today, as in
antiquity, communities based on a foundational document often struggle
not just with the issue of interpretation and leadership but also with the
very grounds on which that authority is assigned.

One of the more intriguing and consequential places where such issues
are clearly visible is the Supreme Court of the United States. The United
States is itself a nation founded on a text, and it is the interpretation of
that text that confers power. Most such authoritative readings of the U.S.
Constitution by the Supreme Court spring from an oracular mode of
reading. It is especially apparent in the legal idea of "originalism," which
sees the judicial task as recovering the true meaning and intention behind
the Constitution (or any statute). The Constitution is seen as a perfect
document written by perfect authors whose will must be recovered. The
frequent and often heated public discussion over how well the Supreme
Court is doing its job—that is, its "right" (outside of a technical formal
one) to advance a particular kind of interpretation—shows how vulnerable interpretive communities are to this kind of challenge.

The example of originalism in the Supreme Court sits at the intersection of oracular reading and normative authority. Today, I would guess,

most people would understand the term "authority of the Bible" in a normative sense. Even those who do not subscribe to any notion that the Bible should have any authority in a civic context might think of it as normative in a personal one. We are a nation of written laws, from the Constitution down, and we naturally conflate writing, authority, and law. Yet, as we have seen, in antiquity texts were rarely considered to be normative. The few occasions when communities did attempt to make texts normative (Josiah, Ezra, the Sadducees) were all within a civic context and largely failed. The idea that texts had personal, normative authority is largely rabbinic, although it also (probably independently) took root in Christian communities in late antiquity.

There is nothing natural about a community based on the writing or reading of texts. Throughout antiquity we have seen in many ways the marginality of texts, even at the very centers of power. Texts so pervade our own communities and lives that it is sometimes difficult for us to imagine a world in which texts play little or no role. This is perhaps the Bible's greatest legacy: the radically implausible notion that one can build a community, a religion, a culture, and even a country around a text.

Chronology

Bold denotes a ruler; *italics* denotes a high priest.

Israel	Judah/Yehud/Judea	Outside of Judah/Yehud/Judea/Galilee
Jeroboam I (922–901)	**Rehoboam** (922–915)	
Omri (876–869)		
Ahab (869–850)		
Jehu (842–815)		
Jeroboam II (786–746)		
Amos		
Hosea		
Hoshea (732–724)	Isaiah	**Shalmaneser V** (726–722; king of Assyria)
722: **Sargon II's** invasion, fall of Israel	701: **Sennacherib's** Invasion of Judah	**Sargon II** (721–705; king of Assyria)
	Hezekiah (715–687/6)	**Sennacherib** (704–681; king of Assyria)
	Manasseh (687/86–642)	
	Josiah (640–609)	
	Jehoahaz (609)	612: Fall of Nineveh to Babylonians
	Jehoiakim (609–598)	**Nebuchadnezzar** (605/4–562)
	Jehoiachin (598/97)	
	Zedekiah (597–587)	
	Jeremiah	
	587/6: **Nebuchadnezzar's** invasion of Judah and the fall of Jerusalem	

BCE 900 — 800 — 700 — 600

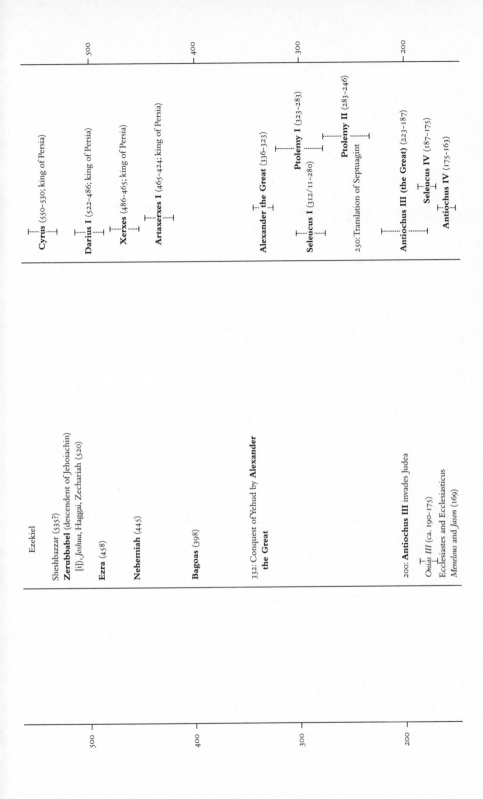

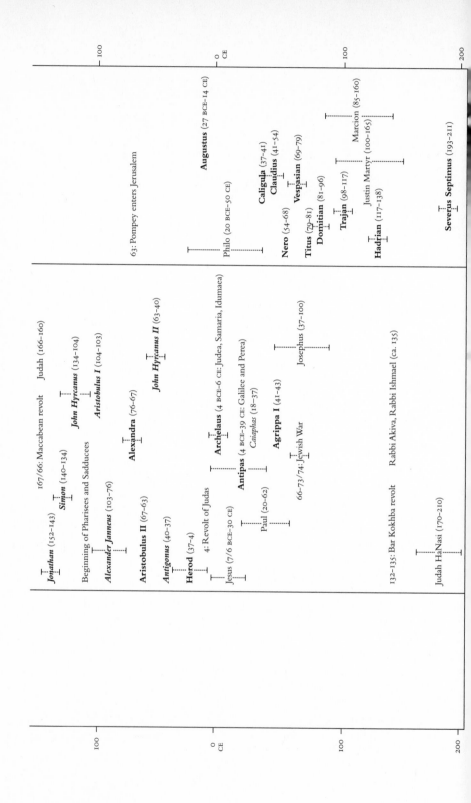

100

0
CE

100

200

63: Pompey enters Jerusalem

Augustus (27 BCE–14 CE)

Philo (20 BCE–50 CE)

Caligula (37–41)
Claudius (41–54)
Vespasian (69–79)

Nero (54–68)
Titus (79–81)
Domitian (81–96)
Trajan (98–117)
Hadrian (117–138)

Justin Martyr (100–165)
Marcion (85–160)

Severus Septimus (193–211)

167/66: Maccabean revolt   Judah (166–160)

Jonathan (152–143)
Simon (140–134)
John Hyrcanus (134–104)
Aristobulus I (104–103)

Beginning of Pharisees and Sadducees

Alexander Jannaeus (103–76)

Alexandra (76–67)

John Hyrcanus II (63–40)

Aristobulus II (67–63)

Antigonus (40–37)

Archelaus (4 BCE–6 CE: Judea, Samaria, Idumaea)

Antipas (4 BCE–39 CE: Galilee and Perea)

Caiaphas (18–37)

Herod (37–4)
4: Revolt of Judas
Agrippa I (41–43)

Josephus (37–100)

Jesus (7/6 BCE–30 CE)

Paul (20–62)

66–73/74: Jewish War

Rabbi Akiva, Rabbi Ishmael (ca. 135)

132–135: Bar Kokhba revolt

Judah HaNasi (170–210)

100

0
CE

100

200

Notes

Introduction

1. There are many fine surveys of Israelite, Jewish, and Christian history from this period, and I do not mean to denigrate them in any way. The approach of this book differs from most of them, though, in presenting a synthetic chronological history focused particularly on the evolving authority of texts. For an entry into these histories, see especially Cohen, *From the Mishnah to the Maccabees*; Jaffee, *Early Judaism*; Efron et al., *The Jews*; and two volumes edited by Shanks, *Ancient Israel* and *Christianity and Rabbinic Judaism*.

Chapter 1. The Northern Kingdom

1. Bright, *History of Israel*, 190–224. The Bible provides multiple explanations for why Saul was succeeded by David rather than his own son. These might well attempt to excuse a messier transition.
2. Athas, *The Tel Dan Inscription*. Both sides of this argument are accessibly presented in Finkelstein and Mazar, *The Quest for the Historical Israel*.
3. Bright, *History of Israel*, 236–41; Parrot, *Samaria*, 53–83; Ahituv, *Echoes from the Past*, 258–59.
4. Finkelstein, "City-States to States," 80.
5. For a sensitive reading of the patriarchal stories as products of Israel, see Fleming, *The Legacy of Israel in Judah's Bible*, 72–90.
6. For a discussion of other such biblical legends that served the political aims of the northern kingdom, see Friedman, *Who Wrote the Bible?* 62–63, 66.
7. There is, admittedly, no firm evidence for the existence of bards in ancient Israel. Nevertheless, the practice of reciting oral stories was widespread throughout antiquity and this seems to be the most plausible social context for such legends.
8. Ahituv, *Echoes from the Past*, 252–57; quote from Seth L. Sanders, *The Invention of Hebrew*, 111, and see there 130–31.
9. On the Samarian ostraca, see Ahituv, *Echoes from the Past*, 258–309. One of the most vocal proponents of the Israelian thesis has been Gary Rendsburg. See, for example, *Linguistic Evidence for the Northern Origin of Selected Psalms*.

10. See Mark S. Smith, *The Early History of God*.

11. One of the principal ways through which we know this is Israelite naming practice, which preferred names that end with "ya/yahu" or "el." Hess, "Aspects of Israelite Personal Names and Pre-exilic Israelite Religion."

12. Ahituv, *Echoes from the Past*, 324–25; Olyan, *Asherah and the Cult of Yahweh in Israel*.

13. See 1 Kings 17–19; Overholt, "Elijah and Elisha in the Context of Israelite Religion."

14. Albertz, "Family Religion in Ancient Israel."

15. See Wiseman, *The Vassal-Treaties of Esarhaddon*.

16. On the applicability of our knowledge of non-Israelite scribes to understanding the Bible, see Schniedewind, *How the Bible Became a Book*; van der Toorn, *Scribal Culture and the Making of the Hebrew Bible*.

17. Horowitz, Oshima, and Vukosavović, "Hazor 18"; Misgav, Garfinkel, and Ganor, "The Ostracon." The guarded interpretation of the inscription that I offer here follows Rollston, "The Khirbet Qeiyafa Ostracon."

18. For a sensitive, if probably overstated, discussion of the Covenant Code as a revision of the Laws of Hammurabi, see David P. Wright, *Inventing God's Law*. I differ with Wright on his historical reconstruction.

19. Hallo and Younger, *The Context of Scripture*, 286, 296.

20. Younger, "Israelites in Exile."

21. On these statistics, see Broshi, "The Expansion of Jerusalem in the Reigns of Hezekiah and Manasseh"; Broshi and Finkelstein, "The Population of Palestine in Iron Age II," 54.

Chapter 2. The Writings of Judah

1. The extent of the refugee influx into Jerusalem is presently a contentious scholarly issue. Jerusalem expanded at this time, but it is unclear why. For a summary of these positions with bibliography, see Geva, "Summary and Discussion of Findings from Areas A, W and X-2."

2. For a description of the tunnel, see Shiloh, "Jerusalem." For a challenge to the dating of the tunnel (although not necessarily the inscription), see Reich and Shukron, "The Date of the Siloam Tunnel Reconsidered." The inscription can also be found in Hallo and Younger, *The Context of Scripture*, 145.

3. Russell, *Sennacherib's Palace*, 152–74; Ussishkin, *The Conquest of Lachish by Sennacherib*.

4. Hallo and Younger, *The Context of Scripture*, 303; 2 Kings 19:35–36.

5. Jars of goods that were destined for the king of Judah would often have a stamp on their handles, frequently reading in Hebrew *lmlk*, "for the king." These goods would generally be brought to administrative centers, where archaeologists have found the stamps in large quantities. For a recent analysis and bibliography, see Lipschits, Sergi, and Koch, "Judahite Stamped and Incised Jar Handles." Monumental inscriptions: Cross, "A Fragment of a Monumental Inscription from the City of David"; and the press release from the Israel Antiquities Authority of another such inscription: http://www.antiquities.org.il/article_Item_eng.asp?sec_id=25&subj_id=240&id=1551&module_id=#as (accessed April 11, 2013).

6. van der Toorn, *Scribal Culture and the Making of the Hebrew Bible*, 63–64.

7. See Shiloh, "Jerusalem," 708–9.

8. See Levinson, *Deuteronomy*, 53–97.

9. Weinfeld, "Deuteronomy, Book of," 177.

10. This is a highly contentious claim, but then, the dating of Deuteronomy is itself a highly contentious topic. For the argument that the core of Deuteronomy was authored in Josiah's time (although with some allowance for a prehistory in the time of Hezekiah), see Weinfeld, *Deuteronomy and the Deuteronomic School*, esp. 158–78. See Haran, *Temples and Temple-Service in Ancient Israel*, 132–48.

11. See Bright, *History of Israel*, 309–23.

12. Levinson, *Deuteronomy*, 96.

13. For example, Handy, "Historical Probability and the Narrative of Josiah's Reform in 2 Kings."

14. Noth, *The Deuteronomistic History*.

15. Van Seters, *In Search of History*, 312–14.

16. See Cross, *Canaanite Myth and Hebrew Epic*, 274–89.

17. Virtually every sentence in this paragraph is highly contested. I have followed here, with modifications, a line of argument developed by Jacob Milgrom and Israel Knohl. See Milgrom, *Numbers*; Knohl, *The Sanctuary of Silence*. Many scholars, though, claim that the H source predates the P source and that the latter was written only after 586 BCE, with others denying that H ever existed.

18. For discussions of such songs and their narrative settings, see Weitzman, *Song and Story in Biblical Narrative*.

19. Barkey et al., "The Amulets from Ketef Hinnom." See Schniedewind, *How the Bible Became a Book*, 24–34.

20. Cited in Seth L. Sanders, *The Invention of Hebrew*, 143.

21. Levenson, "The Last Four Verses in Kings"; Pritchard, *Ancient Near Eastern Texts Relating to the Old Testament*, 308.

Chapter 3. The Second Commonwealth

1. Coogan, "Life in the Diaspora"; Pearce, "'Judean.'"

2. Translation from http://www.britishmuseum.org/explore/highlights/article_index/c/cyrus_cylinder_-_translation.aspx (accessed September 17, 2013). Quote from line 12.

3. Kuhrt, "Babylonia from Cyrus to Xerxes"; Lipschits, "Demographic Changes." The basic authenticity of Cyrus's decree concerning the Judahites (including the text found in Ezra 6) has been argued by Elias Bickerman (whom I am following here) but is not universally accepted. See Bickerman, "The Edict of Cyrus in Ezra."

4. Fried, "'You Shall Appoint Judges'"; Redford, "The So-Called 'Codification' of Egyptian Law under Darius I."

5. See Levtow, *Images of Others*.

6. For a colorful picture of the development of what one scholar has called the "Yahweh-alone" party at this time, see Morton Smith, *Palestinian Parties and Politics That Shaped the Old Testament*, 75–95.

7. See Sommer, *A Prophet Reads Scripture*.

8. Lipschits, "Demographic Changes."

9. For a discussion of the dating of Esther, see Adele Berlin, "The Book of Esther and Ancient Storytelling."

10. For the question of continuity between Israelites and *yehudim*, see Brettler, "Judaism in the Hebrew Bible."

Chapter 4. Ezra and the Pentateuch

1. The identification of the figure on the synagogue wall in Dura Europos is contested. See Kraeling, *The Synagogue*, 234; Fine, *Art and Judaism in the Greco-Roman World*, 172–83, esp. 179. See Tosefta *Sanhedrin* 4:7.

2. See Friedman, *Who Wrote the Bible?*

3. On these wars, see Green, *The Greco-Persian Wars*. The dating of Ezra's mission to 458 BCE is not entirely agreed upon by scholars; it is supported by one reading of the regnal years in the book of Ezra as well as a prosopographical study of some later ostraca. The arguments are complex and not definitive, but to my mind are more convincing than the alternatives. For a succinct discussion and bibliography, see Grabbe, *Judaism from Cyrus to Hadrian*, 88–93.

4. The authenticity of this letter is highly debated by scholars, but many think that at least its core is authentic. For a summary of this debate, see Blenkinsopp, *Ezra-Nehemiah*, 144–52.

5. Blenkinsopp, "The Mission of Udjahorresnet and Those of Ezra and Nehemiah," 418.

6. Finkelstein, "Jerusalem in the Persian (and Early Hellenistic) Period and the Wall of Nehemiah."

7. See Aharoni, *Excavations at Ramat Rahel*.

8. On reading Nehemiah 8 as part of the Ezra narrative, see Blenkinsopp, *Ezra-Nehemiah*, 44–46.

9. The classic statement is Wellhausen, *Prolegomena to the History of Israel*. The literature on this is immense. For some modern evaluations and discussion, see Friedman, *Who Wrote the Bible?*; John J. Collins, *Introduction to the Hebrew Bible*, 47–65; Kugel, *How to Read the Bible*, 2–45.

10. For introductory summaries of some of these models and the intense debate now raging in this field, see Carr, "Controversy and Convergence in Recent Studies of the Formation of the Pentateuch"; Dozeman, Schmid, and Schwartz, *The Pentateuch*. See further Brettler, *How to Read the Jewish Bible*.

11. See Williamson, *World Biblical Commentary*, xxxvii–xxxix.

12. Cohen, "From the Bible to the Talmud."

13. See further Satlow, *Jewish Marriage in Antiquity*, 133–40.

14. Some scholars, most notably Peter Frei, have argued that the law that Ezra returned with was in fact made with Persian backing. For his essay in English translation and several excellent critiques of this thesis, see Watts, *Persia and Torah*.

Chapter 5. Nehemiah to Chronicles

1. Diodorus Siculus, *Bibliotheca historica* XL.3.4–5.

2. Much of the material in the book of Nehemiah is written in the first person. This material is often called by scholars the "Nehemiah Memoir" and is considered to be

genuinely from Nehemiah himself, a position that I take here. The classic defense of this position is von Rad, "Die Nehemia-Denkschrift."

3. Gropp, "Sanballat."
4. Magen, "The Dating of the First Phase of the Samaritan Temple." Josephus attributes the building of the Samaritan Temple to the time of Alexander the Great, but he appears to be mistaken: the archaeology establishes that it was built about a century earlier.
5. Summary of evidence in Grabbe, *Judaism from Cyrus to Hadrian*, 192–98. See Knoppers, "Nehemiah and Sanballat."
6. The Hebrew phrase is unusual. See H. G. M. Williamson, *Ezra, Nehemiah*, 332.
7. See Williamson, *World Biblical Commentary*, 328–30.
8. Morton Smith, "The Dead Sea Scrolls."
9. An argument has been made that Judah in fact revolted from Persia in the mid-fourth century BCE in what is known as the Tennes rebellion. This, however, seems unlikely. See Ephraim Stern, *Material Culture of the Land of the Bible*, 253–55. Judah remained loyal to the Persians through the conquest of Alexander the Great.
10. Goodblatt, *Elements of Jewish Nationalism*, 49–70.
11. Japhet, "Conquest and Settlement in Chronicles."
12. Knoppers, "Hierodules, Priests, or Janitors?"
13. Knoppers, "Intermarriage, Social Complexity, and Ethnic Diversity in the Genealogy of Judah."
14. Japhet, *I & II Chronicles*, 19–23; Knoppers, "Hierodules, Priests, or Janitors?"
15. Publication of the archaeology of the site remains ongoing, particularly in the German series Archäologische Veröffentlichungen. An excellent, if somewhat dated, overview in English can be found in Porten, *Archives from Elephantine*.
16. Porten, *Archives from Elephantine*, 160–64.
17. Porten, *The Elephantine Papyri in English*, 139–47, translation at 143.
18. Ibid., 142.
19. Ibid., 143–44
20. Ibid., no. B13.
21. Porten, *Archives from Elephantine*, 191–92.
22. Ibid., 248–50.
23. Jacob L. Wright, "The Commemoration of Defeat and the Formation of a Nation in the Hebrew Bible."

Chapter 6. The Dawn of Hellenism

1. Thompson, "Economic Reforms in the Mid-Reign of Ptolemy Philadelphus."
2. Tcherikover, "Palestine under the Ptolemies."
3. Applebaum, *Judaea in Hellenistic and Roman Times*, 1–8.
4. Jones, *The Greek City*, 27–50.
5. See Kah and Scholz, *Das hellenistische Gymnasion*.
6. Kloner, "Maresha in the Reign of Ptolemy II Philadelphus"; Kasher, *Jews and Hellenistic Cities in Eretz-Israel*, 24–25.
7. Landau, "A Greek Inscription Found Near Hefzibah."
8. Josephus, *Jewish Antiquities* 12.138–53.

9. Musti, "Syria and the East," 197; Ma, *Antiochus III*, 145–47.

10. Josephus, *Jewish Antiquities* 12.154; Ecclesiasticus 50:1–3; Andrea M. Berlin, "Palestine between Large and Small Forces in the Hellenistic Period," 16.

11. Bickerman, *The Jews in the Greek Age*, 161–76. I disagree, however, with Bickerman's ultimate assessment about the prevalence of Torah education at this time.

12. On paideia, see the classic work of Jaeger, *Paideia*; and for its application in the Hellenistic period, see Morgan, *Literate Education in the Hellenistic and Roman Worlds*, 50–89. Philosophical schools: Dorandi, "Organization and Structure of the Philosophical Schools."

13. For issues of identity and authorship, see Barton, *A Critical and Exegetical Commentary on Ecclesiastes*, 58–65; Seow, *The Anchor Bible*, 96–97, 391–96. The dating is also highly debatable. See the discussion in Murphy, *Ecclesiastes*, xxii–xxiii.

14. This identification of Kohelet might be a later editorial addition. Still, it would have been a reasonable inference. See Fox, *Qohelet*, 311–21.

15. See Braun, *Kohelet*.

16. Bickerman, *Four Strange Books of the Bible*, 147, 153.

17. See Barton, *Qohelet*, 199.

18. On the Cairo Geniza version and the story of its find, see Hoffman and Cole, *Sacred Trash*. Among the Dead Sea Scrolls, the most complete version was found at Masada and is labeled *Mas1h*.

19. Olyan, "Ben Sira's Relationship to the Priesthood."

20. See Benjamin G. Wright, "Biblical Interpretation in the Book of Ben Sira."

21. Gilbert, "L'Éloge de la Sagesse."

22. See Jack T. Sanders, *Ben Sira and Demotic Wisdom*, 29.

23. Murphy, *Ecclesiastes*, xlv–xlvi.

24. See Kraft, "Scripture and Canon in the Apocrypha and Pseudepigrapha."

25. A useful collection is Charlesworth, *The Old Testament Pseudepigrapha*. The English translation is found in 1:5–89.

26. 1 Enoch 1:2.

27. Ibid., 8. See ibid., 14. The account has affinities to Genesis 6:1–4.

28. 1 Enoch 72; Benjamin G. Wright, "'Fear the Lord and Honor the Priest,'" esp. 204–8.

29. See Nickelsburg, "Enochic Wisdom" and the extensive bibliography there; Argall, *1 Enoch and Sirach*. When I refer here to the "author" of 1 Enoch I mean the authors of the various parts of this work that date to the early second century.

30. 1 Enoch 81:1–3 (trans. Nickelsburg, *1 Enoch 1*, 333); 1 Enoch 103:2.

31. See Stuckenbruck, *1 Enoch*, 81–86.

32. See Greenfield, Stone, and Eshel, *The Aramaic Levi Document*.

33. See Fitzmyer, *Tobit*, 18–28, 50–54.

34. Ibid., 35–37.

35. The classic and still useful study is Hengel, *Judaism and Hellenism*.

Chapter 7. The Maccabean Revolt

1. On the Israeli narrative, see Don-Yehiya, "Hanukkah and the Myth of the Maccabees." The Talmudic story can be found at Babylonian Talmud, *Shabbat* 21b.

2. Much of my narrative of the causes of the Maccabean revolt follows the argument of the classic study of Bickerman, *The God of the Maccabees*. I depart from his narrative, however, at the critical juncture of the role of Jewish "Hellenizers."

3. See M. Stern, "'Antioch in Jerusalem'"; Daniel R. Schwartz, *2 Maccabees*, 530–32.

4. On Rome's humiliation of Antiochus, see Polybius 29.27.1–8.

5. On the general historicity of the persecutions, see Daniel R. Schwartz, *2 Maccabees*, 273 (although several of the sources that he details there are dependent on the account in 2 Maccabees). For more discussion of Antiochus's motives, see Tcherikover, *Hellenistic Civilization and the Jews*, 175–203.

6. See Bar-Kochva, *Judas Maccabaeus*.

7. The Animal Apocalypse is 1 Enoch 85–90. Quote from 1 Enoch 89:13–15 (trans. Nickelsburg, *1 Enoch 1*, 365).

8. 1 Enoch 90:9 (trans. Nickelsburg, *1 Enoch 1*, 388).

9. See Tiller, *A Commentary on the Animal Apocalypse of 1 Enoch*, 105–9. Tiller sees a more negative attitude than I do.

10. 1 Enoch 89:62 (trans. Nickelsburg, *1 Enoch 1*, 387).

11. On the dating of these chapters, see especially John J. Collins, *Daniel*, 61n492. Most scholars see more differences than similarities between these texts. See, for example, Boccaccini, *Beyond the Essene Hypothesis*, 81–86. I see these differences as well, but I will argue below that the similarities are more important.

12. Even ancient interpreters noted the discrepancy between Daniel 8:14 and 1 Maccabees 4:52–54. See John J. Collins, *Daniel*, 336.

13. The author's historical grasp is shaky. The scene is set after the temple has been rebuilt, which Daniel seems not to realize. Nevertheless, this misunderstanding makes possible Daniel's prayer and Gabriel's revelation, which follow. See John J. Collins, *Daniel*, 348–49.

14. For discussions of the Hasideans, see Kampen, *The Hasideans and the Origin of Pharisaism*; and, more imaginatively, Hengel, *Judaism and Hellenism*, 1:175–218. A more cautious assessment can be found in John J. Collins, *Daniel*, 67–69.

15. For a literary analysis that dovetails with this assertion, see Henze, "Enoch's Dream Visions and the Visions of Daniel Reexamined."

16. See also Eshel, "Possible Sources of the Book of Daniel."

17. For more on this decree, which is thoroughly Hellenistic in nature, see van Henten, "The Honorary Decree for Simon the Maccabee."

18. Zissu and Amit, "Common Judaism, Common Purity, and the Second Temple Period *Miqwa'ot*."

Chapter 8. The Holy Books

1. Seth Schwartz, "John Hyrcanus I's Destruction of the Gerizim Temple and Judaean-Samaritan Relations."

2. Bartlett, "Edomites and Idumaeans"; Kasher, *Jews, Idumaeans, and Ancient Arabs*, 1–6.

3. Josephus, *Jewish Antiquities* 13.257–58.

4. For a discussion of some of the scholarly controversy, see Kasher, *Jews, Idumaeans, and Ancient Arabs*, 44–78, although his substantive discussion must be treated with caution.

5. In rabbinic tradition, Ruth, whom they date to an earlier period, becomes the proto-typical "convert." This, however, goes far beyond the actual story found in the book of Ruth, which in any case is very difficult to date. See Goldenberg, "How Did Ruth Become the Model Convert?" On the continuation of Idumaeans as Judeans: Josephus, *Jewish War* 4.270–84. See also Cohen, *The Beginning of Jewishness*; Cohen, *Why Aren't Jewish Women Circumcised?* 3–54.

6. Josephus first mentions these groups in his account of the rule of Jonathan around 145 BCE (*Jewish Antiquities* 13.171–73). His discussion there, though, seems to be dis-connected to the actual events that he is relating; it is difficult to know why he in-cludes it where he does. For this story, see Josephus, *Jewish Antiquities* 13.288–92.

7. Ibid., 13.297–98 (trans. Loeb Classical Library, 377)

8. The literature on this topic is vast. For some of the most important treatments, see Cohen, *Josephus in Galilee and Rome*, 144–51; Daniel R. Schwartz, "Josephus and Ni-colaus on the Pharisees"; Seth Schwartz, *Josephus and Judaean Politics*; Mason, *Josephus Flavius on the Pharisees*.

9. This is a much wider and historical expansion of the brilliant insight made by Shem-esh, *Halakhah in the Making*. On the idea that the Pharisees and Sadducees changed their character from political to "religious" parties, see Neusner, *From Politics to Piety*. Josephus's programmatic statement that emphasizes the different beliefs of Pharisees and Sadducees (*Jewish War* 2.119, 162–66), I suggest, more reflects the situation in the first century CE than the second century BCE.

10. Josephus, *Jewish Antiquities* 13.296, with a possible historical echo found in the Mish-nah, *Ma'aser Sheni* 5:15; *Sotah* 9:10.

11. Some scholars connect the term "Sadducee" to the name Zadok and make the claim that the group originated out of the genealogical line of David's priest by that name. Since Onias III was in this line and Josephus testifies that Sadducees were wealthy, this argument goes, the Sadducees are thus portrayed as the old priestly aristocracy, pre-cisely the opposite reconstruction from what I am proposing here. For a discussion of the shaky evidence linking the words "Sadducee" and "Zadok" and some alternative possibilities, see Main, "Sadducees."

12. See Goldstein, *1 Maccabees*, 62–72.

13. Van der Kooij, "The Claim of Maccabean Leadership and the Use of Scripture."

14. See 2 Maccabees 8:23, where the terms are slightly different. This, however, was com-posed in Greek. On the use in Jewish Greek texts, see the next chapter. On the word *holy*, see Botterweck, Ringgren, and Fabry, *Theological Dictionary of the Old Testament*, esp. 12:543–45; Kittel, *Theological Dictionary of the New Testament*, 1:88–97.

15. Bremmer, "From Holy Books to Holy Bible," 338–39.

16. García Martínez, "Temple Scroll." See Yigael Yadin, *The Temple Scroll*.

17. Temple Scroll LIII:14 (my translation; Yigael Yadin, *The Temple Scroll*, 2:240).

18. For an extensive discussion of these regulations, see Yigael Yadin, *The Temple Scroll*, 1:277–343.

19. Temple Scroll LVI:20–LVII:15 (trans. Yigael Yadin, *The Temple Scroll*, 2:254–58, with some minor changes to help readability).

20. Some scholars have also seen in this passage a subtle critique of Hyrcanus, who was known to employ foreign mercenaries. See Schiffman, "The Law of the Temple Scroll and Its Provenance."

21. The Temple Scroll goes on to further constrain the king's actions, limiting beyond Deuteronomy his choice of marital partners; the number of women he can marry at one time; and his ability to appropriate the property of others. For a sensitive treatment of the interpretive activity taking place in this passage (as a reflection of the author's sociohistorical setting), see Fraade, "'The Torah of the King,'" esp. 285–99.

22. See Zahn, *Rethinking Rewritten Scripture*, 179–228; Zahn, "Rewritten Scripture."

23. See VanderKam, "Jubilees, Book of."

24. On the complicated and composite nature of Jubilees, see especially Michael Segal, *The Book of Jubilees*, 11–40, 319–22; Kugel, *A Walk through Jubilees*, esp. 207–26.

25. Jubilees 6:36–38 (trans. O. S. Wintermute, in Charlesworth, *Old Testament Pseudepigrapha*, 2:68).

26. Jubilees 1:4 (trans. O. S. Wintermute, in Charlesworth, *Old Testament Pseudepigrapha*, 2:52). On the "heavenly tablets," see, for examples, 5:13, 6:17, 32:10–15. See García Martínez, "The Heavenly Tablets in the Book of Jubilees." García Martínez links these tablets to the Pharisaic "Oral Torah." Unlike the Oral Torah, though, they are explicitly textual sources of knowledge. On the author's use of previous writings, see Kugel, *A Walk through Jubilees*, 1–205.

27. Jubilees 2:30 (trans. O. S. Wintermute, in Charlesworth, *Old Testament Pseudepigrapha* 2:58). See also Doering, "The Concept of Sabbath in the Book of Jubilees."

28. This socioeconomic stratum is often at the root of sectarian movements. See Baumgarten, *The Flourishing of Jewish Sects in the Maccabean Era*.

29. Damascus Document (CD) I.11–12 (trans. Vermes, *The Complete Dead Sea Scrolls*, 97–98); 1QpHab xi.4–8 (calendar); 4Q171 iv.8–10 (the law); 1QpHab xi.9–12 (council).

30. 1QH xv.9–10 (trans. Vermes, *The Complete Dead Sea Scrolls*, 275). See also 1QH xiv. For a very good, if skeptical, overview of the evidence on the Teacher of Righteousness, see Stuckenbruck, "The Teacher of Righteousness Remembered."

31. Schremer, "[T]he[y] Did Not Read in the Sealed Book."

Chapter 9. The Septuagint

1. Philo, *Life of Moses* 2.40 (trans. Colson, Loeb Classical Library, 6:469).

2. See Thompson, *Memphis under the Ptolemies*, 82–105.

3. Herodotus was the first to write in this mode, but it wouldn't be until the Hellenistic period that the genre became particularly robust. See Munson, *Telling Wonders*; Momigliano, *Alien Wisdom*, esp. 74–96.

4. Diodorus 40.3.1–5, with quote at 40.3.4.

5. The work *On the Athenian Constitution*, falsely attributed to Aristotle, somewhat eccentrically uses the term *politeia* as relating specifically to political organization. See Toye, "Aristotle's Other Politeiai."

6. Diodoros 40.3.6; Bar-Kochva, *The Image of the Jews in Greek Literature*, 115–19, argues that Hecataeus knew the entire Torah. I see no evidence for this. See Grabbe, "Hecataeus of Abdera and the Jewish Law." On Hecataeus and the term "holy book," see Bremmer, "From Holy Books to Holy Bible," 334.

7. Fraser, *Ptolemaic Alexandria*.

8. See Barnes, "Cloistered Bookworms in the Chicken-Coop of the Muses." On the destruction of the library (whose date is debated), see the essays in El-Abbadi and Fathallah, *What Happened to the Ancient Library of Alexandria*.

9. Letter of Aristeas 1:10 (translation R. J. H. Shutt, in Charlesworth, *Old Testament Pseudepigrapha* 2:12).

10. Gruen, "The Letter of Aristeas and the Cultural Context of the Septuagint," 155.

11. This discussion follows, with some modifications, the views of Bickerman, "The Septuagint as a Translation"; and Modrzejewski, "The Septuagint as *Nomos*." For an alternative view that ascribes the translation to Jewish initiative, see Honigman, *The Septuagint and Homeric Scholarship*, 93–118.

12. I do not discount the possibility that this initiative had a domestic dimension as well. According to the Letter of Aristeas 1:11–21, there was an enormous number of Jews in Egypt at this time, and there is some other evidence that also suggests the existence of strong Jewish communities, although not on the scale suggested by the Letter of Aristeas. See Levine, *The Ancient Synagogue*, 75–81. On the Ptolemaic economic policy in Judea, see Tcherikover, "Palestine under the Ptolemies."

13. Letter of Aristeas 1:50; Rajak, "Translating the Septuagint for Ptolemy's Library"; Bar-Kochva, *Pseudo-Hecataeus*, 219–25.

14. For a modern representative of this approach, which sees the Septuagint as an attempt to bring the reader to the underlying Hebrew, see especially Benjamin G. Wright, "The Septuagint and Its Modern Translators." For a more cautious assessment, see Jellicoe, *The Septuagint and Modern Study*, 314–37.

15. Tov, "Theologically Motivated Exegesis Embedded in the Septuagint."

16. See Josephus, *Jewish War* 1.31–33; 7.420–35; Josephus, *Jewish Antiquities* 12.387 (Josephus contradicts himself about the identity of the high priest). See Modrzejewski, *The Jews of Egypt*, 121–33; Hayward, "The Jewish Temple at Leontopolis."

17. For these inscriptions, see Horbury and Noy, *Jewish Inscriptions of Graeco-Roman Egypt*, nos. 29–105, with mention of land of Onias in no. 38.

18. Cowey and Maresch, *Urkunden des Politeuma der Juden von Herakleopolis*. These papyri are known as P. Polit. Iud. It is possible that P. Polit. Iud. 4, a grievance about a broken engagement, contains a term that references the Septuagint's version of Deuteronomy 24:1 and 3 (ibid., 56–71), but the link between the document and Deuteronomy is less than clear. See Kruse, "Das *politeuma* der Juden von Herakelopolis in Ägypten." See also the sensitive review article of Honigman, "The Jewish *Politeuma* at Heracleopolis."

19. Cited in Josephus, *Jewish Antiquities* 14.117 (trans. Marcus, Loeb Classical Library 7:509). See Tcherikover and Fuks, *Corpus Papyrorum Judaicarum*, 1:32–36.

20. See Fraser, *Ptolemaic Alexandria*, 459–67; Morgan, *Literate Education in the Hellenistic and Roman Worlds*, 69–73. Morgan identifies Homer as one of the few "core" texts of Hellenistic education.

21. The history of this textual transmission is typical of such literature. Around the year 80 BCE, a Greek epitomizer named Alexander Polyhistor included some selections of Demetrios, and although Polyhistor's anthology (he also preserved selections of many other now-obscure Greek historians) was lost, some later writers—most nota-

bly Josephus and the church historian Eusebius—learned of Demetrios through their reading of Polyhistor. See Holladay, *Fragments from Hellenistic Jewish Authors*, 1:51–53. See also Eusebius, *Praep. Ev.* 9.21.2, 9.29.16. On the dating, which is a revision from the older view that dates him to the third century BCE, see Niehoff, *Jewish Exegesis*, 38–57.

22. Bickerman, "The Jewish Historian Demetrios"; Niehoff, *Jewish Exegesis*, 38–57.

23. Eusebius, *Praep. Ev.* 8.10.8 (trans. A. Collins in *Old Testament Pseudepigrapha* 2:838), on Exodus 13:9. See ibid., 13.12.12, 13.12.1.

24. Cited in ibid., 9.27.4. This understanding of Artapanus follows that of Gruen, *Diaspora*, 201–11, although I think that Gruen sometimes finds too much playfulness and humor in his writings.

25. See 2 Maccabees 2:11 (citation of a verse not found in our Bible) and 4:11 (reference to laws but not a written law). The date is much debated. I here follow Daniel Schwartz, *The Second Book of Maccabees*, 16–19, and 91 on 2 Maccabees 2:11. Most scholars date it later, which would fit even better into the argument made here.

26. Letter of Aristeas 310 (trans. Hadas, *Aristeas to Philocrates*, 221).

27. Ibid. For the term "charter myth," see Murray, "The Letter of Aristeas."

28. Letter of Aristeas 293–94 (trans. Hadas, *Aristeas to Philocrates*, 215).

29. Letter of Aristeas 145.

30. Letter of Aristeas 31 (trans. Hadas, *Aristeas to Philocrates*, 111), 311 (trans. Hadas, *Aristeas to Philocrates*, 223).

31. Finkelberg, "Canonising and Decanonising Homer"; Honigman, *The Septuagint and Homeric Scholarship*, 119–43; Benjamin G. Wright, "The Letter of Aristeas and the Reception History of the Septuagint."

32. Letter of Aristeas 3, 31, 313, 316 (for reference to "the book"). See Bremmer, "From Holy Books to Holy Bible," 337.

33. For a discussion of the evidence for the formation of the three parts, see Barrera, "Origins of a Tripartite Old Testament Canon." For the suggestion relating this to the Library of Alexandria, see Sarna, *Ancient Libraries*.

34. Philo, *Life of Moses* 2.33–44: Josephus, *Jewish Antiquities* 12.7–118.

35. Cohen, "Sosates, the Jewish Homer"; Jacobson, *The Exagoge of Ezekiel*.

36. Philo, *Life of Moses* 2.216 (trans. Colson, Loeb Classical Library, 6:557).

37. Philo, *Every Good Man Is Free* 86; Philo, *The Contemplative Life* 28, 30–31 (the reading of the texts on the Sabbath is only implied here). For an argument for the existence of the Therapeutae, see Taylor, *Jewish Women Philosophers*.

38. For a review of the evidence regarding pre-70 CE synagogues in general and for what occurred there, see van der Horst, "Was the Synagogue a Place of Sabbath Worship before 70 CE?" although his analysis is less attentive to the chronological argument I make here. My argument here is, to my knowledge, original. I will develop it later, arguing that it helps to explain the later appearance of synagogues in Jerusalem.

39. Daniel R. Schwartz, "Philo, His Family, and His Times," 12–14.

40. See Royse, "The Works of Philo."

41. Philo, *Allegorical Interpretation* 2.19–22 (trans. Colson, Loeb Classical Library, 1: 237–41).

42. Philo, *Life of Moses* 2.37 (trans. Colson, Loeb Classical Library, 6:467), 2.52 (trans. Colson, Loeb Classical Library, 6:475). See Winston, "Sage and Supersage in Philo of Alexandria."

43. For a more developed form of the argument that follows, see Satlow, "Philo on Human Perfection."

44. Philo, *Allegorical Interpretation* 3.140 (trans. Colson, Loeb Classical Library, 1:395).

45. I have not addressed here the issue of to what extent women participated in this intellectual culture. There is very little evidence that would allow us to answer this question. Although Philo's description of the Therapeutae have sometimes been taken as evidence for female Jewish philosophers near Alexandria, there is considerable doubt concerning its accuracy. See Kraemer, *Unreliable Witnesses*, 57–116.

Chapter 10. The Sadducees and the Dead Sea Scrolls

1. It is possible that this Sadducean support of the Hasmoneans is reflected in a fragmentary prayer for "the welfare of King Jonathan," as Alexander was known, found among the Dead Sea Scrolls. This composition, however, might not originate from these circles. See Eshel, Eshel, and Yardeni, "A Qumran Composition." On the riots, see Josephus, *Jewish Antiquities* 13.37 and, in the Dead Sea Scrolls, 4Q169 i.5–6. I think that this riot was likely engineered by the Pharisees on the basis both of Janneaus's actions following it and the particular insult that Josephus records that the people used against him, which echoes one directed against his father by Eliezer the Pharisee. Josephus obscures the connection, probably to advance his own agenda.

2. Josephus, *Jewish Antiquities* 13.402; Josephus, *Jewish War* 1.112 (trans. Thackeray, Loeb Classical Library, 2:55), 97, 113–14. See also Ilan, *Silencing the Queen*, 61–72.

3. Josephus, *Jewish War* 1.114 (trans. Thackeray, Loeb Classical Library, 2:55).

4. The story of the discovery of the scrolls is well told in Shanks, *Understanding the Dead Sea Scrolls*.

5. The Damascus Document (abbreviated CD) was originally found in the Cairo Geniza; fragments of it were later found in the caves around Qumran. Exactly how it survived is still a mystery. Translations of both this and the Community Rule (abbreviated 1 QS) can be found in Vermes, *The Complete Dead Sea Scrolls*, 127–43, 98–117, respectively.

6. Ordering, dating, and understanding the fragments of these two documents is complex and the source of continuing scholarly debate. See Metso, *The Textual Development of the Qumran Community Rule*; Hempel, *The Laws of the Damascus Document*; Hempel, "Shared Traditions." Some of the practices are indeed distinctive, even polemically so (such as the restriction on having more than one wife at a time), but it is unlikely that they would have made the members of this group stand out.

7. See John J. Collins, *Apocalypticism in the Dead Sea Scrolls*; O'Connor, "Damascus."

8. 1QS vi.6–8, and see CD x.6, among other places, where the term "the book of Hagu" might refer to study of the Torah. On the manuscript evidence, see Tov, "Some Thoughts about the Diffusion of Biblical Manuscripts in Antiquity," esp. 156.

9. The dating of the archaeology at Qumran is debated. I follow here the chronology of Magness, *The Archaeology of Qumran and the Dead Sea Scrolls*, esp. 47–72.

10. 4Q397+4Q398+4Q399 (trans. Vermes, *The Complete Dead Sea Scrolls*, 227–28). For ease of readability, I have removed the typographic marks indicating reconstructed and added text.

11. The *Halakhic Letter* has rarely been dated this late, but the arguments against such a late date do not strike me as compelling. For a discussion of the early dating and the relationship between its laws and those of the Sadducees (which we know from later, rabbinic texts), see Schiffman, *Reclaiming the Dead Sea Scrolls*, 83–89.

12. Brooke, "The Explicit Presentation of Scripture in 4QMMT."

13. VanderKam and Flint, *The Meaning of the Dead Sea Scrolls*, 103–53; Ulrich, *The Dead Sea Scrolls and the Origins of the Bible*.

14. Brooke, "Prophecy and Prophets in the Dead Sea Scrolls."

15. VanderKam, *The Dead Sea Scrolls Today*, 97–126.

16. Josephus, *Jewish Antiquities* 13.311–13.

17. See Roller, *The Building Program of Herod the Great*, esp. 85–238.

18. Gabba, "The Finances of King Herod"; Geiger, "Rome and Jerusalem."

19. Josephus, *Jewish Antiquities* 17.205, 15.315 (trans. Marcus, Loeb Classical Library, 8:151), 15.365.

20. Ibid., 15.366–68 (trans. Marcus, Loeb Classical Library, 8:177–79, 17:99). See also Schürer, *The History of the Jewish People*, 1:320–29.

21. Josephus, *Jewish Antiquities* 15.370–79.

22. Ibid., 17.41–44; Josephus, *Jewish War* 1.648–50, with quote at 650 (trans. Thackeray, Loeb Classical Library, 2:309). This part of the speech is omitted from his account of the incident in his later work, *Jewish Antiquities* 17.149–54, perhaps indicating Josephus's desire to distance the episode from the Pharisees.

23. Richardson, *Herod*, 241–47.

24. See John J. Collins, *Apocalypticism in the Dead Sea Scrolls*.

25. On the Qumran "canon" (or better, its lack) see VanderKam, "Questions of Canon Viewed through the Dead Sea Scrolls." Liturgy: Chazon, "Scripture and Prayer in 'The Words of the Luminaries.'"

26. 1QpHab vii.4–5 (trans. Vermes, *The Complete Dead Sea Scrolls*, 343), 1QpHab ii.7–10 (trans. Vermes, *The Complete Dead Sea Scrolls*, 341), 1QS ix.16 (trans. Vermes, *The Complete Dead Sea Scrolls*, 83).

27. See Lim, *Pesharim*.

28. Ulrich, "The Bible in the Making," esp. 53–54.

29. The stone was probably from Jordan; it was not unearthed in a controlled archaeological excavation. See the essays in Henze, *Hazon Gabriel*.

30. Metso, "Biblical Quotations in the Community Rule."

31. Tov, *Scribal Practices*, 125–29.

Chapter 11. Jesus and the Synagogue

1. For a general idea of the economic state of the city, drawn mainly from literary sources, see Jeremias, *Jerusalem in the Time of Jesus*. More recent archaeological finds have vastly increased our understanding of the extent of the city and its wealth. See, particularly, Geva, *Jewish Quarter Excavations in the Old City of Jerusalem*; Geva, *Ancient*

Jerusalem Revealed. For a more evocative essay, see Avigad, "How the Wealthy Lived in Herodian Jerusalem."

2. Josephus, *Jewish Antiquities* 17.304–14.

3. Ibid., 17.317–20.

4. Ibid., 18.26–27.

5. Ibid., 18.3–10; Josephus, *Jewish War* 2.18.

6. This argument follows Knohl, "Between Voice and Silence." See Regev, "Temple Prayer as the Origin of the Fixed Prayer."

7. This, of course, is only a partial explanation for the formation of the book of Psalms, several of which already were thought to be written by David. See Trudinger, *The Psalms of the Tamid Service.* See Mishnah *Tamid* 7:4.

8. Mishnah *Tamid* 5:1. See Hammer, "What Did They Bless?" To my mind, the last selection looks out of place: it is found in Numbers rather than Deuteronomy (at least in our Bible) and is addressed to the individual rather than community. Could it have been added later to the account?

9. There are problems of definition when it comes to discussing "synagogues." Many of the functions that took place in later dedicated buildings undoubtedly took place earlier in other places. See Levine, "The Nature and Origin of the Palestinian Synagogue Reconsidered." My claim is that the reading of scripture was not among these earlier activities.

10. Cotton et al., *Corpus inscriptionum Iudaeae/Palestinae,* 1.1:53–56.

11. Ibid., 1.1:55.

12. Mishnah *Ta'anit* 4:2–3; Tosefta *Ta'anit* 4:2–3.

13. Levine, *The Ancient Synagogue,* 42–73. On what appears to be the earliest of the synagogue structures in Judea, see Onn et al., "Khirbet Umm el-'Umdan."

14. Scholarship on the "historical Jesus" and the methodological issues that accompany it are vast. For an accessible summary, see Ehrman, *Did Jesus Exist?* Less accessible but far more complete is the massive 4-volume collection Holmén and Porter, *Handbook for the Study of the Historical Jesus.* For a sensitive critique of this scholarship, see Ratzinger, *Jesus of Nazareth,* esp. xiv–xxiv.

15. Jesus's education and familiarity with scripture, like much else about his life, are heavily debated. Meier, *A Marginal Jew,* 268–78, acknowledges the sparse evidence but is inclined to think that Jesus was trained to read scripture.

16. Hezser, *Jewish Literacy in Roman Palestine,* esp. 40–89.

17. The issue of Jesus's education also piqued the interest of later rabbis, who portray him as a wayward, and very poor, student. See Schäfer, *Jesus in the Talmud,* 25–51.

18. The claim that Jesus should be seen within a Pharisaic framework has a long history, but the claim itself has largely been marginalized. For a review of the positions, see E. P. Sanders, *Jesus and Judaism,* 51–55. On the Pharisees as explicators of customs rather than written texts, see Mandel, "Scriptural Exegesis and the Pharisees."

19. Luke 4:31–37; Josephus, *Jewish Antiquities* 18.17, 20.168–72, 20.97–98; Acts 5:36.

20. See also Vermes, *The Religion of Jesus the Jew,* 157–73.

21. See Schürer, *The History of the Jewish People,* 1:357–98. The title changes for administrative reasons, but the role is virtually identical.

22. See Bond, *Pontius Pilate*; Taylor, "Pontius Pilate."

23. See, e.g., Josephus, *Jewish War* 2.331–32, which although exceptional indicates that Roman procurators trusted control of their troops to Jewish authorities.

24. Goodblatt, *The Monarchic Principle*, 77–130.

25. Many scholars have seen in this incident the key to understanding Jesus's own perception of himself and his mission. See E. P. Sanders, *Jesus and Judaism*, 61–76; Fredriksen, *From Jesus to Christ*, 111–14.

26. In Matthew 22:15–22 it is the Pharisees who set out on their own initiative to trap him; they are absent from the account in Luke 20:9–19.

Chapter 12. Paul

1. See Saldarini, *Jesus and Passover*.

2. Paul's theology is the stuff out of which bloody wars and inquisitions have been made. I hope that this serves as a relatively uncontroversial and vague encapsulation of it. See E. P. Sanders, *Paul*.

3. According to Acts 22:3, Paul was born in Tarsus and was raised in Jerusalem. This, I think, is an inference made on the part of the author, who had trouble seeing him as purely Judean. See also Frey, "Paul's Jewish Identity."

4. Josephus, *Jewish Antiquities* 19.326–27, 352; Daniel R. Schwartz, *Agrippa*, esp. 157–71.

5. On the increasing influence of the Sadducees under Agrippa, see Daniel R. Schwartz, *Agrippa*, 116–30; Josephus, *Jewish Antiquities* 19.299–311; Meshorer, *Ancient Jewish Coinage*, 2:57.

6. Mishnah *Sotah* 7:8; Josephus, *Jewish War* 2.228–31.

7. Acts 18:3 asserts that Paul was a tentmaker, a solid craft but not the kind that could normally finance an education like Paul's. Perhaps he was, although it is likely that his parents were not. See also Malherbe, *Social Aspects of Early Christianity*, 29–59. See Hengel, *The Pre-Christian Paul*, 18–39, who goes to extraordinary effort to explain how to reconcile this data with his conviction that Paul is best seen as a product of the Diaspora. Three other data can be adduced to support a Jerusalem context for Paul: (1) according to Acts 23:16, he had close family in Jerusalem, which suggests that his entirely family was either born or raised there; (2) Paul self-identifies as a "Benjaminite" (Romans 11:1), which makes most sense as indicating that he was a resident of Jerusalem, which was located within the (long-defunct) tribal area of Benjamin; and (3) he identifies himself as a Pharisee (Romans 11:1). Pharisees are otherwise unknown outside of Judea/Galilee.

8. On Paul from a psychohistorical perspective, see Alan F. Segal, *Paul the Convert*.

9. The literature on the historicity of Acts is vast. See Bauckham, "James and the Jerusalem Church," who argues for a core historicity to Acts, although he does not deal specifically with this issue.

10. See Barclay, *Jews in the Mediterranean Diaspora*, esp. 259–319.

11. Stroup, "Without Patronage"; Hadot, *What Is Philosophy?*, 146–71.

12. Satlow, "Theophrastus's Jewish Philosophers."

13. Orlin, *Temples, Religion, and Politics in the Roman Republic*, 76–115; Plutarch, *Life of Numa,* 22. See Dionysius of Halicanarssus 10.1.4, 11.62.3.

14. See Kraabel, "The Disappearance of the 'God-Fearers'"; Gager, "Jews, Gentiles, and Synagogues in the Book of Acts"; Feldman, *Jew and Gentile in the Ancient World,* 342–82; Cohen, *The Beginnings of Jewishness,* 140–74.

15. Meeks, *The First Urban Christians;* Harland, *Dynamics of Identity in the World of the Early Christians.*

16. For some recent scholarship on Romans, see especially Stowers, *A Rereading of Romans;* Hodge, *If Sons, Then Heirs.*

17. This is not to say that images from and allusions to scripture might not be present, but that they are by-products of Paul's thought rather than deployed as authoritative. See Johnson, "Paul's Reliance on Scripture in 1 Thessalonians."

18. See Stanley, "Paul's 'Use' of Scripture," esp. 149–55.

19. Flint, "Psalms and Psalters in the Dead Sea Scrolls"; J. J. M. Roberts, "The Importance of Isaiah at Qumran." See Flint, *The Dead Sea Psalms Scrolls and the Book of Psalms,* who argues that Psalms 1–90 had largely stabilized as an authoritative collection by then.

20. On the use of psalms in amulets, see Arzt-Grabner, "Psalms as Magic?" esp. the literature cited on 42–43nn19–20. On the numinous power of scriptural texts, see Cohn, *Tangled Up in Text.*

21. See Ehrman, *The Orthodox Corruption of Scripture;* McLay, "Biblical Texts and the Scriptures for the New Testament Church."

22. E. P. Sanders, *Paul,* 18–21.

23. The question of Paul's attitude toward the Jews is immensely vexed and loaded. For a concise summary of positions, see Longnecker, "On Israel's God and God's Israel."

Chapter 13. The Gospels

1. For a more detailed and careful consideration of the causes of the revolt, see Goodman, *The Ruling Class of Judea.*

2. Josephus, *Jewish War* 2.284, 289, 291.

3. See Goodman, *Rome and Jerusalem.*

4. On Mark's date, see Adela Collins, *Mark,* 2–10. See also Marcus, *The Way of the Lord,* 47.

5. See Marcus, *The Way of the Lord,* 153–98.

6. See Evans, "The Beginning of the Good News," esp. 84–85. My argument follows the "skeptical" reading of the Gospels. For an overview that moves in the other direction, see Moyise, "Jesus and the Scriptures of Israel."

7. See Mark 12:26 for a textual note to the reciter. The earliest extant manuscript of Mark, P. Chester Beatty P45, also contains markings that suggest public recitation.

8. On the novels, see Wills, *The Jewish Novel in the Ancient World.* For a discussion of Matthew rewriting Mark, see Allen, *A Critical and Exegetical Commentary on the Gospel according to St. Matthew,* xiii–xl.

9. This is the so-called long ending, Mark 16:9–20.

10. On Q, see Robinson, Hoffmann, and Kloppenborg, *The Critical Edition of Q*. For Matthew's use of it, see Luz, *Matthew 1–7*, 41–43. Not all scholars, though, agree that Q ever existed. See Goodacre, *The Case against Q*.

11. Luz, *Matthew 1–7*, 45; Sim, "Matthew's Use of Mark."

12. Knowles, "Scripture, History, Messiah," 69; Overman, *Matthew's Gospel*, 74–78.

13. On the dating, see Fitzmyer, *The Gospel according to Luke*, 53–57.

14. See Wendel, *Scripture Interpretation*, 112.

15. Brown, *The Gospel according to John*, lxxx–lxxxvi.

16. See Meeks, "'Am I Jew?'" esp. 182.

17. See Barrett, "The Old Testament in the Fourth Gospel"; Brown, *The Gospel according to John*, lix; Menken, *Old Testament Quotations*, esp. 105–22.

18. Dodd, *According to the Scriptures*, 61–110. John does cite scripture occasionally to indicate its fulfillment, e.g., 19:24; 19:28.

19. Brown, *The Gospel according to John*, lxx–lxxv. See John 1:47, where Nathanael is called an "Israelite" rather than a "Jew."

20. See Wasserman, "The Early Text of Matthew."

21. This canonical story can be found in Meyer, *The Gnostic Discoveries*, 13–32.

22. Other genres are represented in the Nag Hammadi writings. See Robinson, *Nag Hammadi Library*. An accessible collection of these and the writings discussed below, unless noted, is Ehrman, *Lost Scriptures*. For the gospel of Judas, see Pagels and King, *Reading Judas*.

23. For the Acts of Pilate, see Elliott, *The Apocryphal New Testament*, 164–85.

24. The "Deutero-Pauline" epistles include 2 Thessalonians, Colossians, 1 and 2 Timothy, Titus, and Ephesians.

25. Ehrman, *Lost Scriptures*, 15–16; "The Paraphrase of Shem (VII, 1)," introduced by Michael Roberge and translated by Frederik Wisse, in Robinson, *Nag Hammadi Library*, 351.

26. The Infancy Gospel of Thomas 15 (in Ehrman, *Lost Scriptures*, 51).

27. On the Ebionites, see Skarsaune, "The Ebionites."

28. Ehrman, *Lost Scriptures*, 158; Stanton, "Jewish Christian Elements in the Pseudo-Clementine Writings."

29. Painchaud, "The Use of Scripture in Gnostic Literature"; "Ptolemy's Letter to Flora," found in Ehrman, *Lost Scriptures*, 201–6.

30. See Revelations 1:3; 1 Timothy 4:13; Justin Martyr, *1 Apology* 67.3–4.

Chapter 14. Early Christians

1. See Matthews, "Hostages, Philosophers, Pilgrims, and the Diffusion of Ideas in the Late Roman Mediterranean and Near East."

2. Josephus, *Against Apion* 1.2.

3. Ibid., 1.37–43 (trans. Thackeray, Loeb Classical Library, 1:177–81).

4. See Leiman, "Josephus and the Canon of the Bible."

5. Mason, "Josephus and His Twenty-Two Book Canon"; Barclay, *Flavius Josephus*, 32n179.

6. Josephus, *Life* 8–9, 12.

7. Josephus, *Jewish War* 1.17 (trans. Thackeray, Loeb Classical Library, 1:11), 5.379–94 (see 6.438–39), 4.530–31, 3.352–53.

8. See Feldman, *Josephus's Interpretation of the Bible*, esp. 14–73; Josephus, *Jewish Antiquities* 1.5–26. He rarely uses the term "holy writings" in *Jewish War*.

9. Josephus, *Life* 418.

10. See Barnard, *Justin Martyr*, 4–13.

11. Justin Martyr, *Dialogue with Trypho*, chapters 2, 7.

12. Wilken, *The Christians as the Romans Saw Them*, 48–67.

13. Justin Martyr, *1 Apology* 17 (trans. A. Cleveland Coxe in Alexander Roberts and James Donaldson, eds., *The Ante-Nicene Fathers* [Edinburgh: T&T Clark, 1867–72], 1:168).

14. Justin Martyr, *1 Apology* 31 (trans. Coxe, in Alexander Roberts and Donaldson, *The Ante-Nicene Fathers*, 1:173).

15. Barnard, *Justin Martyr*, 43–44; Justin Martyr, *1 Apology* 32.

16. See Lieu, *Image and Reality*, 103–53, for a nicely balanced discussion of the historical authenticity of the tract.

17. Justin Martyr, *Dialogue with Trypho* 29, 71–73, 126. See also Barnard, "The Old Testament and Judaism in the Writings of Justin Martyr," esp. 399–400.

18. See Crosgrove, "Justin Martyr and the Emerging Christian Canon."

19. Justin Martyr, *1 Apology* 67.3–4 (trans. Coxe, in Alexander Roberts and Donaldson, *The Ante-Nicene Fathers*, 1:186); Marrou, *A History of Education in Antiquity*, 314–18.

20. Justin Martyr, *1 Apology* 26.

21. See Brakke, *The Gnostics*, 94–99.

22. See Ehrman, *Lost Scriptures*, 103–9.

23. See Brakke, "Scriptural Practices in Early Christianity," esp. 272.

24. Grant, *Irenaeus*, 1–10.

25. Ibid., 21–28. Just as we know Apion primarily through Josephus, so too, with the exception of some tracts from Nag Hammadi, we owe almost all of our knowledge of the Valentinians to Irenaeus.

26. Irenaeus, *Against the Heresies*, 3.11.9 (trans. Grant, *Irenaeus*, 133).

27. McDonald, *The Biblical Canon*, 289–301.

28. Hurtado, "What Do the Earliest Christian Manuscripts Tell Us about Their Readers?"

29. Stroumsa, "Early Christianity"; C. H. Roberts and Skeat, *The Birth of the Codex*.

30. Luijendijke, "Sacred Scriptures as Trash."

Chapter 15. The Rabbis

1. In their imperial propaganda, Vespasian and his descendents heavily used the conquest of Judea, but decades later it is unlikely to have made much of an impact on popular consciousness. See Goodman, *Rome and Jerusalem*. On the Coliseum inscription, see Alföldy, "Eine Bauinschrift aus dem Colosseum."

2. Schremer, "Thinking about Belonging in Early Rabbinic Literature."

3. Josephus, *Jewish War* 5.412 (trans. Thackeray, Loeb Classical Library, 3:331).

4. See also Najman, "How to Make Sense of the Pseudonymous Attribution."

5. 4 Ezra 14:34–35.

6. 4 Ezra 14:42–47 (trans. B. M. Metzger, in Charlesworth, *The Old Testament Pseud-epigrapha*, 1:555).

7. Stone, *Fourth Ezra*, 418–19, 441. See 4 Ezra 4:21, which identifies "the Law" as a physical object that can be burned.

8. For the primary rabbinic account, see Babylonian Talmud, *Gittin* 55b–56b (also *Abot d'Rabbi Natan*, A [11b–12a]), and the discussion in Rubenstein, *Talmud Stories*, 141, 139–75. See also Boyarin, "The *Diadoche* of the Rabbis."

9. Despite the quite understandable desire to know more about these rabbis as actual historical figures, the only relevant information that survives is in the form of much later hagiographical legends. It is likely that these two rabbis actually existed, although it is almost impossible to say much more about their lives. On the different rabbinic approaches, see Azzan Yadin, "Resistance to Midrash?"

10. Mildenberg, *The Coinage of the Bar Kokhba War*, 133; Schäfer, "Bar Kokhba and the Rabbis," esp. 15–20; Bowersock, "The Tel Shalem Arch and P. Nahal Heber/ Seiyal 8."

11. Schäfer, "Bar Kokhba and the Rabbis," 8–15; Cotton, "The Rabbis and the Documents."

12. Palestinian Talmud, *Ta'anit* 4:8; Goodblatt, *Elements of Jewish Nationalism*, 49–70.

13. There has been a lively scholarly debate about whether the renaming of Jerusalem occurred prior to or after the revolt. See Eliav, "The Urban Layout of Aelia Capitolina." On the revolt, see also Isaac, "Roman Religious Policy and the Bar Kokhba War"; Babylonian Talmud, *Berakhot* 61b; Lauterbach, *Mekhilta de Rabbi Ishmael*, 3:142–43 (on Exodus 22:22).

14. See S. Lieberman, "The Martyrs of Caesarea," esp. 424–32.

15. Dio 69.14.1; Seth Schwartz, "Political, Social, and Economic Life in the Land of Israel," esp. 36–38.

16. Lapin, "Rabbis and Cities in Later Roman Palestine." On the lack of a rabbinic "Sanhedrin" at this time, see Levine, *The Rabbinic Class*, 76–83.

17. See Seth Schwartz, *Josephus and Judaean Politics*, 203–8; Sivertsev, *Households, Sects, and the Origins of Rabbinic Judaism*.

18. See Cohen, "The Significance of Yavneh," although he dates this process about a century earlier than I do here.

19. Halivni, "The Reception Accorded to Rabbi Judah's Mishnah."

20. See Cohen, "The Rabbi in Second-Century Jewish Society"; Seth Schwartz, *Imperialism and Jewish Society*, 103–28.

21. See Kugel and Greer, *Early Biblical Interpretation*.

22. See Leiman, *The Canonization of Hebrew Scripture*; and the helpful discussion by Zevit, "The Second-Third Century Canonization of the Hebrew Bible."

23. Fleisher, "On the Beginnings of Obligatory Jewish Prayer."

24. For an overview, see Reif, "The Early Liturgy of the Synagogue."

25. Naeh, "The Role of Biblical Verses in Prayer."

26. Tosefta *Megillah* 3 (4): 10; Heinemann, "The Triennial Lectionary Cycle."

27. Mishnah *Megillah* 3:1.

28. Mishnah *Yadaim* 3:5; Tosefta Yadaim 2:13–14; Lim, "The Defilement of the Hands."
29. See Jaffee, *Torah in the Mouth*, esp. 84–99.
30. Saul D. Lieberman, "The Publication of the Mishnah."
31. Zussman, "Torah she-ba'al peh."
32. Palestinian Talmud, *Megillah* 4:1.
33. Brody, *The Geonim of Babylonia*, 155–70.
34. Jaffee, *Torah in the Mouth*, 147–51.
35. David Stern, "On Canonization in Rabbinic Judaism," 250.
36. Safrai, "The Targums as Part of Rabbinic Literature"; Linder, *The Jews in Roman Imperial Legislation*, 402–11.
37. See Alexander, "Jewish Aramaic Translations of Hebrew Scriptures."
38. See Babylonian Talmud, *Shabbat* 115a–b.

Bibliography

Aharoni, Yohanan. *Excavations at Ramat Rahel*. 2 vols. Rome: Università degli studi, Centro di studi semitici, 1962.

Ahituv, Shmuel. *Echoes from the Past: Hebrew and Cognate Inscriptions from the Biblical Period*. Translated by Anson F. Rainey. Jerusalem: Carta, 2008.

Albertz, Rainer. "Family Religion in Ancient Israel and Its Surroundings." In *Household and Family Religion in Antiquity*, edited by John Bodel and Saul M. Olyan, 89–112. Malden, MA: Blackwell, 2008.

Alexander, Philip S. "Jewish Aramaic Translations of Hebrew Scriptures." In *Mikra: Text, Translation, Reading and Interpretation in Ancient Judaism and Early Christianity*, edited by Martin Jan Mulder, 217–53. Assen: Van Gorcum; Philadelphia: Fortress, 1988.

Alföldy, Géza. "Eine Bauinschrift aus dem Colosseum." *Zeitschrift für Papyrologie and Epigraphik* 109 (1995): 195–226.

Allen, Willoughby C. *A Critical and Exegetical Commentary on the Gospel according to St. Matthew*. 3rd ed. International Critical Commentary. Edinburgh: T and T Clark, 1993.

Applebaum, Simon. *Judaea in Hellenistic and Roman Times: Historical and Archaeological Essays*. Leiden: Brill, 1989.

Argall, Randall A. *1 Enoch and Sirach: A Comparative Literary and Conceptual Analysis of the Themes of Revelation, Creation and Judgment*. Early Judaism and Its Literature. Atlanta: Scholars Press, 1995.

Arzt-Grabner, Peter. "Psalms as Magic? P. Vindob. G 39205 Revisited." In *Septuagint and Reception: Essays Prepared for the Association for the Study of the Septuagint in South Africa*, edited by Johann Cook, 37–43. Supplements to the Vetus Testamentum. Leiden: Brill, 2009.

Athas, George. *The Tel Dan Inscription: A Reappraisal and a New Interpretation*. Journal for the Study of the Old Testament Supplement Series. Sheffield: Sheffield Academic Press, 2003.

Avigad, Nahman. "How the Wealthy Lived in Herodian Jerusalem." *Biblical Archaeology Review* 2:4 (1976): 23–38.

Barclay, John M. G. *Flavius Josephus: Translation and Commentary*, vol. 10, *Against Apion*. Leiden: Brill, 2007.

————. *Jews in the Mediterranean Diaspora: From Alexander to Trajan (323 BCE-117 CE)*. Edinburgh: T and T Clark, 1996.

Barkey, Gabriel, et al. "The Amulets from Ketef Hinnom: A New Edition and Evaluation." *Bulletin of the American Schools of Oriental Research* 334 (2004): 47–71.

Bar-Kochva, Bezalel. *The Image of the Jews in Greek Literature: The Hellenistic Period*. Berkeley: University of California Press, 2010.

————. *Judas Maccabaeus: The Jewish Struggle against the Seleucids*. Cambridge: Cambridge University Press, 1989.

————. *Pseudo-Hecataeus, "On the Jews": Legitimizing the Jewish Diaspora*. Berkeley: University of California Press, 1996.

Barnard, L. W. *Justin Martyr: His Life and Thought*. Cambridge: Cambridge University Press, 1967.

————. "The Old Testament and Judaism in the Writings of Justin Martyr." *Vetus Testamentum* 14 (1964): 395–406.

Barnes, Robert. "Cloistered Bookworms in the Chicken-Coop of the Muses: The Ancient Library of Alexandria." In *The Library of Alexandria: Centre of Learning in the Ancient World*, edited by Roy MacLeod, 61–77. London: I. B. Tauris, 2001.

Barrera, Julio C. Trebolle. "Origins of a Tripartite Old Testament Canon." In *The Canon Debate*, edited by Lee Martin McDonald and James A. Sanders, 128–45. Peabody, MA: Hendrickson, 2002.

Barrett, C. K. "The Old Testament in the Fourth Gospel." *Journal of Theological Studies* 48 (1947): 155–69.

Bartlett, John R. "Edomites and Idumaeans." *Palestinian Exploration Quarterly* 131 (1999): 102–14.

Barton, George Aaron. *A Critical and Exegetical Commentary on Ecclesiastes*. International Critical Commentary. New York: Charles Scribner's Sons, 1908.

Bauckham, Richard. "James and the Jerusalem Church." In *The Book of Acts in Its First Century Setting*, vol. 4, *Palestinian Setting*, edited by Richard Bauckham, 415–80. Grand Rapids, MI: Eerdmans, 1995.

Baumgarten, Albert I. *The Flourishing of Jewish Sects in the Maccabean Era: An Interpretation*. Leiden: Brill, 1997.

Berlin, Adele. "The Book of Esther and Ancient Storytelling." *Journal of Biblical Literature* 120 (2001): 3–14.

Berlin, Andrea M. "Palestine between Large and Small Forces in the Hellenistic Period." *Biblical Archaeologist* 60:1 (1997): 2–51.

Bickerman, Elias J. "The Edict of Cyrus in Ezra." In *Studies in Jewish and Christian History*, edited by Elias J. Bickerman, 1:72–108. Arbeiten zur Geschichte des antiken Judentums und des Urchristentums. Leiden: Brill, 1976.

————. *Four Strange Books of the Bible*. New York: Schocken, 1967.

————. *The God of the Maccabees: Studies on the Meaning and Origin of the Maccabean Revolt*. Translated by Horst R. Moehring. Studies in Judaism in Late Antiquity. Leiden: Brill, 1979.

————. "The Jewish Historian Demetrios." In *Christianity, Judaism, and Other Greco-Roman Cults*, edited by Jacob Neusner, 3:72–84. Leiden: Brill, 1975.

—. *The Jews in the Greek Age.* Cambridge, MA: Harvard University Press, 1988.

—. "The Septuagint as a Translation." *Proceedings of the American Academy for Jewish Research* 28 (1959): 1–39.

Blenkinsopp, Joseph. *Ezra-Nehemiah: A Commentary.* Old Testament Library. London: SCM, 1988.

—. "The Mission of Udjahorresnet and Those of Ezra and Nehemiah." *Journal of Biblical Literature* 106 (1987): 409–21.

Boccaccini, Gabriele. *Beyond the Essene Hypothesis: The Parting of Ways between Qumran and Enochic Judaism.* Grand Rapids, MI: Eerdmans, 1998.

Bond, Helen K. *Pontius Pilate in History and Interpretation.* Cambridge: Cambridge University Press, 1998.

Botterweck, G. Johannes, Helmer Ringgren, and Heinz-Josef Fabry. *Theological Dictionary of the Old Testament,* s.v. צדק, 12:521–45. Translated by Douglas W. Stott. Grand Rapids, MI: Eerdmans, 2003.

Bowersock, Glen W. "The Tel Shalem Arch and P. Nahal Heber/Seiyal 8." In *The Bar Kokhba War Reconsidered: New Perspectives on the Second Jewish Revolt against Rome,* edited by Peter Schäfer, 171–80. Tübingen: Mohr Siebeck, 2003.

Boyarin, Daniel. "The *Diadoche* of the Rabbis." In *Jewish Culture and Society under the Christian Roman Empire,* edited by Richard Kalmin and Seth Schwartz, 285–318. Leuven: Peeters, 2003.

Brakke, David. *The Gnostics: Myth, Ritual, and Diversity in Early Christianity.* Cambridge, MA: Harvard University Press, 2010.

—. "Scriptural Practices in Early Christianity: Towards a New History of the New Testament Canon." In *Invention, Rewriting, Usurpation: Discursive Fights over Religious Traditions in Antiquity,* edited by Jörg Ulrich, Anders-Christian Jacobsen, and David Brakke, 263–80. Frankfurt: Peter Lang, 2012.

Braun, Rainer. *Kohelet und die frühhellenistische Popularphilosophie.* Behiheft zur Zeitschrift für die alttestamentliche Wissenschaft. Berlin: Walter de Gruyter, 1973.

Bremmer, Jan N. "From Holy Books to Holy Bible: An Itinerary from Ancient Greece to Modern Islam via Second Temple Judaism and Early Christianity." In *Authoritative Scriptures in Ancient Judaism,* edited by Mladen Popović, 327–60. Supplements to the Journal for the Study of Judaism. Leiden: Brill, 2010.

Brettler, Marc Zvi. *How to Read the Jewish Bible.* New York: Oxford University Press, 2007.

—. "Judaism in the Hebrew Bible: The Transition from Ancient Israelite Religion to Judaism." *Catholic Biblical Quarterly* 61 (1999): 429–47.

Bright, John. *A History of Israel,* 2nd ed. London: SCM, 1972.

Brody, Robert. *The Geonim of Babylonia and the Shaping of Medieval Jewish Culture.* New Haven: Yale University Press, 1998.

Brooke, George J. "The Explicit Presentation of Scripture in 4QMMT." In *Legal Texts and Legal Issues,* edited by Moshe Bernstein, Forentino García Martínez, and John Kampen, 67–88. Leiden: Brill, 1997.

—. "Prophecy and Prophets in the Dead Sea Scrolls: Looking Backwards and Forwards." In *Prophets, Prophecy, and Prophetic Texts in Second Temple Judaism,* edited by

Michael H. Floyd and Robert D. Haak, 151–65. Library of Hebrew Bible / Old Testament Studies. London: T and T Clark, 2006.

Broshi, Magen. "The Expansion of Jerusalem in the Reigns of Hezekiah and Manasseh." *Israel Exploration Journal* 24 (1974): 21–26.

Broshi, Magen, and Israel Finkelstein. "The Population of Palestine in Iron Age II." *Bulletin of the American Schools of Oriental Research* 287 (1992): 47–60.

Brown, Raymond E. *The Gospel According to John (I-XII)*. Anchor Bible. Garden City, NY: Doubleday, 1966.

Carr, D. M. "Controversy and Convergence in Recent Studies of the Formation of the Pentateuch: A Review of Several Books." *Religious Studies Review* 23 (1997): 22–31.

Charlesworth, James H., ed. *The Old Testament Pseudepigrapha*. 2 vols. Garden City, NY: Doubleday, 1983.

Chazon, Esther G. "Scripture and Prayer in 'The Words of the Luminaries.'" In *Prayers That Cite Scripture*, edited by James L. Kugel, 25–41. Cambridge, MA: Harvard University Press, 2006.

Cohen, Shaye J. D. *The Beginnings of Jewishness: Boundaries, Varieties, Uncertainties*. Hellenistic Culture and Society. Berkeley: University of California Press, 1999.

———. "From the Bible to the Talmud: The Prohibition of Intermarriage." *Hebrew Annual Review* 7 (1983): 27–39.

———. *From the Mishnah to the Maccabees*. Philadelphia: Westminster, 1987.

———. *Josephus in Galilee and Rome: His Vita and Development as a Historian*. Leiden: Brill, 1979.

———. "The Rabbi in Second-Century Jewish Society." In *The Cambridge History of Judaism*, vol. 3, *The Early Roman Period*, edited by William Horbury, W. D. Davies, and John Sturdy, 922–90. Cambridge: Cambridge University Press, 1999.

———. "The Significance of Yavneh: Pharisees, Rabbis, and the End of Jewish Sectarianism." *Hebrew Union College Annual* 55 (1984): 27–53.

———. "Sosates, the Jewish Homer." *Harvard Theological Review* 74 (1981): 391–96.

———. *Why Aren't Jewish Women Circumcised? Gender and Covenant in Judaism*. Berkeley: University of California Press, 2005.

Cohn, Yehudah B. *Tangled Up in Text: Tefillin and the Ancient World*. Brown Judaic Studies. Atlanta: Scholars Press, 2008.

Collins, Adela. *Mark: A Commentary*. Hermeneia. Minneapolis: Fortress, 2007.

Collins, John J. *Apocalypticism in the Dead Sea Scrolls*. Literature of the Dead Sea Scrolls. London: Routledge, 1997.

———. *Daniel*. Hermeneia. Minneapolis: Fortress, 1993.

———. *Introduction to the Hebrew Bible*. Minneapolis: Fortress, 2004.

Coogan, Michael D. "Life in the Diaspora: Jews at Nippur in the Fifth Century B.C." *Biblical Archaeologist* 37:1 (1974): 6–12.

Cotton, Hannah M. "The Rabbis and the Documents." In *Jews in a Graeco-Roman World*, edited by Martin Goodman, 167–79. Oxford: Clarendon, 1998.

Cotton, Hannah M., et al. *Corpus inscriptionum Iudaeae/Palestinae*, vol. 1, *Jerusalem*. Berlin: Walter De Gruyter, 2010.

Cowey, James M. S., and Klaus Maresch, eds. *Urkunden des Politeuma der Juden von Herakleopolis*. Wiesbaden: Westdeutscher, 2001.

Crosgrove, Charles H. "Justin Martyr and the Emerging Christian Canon: Observations on the Purpose and Destination of the Dialogue with Trypho." *Vigiliae Christianae* 36 (1982): 209–32.

Cross, Frank Moore. *Canaanite Myth and Hebrew Epic.* Cambridge, MA: Harvard University Press, 1973.

———. "A Fragment of a Monumental Inscription from the City of David." *Israel Exploration Journal* 51 (2001): 44–47.

Dodd, Charles Harold. *According to the Scriptures: The Sub-structure of New Testament Theology.* London: Nisbet, 1952.

Doering, Lutz. "The Concept of Sabbath in the Book of Jubilees." In *Studies in the Book of Jubilees,* edited by Matthias Albani, Jörg Frey, and Armin Lange, 179–205. Texte und Studien zum Antiken Judentum. Tübingen: Mohr Siebeck, 1997.

Don-Yehiya, Eliezer. "Hanukkah and the Myth of the Maccabees in Zionist Ideology and in Israeli Society." *Jewish Journal of Sociology* 34 (1992): 5–23.

Dorandi, Tiziano. "Organization and Structure of the Philosophical Schools." In *The Cambridge History of Hellenistic Philosophy,* edited by Keimpe Alga, Jonathan Barnes, Jaap Mansfeld, and Malcolm Schofield, 55–62. Cambridge: Cambridge University Press, 1999.

Dozeman, Thomas B., Konrad Schmid, and Baruch J. Schwartz, eds. *The Pentateuch: International Perspectives on Current Research.* Tübingen: Mohr Siebeck, 2011.

Efron, John, Steven Weitzman, Matthias Lehmann, and Joshua Holo. *The Jews: A History.* Saddle River, NJ: Pearson and Prentice Hall, 2008.

Ehrman, Bart D. *Did Jesus Exist? The Historical Argument for Jesus of Nazareth.* New York: HarperOne, 2010.

———. *Lost Scriptures: Books That Did Not Make It into the New Testament.* New York: Oxford University Press, 2003.

———. *The Orthodox Corruption of Scripture.* Oxford: Oxford University Press, 1993.

El-Abbadi, Mostafa, and Omnia Mounir Fathallah, eds. *What Happened to the Ancient Library of Alexandria.* Leiden: Brill, 2008.

Eliav, Yaron Z. "The Urban Layout of Aelia Capitolina: A New View from the Perspective of the Temple Mount." In *The Bar Kokhba War Reconsidered: New Perspectives on the Second Jewish Revolt against Rome,* edited by Peter Schäfer, 241–77. Tübingen: Mohr Siebeck, 2003.

Elliott, J. K. *The Apocryphal New Testament: A Collection of Apocryphal Christian Literature in an English Translation Based on M. R. James.* Oxford: Clarendon, 1993.

Eshel, Esther. "Possible Sources of the Book of Daniel." In *The Book of Daniel: Composition and Reception,* edited by John J. Collins and Peter W. Flint, 2:387–94. Supplements to Vetus Testamentum. Leiden: Brill, 2001.

Eshel, Esther, Hanan Eshel, and Ada Yardeni. "A Qumran Composition Containing Part of Ps. 154 and a Prayer for the Welfare of King Jonathan and his Kingdom." *Israel Exploration Journal* 42 (1992): 199–229.

Evans, Craig A. "The Beginning of the Good News and the Fulfillment of Scripture in the Gospel of Mark." In *Hearing the Old Testament in the New Testament,* edited by Stanley E. Porter, 83–103. Grand Rapids, MI: Eerdmans, 2006.

Feldman, Louis H. *Jew and Gentile in the Ancient World: Attitudes and Interactions from Alexander to Justinian.* Princeton: Princeton University Press, 1993.

————. *Josephus's Interpretation of the Bible*. Berkeley: University of California Press, 1998.

Fine, Steven. *Art and Judaism in the Greco-Roman World: Toward a New Jewish Archaeology*. Cambridge: Cambridge University Press, 2005.

Finkelberg, Margalit. "Canonising and Decanonising Homer: Reception of the Homeric Poems in Antiquity and Modernity." In *Homer and the Bible in the Eyes of Ancient Interpreters*, edited by Maren R. Niehoff, 15–28. Leiden: Brill, 2012.

Finkelstein, Israel. "City-States to States: Polity Dynamics in the 10th-9th Centuries B.C.E." In *Symbiosis, Symbolism, and the Power of the Past: Canaan, Ancient Israel, and Their Neighbors from the Late Bronze Age through Roman Palaestina*, edited by W. G. Dever and S. Gitin, 75–83. Winona Lake, IN: Eisenbrauns, 2003.

————. "Jerusalem in the Persian (and Early Hellenistic) Period and the Wall of Nehemiah." *Journal for the Study of the Old Testament* 32 (2008): 501–20.

Finkelstein, Israel, and Amihai Mazar. *The Quest for the Historical Israel: Debating Archaeology and the History of Early Israel; Invited Lectures Delivered at the Sixth Biennial Colloquium of the International Institute for Secular Humanistic Judaism, Detroit, October 2005*. Edited by Brian B. Schmidt. Atlanta: Society of Biblical Literature, 2007.

Fitzmyer, Joseph A., S.J. *The Gospel according to Luke (I–IX)*. Anchor Bible. Garden City, NY: Doubleday, 1981.

————. *Tobit*. Commentaries on Early Jewish Literature. Berlin: Walter de Gruyter, 2003.

Fleisher, Ezra. "On the Beginnings of Obligatory Jewish Prayer." *Tarbiz* 60 (1991): 397–442 (in Hebrew).

Fleming, Daniel E. *The Legacy of Israel in Judah's Bible: History, Politics, and the Reinscribing of Tradition*. New York: Cambridge University Press, 2012.

Flint, Peter W. *The Dead Sea Psalms Scrolls and the Book of Psalms*. Leiden: Brill, 1997.

————. "Psalms and Psalters in the Dead Sea Scrolls." In *The Bible and the Dead Sea Scrolls*, edited by James H. Charlesworth, 1:233–72. Waco, TX: Baylor University Press, 2006.

Fox, Michael V. *Qohelet and His Contradictions*. Journal for the Study of the Old Testament Supplement Series. Sheffield: Almond, 1989.

Fraade, Steven D. "'The Torah of the King' (Deut 17:14–20) in the Temple Scroll and Early Rabbinic Law." In *Legal Fictions: Studies of Law and Narrative in the Discursive Worlds of Ancient Jewish Sectarians and Sages*, edited by Steven D. Fraade, 285–319. Supplements to the Journal for the Study of Judaism. Leiden: Brill, 2011.

Fraser, P. M. *Ptolemaic Alexandria*. Vol. 1. Oxford: Clarendon, 1972.

Fredriksen, Paula. *From Jesus to Christ: The Origins of the New Testament Images of Jesus*. New Haven: Yale University Press, 1988.

Frey, Jörge. "Paul's Jewish Identity." In *Jewish Identity in the Greco-Roman World*, edited by Jörge Frey, Daniel R. Schwartz, and Stephanie Gripentrog, 285–321. Leiden: Brill, 2007.

Fried, Lisbeth S. "'You Shall Appoint Judges': Ezra's Mission and the Rescript of Artaxerxes." In *Persia and Torah: The Theory of Imperial Authorization of the Pentateuch*, edited by James W. Watts, 63–89. Atlanta: Society of Biblical Literature, 2001.

Friedman, Richard Elliott. *Who Wrote the Bible?* New York: Summit, 1987.

Gabba, Emilio. "The Finances of King Herod." In *Greece and Rome in Eretz Israel: Collected Essays*, edited by A. Kasher, U. Rappaport, and G. Fuks, 160–68. Jerusalem: Yad Izhak Ben-Zvi / Israel Exploration Society, 1990.

Gager, John G. "Jews, Gentiles, and Synagogues in the Book of Acts." *Harvard Theological Review* 79 (1986): 91–99.

García Martínez, Florentino. "The Heavenly Tablets in the Book of Jubilees." In *Studies in the Book of Jubilees*, edited by Matthias Albani, Jörg Frey, and Armin Lange, 243–60. Texte und Studien zum Antiken Judentum. Tübingen: Mohr Siebeck, 1997.

———. "Temple Scroll." In *Encyclopaedia of the Dead Sea Scrolls*, edited by L. S. Schiffman and J. C. VanderKam, 2:927–33. Oxford: Oxford University Press, 2000.

Geiger, Joseph. "Rome and Jerusalem: Public Building and the Economy." In *Herod and Augustus: Papers Presented at the IJS Conference, 21st–23rd June 2005*, edited by David M. Jacobson and Nikos Kokkinos, 157–69. Leiden: Brill, 2009.

Geva, Hillel. *Ancient Jerusalem Revealed*. Jerusalem: Israel Exploration Society, 1994.

———. *Jewish Quarter Excavations in the Old City of Jerusalem Conducted by Nahman Avigad, 1969–1982*, vol. 4, *Area E and Other Studies: Final Report*. Jerusalem: Israel Exploration Society, 2006.

———. "Summary and Discussion of Findings from Areas A, W and X-2." In *Jewish Quarter Excavations in the Old City of Jerusalem Conducted by Nahman Avigad, 1969–1982*, vol. 2, *The Finds from Areas A, W and X-2: Final Report*, edited by Hillel Geva, 520–21. Jerusalem: Israel Exploration Society and Institute of Archaeology, Hebrew University of Jerusalem, 2003.

Gilbert, M. "L'Éloge de la Sagesse (Siracide 24)." *Revue théologique de Louvain* 5 (1974): 326–48.

Goldenberg, Robert. "How Did Ruth Become the Model Convert?" *Conservative Judaism* 61 (2010): 55–64.

Goldstein, Jonathan A. *1 Maccabees*. Anchor Bible. New York: Doubleday, 1976.

Goodacre, Mark. *The Case against Q: Studies in Markan Priority and the Synoptic Problem*. Harrisburg, PA: Trinity, 2002.

Goodblatt, David. *Elements of Jewish Nationalism*. Cambridge: Cambridge University Press, 2006.

———. *The Monarchic Principle: Studies in Jewish Self-Government in Antiquity*. Tübingen: J. C. B. Mohr, 1994.

Goodman, Martin. *Rome and Jerusalem: The Clash of Ancient Civilizations*. London: Penguin, 2008.

———. *The Ruling Class of Judea: The Origins of the Jewish Revolt against Rome, A.D. 66–70*. Cambridge: Cambridge University Press, 1987.

Grabbe, Lester L. "Hecataeus of Abdera and the Jewish Law: The Question of Authenticity." In *Berührungspunkte: Studien zur Sozial- und Religionsgeschichte Israels und seiner Umwelt. Festschrift für Rainer Albertz zu seinem 65. Geburtstag*, edited by Manfried Dietrich and Oswald Loretz, 613–26. Münster: Ugarit, 2008.

———. *Judaism from Cyrus to Hadrian*, vol. 1, *The Persian and Greek Periods*. Minneapolis: Fortress, 1992.

Grant, Robert M. *Irenaeus of Lyons*. London: Routledge, 1997.

Green, Peter. *The Greco-Persian Wars*. Berkeley: University of California Press, 1996.

Greenfield, Jonas C., Michael E. Stone, and Esther Eshel. *The Aramaic Levi Document*. Studia in Veteris Testamenti Pseudepigrapha. Leiden: Brill, 2004.

Gropp, D. M. "Sanballat." In *Encyclopaedia of the Dead Sea Scrolls*, edited by L. S. Schiffman and J. C. VanderKam, 2:823–25. Oxford: Oxford University Press, 2000.

Gruen, Erich S. *Diaspora: Jews amidst Greeks and Romans*. Cambridge, MA: Harvard University Press, 2002.

———. "The Letter of Aristeas and the Cultural Context of the Septuagint." In *Die Septuaginta—Texte, Kontexte, Lebenswelten*, edited by Martin Karrer and Wolfgang Kraus, 134–56. Tübingen: Mohr Siebeck, 2008.

Hadas, Moses. *Aristeas to Philocrates (Letter of Aristeas)*. New York: Harper and Brothers, 1951.

Hadot, Pierre. *What Is Philosophy?* Translated by Michael Chase. Cambridge, MA: Harvard University Press, 2002.

Halivni, David Weiss. "The Reception Accorded to Rabbi Judah's Mishnah." In *Jewish and Christian Self-Definition*, edited by E. P. Sanders et al., 2:204–12. London: SCM, 1981.

Hallo, William W., and K. Lawson Younger Jr., eds. *The Context of Scripture*, vol. 2, *Archival Documents from the Biblical World*. Leiden: Brill, 2002.

Hammer, Reuven. "What Did They Bless? A Study of Mishnah Tamid 5:1." *Jewish Quarterly Review* 81 (1991): 305–24.

Handy, Lowell K. "Historical Probability and the Narrative of Josiah's Reform in 2 Kings." In *The Pitcher Is Broken: Memorial Essays for Gösta W. Ahlström*, edited by Steven W. Holloway and Lowell K. Handy, 252–75. Journal for the Study of the Old Testament Supplement Series. Sheffield: Sheffield Academic Press, 1995.

Haran, Menahem. *Temples and Temple-Service in Ancient Israel: An Inquiry into Biblical Cult Phenomena and the Historical Setting of the Priestly School*. Winona Lake, IN: Eisenbrauns, 1985.

Harland, Philip A. *Dynamics of Identity in the World of the Early Christians: Associations, Judeans, and Cultural Minorities*. New York: T and T Clark, 2009.

Hayward, Robert. "The Jewish Temple at Leontopolis: A Reconsideration." *Journal of Jewish Studies* 33 (1982): 429–43.

Heinemann, Joseph. "The Triennial Lectionary Cycle." *Journal of Jewish Studies* 19 (1968): 41–48.

Hempel, Charlotte. *The Laws of the Damascus Document: Sources, Tradition, and Redaction*. Studies on the Texts of the Desert of Judah. Leiden: Brill, 1998.

———. "Shared Traditions: Points of Contact between S and D." In *The Dead Sea Scrolls: Transmission of Traditions and Production of Texts*, edited by Sarianna Metso, Hindy Najman, and Eileen Schuller, 115–31. Studies on the Texts of the Desert of Judah. Leiden: Brill, 2010.

Hengel, Martin. *Judaism and Hellenism: Studies in the Encounter in Palestine during the Early Hellenistic Period*. 2 vols. Translated by John Bowden. London: SCM, 1974.

———. *The Pre-Christian Paul*. Translated by John Bowden. London: SCM, 1991.

Henze, Matthias. "Enoch's Dream Visions and the Visions of Daniel Reexamined." In *Enoch and Qumran Origins: New Light on a Forgotten Connection*, edited by Gabriele Boccaccini, 17–22. Grand Rapids, MI: Eerdmans, 2005.

————, ed. *Hazon Gabriel: New Readings of the Gabriel Revelation*. Early Judaism and Its Literature. Atlanta: Scholars Press, 2011.

Hess, Richard. "Aspects of Israelite Personal Names and Pre-exilic Israelite Religion." In *New Seals and Inscriptions, Hebrew, Idumean, and Cuneiform*, edited by Meir Lubetski, 301–13. Sheffield: Sheffield Phoenix, 2007.

Hezser, Catherine. *Jewish Literacy in Roman Palestine*. Texts and Studies in Ancient Judaism. Tübingen: Mohr Siebeck, 2001.

Hodge, Caroline Johnson. *If Sons, Then Heirs: A Study of Kinship and Ethnicity in the Letters of Paul*. New York: Oxford University Press, 1997.

Hoffman, Adina, and Peter Cole. *Sacred Trash: The Lost and Found World of the Cairo Geniza*. New York: Nextbook/Schocken, 2011.

Holladay, Carl R. *Fragments from Hellenistic Jewish Authors*. 4 vols. Chico, CA: Scholars Press, 1983.

Holmén, Tom, and Stanley E. Porter, eds. *Handbook for the Study of the Historical Jesus*. 4 vols. Leiden: Brill, 2011.

Honigman, Sylvie. "The Jewish *Politeuma* at Heracleopolis." *Scripta Classica Israelica* 21 (2002): 251–66.

————. *The Septuagint and Homeric Scholarship in Alexandria*. London: Routledge, 2003.

Horbury, William, and David Noy. *Jewish Inscriptions of Graeco-Roman Egypt*. Cambridge: Cambridge University Press, 1992.

Horowitz, Wayne, Takayoshi Oshima, and Filip Vukosavović. "Hazor 18: Fragments of a Cuneiform Law Collection from Hazor." *Israel Exploration Journal* 62 (2012): 158–76.

Hurtado, Larry. "What Do the Earliest Christian Manuscripts Tell Us about Their Readers?" In *The World of Jesus and the Early Church: Identity and Interpretation in Early Communities of Faith*, edited by Craig A. Evans, 179–92. Peabody, MA: Hendrickson, 2011.

Ilan, Tal. *Silencing the Queen: The Literary Histories of Shelamzion and Other Jewish Women*. Tübingen: Mohr Siebeck, 2006.

Isaac, Benjamin. "Roman Religious Policy and the Bar Kokhba War." In *The Bar Kokhba War Reconsidered: New Perspectives on the Second Jewish Revolt against Rome*, edited by Peter Schäfer, 37–54. Tübingen: Mohr Siebeck, 2003.

Jacobson, Howard. *The Exagoge of Ezekiel*. Cambridge: Cambridge University Press, 1983.

Jaeger, Werner. *Paideia: The Ideals of Greek Culture*. 3 vols. Translated by Gilbert Highet. London: Blackwell, 1947.

Jaffe, Martin S. *Early Judaism*. Upper Saddle River, NJ: Prentice Hall, 1997.

————. *Torah in the Mouth: Writing and Oral Tradition in Palestinian Judaism, 200 BCE–400 CE*. New York: Oxford University Press, 2001.

Japhet, Sara. "Conquest and Settlement in Chronicles." *Journal of Biblical Literature* 98 (1979): 205–18.

————. *I & II Chronicles: A Commentary*. Louisville: Westminster / John Knox, 1993.

Jellicoe, Sidney. *The Septuagint and Modern Study*. Oxford: Clarendon, 1968.

Jeremias, Joachim. *Jerusalem in the Time of Jesus: An Investigation into Economic and Social Conditions during the New Testament Period*. Translated by F. H. and C. H. Cave. London: SCM, 1969.

Johnson, E. Elizabeth. "Paul's Reliance on Scripture in 1 Thessalonians." In *Paul and Scripture: Extending the Conversation*, edited by Christopher D. Stanley, 143–62. Early Christianity and Its Literature. Atlanta: Society of Biblical Literature, 2012.

Jones, A. H. M. *The Greek City from Alexander to Justinian.* Oxford: Oxford University Press, 1940.

Kah, D., and P. Scholz, eds. *Das hellenistische Gymnasion.* Berlin: Adademie Verlag, 2004.

Kampen, John. *The Hasideans and the Origin of Pharisaism: A Study in 1 and 2 Maccabees.* Society of Biblical Literature Septuagint and Cognate Studies Series. Atlanta: Scholars Press, 1988.

Kasher, Aryeh. *Jews and Hellenistic Cities in Eretz-Israel.* Tübingen: J. C. B. Mohr, 1990.

———. *Jews, Idumaeans, and Ancient Arabs.* Texte und Studien zum Antiken Judentum. Tübingen: J. C. B. Mohr, 1988.

Kittel, Gerhard, ed. *Theological Dictionary of the New Testament*, s.v. ἅγιος, 1:88–97. Translated by Geoffrey W. Bromiley. Grand Rapids, MI: Eerdmans, 1965.

Kloner, Amos. "Maresha in the Reign of Ptolemy II Philadelphus." In *Ptolemy II Philadelphus and His World*, edited by Paul McKechnie and Philippe Guillaume, 171–81. Leiden: Brill, 2008.

Knohl, Israel. "Between Voice and Silence: The Relationship between Prayer and the Temple Cult." *Journal of Biblical Literature* 115 (1996): 17–30.

———. *The Sanctuary of Silence: The Priestly Torah and the Holiness School.* Minneapolis: Fortress, 1995.

Knoppers, Gary N. "Hierodules, Priests, or Janitors? The Levites in Chronicles and the History of the Israelite Priesthood." *Journal of Biblical Literature* 118 (1999): 49–72.

———. "Intermarriage, Social Complexity, and Ethnic Diversity in the Genealogy of Judah." *Journal of Biblical Literature* 120 (2001): 15–30.

———. "Nehemiah and Sanballat: The Enemy Without or Within?" In *Judah and the Judeans in the Fourth Century B.C.E.*, edited by Oded Lipschits, Gary N. Knoppers, and Rainer Albertz, 305–31. Winona Lake, IN: Eisenbrauns, 2007.

Knowles, Michael P. "Scripture, History, Messiah: Scriptural Fulfillment and the Fullness of Time in Matthew's Gospel." In *Hearing the Old Testament in the New Testament*, edited by Stanley E. Porter, 59–82. Grand Rapids, MI: Eerdmans, 2006.

Kraabel, A. T. "The Disappearance of the 'God-Fearers.'" *Numen* 28 (1981): 113–26.

Kraeling, Carl H. *The Synagogue: The Excavations of Dura-Europos; Final Report VIII, Part 1.* New Haven: Yale University Press, 1956.

Kraemer, Ross Shepard. *Unreliable Witnesses: Religion, Gender, and History in the Greco-Roman Mediterranean.* New York: Oxford University Press, 2011.

Kraft, Robert A. "Scripture and Canon in the Apocrypha and Pseudepigrapha." In *Hebrew Bible/Old Testament: The History of Its Interpretation*, vol. 1, *From the Beginnings to the Middle Ages (until 1300): Pt. 1: Antiquity*, edited by Magne Saebø, 199–216. Göttingen: Vandenhoeck and Ruprecht, 1996.

Kruse, Thomas. "Das *politeuma* der Juden von Herakelopolis in Ägypten." In *Die Septuaginta—Texte, Kontexte, Lebenswelten*, edited by Martin Karrer and Wolfgang Kraus, 166–75. Tübingen: Mohr Siebeck, 2008.

Kugel, James L. *How to Read the Bible: A Guide to Scripture, Then and Now.* New York: Free Press, 2007.

———. *A Walk through Jubilees: Studies in the Book of Jubilees and the World of Its Creation.* Supplements to the Journal for the Study of Judaism. Leiden: Brill, 2012.

Kugel, James L., and Rowan Greer. *Early Biblical Interpretation.* Library of Early Christianity. Philadelphia: Westminster, 1986.

Kuhrt, Amélie. "Babylonia from Cyrus to Xerxes." In *The Cambridge Ancient History*, edited by John Boardman et al., 4:120–29. 2nd ed. Cambridge: Cambridge University Press, 1988.

Landau, Y. H. "A Greek Inscription Found Near Hefzibah," *Israel Exploration Journal* 16 (1966): 54–70.

Lapin, Hayim. "Rabbis and Cities in Later Roman Palestine: The Literary Evidence." *Journal of Jewish Studies* 50 (1999): 187–207.

Lauterbach, Jacob Z., ed. and trans. *Mekhilta de Rabbi Ishmael: A Critical Edition on the Basis of MSS and Early Editions with an English Translation, Introduction and Notes.* 3 vols. Philadelphia: Jewish Publication Society, 1976.

Leiman, Sid Z. *The Canonization of Hebrew Scripture: The Talmudic and Midrashic Evidence.* Hamden, CT: Archon, 1976.

———. "Josephus and the Canon of the Bible." In *Josephus, the Bible, and History*, edited by Louis H. Feldman and Gohei Hata, 50–58. Leiden: Brill, 1989.

Levenson, Jon D. "The Last Four Verses in Kings." *Journal of Biblical Literature* 103 (1984): 353–61.

Levine, Lee I. *The Ancient Synagogue: The First Thousand Years.* New Haven: Yale University Press, 2000.

———. "The Nature and Origin of the Palestinian Synagogue Reconsidered." *Journal of Biblical Literature* 115 (1996): 425–48.

———. *The Rabbinic Class of Roman Palestine in Late Antiquity.* Jerusalem: Yad Izhak Ben-Zvi; New York: Jewish Theological Seminary of America, 1989.

Levinson, Bernard M. *Deuteronomy and the Hermeneutics of Legal Innovation.* New York: Oxford University Press, 1997.

Levtow, Nathaniel B. *Images of Others: Iconic Politics in Ancient Israel.* Winona Lake, IN: Eisenbrauns, 2008.

Lieberman, Saul. "The Martyrs of Caesarea." *Annuaire de l'Institut de philologie et d'histoire orientales et slaves* 7 (1939–44): 395–446.

———. "The Publication of the Mishnah." In *Hellenism in Jewish Palestine*, edited by Saul Lieberman, 83–99. New York: Jewish Theological Seminary of America, 1950.

Lieu, Judith M. *Image and Reality: The Jews in the World of the Christians in the Second Century.* London: T and T Clark, 1996.

Lim, Timothy H. "The Defilement of the Hands as a Principle Determining the Holiness of Scripture." *Journal of Theological Studies* 61 (2010): 501–15.

———. *Pesharim.* Companion to the Qumran Scrolls. London: Sheffield Academic Press, 2002.

Linder, Amnon. *The Jews in Roman Imperial Legislation.* Detroit: Wayne State University Press / Israel Academy of Sciences and Humanities, 1987.

Lipschits, Oded. "Demographic Changes in Judah between the Seventh and the Fifth Centuries B.C.E." In *Judah and the Judeans in the Neo-Babylonian Period*, edited by Oded Lipschits and Joseph Blenkinsopp, 323–76. Winona Lake, IN: Eisenbrauns, 2003.

Lipschits, Oded, Omer Sergi, and Ido Koch. "Judahite Stamped and Incised Jar Handles: A Tool for Studying the History of Late Monarchic Judah." *Tel Aviv: Journal for the Institute of Archaeology of Tel Aviv University* 38 (2011): 5–41.

Longnecker, Bruce. "On Israel's God and God's Israel: Assessing Supersessionism in Paul." *Journal of Theological Studies* 58 (2007): 26–44.

Luijendijke, AnneMarie. "Sacred Scriptures as Trash: Biblical Papyri from Oxyrhynchus." *Vigiliae Christianae* 64 (2010): 217–54.

Luz, Ulrich. *Matthew 1–7*. Hermeneia. Minneapolis: Fortress, 2007.

Ma, John. *Antiochus III and the Cities of Western Asia Minor*. Oxford: Oxford University Press, 1999.

Magen, Yitzhak. "The Dating of the First Phase of the Samaritan Temple on Mount Gerizim in Light of the Archaeological Evidence." In *Judah and the Judeans in the Fourth Century B.C.E.*, edited by Oded Lipschits, Gary N. Knoppers, and Rainer Albertz, 157–211. Winona Lake, IN: Eisenbrauns, 2007.

Magness, Jodi. *The Archaeology of Qumran and the Dead Sea Scrolls*. Grand Rapids, MI: Eerdmans, 2002.

Main, Emanuelle. "Sadducees." In *Encyclopaedia of the Dead Sea Scrolls*, edited by L. S. Schiffman and J. C. VanderKam, 2:812–13. Oxford: Oxford University Press, 2000.

Malherbe, Abraham J. *Social Aspects of Early Christianity*. Rockwell Lecture Series. Baton Rouge: Louisiana State University Press, 1977.

Mandel, Paul. "Scriptural Exegesis and the Pharisees." *Journal of Jewish Studies* 58 (2007): 19–32.

Marcus, Joel. *The Way of the Lord: Christological Exegesis of the Old Testament in the Gospel of Mark*. Edinburgh: T and T Clark, 1992.

Marrou, H. I. *A History of Education in Antiquity*. Translated by George Lamb. London: Sheed and Ward, 1956.

Mason, Steve. "Josephus and His Twenty-Two Book Canon." In *The Canon Debate*, edited by Lee Martin McDonald and James A. Sanders, 110–27. Peabody, MA: Hendrickson, 2002.

———. *Josephus Flavius on the Pharisees: A Composition-Critical Study*. Studia Post-Biblica. Leiden: Brill, 1991.

Matthews, John F. "Hostages, Philosophers, Pilgrims, and the Diffusion of Ideas in the Late Roman Mediterranean and Near East." In *Tradition and Innovation in Late Antiquity*, edited by F. M. Clover and R. S. Humphreys, 29–49. Madison: University of Wisconsin Press, 1989.

McDonald, Lee Martin. *The Biblical Canon: Its Origin, Transmission, and Authority*. Peabody, MA: Hendrickson, 2007.

McLay, R. Timothy. "Biblical Texts and the Scriptures for the New Testament Church." In *Hearing the Old Testament in the New Testament*, edited by Stanley E. Porter, 38–58. Grand Rapids, MI: Eerdmans, 2006.

Meeks, Wayne A. "'Am I Jew?' Johannine Christianity and Judaism." In *Christianity, Judaism and Other Greco-Roman Cults: Studies for Morton Smith at Sixty*, edited by Jacob Neusner, 162–86. Leiden: Brill, 1975.

———. *The First Urban Christians*. New Haven: Yale University Press, 1983.

Meier, John P. *A Marginal Jew: Rethinking the Historical Jesus.* Vol. 1. New York: Doubleday, 1991.

Menken, J. J. Maarten. *Old Testament Quotations in the Fourth Gospel: Studies in Textual Form.* Kampen: Pharos, 1996.

Meshorer, Ya'akov. *Ancient Jewish Coinage.* 2 vols. New York: Amphora, 1982.

Metso, Sarianna. "Biblical Quotations in the Community Rule." In *The Bible as Book: The Hebrew Bible and the Judaean Desert Discoveries,* edited by Edward D. Herbert and Emanuel Tov, 81–92. London: British Library / Oak Knoll, 2002.

———. *The Textual Development of the Qumran Community Rule.* Studies on the Texts of the Desert of Judah. Leiden: Brill, 1997.

Meyer, Marvin. *The Gnostic Discoveries: The Impact of the Nag Hammadi Library.* San Francisco: HarperSanFrancisco, 2005.

Mildenberg, Leo. *The Coinage of the Bar Kokhba War.* Aarau: Saulerländer, 1984.

Milgrom, Jacob. *Numbers.* Philadelphia: Jewish Publication Society, 1990.

Misgav, H., Y. Garfinkel, and S. Ganor. "The Ostracon." In *Khirbet Qeiyafa,* vol. 1: *Excavation Report, 2007–2008,* edited by Y. Garfinkel and S. Ganor, 243–57. Jerusalem: Israel Exploration Society, 2009.

Modrzejewski, Joseph Mélèze. *The Jews of Egypt: From Rameses II to Emperor Hadrian.* Translated by Robert Cornman. Philadelphia: Jewish Publication Society, 1995.

———. "The Septuagint as *Nomos*: How the Torah Became a 'Civic Law' for the Jews of Egypt." In *Critical Studies in Ancient Law, Comparative Law and Legal History,* edited by John W. Cairns, 183–200. Oxford: Hart, 2001.

Momigliano, Arnaldo. *Alien Wisdom: The Limits of Hellenization.* Cambridge: Cambridge University Press, 1975.

Morgan, Teresa. *Literate Education in the Hellenistic and Roman Worlds.* Cambridge Classical Studies. Cambridge: Cambridge University Press, 1998.

Moyise, Steve. "Jesus and the Scriptures of Israel." In *Handbook for the Study of the Historical Jesus,* edited by Tom Holmén and Stanley E. Porter, 2:1137–67. Leiden: Brill, 2011.

Munson, Rosaria Vignolo. *Telling Wonders: Ethnographic and Political Discourse in the Work of Herodotus.* Ann Arbor: University of Michigan Press, 2001.

Murphy, Roland. *Ecclesiastes.* World Biblical Commentary. Dallas: Word, 1992.

Murray, Oswyn. "The Letter of Aristeas." *Studi ellenestici* 54 (1987): 15–29.

Musti, Domenico. "Syria and the East." In *The Hellenistic World,* vol. 7, part 1 of *The Cambridge Ancient History,* 2nd ed., edited by F. W. Walbank et al., 175–220. Cambridge: Cambridge University Press, 1984.

Naeh, Shlomo. "The Role of Biblical Verses in Prayer according to the Rabbinic Tradition." In *Prayers That Cite Scripture,* edited by James L. Kugel, 43–59. Cambridge, MA: Harvard University Press, 2006.

Najman, Hindy. "How to Make Sense of the Pseudonymous Attribution: The Cases of '4 Ezra' and '2 Baruch.'" In *A Companion to Biblical Interpretation in Early Judaism,* edited by Matthias Henze, 308–36. Grand Rapids, MI: Eerdmans, 2012.

Neusner, Jacob. *From Politics to Piety: The Emergence of Pharisaic Judaism.* Englewood, NJ: Prentice Hall, 1973.

Nickelsburg, George W. E. "Enochic Wisdom and Its Relationship to the Mosaic Torah." In *The Early Enoch Literature*, edited by Gabriele Boccaccini and John J. Collins, 81–94. Supplements to the Journal for the Study of Judaism. Leiden: Brill, 2007.

———. *1 Enoch 1: A Commentary on the Book of 1 Enoch, Chapters 1–36, 81–108*. Hermeneia. Minneapolis: Fortress, 2001.

Niehoff, Maren R. *Jewish Exegesis and Homeric Scholarship in Alexandria*. Cambridge: Cambridge University Press, 2011.

Noth, Martin. *The Deuteronomistic History*. Translated from the German. Journal for the Study of the Old Testament Supplement Series. Sheffield: Sheffield Academic Press, 1981.

O'Connor, Jerome Murphy. "Damascus." In *Encyclopaedia of the Dead Sea Scrolls*, edited by L. S. Schiffman and J. C. VanderKam, 1:165–66. Oxford: Oxford University Press, 2000.

Olyan, Saul M. *Asherah and the Cult of Yahweh in Israel*. Atlanta: Scholars Press, 1988.

———. "Ben Sira's Relationship to the Priesthood." *Harvard Theological Review* 80 (1987): 261–86.

Onn, Alexander, et al. "Khirbet Umm el-'Umdan." *Hadashot Arckeologiyot: Excavations and Surveys in Israel* 114 (2002): 74–78 (in Hebrew).

Orlin, Eric M. *Temples, Religion, and Politics in the Roman Republic*. Leiden: Brill, 1997.

Overholt, Thomas W. "Elijah and Elisha in the Context of Israelite Religion." In *Prophets and Paradigms: Essays in Honor of Gene M. Tucker*, edited by Stephen Breck Reid, 94–111. Journal for the Study of the Old Testament Supplement Series. Sheffield: Sheffield Academic Press, 1996.

Overman, J. Andrew. *Matthew's Gospel and Formative Judaism: The Social World of the Matthean Community*. Minneapolis: Fortress, 1990.

Pagels, Elaine, and Karen L. King. *Reading Judas: The Gospel of Judas and the Shaping of Christianity*. London: Allen Lane, 2007.

Painchaud, Louis. "The Use of Scripture in Gnostic Literature." *Journal of Early Christian Studies* 4 (1996): 129–46.

Parrot, André. *Samaria: The Capital of the Kingdom of Israel*. London: SCM, 1958.

Pearce, Laurie E. "'Judean': A Special Status in Neo-Babylonian and Achemenid Babylonia?" In *Judah and the Judeans in the Achaemenid Period: Negotiating Identity in an International Context*, edited by Oded Lipschits, Gary N. Knoppers, and Manfred Oeming, 267–77. Winona Lake, IN: Eisenbrauns, 2011.

Porten, Bezalel. *Archives from Elephantine: The Life of an Ancient Jewish Military Colony*. Berkeley: University of California Press, 1968.

———. *The Elephantine Papyri in English: Three Millennia of Cross-Cultural Continuity and Change*. Leiden: Brill, 1996.

Pritchard, James B., ed. *Ancient Near Eastern Texts Relating to the Old Testament*. 3rd ed. Princeton: Princeton University Press, 1969.

Rajak, Tessa. "Translating the Septuagint for Ptolemy's Library: Myth and History." In *Die Septuaginta—Texte, Kontexte, Lebenswelten*, edited by Martin Karrer and Wolfgang Kraus, 176–93. Tübingen: Mohr Siebeck, 2008.

Ratzinger, Joseph (Pope Benedict XVI). *Jesus of Nazareth*. Translated by Adrian J. Walker. New York: Doubleday, 2007.

Redford, Donald B. "The So-Called 'Codification' of Egyptian Law under Darius I." In *Persia and Torah: The Theory of Imperial Authorization of the Pentateuch*, edited by James W. Watts, 135–59. Atlanta: Society of Biblical Literature, 2001.

Regev, Eyal. "Temple Prayer as the Origin of the Fixed Prayer (On the Evolution of Prayer during the Period of the Second Temple)." *Zion* 70 (2005): 5–29 (in Hebrew).

Reich, Ronny, and Eli Shukron. "The Date of the Siloam Tunnel Reconsidered." *Tel Aviv* 38 (2011): 147–57.

Reif, Stefan C. "The Early Liturgy of the Synagogue." In *The Cambridge History of Judaism*, vol. 3, *The Early Roman Period*, edited by William Horbury, W. D. Davies, and John Sturdy, 326–57. Cambridge: Cambridge University Press, 1999.

Rendsburg, Gary A. *Linguistic Evidence for the Northern Origin of Selected Psalms.* Society of Biblical Literature Monograph Series. Atlanta: Scholars Press, 1990.

Richardson, Peter. *Herod: King of the Jews and Friend of the Romans.* Columbia: University of South Carolina Press, 1996.

Roberts, C. H., and T. C. Skeat. *The Birth of the Codex.* London: British Academy, 1983.

Roberts, J. J. M. "The Importance of Isaiah at Qumran." In *The Bible and the Dead Sea Scrolls*, edited by James H. Charlesworth, 1:273–86. Waco, TX: Baylor University Press, 2006.

Robinson, James M. ed. *The Nag Hammadi Library in English.* Leiden: Brill, 1988.

Robinson, James McConkey, Paul Hoffmann, and John S. Kloppenborg. *The Critical Edition of Q.* Hermeneia. Minneapolis: Fortress; Leuven: Peeters, 2000.

Roller, Duane W. *The Building Program of Herod the Great.* Berkeley: University of California Press, 1998.

Rollston, Christopher. "The Khirbet Qeiyafa Ostracon: Methodological Musings and Caveats." *Tel Aviv* 38 (2011): 67–82.

Royse, James R. "The Works of Philo." In *The Cambridge Companion to Philo*, edited by Adam Kamesar, 32–64. Cambridge: Cambridge University Press, 2009.

Rubenstein, Jeffrey L. *Talmud Stories: Narrative Art, Composition, and Culture.* Baltimore: Johns Hopkins University Press, 1999.

Russell, John Malcolm. *Sennacherib's Palace without Rival at Nineveh.* Chicago: University of Chicago Press, 1991.

Safrai, Zeev. "The Targums as Part of Rabbinic Literature." In *The Literature of the Sages: Second Part*, edited by Shmuel Safrai et al., 243–78. Assan: Royal Van Gorcum; Philadelphia: Fortress, 2006.

Saldarini, Anthony J. *Jesus and Passover.* New York: Paulist, 1984.

Sanders, E. P. *Jesus and Judaism.* London: SCM, 1985.

———. *Paul: A Very Short Introduction.* Oxford: Oxford University Press, 1991.

Sanders, Jack T. *Ben Sira and Demotic Wisdom.* Society of Biblical Literature Monograph Series. Chico, CA: Scholars Press, 1983.

Sanders, Seth L. *The Invention of Hebrew.* Urbana: University of Illinois Press, 2009.

Sarna, Nahum M. *Ancient Libraries and the Ordering of the Biblical Books.* Washington, DC: Library of Congress, 1989.

Satlow, Michael L. *Jewish Marriage in Antiquity.* Princeton: Princeton University Press, 2001.

———. "Philo on Human Perfection." *Journal of Theological Studies* 59 (2008): 500–519.

————. "Theophrastus's Jewish Philosophers." *Journal of Jewish Studies* 59 (2008): 1–20.

Schäfer, Peter. "Bar Kokhba and the Rabbis." In *The Bar Kokhba War Reconsidered: New Perspectives on the Second Jewish Revolt against Rome*, edited by Peter Schäfer, 1–22. Tübingen: Mohr Siebeck, 2003.

————. *Jesus in the Talmud*. Princeton: Princeton University Press, 2007.

Schiffman, Lawrence. "The Law of the Temple Scroll and Its Provenance." *Floria Orientalia* 25 (1989): 85–98.

————. *Reclaiming the Dead Sea Scrolls: The History of Judaism, the Background of Christianity, the Lost Library of Qumran*. Philadelphia: Jewish Publication Society, 1994.

Schniedewind, William M. *How the Bible Became a Book: The Textualization of Ancient Israel*. Cambridge: Cambridge University Press, 2004.

Schremer, Adiel. "[T]he[y] Did Not Read in the Sealed Book: Qumran Halakhic Revolution and the Emergence of Torah Study in Second Temple Judaism." In *Historical Perspectives: From the Hasmoneans to Bar Kokhba in Light of the Dead Sea Scrolls: Proceedings of the Fourth International Symposium of the Orion Center for Study of the Dead Sea Scrolls and Associated Literature, 27–31 January, 1999*, edited by David Goodblatt, Avital Pinnick, and Daniel R. Schwartz, 105–26. Leiden: Brill, 2001.

————. "Thinking about Belonging in Early Rabbinic Literature: Proselytes, Apostates, and 'Children of Israel'; or, Does It Make Sense to Speak of Early Rabbinic Orthodoxy?" *Journal for the Study of Judaism* 43 (2012): 249–75.

Schürer, Emile. *The History of the Jewish People in the Age of Jesus Christ (175 B.C.–A.D. 135)*. 3 vols. Edited by Geza Vermes and Fergus Millar. Edinburgh: Clark, 1973–87.

Schwartz, Daniel R. *Agrippa I: The Last King of Judaea*. Tübingen: J.C.B. Mohr, 1990.

————. "Josephus and Nicolaus on the Pharisees." *Journal for the Study of Judaism* 14 (1983): 157–71.

————. "Philo, His Family, and His Times." In *The Cambridge Companion to Philo*, edited by Adam Kamesar, 9–31. Cambridge: Cambridge University Press, 2009.

————. *The Second Book of Maccabees*. Jerusalem: Yad Ben-Zvi, 2004 (in Hebrew).

————. *2 Maccabees*. Commentaries on Ancient Jewish Literature. Berlin: Walter de Gruyter, 2008.

Schwartz, Seth. *Imperialism and Jewish Society, 200 BCE to 640 CE*. Jews, Christians, and Muslims from the Ancient to the Modern World. Princeton: Princeton University Press, 2001.

————. "John Hyrcanus I's Destruction of the Gerizim Temple and Judaean-Samaritan Relations." *Jewish History* 7 (1993): 9–25.

————. *Josephus and Judaean Politics*. Columbia Studies in the Classical Tradition. Leiden: Brill, 1990.

————. "Political, Social, and Economic Life in the Land of Israel, 66–c. 235." In *The Cambridge History of Judaism*, vol. 4, *The Late Roman-Rabbinic Period*, edited by Steven T. Katz, 23–52. Cambridge: Cambridge University Press, 2006.

Segal, Alan F. *Paul the Convert: The Apostolate and Apostasy of Saul the Pharisee*. New Haven: Yale University Press, 1990.

Segal, Michael. *The Book of Jubilees: Rewritten Bible, Redaction, Ideology and Theology*. Supplements to the Journal for the Study of Judaism. Leiden: Brill, 2007.

Seow, C. L. *The Anchor Bible: Ecclesiastes*. New York: Doubleday, 1997.

Shanks, Hershel, ed. *Ancient Israel: From Abraham to the Roman Destruction of the Temple.* 3rd ed. Washington, DC: Biblical Archaeology Society, 2010.

———, ed. *Christianity and Rabbinic Judaism: A Parallel History of Their Origins and Early Development*. 2nd ed. Washington, DC: Biblical Archaeology Society, 2011.

———, ed. *Understanding the Dead Sea Scrolls*. New York: Vintage, 1992.

Shemesh, Aharon. *Halakhah in the Making: The Development of Jewish Law from Qumran to the Rabbis*. Berkeley: University of California Press, 2009.

Shiloh, Yigal. "Jerusalem." In *The New Encyclopedia of Archaeological Excavations in the Holy Land*, edited by Ephraim Stern, 2:709–12. Jerusalem: Israel Exploration Society, 1993.

Sim, David C. "Matthew's Use of Mark: Did Matthew Intend to Supplement or to Replace His Primary Source?" *New Testament Studies* 57 (2011): 176–92.

Sivertsev, Alexei M. *Households, Sects, and the Origins of Rabbinic Judaism*. Leiden: Brill, 2005.

Skarsaune, Oskar. "The Ebionites." In *Jewish Believers in Jesus*, edited by Oskar Skarsaune and Reidar Hvalvik, 419–62. Peabody, MA: Hendrickson, 2007.

Smith, Mark S. *The Early History of God: Yahweh and Other Deities in Ancient Israel*. New York: Harper and Row, 1990.

Smith, Morton. "The Dead Sea Scrolls in Relation to Ancient Judaism." *New Testament Studies* 7 (1961): 347–60.

———. *Palestinian Parties and Politics That Shaped the Old Testament*. London: SCM, 1987.

Sommer, Benjamin D. *A Prophet Reads Scripture: Allusion in Isaiah 40–66*. Stanford: Stanford University Press, 1998.

Stanley, Christopher D. "Paul's 'Use' of Scripture: Why the Audience Matters." In *As It Is Written: Studying Paul's Use of Scripture*, edited by Stanley E. Porter and Christopher D. Stanley, 125–55. Atlanta: Scholars Press, 2008.

Stanton, Graham. "Jewish Christian Elements in the Pseudo-Clementine Writings." In *Jewish Believers in Jesus*, edited by Oskar Skarsaune and Reidar Hvalvik, 305–24. Peabody, MA: Hendrickson, 2007.

Stern, David. "On Canonization in Rabbinic Judaism." In *Homer, the Bible, and Beyond: Literary and Religious Canons in the Ancient World*, edited by Margalit Finkelberg and Guy Stroumsa, 227–52. Leiden: Brill, 2003.

Stern, Ephraim. *Material Culture of the Land of the Bible in the Persian Period, 538–332 B.C.* Jerusalem: Israel Exploration Society, 1982.

Stern, M. "'Antioch in Jerusalem': The Gymnasium, the Polis and the Rise of Menelaus." *Zion* 57 (1991/92): 233–46 (in Hebrew).

Stone, Michael Edward. *Fourth Ezra: A Commentary on the Book of Fourth Ezra*. Minneapolis: Fortress, 1990.

Stowers, Stanley K. *A Rereading of Romans: Justice, Jews, and Gentiles*. New Haven: Yale University Press, 1994.

Stroumsa, Guy. "Early Christianity—A Religion of the Book." In *Homer, the Bible, and Beyond: Literary and Religious Canons in the Ancient World*, edited by Margalit Finkelberg and Guy Stroumsa, 153–73. Leiden: Brill, 2003.

Stroup, Sarah Culpepper. "Without Patronage: Fetishization, Representation and the Circulation of Gift Texts in the Late Roman Republic." In *The Gift in Antiquity*, edited by Michael L. Satlow, 107–21. Malden, MA: Wiley-Blackwell, 2013.

Stuckenbruck, Loren T. *1 Enoch 91–108*. Commentaries on Early Jewish Literature. Berlin: Walter de Gruyter, 2007.

———. "The Teacher of Righteousness Remembered: From Fragmentary Sources to Collective Memory in the Dead Sea Scrolls." In *Memory in the Bible and Antiquity: The Fifth Durham-Tübingen Research Symposium (Durham, September 2004)*, edited by Loren T. Stuckenbruck, Stephen C. Barton, and Benjamin G. Wold, 75–94. Wissenschaftliche Untersuchungen zum Neuen Testament. Tübingen: Mohr Siebeck, 2007.

Taylor, Joan. E. *Jewish Women Philosophers of First Century Alexandria: Philo's "Therapeutae" Reconsidered*. Oxford: Oxford University Press, 2003.

———. "Pontius Pilate and the Imperial Cult in Roman Judaea." *New Testament Studies* 52 (2006): 555–82.

Tcherikover, Victor. *Hellenistic Civilization and the Jews*. Translated by S. Applebaum. Philadelphia: Jewish Publication Society of America, 1959.

———. "Palestine under the Ptolemies (A Contribution to the Study of the Zenon Papyri)." *Mizraim* 4–5 (1937): 1–90 (in Hebrew).

Tcherikover, Victor A., and Alexander Fuks. *Corpus Papyrorum Judaicarum*. 3 vols. Cambridge, MA: Harvard University Press, 1957–64.

Thompson, Dorothy J. "Economic Reforms in the Mid-Reign of Ptolemy Philadelphus." In *Ptolemy II Philadelphus and His World*, edited by Paul McKechnie and Philippe Guillaume, 27–38. Leiden: Brill, 2008.

———. *Memphis under the Ptolemies*. Princeton: Princeton University Press, 1988.

Tiller, Patrick A. *A Commentary on the Animal Apocalypse of 1 Enoch*. Early Judaism and Its Literature. Atlanta: Scholars Press, 1993.

Tov, Emanuel. *Scribal Practices and Approaches Reflected in the Texts Found in the Judean Desert*. Leiden: Brill, 2004.

———. "Some Thoughts about the Diffusion of Biblical Manuscripts in Antiquity." In *The Dead Sea Scrolls: Transmission of Traditions and Production of Texts*, edited by Sarianna Metso, Hindy Najman, and Eileen Schuller, 151–72. Studies on the Texts of the Desert of Judah. Leiden: Brill, 2010.

———. "Theologically Motivated Exegesis Embedded in the Septuagint." In *The Greek and Hebrew Bible: Collected Essays on the Septuagint*, edited by Emanuel Tov, 257–69. Supplements to Vetus Testamentum. Leiden: Brill, 1999.

Toye, David L. "Aristotle's Other Politeiai: Was the Athenaion Politeia Atypical?" *Classical Journal* 94 (1999): 235–53.

Trudinger, Peter L. *The Psalms of the Tamid Service: A Liturgical Text from the Second Temple*. Supplements to Vetus Testamentum. Leiden: Brill, 2004.

Ulrich, Eugene. "The Bible in the Making: The Scriptures Found at Qumran." In *The Bible at Qumran: Text, Shape, and Interpretation*, edited by Peter W. Flint, 51–66. Studies in the Dead Sea Scrolls and Related Literature. Grand Rapids, MI: Eerdmans, 2001.

———. *The Dead Sea Scrolls and the Origins of the Bible*. Grand Rapids, MI: Eerdmans, 1999.

Ussishkin, David. *The Conquest of Lachish by Sennacherib*. Tel Aviv: Tel Aviv University, 1982.

van der Horst, Pieter W. "Was the Synagogue a Place of Sabbath Worship before 70 CE?" In *Japheth in the Tents of Shem: Studies on Jewish Hellenism in Antiquity*, edited by Pieter W. van der Horst, 55–82. Contributions to Biblical Exegesis and Theology. Leuven: Peeters, 2002.

VanderKam, James. *The Dead Sea Scrolls Today*. 2nd ed. Grand Rapids, MI: Eerdmans, 2010.

———. "Jubilees, Book of." In *Encyclopaedia of the Dead Sea Scrolls*, edited by L. S. Schiffman and J. C. VanderKam, 1:434–38. Oxford: Oxford University Press, 2000.

———. "Questions of Canon Viewed through the Dead Sea Scrolls." In *The Canon Debate*, edited by Lee Martin McDonald and James A. Sanders, 91–109. Peabody, MA: Hendrickson, 2002.

VanderKam, James C., and Peter Flint. *The Meaning of the Dead Sea Scrolls: Their Significance for Understanding the Bible, Judaism, Jesus, and Christianity*. London: T and T Clark, 2002.

van der Kooij, Arie. "The Claim of Maccabean Leadership and the Use of Scripture." In *Jewish Identity and Politics between the Maccabees and Bar Kokhba: Groups, Normativity, and Rituals*, edited by Benedikt Eckhardt, 29–49. Leiden: Brill, 2012.

van der Toorn, Karel. *Scribal Culture and the Making of the Hebrew Bible*. Cambridge, MA: Harvard University Press, 2007.

van Henten, Jan Willem. "The Honorary Decree for Simon the Maccabee (1 Macc 14:25–49) in its Hellenistic Context." In *Hellenism in the Land of Israel*, edited by John J. Collins and Gregory E. Sterling, 116–45. Christianity and Judaism in Antiquity. Notre Dame: University of Notre Dame Press, 2001.

Van Seters, John. *In Search of History: Historiography in the Ancient World and the Origins of Biblical History*. New Haven: Yale University Press, 1983.

Vermes, Geza. *The Complete Dead Sea Scrolls in English*. 4th ed. London: Penguin, 1995.

———. *The Religion of Jesus the Jew*. Minneapolis: Fortress, 1993.

von Rad, G. "Die Nehemia-Denkschrift." *Zeitschrift für die Alttestamentliche Wissenschaft* 76 (1964): 176–87.

Wasserman, Tommy. "The Early Text of Matthew." In *The Early Text of the New Testament*, edited by Charles E. Hill and Michael J. Kruger, 83–107. Oxford: Oxford University Press, 2012.

Watts, James W., ed. *Persia and Torah: The Theory of Imperial Authorization of the Pentateuch*. Atlanta: Society of Biblical Literature, 2001.

Weinfeld, Moshe. *Deuteronomy and the Deuteronomic School*. Oxford: Clarendon, 1972.

———. "Deuteronomy, Book of." In *Anchor Bible Dictionary*, edited by David Noel Freedman, 2:168–83. New York: Doubleday, 1992.

Weitzman, Steven. *Song and Story in Biblical Narrative: The History of a Literary Convention in Ancient Israel*. Bloomington: Indiana University Press, 1997.

Wellhausen, Julius. *Prolegomena to the History of Israel*. Edited by Douglas A. Knight. Atlanta: Scholars Press, 1994.

Wendel, Susan. *Scripture Interpretation and Community Self-Definition in Luke-Acts and the Writings of Justin Martyr*. Leiden: Brill, 2011.

Wilken, Robert L. *The Christians as the Romans Saw Them*. New Haven: Yale University Press, 1984.

Williamson, H. G. M. *World Biblical Commentary*, vol. 16, *Ezra, Nehemiah*. Waco, TX: Word Books, 1985.

Wills, Lawrence Michael. *The Jewish Novel in the Ancient World*. Ithaca: Cornell University Press, 1995.

Winston, David. "Sage and Supersage in Philo of Alexandria." In *Pomegranates and Golden Bells: Studies in Jewish and Near Eastern Ritual, Law, and Literature in Honor of Jacob Milgrom*, edited by D. P. Wright, D. N. Freedman, and A. Hurvitz, 815–24. Winona Lake, IN: Eisenbrauns, 1995.

Wiseman, D. J. *The Vassal-Treaties of Esarhaddon*. London: British School of Archaeology in Iraq, 1958.

Wright, Benjamin G., III. "Biblical Interpretation in the Book of Ben Sira." In *A Companion to Biblical Interpretation in Early Judaism*, edited by Matthias Henze, 363–88. Grand Rapids, MI: Eerdmans, 2012.

——. "'Fear the Lord and Honor the Priest': Ben Sira as Defender of the Jerusalem Priesthood." In *The Book of Ben Sira in Modern Research: Proceedings of the First International Ben Sira Conference, 28–31 July 1996, Soesterberg, Netherlands*, edited by Pancratius C. Beentjes, 189–222. Behiheft zur Zeitschrift für die alttestamentliche Wissenschaft. Berlin: Walter de Gruyter, 1997.

——. "The Letter of Aristeas and the Reception History of the Septuagint." In *Praise Israel for Wisdom and Instruction: Essays on Ben Sira and Wisdom, the Letter of Aristeas and the Septuagint*, edited by Benjamin G. Wright III, 275–95. Leiden: Brill, 2008.

——. "The Septuagint and Its Modern Translators." In *Die Septuaginta—Texte, Kontexte, Lebenswelten*, edited by Martin Karrer and Wolfgang Kraus, 103–14. Tübingen: Mohr Siebeck, 2008.

Wright, David P. *Inventing God's Law: How the Covenant Code of the Bible Used and Revised the Laws of Hammurabi*. Oxford: Oxford University Press, 2009.

Wright, Jacob L. "The Commemoration of Defeat and the Formation of a Nation in the Hebrew Bible." *Prooftexts* 29 (2009): 433–72.

Yadin, Azzan. "Resistance to Midrash? Midrash and *Halakhah* in the Halakhic Midrashim." In *Current Trends in the Study of Midrash*, edited by Carol Bakhos, 35–52. Leiden: Brill, 2006.

Yadin, Yigael. *The Temple Scroll*. 3 vols. Jerusalem: Israel Exploration Society / Institute of Archaeology of the Hebrew University of Jerusalem / Shrine of the Book, 1977–83.

Younger, K. Lawson Jr. "Israelites in Exile." *Biblical Archaeological Review*, 29:6 (2003): 36–45, 65–66.

Zahn, Molly M. *Rethinking Rewritten Scripture: Composition and Exegesis in the 4Q Reworked Pentateuch Manuscripts*. Studies on the Texts of the Desert of Judah. Leiden: Brill, 2011.

——. "Rewritten Scripture." In *The Oxford Handbook of the Dead Sea Scrolls*, edited by Timothy H. Lim and John J. Collins, 323–36. Oxford: Oxford University Press, 2010.

Zevit, Z. "The Second-Third Century Canonization of the Hebrew Bible and Its Influence on Christian Canonizing." In *Canonization and Decanonization: Papers Presented to the International Conference of the Leiden Institute for the Study of Religions (LISOR), Held at Leiden 9–10 January 1997*, edited by A. Van der Kooij and K. Van der Toorn, 133–60. Studies in the History of Religion. Leiden: Brill, 1998.

Zissu, Boaz, and David Amit. "Common Judaism, Common Purity, and the Second Temple Period *Miqwa'ot* (Ritual Immersion Baths)." In *Common Judaism: Explorations in Second Temple Judaism*, edited by Wayne O. McCready and Adele Reinhartz, 47–62. Philadelphia: Fortress, 2008.

Zussman, Yaakov. "Torah she-ba'al peh: Peshutah k'mashamh." *Mehqerei Talmud* 3:1 (2005): 209–384 (in Hebrew).

Acknowledgments

In the course of writing this book I have received much help from institutions, colleagues, and family, and it is a pleasure for me to be able to acknowledge them.

The idea for this book came to me during a leave made possible by a fellowship from the John Simon Guggenheim Memorial Foundation. It was at that time a side project that increasingly began to engage my interest as I returned to my regular duties at Brown University. I developed many of the ideas in this book in conversations with colleagues and students, and I am grateful for their patience, support, and willingness to call a spade a spade when I sometimes wanted to call it a heart. I am particularly grateful to the university library and the Office of the Dean of Faculty for their help and encouragement.

Most of this book was written in Israel, where I served as a Fulbright Senior Scholar at Tel Aviv University (under the auspices of the United States–Israel Educational Foundation) and as the Seymour Gitin Distinguished Professor at the W. F. Albright Institute of Archaeological Research in Jerusalem. These institutions all provided a warm intellectual environment, and I thank them for their support. The National Library of Israel and the library at the École biblique were invaluable resources, and I thank the librarians and staff at both institutions as well as the many colleagues in both places who graciously and generously responded to my questions.

On behalf also of my family, I want to express our profound gratitude to the many people in Israel who helped us in so many ways, both large and small. It made a big practical and emotional difference, and we will always be grateful.

Several colleagues generously read and commented on earlier drafts of the manuscript, in part or whole. The two anonymous referees for Yale University Press read the manuscript with care and saved me from many errors. Aaron Tugendhaft also read the entire manuscript, and his astute comments helped me to sharpen my argument. David Brakke, Naftali Cohn, David Freidenreich, Sylvie Honigman, Jason Kalman, Jonathan Kaplan, Phil Lieberman, Maren Niehoff, Daniel Picus, Ishay Rosen-Zvi, Jordan Rosenblum, Serge Ruzer, Loren Spielman, David Stern, Katja Vehlow, and Steven Weitzman all read and commented on chapters. I thank them for their time and comments, which have greatly improved the book.

My agent, Wendy Strothman, and my editor at Yale, Jennifer Banks, took this project on when it was still in protean form. They have worked tirelessly in helping me shape that project into this one and have taught me much in the process. I thank them for their help and support throughout this process.

I cannot even begin to express my gratitude to my wife, Jacqueline Romm Satlow. Quite apart from what she has contributed directly to this book, she adds purpose to my life and helps to make me a better person.

My children, Daniel, Penina, and Jeremy, all really, really, really wanted me to dedicate this book to them but had too much class to ask outright. You could have, though. You fill my heart with joy, and I hope that I will never miss an opportunity to show it.

General Index

Numbers in *italics* indicate figures.

Aristobulus II, 173

Artapanus, 162–63, 268

Artaxerxes I, 69, 70, 71–72

Asherah, 24

Ashurbanipal, 38, 42, 43

Assyria: alliance with, 26; assault on Judah, 35–36; Babylonian victories over, 42–43; campaign of, against Israel, 29–30; scribes in, 27

Athanasius, 276

Athens, 107

Augustus, 182, 183, 194, 204

authority: meaning of, 4, 278; types of, 4–5, 27. *See also* literary authority; normative authority; oracular authority

Baal, 24

Babylonia: conquest of, 53–55; Judahite court in, 60, 61–62; Judahites in, 54–55; lacking a public cult, 53; taking control of Assyria, 42–43

Balaam, 29; oracle of, 264

Bar Kokhba, 258, 263

Bar Kokhba revolt, 258, 262, 263–65

Bar Kosiba, Shimon. *See* Bar Kokhba; Bar Kokhba revolt

Barnabas, letter of, 237

Baruch, 48

Benjamin, 20

Ben Sira, Jesus, 111, 114–15, 123. *See also* Ecclesiasticus

Beyond the River, 57

Bible: authority of, 2–6, 275, 281; Ben Sira's knowledge of, 117; canonical, 243, 276; development of, 1–3; difficulty of reading, 1–2; English translations of, 277; Gentiles' reading of, 222–23; historical context for, 7; as historical source, 7; as human work, 279; Israel's depiction in, 13–15; legacy of, 278, 281; limited authority of, until 3rd century, 3; literary authority of, 4, 5, 118; normative authority of, 4, 5, 6; oracular authority of, 4–5, 6; origins

of, in Israel, 15; reworked, 185–86; Tobit citing from, 122

"Bible of the Early Church," 233

Bickerman, Elias, 113

blessings, distinct from scripture, 270

books: power of, 216; as signs of culture and status, 215. *See also* texts

Caesarea, 205, 225

calendar, dispute over, 120, 121, 145, 148

Cambyses II, 57

canon: Christian, 251–52, 276, 277; consensus on, 269; four-Gospel, 253–54

charter myth, 164

Christianity: conflicting texts of, 241–42; doctrinal differences within, 242; early centuries of, 234, 239–42; emergence of, 200; literary culture of, 236, 238–40; producing revelatory texts, 242

Christians, activities of, on Sundays, 250–51

Chronicles: consistent style of, 93; read as single book, 92; rewriting history, 93, 94; sources for, 93

churches, Paul setting up, 217–18

church fathers, 237

citation formulas, 268

City of David, 31

clan politics, 71

clans, 73, 82

closed canon, 244–45

Code of Hammurabi, 15, 27, 58

codes of conduct, 151

codices, 255–56

Coele-Syria, 109

coercive authority, 83

communities, formation of, based on texts, 278–79

Community Rule, 176–77, 188, 298n5

Coptic, 235

Council of Holiness, 150–51

councils, in Judea, 206

court historians, 142–43

First Apology (Justin Martyr), 248–49, 250

First Enoch, 7, 105, 111, 118–23, 128, 129, 142, 145, 148, 179–80, 186, 236, 243, 262

First Maccabees, 124, 142–45, 147, 171

First Peloponnesian War, 70

First Thessalonians, letter of, 219, 231

fiscus iudaicus, 257–58

four-Gospel canon, 253–54

4Q41, *187*

4Q201, *119*

4Q258, *176*

Fourth Ezra, 260–62, 267

Frei, Peter, 290n14

functionaries, 25

Gabriel Revelation, 187

Galatians, letter to, 219–20, 251

Galilee, 194, 195; new settlements in, after Bar Kokhba revolt, 265; rabbinic movement in, 258; synagogues in, 197, 200

Gamaliels, 259, 265–66, 267

Gamla, synagogue at, remains of, *199*

genealogical purity, 62, 81–82, 99

Genesis, book of, 238: allegorical commentary on, 168–69; Jubilees and, 148

Geniza (Cairo), 114, 176

Gentiles, Paul's mission to, 214, 216–17

Geshem, 86, 88

Gezer calendar, 21

gnosis, 253

Gnostic heretics, 235

Gnostic literature, 225, 238

God: laws of, established in primal history, 147–48; presence of, 180

God-fearers, 216, 231

gods: Greek pantheon of, 139; household, 25; involvement of, 22–23; private worship of, 24–25

Gospels, 200–201, 205, 210; focus of, 224–25; negative view of the Pharisees, 202

gospels, genre of, 235, 268

Greek: as new lingua franca, 108; in the Septuagint, 158–59; used in Judea, 205

Greeks: education of, 107; political system of, 106–7 (*See also* Ptolemies); religious rites of, 107; theater in culture of, 108

Gregory of Nyssa, 168

gymnasium, 107, 110, 126

Habakkuk, 48, 186

Hadad, 16

Hadrian, 264

Haggai, 62–63

Halakhic Letter, 178–80, 299n11

Haman, 66

Hammurabi, 58. *See also* Code of Hammurabi

Hananiah, 98

Hanukkah, 124, 128

Hasideans, 132

Hasmoneans, 6, 124, 128, 143, 144, 149–50, 171, 182; controlling the Jerusalem temple, 136–37. *See also* Pharisees; Sadducees

heaven: documents written in, 130 (*See also* heavenly tablets); Enoch's ascent to, 120

heavenly tablets, 121, 123, 130, 138, 148–49, 186, 260

Hebrew, 147, 178–79; Bar Kokhba's use of, 264; in Daniel, 130; dialect of, 22; Ecclesiastes and Ecclesiasticus in, 111, 114, 118, 122; in Ezra, 64; Ezra's Torah in, 78; First Maccabees in, 143, 144; gap of, with Aramaic, 78; Hezekiah's officials and, 35; holy books in, first mention of, 144; Jubilees in, 147–48; Judean elites' use of, 94, 137; scripture in, Paul's access to, 212; as vernacular for Israel and Judah, 21, 26

Hebrews, gospel of, 236

Hecataeus of Abdera, 85, 155–56, 158

Hellenism, 103–5, 117, 154–55, 161; Jerusalem encountering, 122–23; polis in, 106–7; popular philosophy in, 113

Heracleopolis, 160, 161

heresy, 277

Herod the Great, 182–85, 191, 193–94, 196, 198, 212

Hezekiah, 32–37, 40–41, 42, 60, 64, 150

Hezekiah's Tunnel, 33, *34*

Hilkiah, 43

Hinduism, 280

history, oral transmission of, 20–21

holiness, hierarchy of, 271

Holiness Code, 75

holy book: first Greek use of term, 155; first Hebrew mention of, 144

holy seed, 80, 81, 82

Holy Spirit, authority of, 219

Homer, 5, 161

Hosayahu, 50

Hosea, 24

Hosea, book of, 186

H (Holiness) source, 49, 75, 76, 77, 81, 99

Huldah, 43

hymns, 49, 196

Hyrcanus, John, 125, 134, 135, 136, 138–43, 146, 147, 172

Hyrcanus, John (II), 173–74, 179, 180, 182, 183

Idumaea, 194–95

Idumaeans, 139, 140

illiteracy, stigma of, 50

"Infancy Gospel of Thomas," 236

inscriptions, 37

intermarriage, 79–84, 89–90, 91, 93, 99

interpretative authority, 280

Irenaeus, 252–55

Isaiah, 36, 48

Isaiah, book of, 43, 60–61, 186, 187, 220, 221

Isaiah scroll, 174

Ishmael (rabbi), 263, 265

Islam, 280

Israel: Assyrian campaign against, 29–30; Assyrian conquest of (722 BCE), 13; as Assyrian vassal state, 26; beginnings of, 16; Bible's origins and, 15; children of, 20; common narrative of, 19, 20; confederation of, 17–19, 20; cultural development of, 15–16; cultural practices of, 25; depiction of, in Chronicles, 92–93; elites from, settling in Jerusalem, 31; elitist ideology in, 82; emergence of, 17; evidence about, 15; fall of (722 BCE), 51; government of, 25–26; history of, in Nehemiah, 88–89; identity of, 19; intermarriage in, 79–84; Jacob's renaming as, 19–20; Judah's depiction of, 13–15; kingdom of, 8; as kingdom of priests, 81–82; language of, 21, 22; naming of, 19–20; refugees from, 30–33; soft power of, 19; strongholds of, 19; subgroup in, resulting from Nehemiah's covenant, 91; worship in, 22–25; written artifacts from, 22; YHWH's election of, 40–41

Israelian language, 22

ivory carvings (Samaria), *18*

Jacob: renaming of, 19–20; sons of, 19–20

James (brother of Jesus), 213

Janneaus, Alexander, 172

Jason (brother of Onias III), 125–26

Jason of Cyrene, 163

Jedaniah, 96–98

Jehoiachin, 50, 58, 92

Jehozadak, 50

Jeremiah, 46, 52, 61, 63, 131

Jeremiah, book of, 131

Jerome, 276

Jerusalem, 16; Antiochus's control of, 109–10; changes in, during Maccabees' time, 133–34; church at, 213; economic position of, 72–73; educational ethos of, 110–11; exiles' return to, 71–74; growth of, 30; gymnasium in, 126; Hellenism's effect on, 105, 122–23;

Jerusalem (*continued*)
Herod's transformation of, 191–92; identity of, developing, 95; institutions in, 206; Israelite elite's presence in, 31–32; Jesus going to, 207; Judahites' return to, 54, 56–57; Judean elite in, 94; library at, 39; moving toward polis status, 123; in Paul's time, 211–12; population of, 30, 62, 72–73, 83; power struggle in, leading to Maccabean revolt, 125, 128; priesthood of, 185; prosperity in, 110; protection of, 33–35; religious life of, 73–74; renamed Aelia Capitolina, 264; renamed Antioch, 125–26; struggling in Nehemiah's time, 86; success of, against the Assyrians, 36; temple culture in, 198; Upper City of, 191–92; walls of, rebuilding, 88; water sources for, 33–35

JE source, 75, 99, 100

Jesus: arrest, trial, and execution of, 207–8; confirming belief in angels and resurrection, 208; death of, 209, 210; divine authority of, 202; early believers in, 213–14, 221–22, 224, 225, 234, 237; followers of, 210–11; going to Jerusalem, 207; life of, 200–201, 208; linked to scripture, 193, 225, 227–28, 230–33; Pharisees and, 193, 202–3, 208; Sadducees and, 203, 208; scriptural knowledge of, 6, 193; scriptural perspective on, 211; supernatural powers of, 232; teachings of, 201–2; virgin birth of, 229; as wonder-worker, healer, and prophet, 203–4

Jesus, son of Phiabi, 185

Jewish Antiquities (Josephus), 244, 246–47

Jewish War, 224, 225–26, 257

Jewish War (Josephus), 246–47

Jews: canon of, 244–45, 277; categorizing scripture, 243–44; holy seed of, 80, 81, 82; identity of, genealogical understanding of, 80; intermarriage by, 81; reputation of, as philosophers, 215;

scriptural authority for, 67; scriptural knowledge of, 4

John, Gospel of, 200, 232–34, 239

John the Baptist, 203

John Maccabee, 133

Jonathan Maccabee, 133

Joseph (father of Jesus), 229

Joseph (son of Jacob), 20

Josephus, 8, 184; on Agrippa, 211; capture of, 243; on closed canon of scripture, 244–46, 252; drawing on the Letter of Aristeas, 166; education of, 246; on the Essenes, 181; governing life according to the Pharisees, 246; on Herod, 184; on the Jewish War, 225–26; on the Judeans, 194; Pharisees and, 246; on the Pharisees and Sadducees, 141–43, 208; receiving gift of holy books, 247; scriptural knowledge of, 246–47; scripture and interpretation coming together in, 268; on the second temple's destruction, 259–60

Joshua, 58–60, 61–63, 64, 82

Joshua, book of, 46

Josiah, 40–48, 60, 64, 65, 79, 150

J source, 74, 75, 89

Jubilees, book of, 7, 143, 147–49, 171, 175, 179–80, 186, 198, 243, 262, 268

Judaea capta coin, *258*

Judah, 20; as Assyrian vassal state, 26; Assyria's assault on, 35–36; Covenant Code taken to, 28; culture of literacy in, 51; fall of, 50; growth of, 30–33; Israelite scribes going to, 26; kingdom of, 8, 13; literary culture of, 31–32, 37; prophetic oracles in, 48; return to, 58–59, 62; transformation of, 16; triumphalist approach of, 13–15; under Babylonian control, 52

Judah (rabbi), 266, 269

Judahites: in Babylonia, 54–55; court of, 70–71; identity of, 67; language of, 22; returning to Jerusalem, 54, 56–57

Judah Maccabee (Maccabeus), 127,
 128–29, 144
Judas (insurrection leader), 195
Judea: councils in, 206; divided into districts, 184; governing of, 85; in Greek
 Empire, 103–5; after the Jewish War,
 257; local institutions in, for law and
 administration, 205–6; political trajectory of, 204; under Ptolemies' control,
 106; Roman administration of, 194–95,
 204–5, 225; under Seleucids' control,
 105, 108–9; self-government of, 206–7;
 synagogues in, 197–98; unification of,
 211
Judeans: becoming, 140; Elephantine,
 religious practices of, 95–99; Hecataeus's account of, 155; in Josephus's
 work, 194; knowledge of, from oral
 recitation, 152; scriptural authority
 for, 67
judges: position of, in Judea, 206; role of,
 in antiquity, 58
Judges, book of, 46, 243
Justinian, 274
Justin Martyr. See Martyr, Justin

Karaite controversy, 275
kingdoms, in ancient Near East, 17
Kings, books of, 46
kingship: institution of, 41; power of,
 17–18; purity of, 146
knights, 204
Kohelet, 105, 111, 123. See also
 Ecclesiastes, book of

language, Israel's emergence and, 21, 22
Latin, 205, 276
law: function of, in Judea, 206; kings'
 subservience to, 41–42; oral pro-
 nouncement of, 15; scribal reworking
 of, 27–28; written, at center of ideal
 state, 146
law codes, 58
law of Moses, 45, 59, 65, 78, 94, 131

Law of Moses, book of, 74, 77, 79, 93, 231.
 See also Pentateuch; Torah
leaders: instruction for, 46–47; punishment of, 46
Letter of Aristeas, 121, 157, 158, 159,
 163–66, 169, 170, 249, 274
Levites, organized into subgroups, 93
Levitical priests, 40, 41
Leviticus, book of, 75–76, 155
libraries, 38–39
Library of Alexandria, 156–57, 158, 159,
 166
library texts, 137
literacy, culture of, 51
literary authority, 4, 5, 27, 118, 149, 159,
 278
liturgy: Christian, 250–51; rabbinic approach to, 269–70
Luke, Gospel of, 200, 230–31, 234
lunar calendar, 120, 148
Lysimachus, 126

Maccabean revolt, 123, 124–25, 128, 130,
 133, 137, 138, 142, 159
Maimonides, 277
Manasseh, 20, 32, 36–37, 42, 46
maps, x–xi, 14, 34, 104
Marcion, 243, 251–52, 253, 254–55
Marduk, 55–56
Maresha (Marisa), 108
Mark, Gospel of, 200, 226–28, 231, 233,
 234
Martyr, Justin, 8, 243, 247, 248–51, 252,
 254–55
Masoretic Text, 180
Mattathias, 127
Matthew, Gospel of, 200, 228–30, 233,
 234
memory, historical, creation of, 21
Menelaus, 126
Micah, book of, 186
Midrash, 268–69
Mishnah, 266–67, 268, 272
Moabite, 21

Persia, 53; administration of, 57–58; conquest of Babylonia, 53–55; empire of, dismantling; life in, 65
pesher texts, 186–88, 268
Peshitta, 276
Peter, 213, 214
Peter, Gospel of, 236
Pharisees, 6, 125, 137, 140–42, 149, 171, 214; Antipas sympathetic to, 202; disagreements among, 151; finding common ground with Sadducees, 258; Gospels' negative view of, 202; Herod's marginalization of, 182; Herod's relations with, 184–85; Jesus and, 202–3, 208; Josephus and, 246; Paul's attraction to, 212; political role of, 172–73, 193; reputation of, as expert interpreters of the law, 200; school of thought descending from, 263
Phillip (son of Herod the Great), 194
Phillip II, 103
Philo, 8, 205, 215, 222, 246; allegorical approach of, 168–69; drawing from Letter of Aristeas, 166; on the Essenes, 167, 181; on the human soul, 169; life of, 168; on the Pentateuch; on the Septuagint, 153, 170; on the Therapeutae, 167
philosophers, 110
philosophy, practice of, 215
Pilate, Pontius, 205, 207–8
Pliny, 181, 248
pluriformity, 221, 227
Plutarch, 216
polis, 106–7
politeia, 155, 156, 158
politeuma, 160–61
political authority: centralized, 40; Dead Sea Scrolls and, 171
Polyhistor, Alexander, 296–97n21
prayer, 116, 270
prayer halls, 167. *See also* synagogues
prefects, 204–5
pride, sin of, 54

Priestly Blessing, 49
priests, 24, 65; benefiting from Jerusalem's growth, 191–92; genealogies of, 81; infusing scripture into the temple cult, 196–97; Israel as kingdom of, 81–82; legitimacy of, 136; Levitical, 40, 41; officiating, private liturgy for, 196; organized into subgroups, 93; relying on scriptural authority, 192; scribes and, 49; shared belief system of, 191–92; wealthy, influence of, 193
procurators, 204, 225
prophecies, 5
prophetic authority, 144, 149
prophets, 24, 28–29; buying off, 88; female, 43, 88; oracles of, recorded, 48; speaking about writing, 48–49
Prophets, books of, 179
Protestantism, 280
proto-Orthodox, 254
Proverbs, book of, 37–38, 113
psalms, 2, 49
Psalms, book of, 49, 179, 186, 187, 220, 221
Pseudepigrapha, 7, 119
Pseudo-Clementines, 237
P source, 49, 75, 76, 77, 78, 81, 99, 100
Ptolemies, 103–6, 154, 157–58
Ptolemy I Soter, 155, 156
Ptolemy II Philadelphus, 105, 156, 158, 163
Ptolemy VI, 160
Ptolemy Epiphanes, 109
public cult, lack of, in Babylonia, 53
Purim, 66, 121
purity: genealogical, 81–82; importance of, 134–35

Q, 200, 230
Qos, 139
questiones, 168
Qumran, 6, 171–74, 177–78, 209; assigning authority to texts, 185–86; canon of, 180; Essenes at, 181; redating of, 8; rule books of, 176–77

rabbinic sources, 8

rabbis, 256, 258–59; elevating scripture, 6; emergence of, 262–63, 265–66; liturgical approach of, 269–70; oral culture of, 273; understanding of Torah, 267–68, 269

readers, communities of, 279

Reformation, 280

religion: ethnicity and, 25; formation of, 279–80; nature of, 79; traditional, Josiah's attack on, 45, 48

religious authority, structure of, 65

revelation, 120; continuing, 267; hidden, 261–62; types of, 261–62

revelatory texts, 236, 242

"Revenue Laws," 105

reverence, 116

reworked Bible (Pentateuch), 147, 185–86

ritualism, condemnation of, 25

ritual purity, 134–35, 145, 271

Romans, letter to, 218

Rome: appointing Jewish high priests, 194; as dangerous place for Christians, 248–49; intellectual culture of, 242–43, 252; power of, growing, 126; ruling Judea, 204–5

Rosh Hashanah, 76, 77

rule books, 176–77

Ruth, book of, 243

Sabbath, 25, 149

sacred documents, appeal to, absent in Esther, 66

sacrifices, 23, 24, 40, 73, 116, 196

Saddok, 195

Sadducees, 6, 125, 133, 137–38, 140–45, 147, 166, 170, 214, 275; assigning divine authority to texts, 149–50; committed to authority of scripture, 192; disagreements among, 150, 151; finding common ground with Pharisees, 258; going to Qumran, 172, 179; Jesus and, 203, 208; political role of, 171, 172–73,

181, 185, 193; prehistory of, 175; renaissance of, 211–12; resurgence of, 182; school of thought, 263; as sons of light, 185

sage, role of, in Ben Sira, 116

Salome (sister of Herod the Great), 193

Salome, Alexandra, 172, 179

salvation: believers' participation in, 251; Christ as key to, 238, 239; source of, 253

Samaria, 17, 105, 138–39, 194–95

Samaritans, 139

Samuel, books of, 46

Sanballat, 86–87, 88, 91

Sanhedrin, 206

Sargon, 29–30

satrapies, 57

Saul, 16, 39

scribes, 4, 5, 25–27, 61; academic activities of, 37–38; accessing hidden wisdom, 262; in the ancient Near East, 27; class of, 92; developing Deuteronomy, 41–42; in Hezekiah's court, 35; Israelite, 26, 27–28; in Jesus's time, 208–9; in Judah, 32; libraries for, 38–39; patrons of, 37; political authority and, 70; priests and, 49; recording prophetic activity, 28–29, 48–49; revisions by, 39–40; reworking laws, 27–28; role of, in Ben Sira, 116; social status of, enhanced, 50; training of, 27–28, 118

scripture: accessibility of, and the targumim, 274–75; authority of, priests relying on, 192; Bar Kokhba and, 264; blessings distinct from, 270; fluidity of, 186; fluid notion of, 180; formal marking of, 268; hidden meaning of, 186–88; interpretation of, revealing God's will, 267–68; Jesus's life linked to, 193, 225, 227–28, 230–33; Jews' categorization of, 243–44; John's use of, 233; Justin Martyr's knowledge of, 249–51; knowledge of, in Jesus's time, 201–2; Luke's use of, 231–32; marginalization of, 273; marginal role of, in Jesus's life, 208; Mark's use of, 226–28; Matthew's use of, 230; omnisignificance of, 268, 269; oracular authority of, 220–21; Paul's use of, 218–23; perfection of, 268; prophetic authority of, 239; public reading of, 215, 216; Qumran community's valuing of, 180; recitation of, 270–71; sacred, treatment of, 255–56; soft power of, 212; as source of all true knowledge, 268, 269; as vague term, in Jesus's time, 209. *See also* Bible; New Testament; Old Testament; Septuagint

scroll of the Law, symbolic nature of, 239–40

scrolls, 255–56; religious authority of, 44–45; ritual impurity and, 271; significance of, 270–71

Second Apology (Justin Martyr), 248–49, 250

Second Chronicles, 131

Second Maccabees, 124, 163

Seleucids, 103–5, 108–9, 127, 128, 133, 136, 138

semicanonical works, 7

Semitic languages, 21

Sennacherib, 35–36

Septuagint, 2, 152, 274, 276; appropriation of, by Jewish intellectuals, 162–63, 170; becoming a holy book, 153–54; as collection of laws, 165; Jewish knowledge of, 166–68, 170; knowledge of, in 1st-century Jerusalem, 195; language of, 158–59; literary authority of, 159; oracular authority of, 247; Paul's knowledge of, 221; as perfect, holy text, 165; Philo's praise for, 153; prestige associated with, 5; public knowledge of, increasing, 167–68; study of, among Jewish intellectuals, 153

Sermon on the Mount, 201, 202

Shalmanseer V, 29

Shavuot (Pentecost), 75

Shebna, 35

Sheol, 112

Shepherd of Hermas, 242

Sheshbazzar, 56, 57, 59, 64, 86

Shimon (rabbi), 265

shrines, 24

Sibylline Books, 216, 250

Siloam inscription, 33

Simon (son of Onias), 115, 117, 128

Simon Maccabee, 133

soft power, 19

solar calendar, 120, 121, 145, 148, 179

Solomon, 16–17, 38, 80, 111, 114

soul: human, 169; survival of, 185

step-pools, 134

Strabo, 160–61

Sukkot. *See* Tabernacles

Sumerian language, 27

supersessionism, 223

synagogues, 167, 168, 170, 188; establishment of, 197–200; Gentiles attracted to, 216; Paul preaching in, 214–15, 216–17; scripture read in, for the public, 192–93

synoptic Gospels, 200, 207–8

Syria, 105, 106–7

Syriac, 276

Tabernacles (Sukkot), 75–76, 77

Talmud, 272–73

Tanak, 2, 277

tannaim, 272

targumim, 273–75

Tatian, 252, 254–55

tax farmers, 105–6

Teacher of Righteousness, 150–51, 172, 173, 175, 180, 186

Tell el-Yehoudieh, 160

temple: Antiochus's support of, 109; as central feature for worshiping YHWH, 59; construction of, 145–46; Elephantine, 96–98; library at, 39; local, 24; at Mt. Gerizim, 87, 138; prophets of, 24 temple, first: building of, 16; destruction of, 50–51, 54, 260–61; implements from, 64

temple, second, 52, 53; administration of, 195–96; continuity of, with the first temple, 64; destruction of, 223, 224, 226, 259–60; in Ezra's time, 73; God's return to, 65; Hasmonean control of, 136–37; purity of, 134–35, 136; rebuilding of, 59–60, 62–64; reestablishing, Nehemiah's interest in, 90; renovations of, in Herod's time, 183; resanctification of, 127–28

Temple Scroll, 143, 145–47, 149, 151, 175, 243

texts: customs following, 142; fluidity of, 147; function of, for early Christian community, 238–39; heightened concern for, 148–49; hidden meanings of, 186–88; marginal role of, in antiquity, 9; physical aspects of, 256; power of, 9; primacy of, over message, 259, 277; Qumran community assigning authority to, 185–86; reflection on, as philosophical activity, 215; religious authority of, 79; rising authority of, 154; Sadducees assigning divine authority to, 149–50; shifting view of, 125; used as models, 4

textual authority, 32, 142; attitudes toward, 3–4; Dead Sea Scrolls and, 171–72; given to written texts, 44

textual studies, discipline of, 165

theater, 107–8, 166, 167, 170

theodicy, 120

Theodotus (son of Vettenos), 197–98

theophoric names, 30, 86, 95–96

Therapeutae, 167, 298n45

Thessalonica, 219

Third Corinthians, 237

Thomas, Gospel of, 7, 235, 236

Tiglath-pilesar III, 29

Tisha B'Av, 50–51

Tobiads, 87, 90

Tobiah, 86, 87, 88, 91

Tobit, 121, 131

Torah: as academic text, 85–86; existence of, first evidence of, 69; Ezra's reading of, 74, 77–79, 91; holiness of, 271; introducing new source of religious authority, 79; as law, 69; liturgical reading of, linked to Ezra, 69; Oral and Written, 272–75; oral transmission of, 271–72; rabbis' understanding of, 267–68, 269; requiring explanation, in Ezra's time, 78; scroll of, discovery of, 43–45, 47–48; scrolls produced for reading of, 270–71; written on single scroll, 78

Tosefta, 268

Tov, Emanuel, 188

Trajan, 248

tribes, differences between, 20

Trito-Isaiah, 60

Ugaritic, 21

United Monarchy, 16, 17

U.S. Constitution, 280, 281

U.S. Supreme Court, 280

Valentinians, 253

Valentinus, 235, 253, 254–55

vassal states, 26

visions, genre of, 236

Vulgate, 276

water, immersion in, 134, 199

wealth, wisdom and, 37–38

Wellhausen, Julius, 74

Wicked Priest, 150, 151

wisdom: linked with the law, 117; wealth and, 37–38

Wisdom of Solomon, 250

writers, communities of, 278–79

writing: appearing in prophecies, 48–49; numinous quality of, 49; prestige of, increasing, 48–50; status related to, 32. *See also* texts

Writings, the, 179

Written Torah, 272–74, 275

Xerxes I, 69

Yah, 95–96
Yehud (Judah), 53; governing of, 85, 92;
population of, 62; priestly influence in,
99–100; return to, 58–59, 62. *See also*
Judah
yehudi, 67
YHWH (Yahweh, Jehovah), 22–24;
consolidation around, 60, 62; cult of,
23, 36, 41; as the only god, 60–61; rules
of, following, 46–47; sacrifice to, 24,
40–41; worship of, changes in, 52. *See
also* Elohim
Yom Kippur, 76, 77

Zadok, 294n11
Zechariah, 63
Zenon, 106
Zerubbabel, 58–65, 82, 86

Index of Scripture and Other Ancient Sources